RENEWALS 458-4574
DATE DUE

**WITHDRAWN
UTSA LIBRARIES**

Managing Opportunity Development in Business Networks

Managing Opportunity Development in Business Networks

Edited by

Pervez Ghauri

Amjad Hadjikhani

and

Jan Johanson

© Pervez Ghauri, Amjad Hadjikhani and Jan Johanson 2005

All rights reserved. No reproduction, copy or transmission of this publication may be made without written permission.

No paragraph of this publication may be reproduced, copied or transmitted save with written permission or in accordance with the provisions of the Copyright, Designs and Patents Act 1988, or under the terms of any licence permitting limited copying issued by the Copyright Licensing Agency, 90 Tottenham Court Road, London W1T 4LP.

Any person who does any unauthorized act in relation to this publication may be liable to criminal prosecution and civil claims for damages.

The authors have asserted their rights to be identified as the authors of this work in accordance with the Copyright, Designs and Patents Act 1988.

First published in 2005 by
PALGRAVE MACMILLAN
Houndmills, Basingstoke, Hampshire RG21 6XS and
175 Fifth Avenue, New York, N.Y. 10010
Companies and representatives throughout the world.

PALGRAVE MACMILLAN is the global academic imprint of the Palgrave Macmillan division of St. Martin's Press, LLC and of Palgrave Macmillan Ltd. Macmillan® is a registered trademark in the United States, United Kingdom and other countries. Palgrave is a registered trademark in the European Union and other countries.

ISBN-13: 978–1–4039–4769–7
ISBN-10: 1–4039–4769–4

This book is printed on paper suitable for recycling and made from fully managed and sustained forest sources.

A catalogue record for this book is available from the British Library.

Library of Congress Cataloging-in-Publication Data

    Managing opportunity development in business networks / edited by Pervez Ghauri, Amjad Hadjikhani and Jan Johanson.
      p. cm.
    Includes bibliographical references and index.
    ISBN 1–4039–4769–4 (cloth)
    1. International business enterprises – Management. 2. Entrepreneurship. 3. Business networks – Management. 4. Globalization – Economic aspects. 5. Competition, International. I. Ghauri, Pervez N., 1948– II. Hadjikhani, Amjad. III. Johanson, Jan, 1934–

HD62.4.M3672 2005
658'.044—dc22
                                                                                   2005046304

10 9 8 7 6 5 4 3 2 1
14 13 12 11 10 09 08 07 06 05

Printed and bound in Great Britain by
Antony Rowe Ltd, Chippenham and Eastbourne

Contents

List of Figures vii

List of Tables ix

List of Contributors x

Introduction: Opportunity Development in Business Networks 1
Amjad Hadjikhani, Pervez Ghauri and Jan Johanson

Part I Opportunity Development in Business Networks: Conceptual Development

1 Opportunities, Relational Embeddedness and Network Structure 27
 Ulf Andersson, Desireé Blankenburg Holm and Martin Johanson

2 The Importance of Competition and Cooperation for the Exploration of Innovation Opportunities 49
 Maria Bengtsson, Jessica Eriksson and Sören Kock

3 International Entrepreneurial Culture, International Opportunity Perception and Pattern of International Exploitation: Towards an Integrated Model 67
 Pavlos Dimitratos and Marian V. Jones

4 Subsidiary Business Networks and Opportunity Development in Multinational Enterprises: A Comparison of the Influence of Internal and External Business Networks 91
 Mohammad Yamin

5 Value Processes in Industrial Networks: Identifying the Creation and Realisation of Value 110
 Martin Johanson and Torkel Strömsten

Part II Opportunity Development in International Business

6 Business Opportunities, Subsidiaries and Interpreneurial Activity 127
 Cecilia Pahlberg and Magnus Persson

7   International Experience and the Recognition
    of Business Opportunities in Foreign Markets – A Study
    of SME's International Experiences and
    Choice of Location   146
    Jukka Hohenthal and Jessica Lindbergh

8   Opportunities of Being Multinational: A Study of
    Organizational Rejuvenation, Relationships and Knowledge   164
    Maria Adenfelt and Katarina Lagerström

9   Learning across the Border? Innovations, Knowledge
    Sharing, and Business Opportunities in MNCs   180
    Fang Lee Cooke

10 Network Opportunities and Obstacles in Mergers and
    Acquisitions: The Role of Resource Embeddedness   202
    Enrico Baraldi and Torkel Strömsten

11 Reputation as Opportunity and Risk   219
    Carin Eriksson and Jan Lindvall

Part III   Opportunity Development and Networks

12 The Role of Business Opportunity Mediators in
    the Entrepreneurial Process   235
    Björn Berggren and Lars Silver

13 Opportunity Development for Ongoing Business
    Relationships   250
    Cecilia Pahlberg and Peter Thilenius

14 Opportunities and Obstacles in Using IT Systems:
    Embedding Movex in Edsbyn's Resource Network   269
    Enrico Baraldi

15 Creating New Opportunities from Old Resources through
    Contextually Determined Information Asymmetries   288
    Anna Bengtson and Susanne Åberg

16 The Emergence and Exploitation of Opportunities in
    Business Networks   306
    Benjamin Ståhl

Epilogue: Opportunity Development in Business Networks   325
Amjad Hadjikhani and Jan Johanson

Index   332

List of Figures

I.1	Opportunity development process	12
I.2	Balance/imbalance in the opportunity elements	14
1.1	Relational embeddedness	31
1.2	Open (A) and closed (B) networks	34
1.3	The rent accruing position in an open network	35
1.4	Rational use of limited resources in an open network according to Burt (1992a)	36
1.5	Impact on finding and exploiting opportunities by embeddedness and network structure	37
1.6	An open network with a low degree of relational embeddedness	38
1.7	A closed network with a low degree of relational embeddedness	39
1.8	An open network with a high degree of relational embeddedness	41
1.9	A closed network with a high degree of relational embeddedness	42
1.10	A semi-open network with different degrees of relational embeddedness	45
2.1	Networks characteristics and opportunity seeking patterns	57
2.2	Network slack and network dynamics	61
3.1	A Simple integration: international entrepreneurial culture, international opportunity perception and international opportunity exploitation	68
3.2a	The entrepreneurial process	70
3.2b	The international entrepreneurial process	71
3.3	Towards a detailed integration: international entrepreneurial culture, international opportunity perception and international opportunity exploitation	72
5.1	A model of the creation and realisation of value	119
5.2	An illustration of the creation and realisation of value	120
6.1	The characteristics of business opportunities	130
6.2	The locus of interpreneurial activity	139
7.1	Percentage of first entries in the same cultural block as the home market	155
7.2	The relationship between international presence, managerial experiential knowledge and choice of location	157
9.1	Corporate entrepreneurship: the link between innovations and business opportunities	185

9.2	Communication links in knowledge sharing in the MNCs	190
13.1	Opportunity development for ongoing business relationships	257
14.1	The effects of an IT system on resources	273
14.2	Movex and the surrounding network of resources	279
14.3	Four types of IT-related opportunities, closer to and farther from the IT core	283
14.4	Classifying IT-related opportunities and obstacles for Edsbyn	285
15.1	The electronic payment resource network	291
15.2	Some of the actors involved in the ISDN network	295
16.1	ATD stock, data/product flow	315
16.2	Mutual opportunity in business networks	319

List of Tables

4.1	Subsidiary business network: Internal versus external business networks	97
7.1	The indicators	157
9.1	Strategies for creating business opportunities and activities of knowledge management in the case study MNCs	187
10.1	Three types of opportunities driving mergers and acquistions	206
12.1	The role and contribution of the business opportunity mediator in the four cases	246
13.1	Indicators of areas of change in the business relationship	260
13.2	Indicators of connections in the business network	261
13.3	Areas of changes and connections as opportunity development	262

List of Contributors

Maria Adenfelt, Department of Business Studies, Uppsala University, Sweden
Ulf Andersson, Department of Business Studies, Uppsala University, Sweden
Enrico Baraldi, Department of Business Studies, Uppsala University, Sweden
Anna Bengtson, Department of Business Studies, Uppsala University, Sweden
Maria Bengtsson, Department for Business Administration, Umeå University, Sweden
Björn Berggren, Centre for Banking and Finance, Royal Institute of Technology, Stockholm, Sweden
Desireé Blankenburg Holm, Department of Business Studies, Uppsala University, Sweden
Fang Lee Cooke, Manchester Business School, The University of Manchester, UK
Pavlos Dimitratos, University of Strathclyde and University of Glasgow, UK
Carin Eriksson, Department of Business Studies, Uppsala University, Sweden
Jessica Eriksson, Department for Business Administration, Umeå University, Sweden
Pervez Ghauri, Manchester Business School, The University of Manchester, UK
Amjad Hadjikhani, Department of Business Studies, Uppsala University, Sweden
Jukka Hohenthal, Department of Business Studies, Uppsala University, Sweden
Jan Johanson, Department of Business Studies, Uppsala University, Sweden
Martin Johanson Department of Business Studies, Uppsala University, Sweden and Mid Sweden University
Marian Jones, University of Strathclyde and University of Glasgow, UK
Sören Kock, Hanken, Swedish School of Economics and Business Administration, Finland
Katarina Lagerström, School of Business, Economics and Law, Göteborg University, Sweden
Jessica Lindbergh, Department of Business Studies, Uppsala University, Sweden
Jan Lindvall, Department of Business Studies, Uppsala University, Sweden
Magnus Persson, Department of Business Studies, Uppsala University, Sweden
Cecilia Pahlberg, Department of Business Studies, Uppsala University, Sweden
Lars Silver, Centre for Banking and Finance, Royal Institute of Technology, Stockholm, Sweden

Benjamin Ståhl, Department of Business Studies, Uppsala University, Sweden
Peter Thilenius, Mälardalens Business School, Sweden
Torkel Strömsten, Stockholm School of Economics, Sweden
Mohammed Yamin, Manchester Business School, The University of Manchester, UK
Susanne Åberg, Department of Business Studies, Uppsala University, Sweden

Introduction: Opportunity Development in Business Networks

Amjad Hadjikhani, Pervez Ghauri and
Jan Johanson

During the last few decades entrepreneurship has attracted a growing interest in both the business world and academia. It seems to be a general agreement that accelerating technological development and globalization require that national economies and industries grow rapidly enough to be competitive in this new world order. It is also believed that entrepreneurship is critical in promoting the necessary industrial growth and development. Opportunity is one of the core concepts in the entrepreneurship literature since it is generally assumed that opportunity seeking has a central role in entrepreneurship. The objective of this volume is to explore some issues in the landscape of business opportunity. Our exploration aims at examining business opportunity in a network perspective. The reasons are that cooperative inter-firm networks are frequently said to be effective in managing the forces of technological development and globalization, and that research has demonstrated that firms are engaged in networks of interconnected relationships.

In the first section of this introductory chapter we discuss some general, almost common-sense, aspects of opportunities. In the following section, we review the relevant research literature.

Some basic considerations

Opportunities are central in the dynamics of the market economy. In business contexts we frequently meet the word 'opportunity' and it usually refers to the beginning of a successful business. But the word is more often used in a rather specific sense. Often it is specified as business opportunity, market opportunity or exchange opportunity. Market opportunity concerns opportunities in the market. Similarly business opportunities are about opportunities to do business which seems to be a matter of selling and buying in the market. Exchange opportunities are related to market exchange. However, these concepts refer to the same phenomenon. We are, however, not dealing with opportunities for rationalization or internal relations unless they are directly related to business opportunities in the market. Penrose (1959: 31) provided an early explanation of 'opportunity' and defined a firm's 'productive opportunity' as 'all of the productive possibilities that its "entrepreneurs" see and can take advantage of'. Kirzner (1997: 71) talks about profit opportunities, defined as opportunities for pure entrepreneurial profit that tend to be discovered and grasped by routine-resisting entrepreneurial market participants.

However, an opportunity for pure profit cannot be systematically searched, as one is not aware that one has missed the opportunity of grasping any profit. Opportunity is thus related to entrepreneurial alertness that one is, at all times, spontaneously looking for unnoticed features of the present or the future environment. In other words, an entrepreneur without knowing what he is looking for, is all the time scanning the horizon and is ready to discover (Kirzner, 1989).

Smith (1967) identified two types of entrepreneurs; 'craftsman' and 'opportunistic'. Craftsman is characterized by narrowness of education and lack of confidence, while 'opportunistic' entrepreneurs are characterized by high social awareness and involvement and confidence to deal with present and future environment (see also Manimala, 1999). Although these categories have been further developed to four (Lafuente and Salas, 1989) and later to five (Webster, 1977) categories, the opportunistic entrepreneur fits into one line of thinking. However, 'opportunity' as a concept has not been properly discussed in the literature and needs more attention from researchers. We can find general definitions; for example, according to Longman Dictionary of Contemporary English (1995) opportunity is a 'chance to do something or an occasion when it is easy for you to do something'.

A potentially interesting distinction concerns the time dimension. If we view opportunity as an opening we can perhaps distinguish between those openings that are very temporary and those which are more or less permanently opened. They are sometimes called strategic windows which may be closed almost immediately or are opened for being exploited. However, to seize an opportunity implicitly assumes that the opening is temporary.

From another point of view we can make a distinction between opportunities which are very specific in that they are related to one or a few particular actors in the market or elsewhere and those which are general in that they concern general demand and supply relations in a market. Perhaps it can be fruitful to consider this as a basis for a two-by-two typology in which we have first very temporary and specific opportunities and, second, the more permanent and specific ones. Third, there are temporary and general opportunities and finally some which are permanent and general. It might be worthwhile to take a look at these four types and examine the kind of competence and resources that are useful in each one. Assuming that opportunity is a matter of combination of resources we have to consider the resources involved in the combination, potential combinations of those resources and the competence regarding the use.

A further understanding of the nature of opportunities may be gained by considering how you find an opportunity. Finding may be a result of search or discovery. Search means that you look for something that you believe is in the direction where you are searching. In the present context you search for a business opportunity that can match your competence and resources. Sometimes your search is interrupted by a finding which is completely unexpected, a discovery. But discoveries can also be the outcome of ongoing activities. You may stumble on something in the market which you had no idea of. This suggests, in turn, that opportunity is a matter of seeing or realizing. According to some researchers there is no opportunity until you have seen it (Kirzner, 1973). A discovery may also be the result of someone else approaching you with an offer or request or proposal or suggestion.

You can also give someone an opportunity. The implicit assumption behind getting and giving opportunities is that opportunities are closely related to exchanges in which you give something and get something else. A reasonable idea is that opportunities to a great extent are created through exchange between two parties who both have an interest in the realization of the opportunity.

The view of opportunities discussed above suggests that opportunities should be studied as some kind of process in which the opportunity is found and realized, or more generally, developed. And that this process, at least sometimes, takes place as exchange between two or more parties. The process means that the focal actor successively increases its commitment to the realization of the opportunity and, in parallels its knowledge about development of the opportunity.

A consequence of this process view is that it might be fruitful to consider, in addition to the resources directly combined in the opportunity, the resources and competencies involved in the process preceding the exploitation of the opportunity. For instance, what kind of competence and resources help the firm to develop opportunities?

The basic concern of the book

Inspired by the pioneering studies of the Austrian economists Mises (1949), Hayek (1945) and Penrose (1959) researchers attach firms' growth to opportunity-seeking and entrepreneurship. By dividing firm activities into routinized and creative, researchers in the field of entrepreneurship postulate that it is opportunity-seeking that creates change and dynamics in firms and markets. The researchers, however, choose different theoretical perspectives when analysing the phenomenon. Irrespective of their theoretical tracks, as Foss and Klein (2002) pinpoint, these authors have shortcomings in exploring opportunity and entrepreneurship at the firm level. Those few, who spotlight the firm, are inspired by traditional organizational and management theories (Alvarez and Busenitz, 2001). Their attention is on the individual entrepreneurs and the analysis of factors influencing firms' opportunity is based on conceptions of a 'diffuse and abstract environment' (Kirzner, 1999; McKendall and Wagner; 1997). The theoretical foundation obtains no impulse from more recent theories.

Joseph Schumpeter (1942: 83) refers to entrepreneurial ventures as, 'the fundamental engine that sets and keeps the capitalist system in motion'. This is done by creating new goods, inventing new markets and devising new business models. Entrepreneurship is not necessarily related to small businesses, as the distinguishing elements of entrepreneurship are novelty and dynamism and not the size (Hart, 2003). Moreover, Schumpeter's entrepreneurship refers to the creation of technologically dynamic, high value added, high-growth firms that is strongly linked to creativity (Florida, 2003; Mokyr, 1990; Schumpeter, 1947).

Against this background we believe that there is a need for considering opportunity development in a theoretical perspective placing the opportunity-seeking firm in a less diffuse and abstract market environment. Therefore, we think that business network theory can contribute to a better understanding of business opportunity and entrepreneurship. Business network theory was developed on the basis of research on business markets, that is markets where both suppliers and customers are firms (Håkansson, 1995). It was demonstrated that supplier firms and customer firms develop close and lasting relationships with each other and that most firms are engaged in a limited network of relationships with important customers and suppliers. Since the relationship partners in turn are engaged in other relationships, the network of relationships extends far beyond the single firm so that markets are networks. This perspective lies behind most of this volume and a primary objective of the volume is to explore opportunity development in business networks.

In addition, we think that placing opportunity development and entrepreneurship in a business network setting may cast some further light on business network dynamics. The network perspective stresses relationship change which contains the two dimensions of present and past. Simply stated, interdependence in the network relationships is present because of changes in the past and those changes are assumed to be stable and smooth. Firms' 'extra' resource input for the sake of change of relationships is omitted. In other words, concepts for analysis of discontinuous changes are missing. Business opportunity contains such changes and by discussing them in a network perspective the volume will hopefully contribute to a further understanding of business network theory. This is a secondary objective of the book.

Steps of integration of the two theoretical areas are taken by some articles treating various problems and possibilities associated with combining the two (Dess, *et al.*, 2003; Jack and Anderson, 2002). Prior to a short presentation of the articles, this introductory chapter offers a review of opportunity literature and an analytical framework for studying business network and opportunity development.

Previous studies

Research on opportunity has followed different theoretical tracks. In the past 50 years, the concepts of opportunity and entrepreneurship have occupied the focus of a large number of researchers. The selected views broadly have followed two different and contradictory lines of thoughts. While some confer to economic theories and elevate the matter of perfect information, others follow the theoretical view of Hayek (1945) on incomplete and frequently contradictory knowledge (Khilstrom and Laffont, 1979). Some lines of thoughts are discussed briefly in the following. The first section concerns the economic theory and opportunity, the second, provides some reflection on studies connected to opportunity and business theories and finally the last section is devoted to the later studies on opportunity and entrepreneurship.

Opportunity and economic theories. In its early stage, the analytical tools of the majority of the researchers on opportunity seeking by entrepreneurs were conceived from economic theories. These tools were developed to approach the smallest unit of the market – individual entrepreneurs' opportunity seeking. The equilibrium perspective is perceived to drive opportunity development. Disequilibrium in the market price and information were determinant in the use of resources and decision optimization; that is, opportunity. It was conceived as an outcome of the entrepreneurs' rational behaviour. Market equilibrium itself is argued to be the outcome of new market opportunities, that is, growth of the market is geared by opportunity-seekers' actions. Following this construction, researches initiated empirical studies to signify the reliability of the postulations. Studies of Geroski (1990) and Vihanto (2002) are excellent examples in this field. Opportunity seeking is dissected by mechanical process containing standardized mathematical devices. There are many who have questioned these assumptions. Defining opportunity by measurable and rational behaviour is condemned to miss aspects like resource heterogeneity or cases of opportunity failures. The assumption that single entrepreneurs act intentionally and mechanically to fulfil the needs (defined by the market) is criticized to be far from the real business life.

In this critical stream, researchers like Shackle (1982) utterly destroy the earlier view. The assumptions of the earlier researchers that (1) firms have no incentive to change the present actions because of their current satisfaction, that (2) current market prices convey all the relevant information necessary to direct resources, and that (3) perfection of knowledge is not essential (Pearce, 1992) have been established as incomplete tools to define the opportunity behaviour (see e.g. Hayek, 1945). In the Austrian view (see e.g., Foss and Klein, 2002; Vaughn, 1994), researchers like Kirzner (1997) and Shane (2000) explain the failure of the economic views and offer other theoretical frames. Kirzner (1973), for example, had vigorously rejected the orthodox emphasis on entrepreneurs' full access of information. They instead, have offered views on, lack of information, asymmetry in the resources and non-obviousness of opportunity constructed on behavioural theory (grounded in studies like, Mises, 1943). Researchers in this field state that opportunity development cannot be explained by automatic response to disequilibrium. More precisely, they turn their standpoint from the perfect market to individual entrepreneurs. Opportunity itself is defined as situations in which new goods and services or organization methods are introduced through formation of new means–ends relationships (Eckhardt and Shane, 2003). Contrary to the first view, they denote that opportunity finding is an imaginative original action of individuals. Instead of approaching opportunity with market devices, they ground their perspectives in the behaviour of entrepreneurs. These researchers turn from external, market factors to internal, entrepreneurial factors (entrepreneurs) to explain opportunity behaviour.

While researchers had their major attention on connecting economic theory to opportunity and individual entrepreneurs, research on elevating opportunity and firm behaviour have been neglected (Foss and Klein, 2002). Following the study by Penrose (1959) some recent studies have initiated research to overcome this shortcoming. But, a large number of studies have the tendency to regard firms and entrepreneurs (individuals or small firms) as one and united phenomenon (Shane, et al., 2003; Venkataraman, 1997). They base their discussions on Mises' (1981) four factors: (1) autonomy of individual choice, (2) the uncertainty in the environment within which the choices are made, (3) the character of the entrepreneur's market decisions, and (4) the overriding importance of human purposefulness. These factors, instead of market forces, are assumed to explain the behaviour of opportunity seekers – entrepreneurs (see also Geroski, 1990; Kirzner, 1997; Vaughn, 1994).

Opportunity and business theories. When exploring the concept, Penrose (1959) and later studies like Graver (2003) place attention on firms' resources and uncertainty. They leave the definition of *entrepreneurs as small firms* and expose that any firm, no matter of its size, can act and behave as entrepreneurs to gain business opportunity. In this approach, opportunity behaviour is regarded as a matter of competence management. It focuses the ability of the firm to differentiate the existing activity patterns for generation of new activities and visions. Therefore, firms, for their survival, diversify and separate the administrative competence (routine tasks) from the opportunity creation competence. In this track, the competence for opportunity development is internal, that is, every individual firm possesses the needed competence.

The origin of opportunity, that is, whether the opportunity is developed because of the internal or external factors, has engaged different groups of researchers (see e.g., Shane, 2000). A significant number of studies put forth theoretical views on external environmental forces (Aldrich, 2000), characteristics of firms (McKendall and Wagner, 1997), characteristics of entrepreneurs and characteristics of the opportunity itself (Shane and Venkataraman, 2000). A group of researchers borrow views from organizational behaviour and emphasize the internal nature of opportunity, that is, opportunity is developed because of individual entrepreneurs (Kirzner, 1973; Stigler, 1961). Researchers like Shane et al. (2003) ground their theoretical views on individual entrepreneurs and study their motivations. In their analytical context, the opportunity seekers' motivation, intelligence and skills are presented as the main factors affecting opportunity success. While researchers in this group use organization theory for understanding opportunity, others focus motivational and cognitive factors. In this track, business opportunity is regarded as a consequence of entrepreneurs' willingness to bear risk (Brockhaus and Horowitz, 1986), motivational and self-sufficiency behaviour of individuals (Chen, 1998), and their tolerance for ambiguity (Baron, 1998; Begley and Boyd, 1987).

The short review above manifests how researchers, in spite of their first attempt to individualize firms, stand on different analytical standpoints. They can simply be placed in a continuum. In one end we have those analytical tools relying on individual behaviour and psychological variables and at the other end we have those using external economic factors. In between these two extreme fields, we have researchers like Penrose (1956) that explicitly offer the theoretical tool of competence to connect opportunity development to firms behaviour.

Business opportunity and development process. Some researchers introduced a process view for understanding business opportunity (Kirzner, 1997). In this vein the definition of opportunity as a strategic goal (Vihanto, 2002) loses its significance and opportunity development, that is, means–end relationship comes in focus. In approaching a process view, Dess (2003) behold that it permits a deeper understanding of a firm's opportunity behaviour. The first proposal of the authors in this track is that firms' growth is directly related to how they can manage the opportunity process. Some in this group observe business opportunity as the fundamental market strategy tool (Graver, 2003; Woodruff and Gardial, 1996) and emphasize the ability of organizations to permit individuals in the firms to search and discover opportunity. Opportunity development is explained by the uniqueness of the resource combination – with emphasis on information possession (Hayek, 1945; Shane, 2000). Later studies like Alvarez and Busenitz (2001), Shane et al. (2003), Eckhardt and Shane (2003), Venkataraman (1997) develop phases to study this process. They assume that the process contains phases of entrepreneurial recognition and exploitation. The search process is regarded as a conscious action of the firms to find a place far from competition. Some authors explain the process as search, which develops to discovery, and then to the final stage by acting on the reached discovery. Others explain it by the process of discovery, evaluation and exploitation. In this process the two phases of search and discovery are separated from the pursuit of opportunity. But the process is divided into specific phases. There are two main reasons why these authors divide the process into phases. One is related to the internal organizational processes that vary in different phases. The second is related to the perceptions of the exogenous factors that are specific in each phase.

Later development. The review reveals that during the last two decades the researchers apply views borrowed from the traditional management theories. Aspects like heterogeneity in the information and organizational resources have become more apparent in their analytical approaches. Alvarez and Busenitz (2001), for example, extend the view on information possession and connect business opportunity to the resource-based theory. They extend the resource view and state that individuals' cognitive ability and information possession are only two types of resources. From their point of view business opportunity is apparent when different firms or agents have an insight into the value of different resources that others do not. As discussed, some further develop the notion and employ concepts like strategy that frequently are used in the marketing and organizational studies. Stevenson and Jarillo (1990), in their process model connect strategy to opportunity (see also Brown, *et al.*, 2001) driven to change in the use of endogenous resources. These theoretical perspectives, however, have a limit. The intrinsic process view on resource values and commitment beholds the single organization as the unit of analysis. Somewhat similar to those following the economic theories, the driving force is presumed to have its origin in the environment or individuals in the firms and not in the values obtained by combination of external and internal resources. Environment is treated as a source of impact and uncertainty and not as a source that firms can get needed resources from.

Authors like Thakur (1998), Alvarez and Busenitz (2001) argue that the opportunity process is influenced by a combination of external and internal factors. They introduce factors like, (1) political ones, (2) market forces, (3) resources and finally, (4) the motivation of the entrepreneurs. The discovery process, for example, is assumed to be affected by the impact from the individual in the organization as well as the impact from external organizations like government. A similar perspective is selected by Morris and Paul (1987) for studying market penetration and Rice, *et al.* (2001) for technological innovation. In line with Jack and Anderson's (2002) thoughts, these authors introduce the concept of embeddedness in the entrepreneurial process. They define embeddedness as the social structure and connect it to the opportunity development (see also Hoang and Antoncic, 2003; Sarah and Anderson, 2002).

In spite of the contributions of these studies, the later development also seems to gain its strength from the traditional organizational and marketing principles that assume that firms have sufficient knowledge to formulate their strategies and manage the environmental factors. Opportunity is explained by the act of individual entrepreneurs with visions and coordinative capability aiming at an end of a 'short term' means and end relationship. Opportunity seeking is an end of short-term interactions with given plans. The strategy view of these researchers assumes that opportunity can be measured and computed. Firms' have calculative ability to design the process, understand and eliminate environmental uncertainty and develop new opportunities and reach their strategies. Opportunities are measured as calculative ends and strategies that firms are aiming at. The process view on opportunity and entrepreneurship is constructed as a short-term dynamic process. These are, as we realize, consequences of the views selected. In the following section, we make an attempt to characterize opportunity in terms of networks.

Opportunity and business networks

The process of combining heterogeneous resources raises the question on resource control. The endogenous view in the earlier studies (i.e., firm or entrepreneurs – as the focal unit of the analysis), has the presumption that individual firms possess all of the required unique and heterogeneous resources (Alvarez and Busenitz, 2001; Jack and Anderson, 2002). Environment is treated as a factor mostly threatening opportunity development. The view avoids the problem that all unique resources cannot be accumulated in a single organization for two main reasons: (1) the matter of efficiency and lack of capital to internalize all resources; (2) firms do not know in advance what resources are needed. Against this line of thought, there are other studies on business firms that see new product development with cooperative perspectives (Håkansson, 1987). As a response to the traditional view on opportunity development, Ardichvili, *et al.* (2003) integrate social network into their theoretical framework to highlight the firms' interdependency with others in their environment (Thakur, 1998) within the context of the social network. The answer of Busenitz *et al.* (2003), (see also Dubini and Aldrich, 1991; Scott, 1991) to the question how opportunity visions are generated and how capital is attracted relies on the network management. But the attention of these studies is on small entrepreneurial firms (the unit of analysis) and the construction of network concerns social interactions aiming to raise capital resources. Cooperation between firms for accumulation of heterogeneous technological or knowledge resources for unique and unclear opportunities is not considered. One way of resolving this deficiency is to change the perspective of firm–environment to the firms as cooperative units. In this perspective, which is also touched by Busenitz, et al. (2003), business opportunity is conceived in terms of cooperative activities of firms to generate and introduce new solutions.

In this spirit and as a contrast to the view of 'diffuse and abstract environment' a line of research sees business firms as units interwoven in networks of interdependent relationships (Håkansson and Snehota, 1995; Johanson and Mattsson, 1988). A basic assumption underlying this business network theory is that resources are heterogeneous (Penrose 1959) which implies that their values are dependent on which other resources they are combined with. A second assumption is that knowledge is dispersed among actors in the market (Hayek, 1945; Kirzner, 1973). These assumptions which are consistent with important lines of opportunity research are also consistent with one of the central observations in business network research – firms develop close and long lasting business relationships with important supplier and customer firms as well as other partner firms. Relationship development is a matter of gradual and interactive adaptations and combinations of heterogeneous resources of the firms to each other so that the value of the relationship is enhanced. Thus, the firms become committed to future business with each other and know each others' capabilities, needs and strategies. In this way the firms get some control over each other. The theory also posits that those relationships are connected in that they have an impact on each other. Thus, connected relationships may deploy and combine heterogeneous resources so that the relationships become interdependent with each other. Like relationship development relationship connection is a matter of gradual learning of how to best combine the heterogeneous resources. Since the firms with which the focal firm has relationships in turn are engaged in relationships with other firms they are all engaged in networks of business relationships – business networks (Ghauri and Prasad, 1995). Thus each firm is engaged in a network which extends further and further away from the focal firm.

If we assume that opportunity development is a matter of recognizing and having access to the resources and competencies that may be required, business network theory might have something important to say about opportunity development and entrepreneurship. First of all, the partner firms with which the firm has close relationships are likely to have the complementary competence and resources needed for opportunity development and are likely to be able to see how the heterogeneous resources involved can be combined. Moreover, these are the firms which our focal firm knows best and, in particular knows better than potentially competing opportunity developers. Second, it is likely that the focal firm is better equipped than other firms to understand opportunities that are more or less concealed and waiting for being exploited in the network context. Third, this surrounding network contains heterogeneous resources that the focal firm has a relative advantage compared to outside firms for opportunity development. In addition to knowing the resources of the firm's network partners, due to interdependence, it has some possibility to control the use of these resources in potential opportunity development. Fourth, each network is a structure to which the firms are committed and understanding this structure makes it better equipped than outsider firms to analyse many difficulties associated with opportunity development in the network setting. But let us remember that opportunity development in a business network context is likely to be a matter of interaction processes involving two or several actors. This implies, in fact, that in some situations opportunity development is also a matter of opportunity creation.

An analytical perspective

In the context of this book, opportunity development is the process of knowledge and resource combinations to attain new markets or products. Firms exchange knowledge and combine old and new resources for favourable junctions necessary for growth. Knowledge about markets and technologies, and about opportunities where the two come together, is the most vital asset that entrepreneurs possess. At the outset of the entrepreneurial process, it is the only asset they have (Hart, 2003: 230). The only other actors who might possess the relevant knowledge are the firms that are members of the same network or who are potential targets for entrepreneurial entry. Technology network (TechNet) in Silicon Valley, USA, is such an example (Miles, 2001). The opportunity process is the incremental knowledge and resource combinations by which exchange partners stepwise increase their accumulative value. Thus, opportunity development consists of components of knowledge and resources. These components, which are driven by hopes, wishes or diffuse ideas, have somewhat different characteristics than those commitments and knowledge needed for general and standardized managerial coordination. The standardized knowledge and resource exchange represents stability with established managerial roles. This view follows Penrose's (1959) distinction between routine and creative activities. Actors' commitment and knowledge in the relationship can thus be divided into general and specific. While general knowledge and commitment structure a process of standardized exchange and consistent values, specific knowledge and commitment engenders surpass value. Surpass value contains new knowledge and demands for additional commitments, and so the process continues. The length of the process varies. A firm can enjoy an opportunity episode and stop the process for a short-term benefit. The presumption is that there are two different (somehow interrelated) processes that prevail in the relationships. One represents network stability with institutionalized relationships and the other concerns change and dynamics. Firms gain visions for some 'perception or knowledge' and in seeking for that commit new resources. The contents of the relationships are changing and the outcomes are unclear. While the first one contains a low uncertainty and clear outcome, the other one contains high uncertainty and unknown future benefits.

As Figure I.1 depicts, opportunity development can be explained by the three interrelated elements of specific knowledge, specific commitment and surpass value. For the sake of efficiency, these interrelated elements develop incrementally. The process can be initiated by a specific knowledge of an actor (individual or unit). Distribution of that knowledge to others will add new values and that affects commitment of the interacting parties. Contrary to the traditional perspectives that presume individual firms as the foundation of knowledge and commitment for opportunity, the network-based opportunity process is driven by dispersed and complementary knowledge and commitments in the network. While traditional views emphasize organizational learning and structure to explain opportunity development, the concern of network perspective focuses on business relationships and interacting parties' ability to combine their knowledge and experiences. It is an ongoing process initiated by a thought or vision of a firm or a unit or individual and proceeds through cooperation with other network actors to exchange knowledge and resources.

Different types of resources are available among different interdependent actors. Each actor has access to specific resources and knowledge. It is the interaction between actors in adding new knowledge and resources that generates the surpass value. Surpass value is the extra value which is developed by interaction. This value is beyond the ordinary standardized added values which reflect a more routinized interaction. This, the surpass value, is presumed here to be developed when actors combine dispersed knowledge and heterogeneous resources. There is a number of studies that manifests how

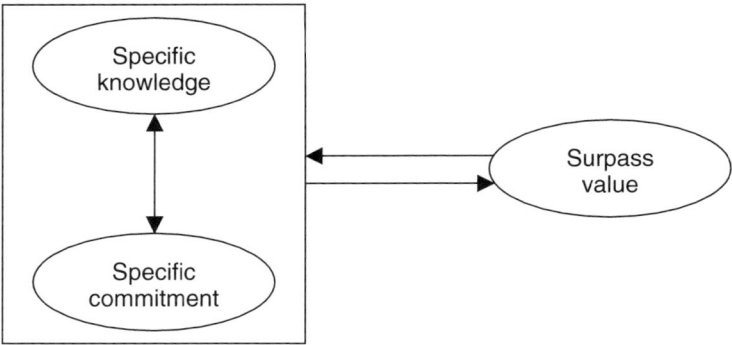

Figure I.1 Opportunity development process

the connected actors' resources and knowledge drive change in the focal relationship (Andersson and Forsgren, 2000; Blankenburg-Holm, 1996; Easton and Araujo, 1992). But for a focal firm opportunity development depends on how the firm succeeds in integrating knowledge and resources in a way that benefits not only itself but also the interrelated actors.

The view of incrementality also implies that the routine behaviour and institutionalized relationship may induce new understandings of the exchange; and that the subsequent commitment destroys the old routine relationship and provokes a new relationship. The process may have long-term interplaying surpass values but also a short-term problem-oriented phase. A process that engenders a temporary suboptimal situation (see Egidi and Narduzzo, 1996), reaches its end after a short period and stops. This can occur in an isolated episode for development of a new idea. Firms may reach a unique position, which satisfies them, and thereby standardize the production and management. In contrast, firms may have several interconnected and/or sequential thoughts for their growth in the future. In such situations, the firms are likely to go in for those partners who possess the needed knowledge and resources they have experience of. Firms' R&D units, for example, do not stop their commitments when they have reached one suboptimum.

There is no specific routine for how and by whom an opportunity process in a business network is initiated. But all studies postulate that specific knowledge of firms is the main factor. In the received perspectives researchers have developed stage models positing that opportunity is created and developed by conscious search processes of individuals who have a unique knowledge (Garrouste, 2002; Kirzner, 1997). Dess *et al.* (2003), when studying corporate entrepreneurship in international markets, introduce a different view. They argue that the factor of experiential knowledge is the key element. Similarly, Kirzner (1997) defines opportunity as the 'piece of missing information' (p. 71). According to his point of view opportunity beholds knowledge produced by both standardized search and 'pure chance'. The crucial factor elevated by the recent research is the incrementality in the experiential knowledge. Specific knowledge necessary for the opportunity creation is assumed to be constructed, based on experience and learning (Shane, 2000). But the opportunity process does not rise up from a void. The start and the termination of opportunity are unclear. But it has a history and a future. This is different from the view of purposeful strategic opportunity behaviour in which means and ends are clear. Based on the behavioural perspective, Shane (2000), Kaish and Gilad (1991) and Venkataraman (1997) connect knowledge heterogeneity to the opportunity seekers' earlier stock of knowledge and their idiosyncratic experience. In terms of business networks, the process is connected to the involved parties' earlier experiential knowledge. The prior cooperative experience of product, market or technology, can generate new knowledge which implies changes in their relationship commitment. The new perceived knowledge complements the prior knowledge. In this vein opportunity development becomes accumulative. The view also beholds that in the process of opportunity development the perceived knowledge refines and modifies the earlier experience. The accumulative knowledge on how to combine a number of heterogeneous resources in new and unique conditions is interwoven with different ranges of uncertainty (see also Ingram and Baum, 1997).

This expression infuses two interrelated and interesting concepts. One reflects the correlation between opportunity development and incrementality in the experience and knowledge. The second concerns the exploitation of opportunity; all opportunities do not produce what firms have planned. They mostly generate failures. It can be explained by the imbalance between the three components of surpass value, specific knowledge and commitment of the involved actors. Since, actors in developing new ideas or products are interdependent with each other, insufficiency in the knowledge and commitment of the focal actors can easily cause imbalance.

The factor of balance/imbalance is an outcome of the degree of input of specific knowledge and commitment. Whereas the synchronized and balanced specific commitment and knowledge development is correlated with positive surpass and low uncertainty, the imbalance is associated with unclear surpass value and higher uncertainty. Combination of low and high specific knowledge and commitment can be elaborated in a matrix illustrating four different situations (see Figure I.2). The four situations in the figure illustrate the balance and imbalance in the opportunity elements. Having reached a balanced situation, developing opportunity requires more knowledge that creates an imbalanced situation. Earlier knowledge is a key that smooth the dynamic of change from imbalance to balance state of condition. In reaching the state of condition 4, for example, firms incrementally pass different states of conditions. When developing opportunity, firms are

	Specific commitment	
	Low	High
Specific knowledge — Low	(1) Simple incremental entrepreneurship	(2) Opportunity failure high risk taking and chancing
Specific knowledge — High	(3) Unnoticed opportunity	(4) Complex incremental opportunity development

Figure I.2 Balance/imbalance in the opportunity elements

always acting with lack of sufficient knowledge and incrementality in development of the elements are to reduce uncertainty. Thus, opportunity development process is like an orchestra that focal actors are to follow accordingly; that is, incrementality in these elements is a mean to avoid failure. Naturally, firms fall into different conditions of imbalance but incrementality in development of elements reduces the harm caused by uncertainty.

These conditions also differentiate between the views of incrementality in opportunity development from other general explanation. Since the element of specific knowledge explained in this volume is fundamentally related to the factor of uncertainty, a process of opportunity development can move from one cell to another. Opportunity development involves dynamic and change which is the interplay of the balance and imbalance between elements. For understanding of different conditions that firms are generally challenging with, a simple explanation is provided in the following.

While conditions 1 and 4 rely on the balance in the development of opportunity elements, conditions 3 and 4 reflect on imbalance. A crucial difference between conditions 1 and 4 lies in the degree of commitment and knowledge. In the first condition a firm can be a small entrepreneur that cautiously develops its vision and makes small commitments. It can also reveal the first episode in the opportunity development process. The exchanged resources are simple and few. Thakur (1998), Coviello et al. (1998) and Ghauri et al. (2004) for example, are among those inspired by opportunity coupling of small firms for new ventures and entrepreneurships. There, firms for their needs, like financial resources, use their social network. Condition 4 replicates a situation in which the exchange relationships are developed and the firms have knowledge about each other's organizational and technological capabilities. Studies on industrial technological development conducted by Håkansson (1987) or Håkansson and Waluszewski (2002) are examples for how firms cooperate to develop new products. In this condition exchange relationships are complex and embedded in multifaceted heterogeneous resources. Partners have a long-term exchange relationship with each other. Cell 2 in the figure, on the other hand, can replicate a condition containing high risk taking 'opportunities' and fails in the production of a surpass value. Firms imitating others decide to enter into, for example, new markets. In a critical and risky situation when the level of specific knowledge is very low, like political crises, firms may maintain a high commitment only for the future expectations for market prosperity (Hadjikhani, 1996, 1997). For these firms, high commitment with a low specific knowledge is chance taking. While interacting parties in conditions 1 and 4 reduce uncertainty with reliance on their specific knowledge, firms in condition 2 voluntarily make a large commitment based on subjective feeling of future gains. Condition 3 reflects episodes or processes that cause firms fail to discover opportunities because of being very cautious or lack of resources.

When the elements of knowledge are of a low degree (or experiential knowledge has a general nature) but commitment is high, uncertainty in the added value will be high and subsequently opportunity development fails. With this proposition, it becomes easy to understand why more than 90 per cent of all new ideas lead to bankruptcy. We have already experienced the results from the 'opportunity' declaration of the IT businesses during 1990s, wherein firms with a low experience and market knowledge made a large commitment and gained no value. The proposition suggests that the incremental process in opportunity development has its base on balance between the elements. An imbalance between these elements genders high uncertainty and failure. A high specific commitment with a low specific experiential knowledge will gender low surpass values. Visions constructed on general knowledge develop high uncertainty and low or negative added value. Success in such a condition is only based on 'pure chance'. Logically firms cannot afford to commit resources in a number of cases with the hope that 'chance' will help them. High resource commitment based on low and general knowledge, is far from the process of opportunity development. While 'chancing' normally holds waste of resources, the process of opportunity development increases the efficiency. The elements of specific knowledge and resource commitment reduce uncertainty in gaining surpass values.

A condition that is often discussed in recent research on opportunity is when firms miss their chances to develop opportunity process because it goes unnoticed. This is when firms potentially have some specific knowledge but miss to commit specific resources. This follows the statement of Kirzner (1997), that gaining specific knowledge to commit resources is not an intentional action. The interesting statement is that opportunity seekers do not really know beforehand if an opportunity will arise and will be exploited. Therefore, 'one' cannot search for something that one does not know exists. Opportunity notion contains phases and each phase has an unclear start and unknown outcome. The correlation between the knowledge and commitment cannot be understood through mechanical computation (see Shane, 2000). Opportunity development resides on the knowledge and commitments of interrelated actors. According to this point of view, the surpass value added in each phase of opportunity development is unknown until it has passed a long-term process wherein the correlation between the elements have become apparent. Though, opportunity development contains a process which is constructed on incrementality in the exchange of specific knowledge and heterogeneous resources, the surpass values induce actors to continue cooperation and to add new knowledge and resources.

An overview of this volume

The previous section has introduced the opportunity development concept and sets the scene by connecting it to business networks. Now, we can present the rest of the volume. Chapter 1 (Andersson, *et al.*) explores how firms find and exploit market opportunities. The paper suggests that each firm is constrained in terms of resources and therefore seeks relationships and networks to find and exploit opportunities. Based on network approach the authors suggest how these relationships should be configured to exploit opportunities. Chapter 2 (Bengtsson, *et al.*) deals with different cooperative and competitive relationships and how these relationships can enable firms to develop/explore technological innovation opportunities. They introduce the concept of 'network slack' and positive and negative contents/dimensions of relationships. These relationship are considered to lead towards evolutionary process of opportunity seeking. They present four different contexts in which network slack and network dynamics can be combined to explore innovation opportunities. Chapter 3 (Dimitratos and Jones) discusses the relationship between internationalization, opportunity perception and internationalization pattern of a firm and how these three aspects influence entrepreneurial activities of the firm. Based on resource-based and head-office assignment theories, they present a conceptual framework for the study of international entrepreneurship. The key contribution of this chapter is that it identifies the primary role of international opportunity patterns. Chapter 4 (Yamin) presents opportunity development as new technical resource combinations and capability development in multinational enterprises (MNEs). It suggests that MNE subsidiaries are often important sources of entrepreneurship and opportunity development. It also suggests that subsidiaries are embedded in networks and business relationships with customers and suppliers externally and with the head office and other subsidiaries internally. These internal and external networks play an important role in opportunity and business development in MNEs. Chapter 5 (Johanson and Strömsten.) considers the ability to create value as the key to growth and prosperity of a firm in industrial networks. The value is described as the combining and re-combining of resources within and between firms in a network. The value concept is treated as a process of value creation and realization, where value is created at one place and realized at another place in the network. The process of value creation and realization is further explained with the help of a case study from the European pulp and paper industry.

Part II looks at the opportunity development in international business. The first chapter in this section (Chapter 6 by Pahlberg and Persson) professes that MNEs need to explore opportunities in their environment in order to achieve sustainable competitive advantage. They also relate this to the local embeddedness of MNE subsidiaries. They claim that opportunity detection is strongly related to market knowledge, which is dependent on networks and relationship activities of subsidiaries in the local market. The transition from the awareness to exploitation of a subsidiary is dependent on the decision-making powers and cognitive capabilities. This leads to the conclusion that subsidiaries play a major role in MNE's capabilities to detect and explore opportunities. Chapter 7 (Hohenthal and Lindbergh) deals with SMEs internationalization activities and how this experience helps them to recognize opportunities in foreign markets. The chapter starts with the internationalization process of the firm and introduces and discusses concepts such as cultural distance, management experiential knowledge and offers an explanation as to why management's experiential knowledge influences the discovery of new business opportunities. The results of the study confirm that firms with more international experience have a higher level of managerial experiential knowledge and have more international presence. Chapter 8 (Adenfelt and Lagerström) discusses how multinationals seize opportunities by being multinational through relationships. The authors claim that all MNEs consider pursuit of entrepreneurial opportunities as a critical means of achieving competitive advantage. This is done through organizational rejuvenation. The authors use network theory to explore opportunity development through gaining access to complementary knowledge in network of relationships. An in-depth study of one MNC, Heitz, is presented to support their argument. They conclude that the MNC took advantage of dispersed knowledge and used it at global level for developing global IT-systems. This was done through existing relationships and knowledge combinations in the network. Chapter 9 (Cooke) claims that although much has been written on inter-organizational learning and knowledge among network organizations, insufficient attention has been given to knowledge sharing among MNEs as specific networked organizational form. It also claims that little is known about how MNEs plug into local centres and coordinate locally held knowledge across both national and organizational borders. This chapter tries to explain how MNEs exercise entrepreneurship by exploiting innovations that have taken place elsewhere and turn them into business opportunities for their own establishment. The chapter presents two case studies of UK MNEs. It examines formal as well as informal mechanisms used in generation and integration of corporate innovations. The chapter concludes that strategic knowledge management and interorganizational learning are important mechanisms for identifying business opportunities. Chapter 10 (Baraldi and Strömsten) deals with opportunities and obstacles a firm facess in its merger and acquisition (M&A) activities. The authors suggest that the major problem in M&As is that the value that it is supposed to be created is seldom realized. They focus on the network in which both firms are embedded as a unit of analysis. They study three cases; Ericsson, the Swedish Brewery Spendrups and a biotech merger between Toro and BEE. The chapter concludes that the opportunities and risks associated with M&A are hidden in the network of relationships and resources in which the acquired firm is embedded. Chapter 11 (Eriksson and Lindvall) treats reputation as an opportunity or risk. The authors define opportunity as 'potentialities' for profit making and explain that it is the reputation of the firm that determines potential for profit making. However, it is not the reputation *per se*, but a firm's reputation in a specific network of relationships that is important for opportunity development. The chapter presents data from Sweden's ten biggest consulting firms and concludes that the best way to create opportunities is to keep the old clients, as trust is built through experience. To attract new clients, the firm first has to build a reputation. This network reputation, particularly in service industry, would lead the firm towards new opportunities.

Part III particularly connects the two central concepts; opportunity development and networks. Here, Chapter 12 (Berggren and Silver) introduces the concept of mediators in opportunity development. In contrast to earlier understanding in which entrepreneur is considered as a lone ranger, it argues that other actors in the network play important role in shaping the entrepreneurs. The chapter presents form cases to illustrate the supporting role played by mediators. The mediators' contributions are directed towards links with customers as well as transferring an established business platform. The chapter provides empirical evidence to establish that how mediators in the network help entrepreneurs to develop opportunities and grow. Chapter 13 (Pahlberg and Thilenius) takes up opportunity development in an ongoing business context. The opportunity is defined as something valuable occurring in the market which can be discovered and put to use by a company with a capability to do so. For a firm, this means being continuously active in the market to realize the opportunity and to change its operations accordingly. They argue that some opportunities can only be developed through ongoing business relationships and a continuous change in these relationships. Opportunity development is thus dependent on the input from a wider network of relationships. Without this change induced by the network, business relationships would stagnate and become routine thus creating obstacles to opportunity development. Analysing 279 business relationships between buyers and suppliers, the chapter concludes that opportunity development is a continuous process that takes place in ongoing business relationships. Chapter 14 (Baraldi) takes up the emerging phenomenon of the role played by information technology (IT) in opportunity development. It examines the opportunity offered by IT solutions such as ERP (Enterprise Resource Planning) and obstacles towards seizing these opportunities. The chapter aims to develop a framework to illustrate the above. This is done through in-depth study of a firm (Edsbyn) that has recently implemented the ERP-system. The IT-influenced opportunities and hindrances are studied through the implementation process and the daily use of the particular IT system. The authors identify a series of opportunities and obstacles. They conclude that the IT system helps the firm to detect and develop opportunities as regards information handling, intra- and inter-organizational efficiency and resource development at network level. Chapter 15 (Bengtson and Åberg) discusses the notion of information asymmetry and whether it is a prerequisite for the existence of entrepreneurial opportunities. They argue that the type of information from which opportunities are created is situation-specific rather than generally applicable and is connected to the context of a specific actor. They present some theoretical implications that differ from the earlier studies. They illustrate their point by studying the development and use of ISDN-net's D-channel for electronic payment services in six different firms. They explain how the resource context of the different actors influence opportunity creation and exploitation. Chapter 16 (Ståhl) elaborates on the emergence and exploitation of opportunities in business networks and how these enhance our understanding of change in business networks. The chapter presents an in-depth study of a leading Industrial Tooling Company (ITC) and how it develops and exploits an opportunity. It is based on the concept of 'preferred supplier' developed in the UK subsidiary since 1990s. The study reveals that development and exploitation of opportunity depends upon an interplay between internal resources, judgements and development of new resources and relationships coupled with network trends. The opportunity was exploited by creating a holistic approach to tooling in the production process common to both counterparts, thus improving productivity. They conclude that opportunities are inter-active phenomena. Finally, the epilogue (Hadjikhani and Johanson) ties the whole volume up and suggests some avenues for future research.

Summary

This introductory chapter is devoted to introduce the concept of opportunity development and develop a notion connecting opportunity development to the business network perspective. There are two reasons for the development of this framework. One was to give a new definition to the concept of entrepreneurship that traditionally is coupled with individuals and small organizations and the second was to encapsulate the dynamism in the business network theory. In this vein the development of business opportunity apprehends an interdependent relationship between individuals/units/organizations. The theoretical framework that is introduced has a strength to be generally applicable for different conditions. No matter if the focal developer of opportunity is individuals or organizations. The notion, similar to some later studies in entrepreneurship, holds the view that opportunity contains an incremental development process. In line with business network thoughts we introduced a theoretical framework containing the three variables of specific knowledge, resource commitment and surpass value. The crucial assumption is that the extra value in opportunity development is related to the knowledge and resource contribution of actors. Shortcomings in knowledge or resource contributions affect the extra value added and results in economic failure. The process initiated by a focal actor combines heterogeneous resources from interrelated actors. The initiator is not necessarily the same as one who explores it. After reaching the exploration stage, the activities become standardized and opportunity development has its strength as far as it provides extra value to the focal and connected actors. Opportunity development comes to an end when actors like competitors gain a better market position and the extra value ceases to flow into the organizations.

References

Longman Dictionary of Contemporary English. (1995). Pearson Education.
Aldrich, H. (2000). Many are Called but Few are Chosen: An Evolutionary Perspective for the Study of Entrepreneurship, in P. Westhead and M. Wright (Eds) *Advances in Entrepreneurship*, London: Edward Elgar Publishing Ltd.
Alvarez, S. A. and Busenitz, L. W. (2001). The Entrepreneurship of Resource-Based Theory, *Journal of Management*, 27, 755–75.
Andersson, U. and Forsgren, M. (2000). In Search of Centre of Excellence: Network Embeddedness and Subsidiary Roles in Multinational Corporations, *Management International Review*, 40(4), 329–50.
Ardichvili, A., Cardoza, R. and Ray S. (2003). A Theory of Entrepreneurial Opportunity Identification and Development, *Journal of Business Venturing*, 18, 105–23.
Baron, J. (1998). Cognitive Mechanisms in Entrepreneurship: Why And When Entrepreneurs Think Differently Than Other People, *Journal of Business Venturing*, 13, 275–94.
Begley, T. M. and Boyd, D. P. (1987). A Comparison of Entrepreneurs and Managers of Small Business Firms, *Journal of Management*, 13, 99–108.
Blankenburg Holm, D. (1996). Business Network Connections and International Business Relationships, doctoral thesis, No. 65, Department of Business Studies, Uppsala University, Uppsala.
Brockhaus, R. and Horowitz, P. (1986). The Psychology of the Entrepreneur, in D. Sexton and R. Smilor (Eds) *The Art and Science of Entrepreneurship*, Cambridge, MA: Ballinger.
Brown, T. E., Davidsson, P. and Wiklund, J. (2001). An Operationalization of Stevensons's Conceptualization of Entrepreneurship as Opportunity-Based Firm Behaviour, *Strategic Management Journal*, 22, 953–68.
Busenitz, L. W. (2003). Entrepreneurship Research in Emergence: Past Trends and Future Directions, *Journal of Management*, 29(3), 285–308.
Chen, C. P. (1998). Does Entrepreneurial Self-Efficacy Distinguish Entrepreneurs from Managers?, *Journal of Business Venturing*, 13(4), 295–316.
Coviello, N., Ghauri, P. and Marin, K. (1998). International Competitiveness: Empirical Findings from SME Services Firms, *European Journal of Marketing*, 30(2), 75–88.
Dess, G. (2003). Emerging Issues in Corporative Entrepreneurship, *Journal of Management*, 29(3), 351–78.
Dubini, P. and Aldrich, H. (1991). Personal and Extended Networks are Central to the Entrepreneurial Process, *Journal of Business Venturing*, 6, 305–13.
Easton, G. and Araujo, L. (1992). Non-economic exchange in industrial network, in B. Axelsson and G. Easton (Eds) *Industrial Networks – A New View of Reality*, London: Routledge.
Eckhardt, J. T. and Shane, S. A. (2003). Opportunities and Entrepreneurship, *Journal of Management*, 29(3), 333–49.

Egidi, M. and Narduzzo, A. (1996). The Emergence of Path-Dependent Behaviors in Cooperative Contexts, *International Journal of Industrial Organization*, 5, 677–709.
Florida, R. (2003). Entrepreneurship Creativity and Regional Economic Growth, in D. M. Hart (Ed.) *The Emergence of Entrepreneurship Policy*, Cambridge: Cambridge University Press.
Foss, N. J. and Klein, P. G. (Eds) (2002). *Entrepreneurship and the Firm. Austrian Perspectives on Economic Organization*, Cheltenham: Edward Elgar Publishing Ltd.
Garrouste, P. (2002). Knowledge: A Challenge for the Austrian Theory of the Firm, in N. J. Foss and P. G. Klein (Eds) *Entrepreneurship and the Firm*, Cheltenham: Edward Elgar.
Geroski, P. A. (1990). Innovation, Technological Opportunity, and Market Structure, *Oxford Economic Papers*, 42(3), 586–602.
Ghauri, P. N. and Prasad, S. B. (1995). A Network Approach to Probing Asia's Interfirm Linkages, in Prasad, S. B. (ed.), *Advances in International Comparative Management*, 10, Stamford, CT: JAI Press, 63–8.
Ghauri, P. N., Clemens Lutz and Goitom Tesfom (2004). Using Networks to Solve Export-Marketing Problems of Small- and Medium-Sized Firms from Developing Countries, *European Journal of Marketing*, 37(5/6), 728–52.
Ghauri, P. N. (Ed.) (1999). *Advances in International Marketing: International Marketing and Purchasing*, Stamford, CT: JAI Press.
Graver, M. S. (2003). Best Practices in Identifying Customer-Driven Improvement Opportunities, *Industrial Marketing Management*, 32, 455–66.
Hadjikhani, A. (1996). *Political Crises and International Business: Swedish MNCs in a Turbulent Market*, Acta Universitatis Upsaliensis, Studia Oeconomiae Negotiorum, No. 40, Uppsala University, Stockholm: Almqvist & Wiksell International.
Hadjikhani, A. (1997). A Note on the Criticism against the Internationalization Process Model, *Management International Review*, Special Issue, 37, 43–66.
Hadjikhani, A. (2000). The Political Behavior of Business Actors, International Studies of Management and Organisation, 30(1), 95–119.
Håkansson, H. (1987). *Industrial Technological Development: A Network Approach*, London: Croom Helm.
Håkansson, H. and Snehota, I. (1995). *Developing Relationships in Business Networks*, London: Routledge.
Håkansson, H. and Waluszewski, A. (2002). *Managing Technological Development: IKEA, the Environment and Technology*, London: Routledge.
Hart, D. M. (2003). Entrepreneurship Policy: What It Is and Where It Came From, in D. M. Hart (Ed.) *The Emergence of Entrepreneurship Policy*, Cambridge: Cambridge University Press.
Hayek, F. A. (1945). The Use of Knowledge in Society, *American Economic Review*, 35(4), 519–30.
Hoang, H. and Antoncic, B. (2003). Network-based Research in Entrepreneurship – A Critical View, *Journal of Business Venturing*, 18, 165–87.
Ingram, P. and Baum, J. A. C. (1997). Opportunity and Constraint: Organizations' Learning from the Operating and Competitive Experience of Industries. *Strategic Management Journal*, 18, 75–98.
Jack, S. L. and Anderson, A. R. (2002). The Effect of Embeddedness on the Entrepreneurial Process, *Journal of Business Venturing*, 17, 467–87.
Johanson, J. and Mattsson, L-G. (1988). Internationalization in Industrial Systems – A Network Approach, in N. Hood and J-E. Vahlne, J-E. (Eds) *Strategies in Global Competition*, London: Croom Helm, 286–314.

Kaish, S. and Gilad, B. (1991). Characteristics of Opportunities Search of Entrepreneurs Versus Executives: Source, Interests, General Alertness, *Journal of Business Venturing*, 6, 45–61.

Khilstrom, L. and Laffont, N. (1979). A General Equilibrium Entrepreneurial Theory of Firm Formation Based on Risk Aversion, *Journal of Political Economy*, 87(4), 719–48.

Kirzner, I. M. (1973). *Competition & Entrepreneurship*, Chicago: University of Chicago Press.

Kirzner, I. M. (1989). *Discovery, Capitalism and Distributive Justice*, Oxford: Basil Blackwell.

Kirzner, I. M. (1997). Entrepreneurial Discovery and the Competitive Market Process: An Austrian Approach. *Journal of Economic Literature*, 35(1), 60–85.

Kirzner, I. M. (1999). Creativity and/or Alertness: A Reconsideration of the Schumpeterian Entrepreneur. *Review of Austrian Economics*, 11, 5–17.

Kreizner, I. (1973). *Competition and Entrepreneurship*. Chicago: The University of Chicago Press.

Lafuente, A. and Salas, V. (1989). Types of Entrepreneurs and Firms: The Case of New Spanish Firms. *Strategic Management Journal*, 10(1), 17–30.

Manimala, M. J. (1999). *Entrepreneurial Policies and Strategies: The Innovator's Choice*, New Delhi: Sage.

McKendall, M. A. and Wagner J. A. (1997). Motive, Opportunity, Choice, and Corporate Illegality. *Organization Science*, 8(6), 624–47.

Miles, S. (2001). *How to Hack a Party Line: The Democrats and Silicone Valley*, New York: Farrar, Straus and Giroux.

Mises, L. V. (1943). Elastic Expectations and the Austrian Theory of the Trade Cycle, *Economica*, X (N.S.), (37) Feb. 12–23.

Mises, L. V. (1949). *Human Action. A Treatise on Economics*, Chicago IL: Henry Regnery.

Mises, L.V. (1981). *The Theory of Money and Credit*, Indianapolis, IN: Liberty Fund.

Mokyr, J. (1990). *The Lever of Riches*, New York: Oxford University Press.

Morris, M. H. and Paul, G. W. (1987). The Relationship between Entrepreneurship and Marketing in Established Firms. *Journal of Business Venturing*, 2, 247–59.

Pearce, W. (1992). *The MIT Dictionary of Modern Economics*, Cambridge, MA: MIT Press.

Penrose, E. (1956). Foreign Investment and the Growth of the Firm. *Economic Journal*, 66(262), 220–35.

Penrose, E. (1959). *The Productive Opportunity of the firm and the 'Entrepreneur', The Theory of the Growth of the Firm*, 3rd edn, Oxford: Oxford University Press.

Rice, M. P., A, B and C (2001). Radical Innovation: Triggering Initiation of Opportunity Recognition and Evaluation. *R & D Management*, 31(4), 409–20.

Sarah, L. J. and Anderson, A. R. (2002). The Effect of Embeddedness on the Entrepreneurial Process *Journal of Business Venturing*, 17, 467–87.

Schumpeter, J. (1942). *Capitalism, Socialism and Democracy*, New York: Harper Brothers.

Schumpeter, J. (1947). The Creative Response in Economic History. *Journal of Economic History*, 7, 149–59.

Scott, J. (1991). *Social Network Analysis. A Handbook*, Newbury Park, CA: Sage Publications.

Shackle, N. (1982). *Imagination of Nature of Choice*. Edinburgh University Press, Edinburgh, Scotland.

Shane, S. A. (2000). Prior Knowledge and the Discovery of Entrepreneurial Opportunity. *Organization Science*, 11(4), 448–79.

Shane, S. A. and Venkataraman, S. (2000). The Promise of Entrepreneurship as a Field of Research! *Academy of Management Review*, 25, 217–26

Shane, S., Locke, E. and Collins, C. (2003). Entrepreneurial Motivation. *Human Resource Management Review*, 13, 257–79.

Smith, N. R. (1967). *The Entrepreneur and his Firms: The Relationship between Type of Man and Type of Company*, East Lansing, MI: Michigan State University.

Stevenson, H. H. and Jarillo, J. C. (1990). A Paradigm of Entrepreneurship: Entrepreneurial Management. *Strategic Management Journal*, 11, 17–27.

Stigler, G. J. (1961). The Economics of Information. *Journal of Political Economy*, 69, 213–25.

Thakur, S. P. (1998). Size of Investment, Opportunity Choice and Human Resources in New Venture Growth: Some Typologies. *Journal of Business Venturing*, 14, 283–309.

Vaughn, K. (1994). *Austrian Economics in America – The Migration of a Tradition*, Cambridge: Cambridge University Press.

Venkataraman, S. (1997). The Distinctive Domain of Entrepreneurship Research: An Editors' Perspective, in J. Katz and R. Brockhaus (Eds) *Advances in Entrepreneurship, Firm Emergence, and Growth*, Greenwich, CT: JAI Press.

Vihanto, M. (2002). Costs of Contracting, Psychology of Entrepreneurship and Capabilities of Firms, in N. J. Foss and P. G. Klein (Eds) *Entrepreneurship and the Firm. Austrian Perspectives on Economic Organization*, Cheltenham: Edward Elgar Publishing Ltd.

Webster, F. A. (1977). Entrepreneurs and Ventures: An attempt at classification and clarification. *Academy of Management Review*, 2(1), 54–61.

Woodruff, R. B. and Gardial, S. F. (1996). *Know your Customer New Approaches to Understanding Customer Value and Satisfaction*, Cambridge, MA: Blackwell.

Part I

Opportunity Development in Business Networks: Conceptual Development

1
Opportunities, Relational Embeddedness and Network Structure

Ulf Andersson, Desireé Blankenburg Holm and Martin Johanson

Introduction

The thesis of this chapter is that the characteristics of the business network surrounding the firm have a profound impact on how the firm finds and exploits opportunities. Characteristics of networks and relations between network actors have been increasingly researched during recent decades (see e.g. Dyer and Chu, 2000; Grabher, 1993; Granovetter, 1985, 1992; Gulati, 1998, 1999; Gulati *et al.*, 2000; Håkansson and Snehota, 1995; Halinen and Törnroos, 1998; Kogut, 2000; McEvily and Zaheer, 1999; Rowley *et al.*, 2000; Uzzi, 1996, 1997; Zukin and Di Maggio, 1990). In parallel, a wide and strong tradition of research has emerged on the nature of opportunity, especially among entrepreneurship researchers (see e.g. Ardichvili *et al.*, 2003; Eckhardt and Shane, 2003; Shane, 2000). We aim to combine these two traditions and seek to develop a model for analyzing the relation between different types of opportunities and different types of relationships and networks. Entrepreneurial behavior and social networks have previously been explored (Ardichvili *et al.*, 2003; Ellis, 2000; Jack and Anderson, 2002; Kenney and Goe, 2004; Simsek *et al.*, 2003). These studies have observed that there seems to be a relation between finding an opportunity and the characteristics of the social network, but to our knowledge there are no studies investigating the character of relationships and network configurations and how it influences the firm's way of finding and exploiting opportunities. This chapter aims to fill this void.

We begin by highlighting the questions that this chapter tries to answer. After that follows a discussion where we define the opportunity concept and distinguish two activities in the opportunity-process, finding and exploiting opportunities. Thereafter, we propose that different types of knowledge tend to have different influences on how the firm finds and exploits opportunities, depending on the nature of its relationships and networks. The subsequent section deals with the concept of relational embeddedness, before we discuss open and closed network structures. Based on that discussion, we distinguish four situations characterized by various degrees of relational embeddedness and different network closure. Finally, the chapter concludes with managerial suggestions for finding and exploiting opportunities, given different degrees of relationship embeddedness and network structures which depend on the type of knowledge.

Key considerations

In our attempt to conceptualize how opportunities are found and exploited in different relationships and network settings, we identify four key considerations, from which the discussion begins. *First*, the characteristics of the firm and its network structure constitute the framework for its performance and since both finding and exploiting opportunities is contingent on the firm's behavior, the relationships and network are both a possibility and a constraint. The network structure is discussed in terms of open and closed networks (Coleman, 1990) and we focus on the flow of knowledge and how firms can assimilate, reflect and compare the knowledge received. We build the analysis on the notions of relational embeddedness and open and closed networks. Zukin and DiMaggio (1990) classify embeddedness into four types but three are sufficient here: cognitive, cultural and political. These are often merged into relational embeddedness, which primarily concerns the qualitative aspects and the nature of relationships.

Second, we do not believe that all relationships and networks foster a variety of opportunities; instead it seems likely to expect that the type of opportunity found is dependent on the nature of the firm's relationships and the network structure. We make a distinction between market opportunities and technological opportunities, where market opportunity refers to the exchange of resources and technological opportunities are concerned with how firms combine resources.

Third, we discuss what type of knowledge is likely to be the source of the opportunity. This discussion builds on findings made primarily by social network scholars, but also on results produced by the Industrial Marketing and Purchasing Group (Ford *et al.*, 2003; Håkansson, 1982). One important aspect of knowledge is whether the opportunity is based on new or existing knowledge. New knowledge implies that the firm does not know about the character and nature of the opportunity. Existing knowledge, on the other hand, is either the firm's own knowledge, which it is already using, or what they know is being used by other firms in the network. The other aspect of knowledge concerns whether it can be codified or not. This is important, because as relationships and networks are supposed to provide opportunities, the flow of knowledge in the network has an impact on how firms find opportunities. In general, we expect codified knowledge to be transferred more easily in the network than non-codified knowledge.

Fourth, and finally, once opportunities are found, the firm can decide to exploit them, but also, in this case, relationships and networks surrounding the firm have an impact on how the fruits of the opportunities are divided between the firms in the network. We make a distinction between the likeliness that some or a few firms in the network can earn rent or if the benefits produced by the opportunities exploited are more evenly shared between a large number of firms.

Opportunity

Opportunity is the focus of this section. It refers to new ways of using resources, both internally and externally. New ways which are more efficient, profitable or produce more value for the actors involved than the existing ways of using the resources. Eckhardt and Shane (2003: 336) define opportunities as situations in which new ways of using resources – through exchange or combination – can be introduced by transforming the existing ends and/or means. New ways imply that an opportunity for the enterprises involved has a high degree of originality in itself (Casson, 1982; Choi and Shephard, 2004). Finding opportunities is contingent on the fact that knowledge is imperfectly distributed among different actors in the economy (Hayek, 1945), which means that opportunity is a subjective and perceptual concept, based on what the individuals know and perceive. Burt (1992b) has a similar starting point as he relates an actor's opportunity to his social capital, which in turn creates a competitive advantage. Each actor has a network of contacts in the [competitive] arena. Certain actors are connected to certain others, trusting certain others, obligated to support certain others, dependent on exchange with certain others (57). It then follows that there is no such thing as an objective opportunity, which is waiting to be found by any firm. Nor is any firm able to discover or recognize all opportunities. Instead, we assume that a firm's competitive advantage is based on its capability to find and exploit opportunities in a network. Two well-known economists help to divide the new ways of using resources into two types of opportunities:

First, there are *market opportunities*, which refer to exchange of resources between at least two actors. Kirzner (1973, 1992, 1997) discusses entrepreneurial behavior in a market process characterized by disequilibrium. A driving factor in the market process is firms' capability to be alert to discover new ways of exchanging resources and new counterparts in the market. Kirzner makes a distinction between known ignorance and unknown ignorance. Finding market opportunities based on known ignorance implies that the firm can identify and specify what they are searching for, that is, it is based on existing knowledge. However, Kirzner also means that sometimes firms find market opportunities based on unknowable, that is, completely new knowledge. It is the finding of market opportunities based on new knowledge that drives the market process, according to Kirzner (1997).

Second, there are also *technological opportunities*, which can be viewed as new ways of combining resources without necessarily exchanging the new combination of resources with other actors. Technological opportunities correspond well to four of the five loci, which Schumpeter (1934) suggests are sources for change: creation of new products or services, discovery of new raw materials, new methods of production and new ways of organizing. The fifth locus refers to new geographical markets, which fall under the definition of market opportunities.

Finding opportunities is accomplished through the execution of activities like search, exploration, discovery and recognition (March, 1991), which means that finding an opportunity can be more or less planned, and thus appear after a more or less deliberate process. Exploiting opportunities involves activities like assimilation, absorption, deployment, implementation and utilization and it is thus a question of doing business with other actors and/ or utilizing technologies. From the above, it follows that market and technological opportunities have to be found before they can be properly exploited. Opportunity implies finding something new and incorporating it into something which already exists, which means that there is need for fit (Ardichvili *et al.*, 2003) between the opportunity and the firm's existing relationships and network, that is, the new knowledge, represented by the opportunity, must be able to be absorbed in the prevailing knowledge structure.

Dispersed knowledge is a prerequisite for the existence of opportunities, but dispersed knowledge also implies that firms learn. Since opportunities are new ways of using resources, the degree of novelty of the opportunities has an impact on how firms are able both to find and to exploit them. Finding opportunities is thus related to the firm's prior experience (Shane, 2000) while the decision to exploit opportunities is more likely to be made when the firm perceives that it has knowledge about the new way of using resources (Choi and Shepherd, 2004). The need for fit between opportunities and structure is thus relevant both for finding and exploiting opportunities. In furthering our understanding on how the firm can optimize the search and exploitation of opportunities, we have reason to focus on structural issues in terms of relationships and networks.

Relational embeddedness

One notion that is often put forward when discussing relationships and networks is relational embeddedness. Being embedded in a social context has been observed to create opportunities, and even sometimes to be a prerequisite for finding any opportunities (Burt, 1992a; Ellis, 2000; Jack and Anderson, 2002). Much of our reasoning around embeddedness goes back to

Granovetter's (1985) seminal article, where his stance was that economic behavior is not an autonomous activity, which is performed in isolation from institutions, technology, political or cultural conditions and the social context.

The point of departure for relational embeddedness is that a relationship between actors has several dimensions and that several types of activities are simultaneously performed. However, dimensions and activities are not isolated from each other. Instead, the embeddedness concept implies that they are interdependent. Consequently, strong interdependence between these dimensions means a high degree of embeddedness.

In this chapter, we focus on three specific dimensions of relationships: *social relations, exchange of resources, and combination of resources*. Thus, we assume that exchange between two firms in a relationship (economic action in Granovetter's terminology (*ibid.*)) can be more or less embedded in a technological structure, where the firms combine resources and invest and adapt their resources towards the counterpart, and that this exchange is more or less embedded in a set of social relations. We define relational embeddedness as the interdependence between social relations, exchange of resources, and combination of resources in the relationship. The reason for this definition is twofold. First, we assume that it is in line with Granovetter's (1985) ideas and, second, it seems consistent with the definition of opportunity. Thus, a high degree of embeddedness is a result of a high interdependence between how, when and why two actors exchange resources and how and what types of resources the actors combine in the relationship. In this case, the business performed in the relationship is embedded in the two actors' technological structure and social relations.

This means that market opportunities are more or less embedded in a technological structure and a set of social relations. When firms try to find and exploit market opportunities they have to consider both social relations and technological issues (see Figure 1.1). On the other hand, technological opportunities are embedded in an exchange structure and a set of social relations. The way firms exchange resources and handle social relations will consequently influence the process of finding and exploiting technological opportunities. A high degree of relational embeddedness

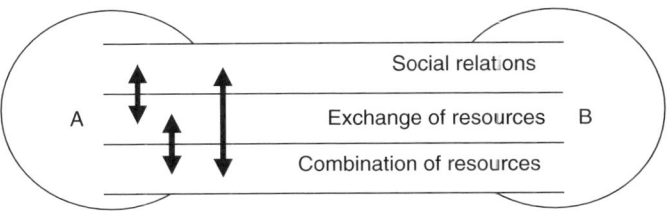

Figure 1.1 Relational embeddedness

seems to be a crucial condition or at least a favored circumstance for finding and exploiting opportunities based on non-codified knowledge (see e.g. Hansen, 1999). For instance, technology development research has analyzed the troublesome flow of complex knowledge, including non-codified knowledge (Zander and Kogut, 1995) and knowledge dependent on a larger system (Winter, 1987). Further, the market as network perspective, mainly interested in activity relationships between firms, has rather emphasized the importance of close and interdependent relationships, especially in the case of product development (see e.g. Andersson and Forsgren, 1996, 2000; Håkansson, 1989; Laage-Hellman, 1989). The advantage of a high degree of relational embeddedness has also been observed by Uzzi (1997). He argues that a high degree of relational embeddedness enhances a flow of fine-grained knowledge between two firms and joint problem solving, while a low degree of relational embeddedness may cause problems in the flow of non-codified knowledge between firms. When exchange is strongly embedded in a technological structure and a set of social relations, the relationship tends to be characterized by extensive interaction, mutual trust, and relationship-specific advantage, which, in turn, means good knowledge about the counterpart. Finding technological opportunities, therefore, can be a result of solving problems which have occurred while interacting, and which, in turn, force the firms to cooperate to solve the problem. Altogether this means that changes concerning, for instance, exchange and technology, often are incremental and must fit into the present character of the relationship.

Hansen (1999) has shown that the advantage of relationships with a low degree of embeddedness as a source of opportunities prevails if the knowledge found is of a codified type. When the knowledge is of a non-codified complex type, there has to be a certain depth in the relationship, that is, a higher degree of relational embeddedness has its advantages when the firm exploits knowledge that originally resides in other relationships. Moreover, when the relationships are characterized by a high degree of relational embeddedness, firms tend to search for opportunities locally in their direct relationships. This corresponds to the idea that opportunities based on problem solving occur in a situation when the ends sought are defined but the means are still not defined (Ardichvili *et al.*, 2003).

A high degree of relational embeddedness not only affects the opportunities found, but also influences how they are exploited. Relationships with a high degree of relational embeddedness are characterized by informal contracts, mutual trust and wide and intensive cooperation and interaction, where the exchange is dependent on social relations between people involved in the interaction and the combination of resources deployed in the technology. Therefore, changing the character of, for instance, the exchange of resources, cannot be done autonomously from the social relations in the relationships. This makes exploitation of opportunities a more complicated process than in relationships with a low degree of embeddedness. Thus, exploitation of opportunities based on non-codified knowledge tends to be promoted by more deep and intense relationships between the firm and its counterparts, that is, a high degree of relational embeddedness. This means that high degrees of embeddedness often promote technological opportunities, while relationships with low degrees of embeddedness tend to favor market opportunities. The reason for this is that technological opportunities usually contain a large element of non-codified knowledge (Andersson and Forsgren, 1996, 2000; Andersson et al., 2001; Håkansson, 1989; Hansen, 1999). Firms that share deep and intense relationships with each other are likely to possess more common knowledge of each other compared to actors which have relationships with a low degree of embeddedness. Moreover, a high degree of relational embeddedness means that the two firms are likely to develop a shared understanding of each others' capabilities and trustworthiness. A high degree of relational embeddedness can be viewed as the capacity of the relationship to hold knowledge that diminishes uncertainty (Granovetter, 1973).

Moreover, a high degree of relational embeddedness implies a strong link between finding opportunities, which often is a result of problem solving or firms jointly searching for innovation, and exploitation. Finding and exploiting opportunities are, thus, integrated activities. The degree of embeddedness thus gives the relationship a certain structure that can be more or less dense, to put it simply. However, there is also reason to investigate the structure of the network to ascertain different bases needed for finding and exploiting opportunities with different characteristics.

Network structure as open and closed systems

A common way to describe network structures is as open or closed systems (see e.g. Burt, 1992a; Coleman, 1990; Kogut, 2000; Uzzi, 1996). The open network structure is the outcome of the competitive struggle between parties motivated by self-interest. The main construct in this type of network is the unique, that is, non-redundant, relationship (Figure 1.2). A relationship is non-redundant if it is the only path between two actors. Thus, a completely open network consists only of non-redundant relationships, where there is only one path between the firms in the network (see Figure 1.2). This, in turn, means that open networks promote the flow of new knowledge as it is less likely that a firm will receive the same knowledge from other counterparts.

Further, actors that have multiple non-redundant relationships to other actors who are not connected to each other have a strong brokerage position called "structural holes" (Burt, 1992a). Firms positioned in structural holes have a more powerful position than others do because they control the knowledge flows between different networks (*ibid.*). Networks of this type

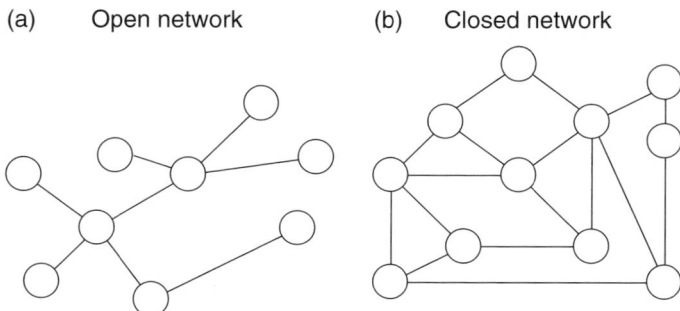

Figure 1.2 Open (A) and closed (B) networks

tend to have a "hierarchical" structure although there are several hierarchies, and the firm bridging the structural holes earns the credit (Kogut, 2000).

The closed network, on other hand, builds on the notion that firms in the network coordinate their efforts and actions (Figure 1.2). Coordination is improved through the continuous knowledge flows between the actors in the network (Coleman, 1990). A closed network does not give the firms so much new knowledge because it is always likely that knowledge received from one counterpart will later be received from another counterpart as well. The redundant relationships between the network partners result in a resolution to collective action problems (Kogut, 2000), but also allows the firm to check the quality of the knowledge and to reflect, compare and evaluate the received knowledge. Network structure focuses on the position a firm occupies in the network beyond the immediate relationships. In these positional perspectives, the frame of reference shifts from the dyad or triad to the system. Different positions in a network have different advantages, for example, a firm positioned between two other unconnected firms, which characterizes an open network, can control the knowledge flow between the other actors and thereby also influence the other actors' access to knowledge (see e.g. Burt, 1992a, 1992b; Cook and Emerson, 1978). Thereby, a completely open network gives each firm in the structure a possibility to control how and what knowledge is flowing through the network, which combined with the relatively large portion of new knowledge makes it easy to keep critical knowledge (privileged knowledge) within the boundaries of the firm. But this is the same for all firms in the network.

On the other hand, we believe that a closed network causes technological opportunities, which are based on cooperation and coordination, but at the same time firms will find few market opportunities as there is a limited flow of new knowledge inside the closed network. Thus, it is less likely that the

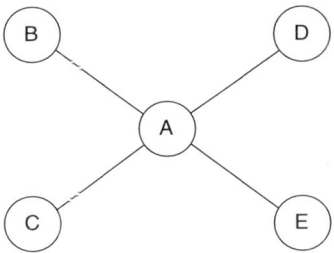

Figure 1.3 The rent accruing position in an open network

opportunities will be characterized by novelty than in an open network. Therefore in an open network, joint search and learning is usually absent. But, on the other hand, the open network makes it possible for a firm to earn rent based on its position in the network. Consider for example a situation, as in Figure 1.3, where the Firm [A], has received new, and for some reason important, knowledge from its counterparts [B] and [C]. The Firm [A] can now charge each of its other counterparts [D] and [E] arbitrage for supplying this knowledge, as they are not connected with each other or connected to any one else that can provide the knowledge except for firm [A]. This means that in open networks it is relatively easy to keep the benefits within the boundaries of the firm. In open networks, one can expect to see that firms which find opportunities strive to limit knowledge about them in order to fully exploit those opportunities, without sharing the benefits with other actors in the network.

In contrast to the broker earning rent in the open network, the closed network benefits the whole. The benefits of the closed network are not attributed to efficient flow of new knowledge, but rather to the fact that a large quantity of redundant relationships promotes cooperative behavior and coordination. Thereby the share of new knowledge in relation to the total amount of knowledge is smaller than in an open network (Burt, 1992a). Although a more open network often provides a better structure for flow of new knowledge into and out of the network, it does at the same time give some actors a position to control the flow of knowledge in the network. The open network therefore tends to limit the reasons to cooperate and coordinate the actors' activities. Apparently closed and open networks both have their pros and cons when put in these absolute terms. To put it differently, given that the firm has a fixed amount of resources, if a firm has a relationship to counterpart [A], which in turn has a relationship to [B], it is better to relinquish a relationship to [B] and instead use the limited resources to engage in a new relationship with counterpart [C] (see the dotted lines in Figure 1.4). This is because the knowledge received from [A] already contains the knowledge from [B], as they are connected (Burt, 1992a). For instance, Uzzi (1997)

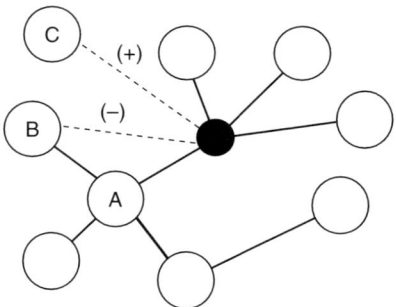

Figure 1.4 Rational use of limited resources in an open network according to Burt (1992a)

argues that there is a risk of becoming locked-in in closed networks. It happens when the firms are too involved in too many relationships, which are connected with each other. In this network, there are few or no relationships with outside firms, who can potentially contribute new knowledge (Burt, 1992a). A network which is too closed reduces the flow of new knowledge into the network, because it is likely that the same knowledge circulates in the network, that the knowledge flowing is of the same character as that already used in the relationship. Extensive novelty is usually difficult to transform into incremental changes. Thus, we can conclude that an open network structure very much repeats the hierarchical structure, but in multiple ways, and that the benefits accrue to the bridging firm (Burt, 1992a; Kogut, 2000). On the other hand, a closed network facilitates a positive development of the whole network, through cooperation and coordination among the firms, where the gain is in being a part of the network structure.

Finding and exploiting opportunities

Bringing together what is said above about relationships, structures and opportunity, we can conclude that a firm's ability to find and exploit opportunities is dependent on its network structure, in terms of closure, as well as on the characteristics of its relationships, in terms of depth. Being embedded in a set of social relations and technological structures provides not only knowledge, resources, support and advice, but can also help the firm to find opportunities (Jack and Anderson, 2002).

This discussion reveals two contradicting forces influencing a firm's position to find opportunities and the configuration of the network and content of the relationships. First, there is the aspect of having sources, which provide new knowledge, which can be turned into opportunities. This seems to

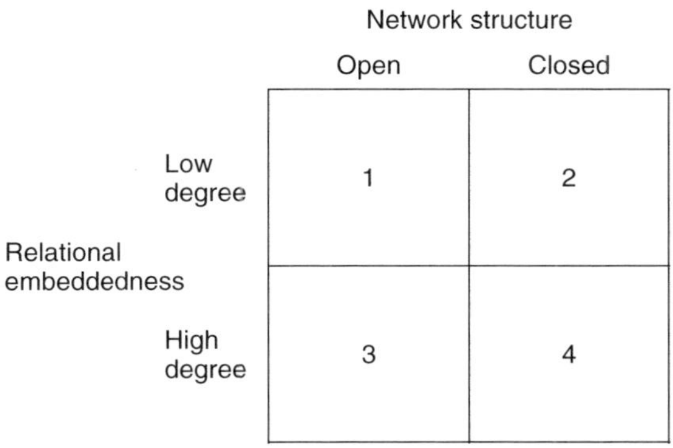

	Network structure	
	Open	Closed
Relational embeddedness — Low degree	1	2
Relational embeddedness — High degree	3	4

Figure 1.5 Impact on finding and exploiting opportunities by embeddedness and network structure

require that the firm has relationships with a low degree of embeddedness and that at least part of its network is open. Second, the firm's ability to absorb knowledge (Cohen and Levinthal, 1990; Lane and Lubatkin, 1998) and exploit those opportunities that are found is dependent on having relationships with a high degree of embeddedness and being in a position which enables cooperation and coordination with other actors, that is, being part of a closed network. This is because the more new knowledge of a non-codified type the opportunity contains, the greater the need for deep relationships in order for the firm to have good possibilities to assimilate the knowledge. Based on the discussion above, we are then facing four theoretical situations, summarized in Figure 1.5. These theoretical situations are by no means situations commonly found in reality but rather archetypes helping to clarify the subsequent discussion.

The theoretical situations are (1) an open network with a low degree of embeddedness, (2) a closed network with a low degree of embeddedness, (3) an open network with a high degree of embeddedness, and (4) a closed network with high degree of embeddedness. These four situations will be further discussed below.

An open network with low degree of relational embeddedness

If we first of all consider the critical issue of knowledge as a source of opportunity, the possibilities for the firm to receive new knowledge increases if the firm has relationships to many counterparts that can provide such knowledge. From a structural point of view, this is the case when the firm's relationships are unrelated to each other, that is, cell 1 in Figure 1.5. In an open structure (Burt, 1992a), the probability of each counterpart contributing

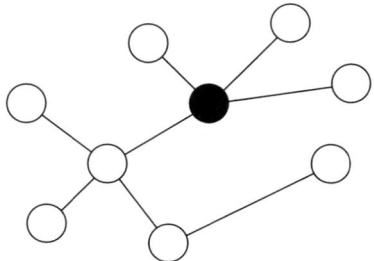

Figure 1.6 An open network with a low degree of relational embeddedness

unique knowledge increases, as the firms are not connected to each other. Moreover, when an open network contains relationships with a low degree of relational embeddedness as shown in Figure 1.6, it seems likely to expect that the firm is in a good position to find opportunities if they are based on knowledge that is codified.

Thus, this situation implies that the opportunities found will be based on a large proportion of new, but codified knowledge. Such a situation also tends to be a good basis for finding market opportunities, while finding and exploiting technological opportunities is less likely. The reason for this is that assimilation of opportunities based on non-codified knowledge is difficult, thus, the more the knowledge is of a non-codified kind, the more difficult it is to assimilate the opportunities. We have reason to assume that the coordination and cooperation that is needed for integration of more complex knowledge is difficult to achieve as the relationships are not connected and therefore lack a common knowledge base (Cohen and Levinthal, 1990; Coleman, 1990; Lane and Lubatkin, 1998). Another characteristic of this type of situation is that the firm in focus can relatively easily earn rent at the expense of other firms (see Burt, 1992a; Kogut, 2000), as it can keep critical knowledge inside the firm and not let other firms, with which it has relationships, know about the exploitation of the opportunity.

This observation has much in common with what a stockbroker does. By connecting buyers and sellers of different stocks, having a position such as the firm portrayed in black in Figure 1.6 is beneficial. For a stockbroker, the only crucial knowledge needed is who wants to sell a particular stock and who wants to buy that stock. By being the connecting link between the buyers and sellers, the brokerage firm earns rent. The minute there is a direct relationship between the buyer and the seller they can commence the deal without having to pay extra for the knowledge of the potential buyer or seller residing in the brokerage firm. Also, the stockbroker does not benefit to any large extent by adapting and learning more about its selling counterpart, price and quantity is sufficient to conduct a deal. Opportunities arise as the broker has a matching pair of buyers and sellers, in fact business and opportunity is very much the same thing in this example.

We summarize the above discussion by formulating the following propositions:

P1: Firms operating in an open network structure with a low degree of relational embeddedness are likely to find market opportunities based on codified and new knowledge.

P2: Firms finding market opportunities in an open network structure with a low degree of relational embeddedness are likely to earn rents from exploitation of the opportunities.

A closed network with low degree of relational embeddedness

However, we can also imagine a situation, which corresponds to cell 2 in the matrix (i.e. Figure 1.5), where there is a closed network with a low degree of relational embeddedness (Figure 1.7). In such a system, we have reason to anticipate that there is more coordination and cooperation between the firms in the network than in the previous situation, where the network had an open structure (Coleman, 1990; Kogut, 2000). But this situation can provide difficulties for the firm. On the one hand, the closed structure in the network increases the possibility for finding and exploiting technological opportunities, as this type of structure imposes a similar knowledge base on the firms (Cohen and Levinthal, 1990; Lane and Lubatkin, 1998). On the other hand, it is likely that the low degree of relational embeddedness and the closed network tend to give the firm advantageous search options if knowledge is codified, which means that assimilation based on non-codified knowledge is difficult. Opportunities tend in this situation to be based on existing knowledge. Finally, it seems that this structure does not allow the firm to make arbitrary profits at the other firms' expense, as is the case in the

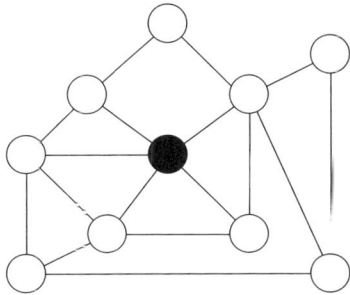

Figure 1.7 A closed network with a low degree of relational embeddedness

open structure in Figure 1.6, as the need for cooperation means that benefits are shared. Thus, we let propositions 3 to 4 summarize some of the recognized conditions in this situation.

P3: Firms operating in a closed network structure with a low degree of relational embeddedness are likely to find market opportunities based on codified and existing knowledge.

P4: Firms finding market opportunities in a closed network structure with a low degree of relational embeddedness are likely to share the benefits from exploitation of the opportunities with other firms in the network.

It seems that this structure is not a very common one in real life, at least not for long periods of time. To some extent this structure can be found in the clothing industry where a designer in a particular country sends patterns to tailors in countries where labor-intensive tasks are cheaper. At the same time the designer orders a specific fabric from firms in maybe several other countries. The fabric is directly shipped to the tailors who, for instance, manufacture a certain type of jacket. At the same time, advertising firms in the end markets prepare the advertising campaigns. When the jacket is finished it is shipped directly by a transportation company to the countries where it is sold in stores. The tailors get a specific amount of jackets to be sewn depending on their spare capacity at that particular time and it is also easy to imagine that the tailors back up each other and change the original order from the designer. As long as the end result is the same the designer has, probably, no opinion about who has actually manufactured the jacket. It is also easy to imagine how several stores or outlets in the same region or country cooperate to get cheaper shipment by sharing the same distributor. In this example, opportunities appear when quantities or prices are changed for some reason and are ended by the flexibility and information processing speed of the involved firms.

An open network with high degree of relational embeddedness

An almost opposite situation is illustrated by cell 3 in Figure 1.5. Here, an open network surrounds the firm with a high degree of relational embeddedness (Figure 1.8). This is a complicated situation, because a high degree of relational embeddedness and an open network represent to some extent contradictory forces. One the one hand, a high degree of relational embeddedness promotes acquisition of complex knowledge and joint problem solving while an open network means a possibility to control knowledge flows and to acquire codified knowledge. We expect that much of what typifies the opportunities in this situation is based on how the firm cooperates

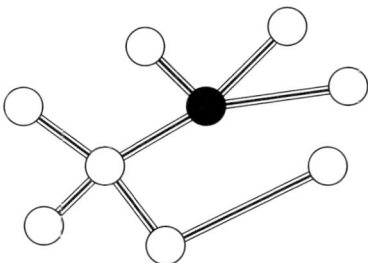

Figure 1.8 An open network with a high degree of relational embeddedness

with its counterparts, which especially concerns exploitation of opportunities, since the relational embeddedness means good conditions to assimilate complex and non-codified knowledge. The fact that the firm has only one path to all the other firms in the network means that much of the knowledge that travels through the network is new. This seems to promote technological opportunity. Exploitation of opportunities in this situation usually takes place within the boundaries of the firm or in dyadic relationships and mostly concerns integration of the firms' activities and resources. This is, for instance, the case in the running operations in the car manufacturing industry, where there are strong and deep relationships between different actors, but where the network to a large extent consists of a set of separate relationships and where technical development is a continuous activity. There is also much adaptation between the involved firms concerning logistics and administrative systems in order to accomplish just-in-time deliveries and lean and efficient production. The network gives each firm a possibility to keep that knowledge within the firm and to earn rents from exploitation of that knowledge as long as the firm has power in relation to its counterpart. The situation resembles a value chain (Porter, 1986) or a distribution channel (see El-Ansary and Stern, 1972; Gaski, 1984; Hunt and Nevin, 1974) where power and control are sources to earn rents and where conflict between the firms in the dyadic relationship are likely as the high degree of relational embeddedness gives the firm good insight in the counterparts' operations.

However, the high degree of relational embeddedness can force the firm to share the benefits with some specific counterparts, since it is likely that, due to the high degree of relational embeddedness, it is able to fully exploit the opportunities. But this situation also gives rise to another type of opportunities, which are based on dyadic cooperation, joint learning and not on the flow of knowledge in the network. If that is the case, there are good possibilities to keep the knowledge within the boundaries of specific relationships and to assure that it is not spread.

P5: Firms operating in an open network structure with a high degree of relational embeddedness are likely to find technological opportunities based on non-codified and new knowledge.

P6: Firms finding technological opportunities in an open network structure with a high degree of relational embeddedness are likely to earn rents from exploitation of the opportunities.

However, this view of the network is perhaps too simple, in the sense that the role of the firm is not only to absorb new knowledge. The firm's role is also to participate in a development process which includes several actors. The following proposition is seen as an important consequence to be handled by management to see that the firm does not loose the advantage from opportunities created by receiving new and non-codified knowledge.

P7: An open network with a high degree of embeddedness will force the firm to carefully choose among counterparts when it comes to deepen the cooperation and coordination.

A closed network with high degree of relational embeddedness

In the situation portrayed in Figure 1.9, the firm has strong and tight relationships to its business partners, that is, a closed network structure. As the relational embeddedness is high, cooperation and coordination of activities is deep, which implies that the possibilities for technological opportunities are good, but there is a risk of receiving mostly existing knowledge through the different relationships. This is the case when an actor is connected to other actors, which in their turn are connected with each other, the actor is locked in and receives existing knowledge.

On the other hand, this situation gives the firm a good position to compare the existing knowledge with the little new knowledge, which pours

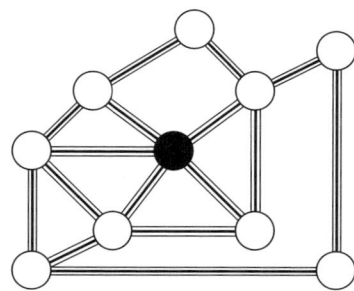

Figure 1.9 A closed network with a high degree of relational embeddedness

into the network. Through repetition and reflection, firms can check the content and quality of the new knowledge and together with other firms jointly solve problems. In such a process, the problem is not to find the one missing piece in the puzzle, it is rather to learn and understand how to modify your own puzzle to better fit the other actors' puzzles. In such a situation where learning complex knowledge is important, the high degree of relational embeddedness and networks with strong connectivity are clearly superior (Coleman, 1990; Hansen, 1999; Kogut, 2000). This means that most opportunities are a result of joint learning in the network, which, in turn, has effects on how the benefits of the opportunity found are later exploited. Since finding the opportunity is a result of joint efforts and cooperation it is difficult for a single firm in the network not to share the benefits with other actors. Instead, a high degree of relational embeddedness and the closed network structure tend to distribute the fruits more evenly over the network than in the other three situations discussed. As there is a risk for inbreeding in this situation, firms will have to look for ties that might give new inputs and opportunities.

This type of network is time-limited in one way or another, it perfectly portrays a firm that is over-embedded in Uzzi's (1997) terms. A situation where this form of network does appear is in large, technically advanced projects like developing a new fighter jet, for instance. All included subsystems and materials are developed at the edge of their technical capabilities, and often even in advance of this, adaptation between all or most of the involved firms is crucial to the success of the project. Opportunities occur in the intersection between different subsystems and their development, meaning that the development in one system forces or opens up for development and changes in another subsystem. At the same time these joint developments of two of the included subsystems affect a third and require changes to it, and so on. Much of the development and opportunities happen when the firms involved solve problems together. Much of the exploitation of the opportunities comes about when the whole system (the fighter jet) is delivered, but also after completion of the project when each firm tries to exploit its learning by applying the developments in different networks. This can be summarized by the following propositions:

P8: Firms operating in a closed network structure with a high degree of relational embeddedness are likely to find technological opportunities based on non-codified and recombined existing knowledge.

P9: Firms finding technological opportunities in a closed network structure with a high degree of relational embeddedness are likely to share the benefits from exploitation of the opportunities with other firms in the network.

P10: A closed network with a high degree of relational embeddedness is only likely to exist for a limited time.

Final discussion

The pros and cons of closed and open networks and high or low degrees of relational embeddedness depend on the specific situation. The more the firm's network contains intense and deep relationships, that is, a high degree of relational embeddedness, the larger the extent that its opportunities are founded on complex knowledge. If the network configuration is also of a closed type we can expect that the exploitation of these opportunities will be facilitated by the cooperative and coordinative character such networks have. On the other hand, new knowledge is more easily accessed in a network of many unconnected participants having relations with a low degree of embeddedness to each other. In such a network the firm detecting the opportunity also has a better possibility to keep the knowledge inside the firm and can earn rent during the exploitation phase.

It is in a sense difficult to imagine any firm being situated in any of the above-mentioned situations; in reality a firm has relationships characterized by both high and low degrees of embeddedness. Likewise, no system, that is, network, is totally open or totally closed, even if parts of the system could reflect such a homogenous character. One important conclusion from the reasoning above ought to be that an ideal network should contain relationships of varying degrees of embeddedness and be of a semi- open/closed structure to ensure survival of the firm in the long run.

Extending the boundaries of the studied network will reveal different and even contradictory results from the reasoning above. It is important in this chapter to remember that we are dealing with "arche types" to be able to draw conclusions and that the archetypes developed seldom appear in real life. For example, think of a firm producing goods. Figure 1.10 shows a plausible picture of how this firm's network may look, in terms of relational embeddedness and network structure. Viewing Figure 1.10 from left to right we can think of suppliers in the left end and customers in the right end of the figure. The firm's direct relationships are of a relatively high degree of embeddedness while its connected relationships are of a lower degree of embeddedness. Further the firm's network contains both closed and open structures depending on where we draw the line of inquiry. It is easy to see how new knowledge enters the central parts of the network depicted in Figure 1.10 from different unconnected actors having relations with low degrees of embeddedness. It is also straightforward to understand the preconditions for problem solving processes in the highly embedded relationships between the firm and its customers, allowing knowledge of a more complex and fine-grained type to flow between the parties. It is further, rather easy to depict how the "triad" of firm and suppliers develop together as the structure in which they pursue their activities fosters coordination and cooperation.

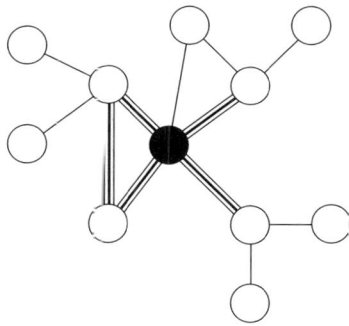

Figure 1.10 A semi-open network with different degrees of relational embeddedness

Summarizing the idea of this chapter would be to say that optimal findings and exploitation of opportunities are recognized to have different prerequisites. These are manifested through the network thus showing the different roles that the network has from a market as well as technological aspect.

As the concept of a network is getting more and more used in business research, it is important to conclude from this chapter that a network is not always the same thing. It differs in closure as well as in the depth and intensity of the relationships. If network as a concept is used in business research it should be thoroughly defined in terms of the characteristics brought up in this chapter. As is evident from our discussions, the characteristics of the network, in terms of relational embeddedness and closure, have very different implications for how firms find and exploit opportunities.

Further, we can see that the impact of relational embeddedness on the firm's possibilities of finding and exploiting opportunities is dependent on whether the network is closed or open; also that the influence the network structure has on the firm's possibilities of finding and exploiting opportunities is dependent on the degree of relational embeddedness it has with its network partners. Taken together this means that a lot more research is needed in order to fully expose how network structures and relationship characteristics influence opportunities.

References

Andersson, U. and Forsgren, M. (1996). Subsidiary Embeddedness and Control in the Multinational Corporation, *International Business Review*, 5(5), 487–508.

Andersson, U. and Forsgren, M. (2000). In Search of Centre of Excellence: Network Embeddedness and Subsidiary Roles in Multinational Corporations, *Management International Review*, 40(4), 329–50.

Andersson, U., Forsgren, M. and Pedersen, T. (2001). Subsidiary Performance in multinational corporations: The Importance of Technology Embeddedness, *International Business Review*, 10(1), 3–23.

Ardichvili, A., Cardozo, R. and Ray, S. (2003). A Theory of Entrepreneurial Opportunity Identification and Development, *Journal of Business Venturing*, 18(1), 105–23.

Burt, R. (1992a). *Structural Holes: The Social Structure of Competition*, Cambridge, MA: Harvard University Press.

Burt, R. (1992b). The Social Structure of Competition, in N. Nohria and R. Eccles (Eds) *Networks and Organizations. Structure, Form and Action*, Cambridge, MA: Harvard Business School Press.

Casson, M. (1982). *The Entrepreneur*, Totowa, NJ: Barnes and Noble Books.

Choi, Y. R. and Shephard, D. A. (2004). Entrepreneurs Decisions to Exploit Opportunities, *Journal of Management*, 30(3), 377–95.

Cohen, W. and Levinthal, D.A. (1990). Absorptive Capacity: A New Perspective on Learning and Innovation, *Administrative Science Quarterly*, 35(1), 128–52.

Coleman, J. (1990). *Foundations of Social Theory*, Cambridge, MA: Harvard University Press.

Cook, K. S. and Emerson, R. M. (1978). Power, Equity and Commitment in Exchange Networks, *American Sociological Review*, 43, 721–38.

Dyer, J. H. and Chu, W. (2000). The Determinants of Trust in Supplier–Automaker Relationships in the U.S., Japan, and Korea, *Journal of International Business Studies*, 31(2), 259–85.

Eckhardt, J. T. and Shane, S. A. (2003). Opportunities and Entrepreneurship, *Journal of Management*, 29(3), 333–49.

El-Ansary, A. I. and Stern L. W. (1972). Power Measurement in the Distribution Channel, *Journal of Marketing Research*, 9(1), 47–52.

Ellis, P. (2000). Social Ties and Foreign Market Entry, *Journal of International Business Studies*, 31(3), 443–69.

Ford, D., Gadde, L-E., Håkansson, H. and Snehota, I. (2003). *Managing Business Relationships*, Chichester: Wiley.

Gaski, J. F. (1984). The Theory of Power and Conflicts in Channels of Distribution, *Journal of Marketing*, 48 (Summer), 9–29.

Grabher, G. (1993). Rediscovering the Social in the Economics of Interfirm Relations, in G. Grabher (Ed.) *The Embedded Firm*, London: Routledge.

Granovetter, M. (1973). The Strength of Weak Ties, *American Journal of Sociology*, 78(6), 1360–80.

Granovetter, M. (1985). Economic Action and Social Structure: The Problem of Embeddedness, *American Journal of Sociology*, 91(3), 481–510.

Granovetter, M. (1992). Problems of Explanation in Economic Sociology, in N. Nohria and R. Eccles (Eds) *Networks and Organizations: Structure, Form and Action*, Boston: Harvard Business School Press.

Gulati, R. (1998). Alliances and Networks, *Strategic Management Journal*, 19(4), 293–18.

Gulati, R. (1999). Network Location and Learning: The Influence of Network Resources and Firm Capabilities on Alliance Formation, *Strategic Management Journal*, 20(5), 397–420.

Gulati, R., Nohria, N. and Zaheer, A. (2000). Strategic Networks, *Strategic Management Journal*, 21(3), 203–15.

Håkansson, H. (1989). *Corporate Technological Behaviour: Co-operation and Networks*, London: Routledge.

Håkansson, H. (Ed.) (1982). *International Marketing and Purchasing: An Interaction Approach*, Chichester: John Wiley and Sons.
Håkansson, H. and Snehota, I. (1995). *Developing Relationships in Business Networks*, London: Routledge.
Halinen, A. and Törnroos, J-Å. (1998). The Role of Embeddedness in the Evolution of Business Networks, *Scandinavian Journal of Management*, 14(3), 187–205.
Hansen, M.T. (1999). The Search-transfer Problem: The Role of Weak Ties in Sharing Knowledge across Organization Subunits, *Administrative Science Quarterly*, 44(1), 82–111.
Hayek, F. A. (1945). The Use of Knowledge in Society, *American Economic Review*, 35(4), 519–30.
Hunt, S. D. and Nevin, J. R. (1974). Power in a Channel of Distribution: Sources and Consequences, *Journal of Marketing Research*, 11 (May), 186–93.
Jack, S. L. and Anderson, A (2002). The Effects of Embeddedness on the Entrepreneurial Process, *Journal of Business Venturing*, 17(5), 467–87.
Kenney, M. and Goe, W. R. (2004). The Role of Social Embeddedness in Professorial Entrepreneurship: A Comparison of Electrical Engineering and Computer Science at UC Berkeley and Stanford, *Research Policy*, 33(5), 691–707.
Kirzner, I. M. (1973). *Competition & Entrepreneurship*, Chicago: University of Chicago Press.
Kirzner, I. M. (1992). *The Meaning of Market Process: Essays in the Development of Modern Austrian Economics*, London: Routledge.
Kirzner, I. M. (1997). Entrepreneurial Discovery and the Competitive Market Process: An Austrian Approach, *Journal of Economic Literature*, 35(1), 60–85.
Kogut, B. (2000). The Network as Knowledge: Generative Rules and the Emergence of Structure, *Strategic Management Journal*, 21(3), 405–25.
Laage-Hellman, J. (1989). *Technological Development in Industrial Networks*. PhD Dissertation, Uppsala: Acta Universitatis Upsaliensis.
Lane, P. J. and Lubatkin, M. (1998). Relative Absorptive Capacity and Internorganizational Learning, *Strategic Management Journal*, 19(5), 461–77.
March, J. G. (1991). Exploration and Exploitation in Organizational Learning, *Organization Science*, 2(1), 71–87.
McEvily, B. and Zaheer, A. (1999). Bridging Ties: A Source of Firm Heterogeneity in Competitive Capabilities, *Strategic Management Journal*, 20(12), 1133–56.
Porter, M. E. (1986). *Competition in Global Industries*, Boston: Harvard Business School Press.
Rowley, T., Behrens, D. and Krackhardt, D. (2000). Redundant Governance Structures: An Analysis of Structural and Relational Embeddedness in Steel and Semiconductor Industries, *Strategic Management Journal*, 21(3), 369–86.
Schumpeter, J. (1934). *Theory of Economic Development*, Cambridge, MA: Harvard University Press.
Shane, S. (2000). Prior Knowledge and the Discovery of Entrepreneurial Opportunities, *Organization Science*, 11(4), 448–69.
Simsek, Z., Lubatkin, M. H. and Floyd, S. W. (2003). Inter-Firm Networks and Entrepreneurial Behavior: A Structural Embeddedness Perspective, *Journal of Management*, 29(3), 427–42.
Uzzi, B. (1996). The Sources and Consequences of Embeddedness for Economic Performance of Organizations: The Network Effect, *American Sociological Review*, 61(4), 674–98.
Uzzi, B. (1997). Social Structure and Competition in Interfirm Networks: The Paradox of Embeddedness, *Administrative Science Quarterly*, 42(1), 35–67.

Winter, S. (1987). Knowledge and Competence as Strategic Assets, in D. Teece (ed.), *The Competitive Challenge – Strategies for Industrial Innovation and Renewal*, Cambridge, MA: Ballinger.

Zander, U. and Kogut, B. (1995). Knowledge and the Speed of Transfer and Imitation of Organizational Capabilities: An Empirical Test, *Organization Science*, 6(1), 76–92.

Zukin, S. and Di Maggio, P. J. (Eds) (1990), *Structure of Capital*, Cambridge: Cambridge University Press.

2
The Importance of Competition and Cooperation for the Exploration of Innovation Opportunities

Maria Bengtsson, Jessica Eriksson and Sören Kock

Introduction

The business landscape is continuously changing. Markets as well as technologies develop, sometimes rapidly, as innovations destroy old technologies and disrupt markets, at times incrementally, while products and processes are adjusted and refined (see e.g. D'Aveni, 1994; Hamel and Prahalad, 1994; Makadok, 1998; Nagarajan and Mitchell, 1998). Consequently, the ability to explore new opportunities and develop new technology has become increasingly important. Technological development is crucial for business and market opportunities and for the competitiveness of firms in many industries (cf. Rice, *et al.*, 2001). In this chapter, we focus on the exploration of opportunities related to technological innovations.

The organization is one important base for discovery of opportunities and for innovation processes, but this organization is also dependent on the interaction with other organizations for its innovation activities (Eisenhardt and Schoonhoven, 1996; Hamel, 1991; Teece and Pisano, 1994). Powell, *et al.* (1996) argue that learning and exploration to a great extent is generated through cooperative ventures. Others however, connect exploration and innovative performance to dynamic competition (Harari, 1999), often with references to Schumpeter (1942). The argument put forward is that intense competition stimulates or forces firms and entrepreneurs to search for new opportunities in the marketplace.

These two views are compatible, given further scrutiny. Oliver (2004) states that competitive as well as cooperative relationships in networks influence the inclination to explore opportunities, and following her analysis; we argue that there is a need for a comprehensive approach that integrates the different perspectives and contextualizes the exploration of opportunities. We therefore apply a network perspective on opportunities for technological development that includes both positive and negative relationships (cf. Granovetter, 1973). The article follows the theoretical view discussed in the first chapter and focuses on the concept of cooperative and competitive nature of relationships in opportunity development.

Positive and negative relationships among firms within business networks can enhance as well as hamper the firms' abilities to discover opportunities. Through the discovery process, resources (Ingram and Baum, 1997) and information (Törnquist, 1986) are combined into new technological solutions that are introduced on the market. Different relationships can enhance as well as constrain the flow of resources and information that are needed. For example, cooperation and competition are diverse phenomena that work differently depending on the setting. Interaction among competitors can be more or less intense, hostile, and emotional. Similarly, interaction among cooperating actors can be more or less formalized and more or less closely coupled. The type of interaction influences the exchanges taking place and hence the possibilities to discover opportunities. Resources and information available in networks that can be shared and used for many purposes but are not utilized, create a network slack, or inefficiency, since they could be better put to use through exchanges between firms (cf. Cyert and March's (1963) discussion on organizational slack).

We argue that an understanding of the accumulation of resources and information within networks as well as an understanding of the flows of resources and information in different cooperative and competitive relationships is very important for the ability to develop technological innovations (cf. Bengtsson and Eriksson, 2002). The purpose of this chapter is therefore to explore how different cooperative and competitive relationships enable and constrain the exploration of technological innovation opportunities. Before elaborating on the different forms of interactions and how they shape the ability to discover new opportunities, we first need to know more about the process of opportunity exploration, about the flows of resources, and the information needed in these processes.

Exploring opportunities

The exploration of opportunities is at the core of Schumpeters' (1942) discussion of innovation and creative destruction, where concepts of product quality and design, process technology, logistics, distribution and organization fundamentally change. However, innovation is not only a matter of exploration. Bresman and Sölvell (1997) argue that the process of innovation consists of three different phases; an initial phase with scanning or monitoring that provides information and ideas, a creative phase where the generated pieces of information are combined in novel ways (cf. Schumpeter, 1942), and a final phase of commercialization or implementation. This description of the innovation process is in line with recent research on opportunity discovery processes. The discovery of opportunities is described as phases of entrepreneurial recognition and exploitation (cf. Alvarez and Busenitz, 2001; Eckhardt and Shane, 2003; Shane, et al. 2003) or processes of discovery, evaluation, and exploitation (cf. Rice, et al., 2001). The different descriptions of opportunity discovery or innovation processes illustrate the difficulty in dividing the processes into definite phases. It can also be questioned if the processes are sequential. We rather believe that innovations and discoveries contain different developmental activities, and that these activities dominate during different parts of innovation processes. Different activities in innovative processes can be divided into explorative activities and exploitative activities (cf. March, 1991). Monitoring, search, and creation are examples of explorative activities, which are more or less deliberate. Evaluation, exploitation, and commercialization are examples of exploitative activities through which new ideas are materialized and introduced in the organization or on the market. The focus in this chapter is on the former activities, namely the exploration of opportunities, but we want to emphasize that exploitation is also needed for the realization of innovations. Through successful commercialization, it is possible to gain financial resources to support a sustained exploration of markets and technology. March describes the paradox in focusing solely on exploration; "Adaptive systems that engaged in exploration to the exclusion of exploitation are likely to find that they suffer the costs of experimentation without gaining many of its benefits" (March, 1991: 71). With that in mind, we turn to the question of how technological innovation opportunities are explored.

Researchers provide different descriptions of the identification of pieces of information and resources that can be combined in novel ways. Deliberate monitoring and search for new resources and information are described as essential parts of innovation processes in the literature on technological development, whereas surprise, chance, and accident are important features of discoveries in the literature on entrepreneurial opportunities. In studies on technological development, discoveries are considered a result of a conscious and deliberate search for opportunities. Competitors are monitored and routines are developed to gather information about end customers and their attitudes. Planned search can provide firms and individuals with more pieces of information and thereby create a situation that is favorable for discoveries.

Törnquist (1986) however, argues that the transference of information in innovation processes cannot be planned but developed, as new combinations and unexpected constellations of pieces of information continuously occur. He argues that it is the possibility to combine fragmentary pieces of tacit information in new ways that make the creation and the exploration of opportunities possible. He describes the information necessary for creative processes as unstructured and heterogeneous information that does not follow well-established, formal information channels. The heterogeneity of information and the presence of incomplete and contradicting knowledge (cf. Hayek, 1945) enable the combination of unique resources and hence discoveries; however Törnqvist (1986) argues that the search for information is largely unconscious and integrated into the creation of new solutions.

Kirzner (1997) also suggests that the discovery of opportunity includes an element of surprise, as "sheer ignorance" is reduced when a discovery is made through the combination of fragmented information. This view on discoveries, or the exploration of opportunities, can be compared with the garbage can model description of decision-making (March and Olsen, 1979). According to the garbage can model, problems and solutions float around, and sometimes a problem and a solution come together and the problem is solved. In the same way, opportunities in the shape of both tangible and intangible recourses and information are exchanged and float around in organizations and networks creating a network slack. When these are combined in novel ways and realized, a technological discovery is made.

Planned search for ideas and monitoring of the environment is important even when the exploration of opportunities is described as an irrational and unplanned process. Through search and monitoring, more pieces of information and resources such as knowledge are made available, and the possibility to detect a solution by chance therefore increases. Search is a more frequent activity than discovery, but discovery is most often the outcome of a non-expected search result. A discovery can hence be stimulated both by deliberate search and by unconscious combinations of information and resources floating around in organizations and networks of firms.

Flows of resources and information in opportunity exploration

If the context for opportunities is extended to include the network, as in this chapter, the possibility to utilize network slack by consciously and unconsciously combining different pieces of information or resources increases. The combination of these pieces is obtained through the interaction among people and organizations and the formal or informal exchange of information and resources that follows. These exchanges are dependent on flows of information and resources. Flows can however be characterized by both "leakiness" and "stickiness" (cf. Brown and Duguid, 2001; Szulanski, 1996). Leakiness refers to mechanisms facilitating flows and exchanges, whereas stickiness refers to mechanisms hindering flows and exchanges. Thus, stickiness is largely negative for the exploration of opportunities.

Leakiness and stickiness are found both within organizations and within networks, enabling as well as constraining opportunity discovery. The formation of a network allegedly facilitates transfer of knowledge and information pieces (cf. Eisenhardt and Schoonhoven, 1996; Hamel, 1991; Inkpen and Crossan, 1996; Teece and Pisano, 1994). Information and resources may even flow easier between organizational departments in different organizations than within an organization having similar practices (Brown and Duguid, 2001).

This is due to the indivisibility between knowledge and practice. For example, a marketing division may have information that is provided to the development division, but they cannot interpret the information in the same manner as the information from another development division in another firm. Differences in goals, corporate cultures, rules, distances in space, and other factors can however also lead to stickiness, and constrain flows of resources and information and hinder opportunity discovery within networks (see e.g. Bengtsson and Eriksson, 2002; Larsson et al., 1999). Further, it has been noted that while successful firms and successful groups of firms provide incentives for exploration, success can also create blindness and reduce exploration (cf. Pouder and St John, 1996).

Certain preconditions can enhance the leakiness of resources and information and hence the utilization of network slacks. First, *meeting places* for random contacts are needed to combine different pieces of tacit knowledge, pieces of new information and fragments of new ideas. These random contacts stimulate the discovery of ignorance that is a prerequisite for the exploration of opportunities. Brown and Duguid (2001) argue that leakiness of knowledge is facilitated in "communities of practice." A prerequisite is that the organizations in some way are proximate, which is in line with Törnquist's (1986) argument that meeting places for face-to-face interaction is important. Similarly, Porter (1990) argues that proximity among competitors improves leakiness of information etcetera and pressures firms to improve their business.

Second, *absorptive capacity* is important in overcoming the stickiness due to different practices, routines and knowledge bases in different projects, units, and organizations. Absorptive capacity is considered as the gathering and filtering of knowledge accessed from different units and from the external environment for utilization within organizations (Cohen and Levinthal, 1990). Some employees can act as centralized gatekeepers or boundary-spanners when the expertise of most employees differs from the expertise of external interacting actors (Cohen and Levinthal, 1990; Powell, 1990). For example, one or a few employees can act as gatekeepers by monitoring and translating external technological information for the rest of the employees of the organization. In ongoing activities, the actors embedded in a different and proximate relationship are the most ready to assimilate external information (cf. Bengtsson and Eriksson, 2002). Cohen and Levinthal (1990) focus on the firm level, but according to Van den Bosch *et al.* (1999), absorptive capacity could be better considered in an intra-organizational context, for example analyzing how absorptive capacity influences the input and output levels of innovative firms. Absorptive capacity is achieved in different ways. According to Cohen and Levinthal (1990), and the studies they recount experience is important for absorptive capacity. For example, organizations conducting their own R&D are more capable of understanding and exploiting external information and resources.

Third, *communicative capacity* is of importance for the leakiness of resources and information. The concept communicative capacity has been developed to complement absorptive capacity (Larsson *et al.*, 1998). It refers to the ability to be transparent and to give out information and knowledge so that a new connection, or inter-organizational learning, is possible (Larsson *et al.*, 1999). Larsson *et al.* (1999) point out that familiarity and prior interaction, trust of various types as well as commitment help generate communicative capacity. Although they primarily deal with partner-specific relationships, the reasoning applies to networks as well. A history of interaction within a network thus reduces the time required to identify relevant counterparts with whom it is possible to exchange resources and information. The development of a shared language or other means of communication within a network can give rise to a communicative capacity that improves the flow of knowledge in all relationships within that technological field (cf. Bengtsson and Eriksson, 2002).

We thus argue that meeting places, absorptive capacity and communicative capacity enable exploration and opportunity discovery through improved leakiness. However, the leakiness and stickiness of flows in networks, and consequently the opportunity discovery, are connected to the character of the cooperative and competitive relationships. Different cooperative and competitive relationships enable and constrain the exploration of technological innovation opportunities. The next section therefore, outlines the characteristics of cooperative and competitive relationships.

Characteristics of cooperative and competitive relationships

The base for creating opportunities and constraints is the organization itself and the content of its indirect and direct relationships with other organizations. The content of the relationships can be described as cooperation and competition. Traditionally, arguments in favor of competition and cooperation have been rather stereotypical and polarized, being rooted in different theoretical perspectives. Recently however, attempts have been made to overcome this polarization and bring the different perspectives together (see e.g. Oliver, 2004).

Organizations can cooperate and compete simultaneously, which implies that competition and cooperation are not mutually exclusive. Instead of portraying either cooperation or competition as stimulating innovation, both competition and cooperation can have positive as well as negative effects for innovation. Both types of interaction can enhance as well as hamper firms' abilities to discover opportunities, depending on the situation. The different interactions can also enhance as well as overcome the constraints for discoveries, again depending on the circumstances. We will therefore elaborate further on how opportunities are explored and constrained in different business contexts.

Strong and weak competitive relationships

Competition cannot be described along traditional market structures and market behavior dimensions as in neo-classical economic theory. Kirzner (1973), among others, states that the market is never in equilibrium, since there are always gaps between supply and demand. The gaps can be viewed as market opportunities for entrepreneurs. However we argue that competition is more than a matter of supply and demand, and that relational dimensions need to be included in the analysis if we want to understand the role of competition in opportunity exploration. Following a network perspective, we rather consider opportunities for technological development as contained in relationships, than as a result of a gap between supply and demand. Through interaction among competitors, relationships are created, even if no economic exchanges are made (cf. Bengtsson and Kock, 1999; Easton, 1990).

Given the network perspective applied in this chapter, opportunities need to be seen as possibilities arising from strong and weak competitive relationships. Content characteristics of the relationship determine whether there is a strong or a weak competitive relationship. Bengtsson (1998) offers a detailed view of the relational dimension of competition. She has coined four types of climates of competition within an industry, but the argumentation is transferable to business networks. The climates, or the relationships in a network, vary depending on if the competition is active or passive and if there is symmetry or asymmetry between the competitors' businesses. These dimensions are further operationalized, and when there is functional proximity between the competitors (as they are doing business in the same network and product areas), the interactions between the actors are direct and intense. If firms sell similar products to the same markets, they often meet each other, and need to relate to the actions taken by the other firm. The opportunity to survey the moves of competitors in such a relationship is of importance for the ability to find new combinations of resources and information. If different competitors operate in various markets, the intensity in interaction is much lower.

Bengtsson's (1998) classification can be used to categorize different types of competitive relationships, and provide an understanding of how competition affects exploration. Competition is at its weakest when competitors do not confront each other, but adapt to each other, when functional distance is great, and when firms can be said to live in symbiosis with low intensity in competition, and when they only collect and analyze limited amounts of data about each other. Competition is at its strongest when firms confront each other within many product and market areas, when firms collect and analyze large amounts of data about each other, and when there are no accepted rules-of-play. Both high and low degrees of intensity in competition can be advantageous for certain activities and in some situations but harmful where others are concerned. However, the outcomes of competitive relationships need to be considered in context of the ongoing cooperative interaction.

Strong and weak cooperative relationships

Sociological studies have shown how cooperation benefits exploration, if cooperation facilitates the flow of knowledge between organizations as well as provides different viewpoints and input to the creative process (cf. Oliver, 2004; Pouder and St John, 1996; Powell, 1990). Cooperative relationships between organizations give access to heterogeneous resources (cf. Kock, 1991), for example, explicit and tacit knowledge, and business opportunities can therefore be explored in cooperative activities (cf. Busenitz, et al., 2003). A business opportunity can be viewed as an organization's exploration of new layers in existing relationships or the access to new relationships through connected relations in the business network. However, all cooperative relationships do not enhance opportunity exploration in all situations and it is therefore of importance to discuss the content of cooperative relationships.

Cooperation in social networks has often been described using the concepts of strong and weak ties between individuals within and between networks (Granovetter, 1973). Strong cooperative ties are often assumed as the most beneficial for organizations, but Granovetter (1973) emphasized that there is a risk in considering only strong ties; information can flow within weak ties as well. Whereas information in strong ties is uniform, new and heterogeneous information can also be found in relationships with weak ties. Following Granovetter (1973), Marsden and Campbell (1984) put forward a number of different features as measurements of the strength of a tie, such as closeness/intimacy, duration, frequency of contact, reciprocity of support and aid, and overlapping group memberships. Similarly, characteristics were applied to analyze relationship strength (or bond strength) in industrial networks. For example, the concepts of commitment, identity and trust put forward by Håkansson and Snehota (1989) correspond to the more detailed features mentioned above.

Applying this perspective to industrial networks, it follows that organizations within a network that have frequent exchanges, a long-standing relationship, high levels of trust and commitment (or reciprocity) and have well-established roles in relation to each other, have a stronger cooperation that others. Weak cooperative relationships are characterized by infrequent interactions, un-established relationships and distance, limited trust and commitment and uncertain roles. This is related to issues of embeddedness; relationships can be more or less embedded in different cooperative dimensions (Hite, 2003). Strong ties are likely to be structurally and culturally embedded, whereas weak ties are at least less structurally embedded.

This reasoning can be further developed on the basis of results from Uzzi (1997). He shows that "overembeddedness" in social norms, for example, thwarts new ways of acting. One could thus claim that constraints for exploration can be found in strong relationships; the partners are so closely connected that the information is seldom unique, or even different. Exploration challenges existing conformity and can be considered as illegitimate behavior (cf. Gnyawali and Madhavan, 2001). Existing relationships can even prevent a partner from building or increasing the relationships to a third counterpart due to the loyalty to the old partners. Cooperative relationships can accordingly both constrain and stimulate exploration and exploitation. An understanding of this is closely related to content characteristics of cooperative relationships and the combination of cooperation and competition in these relationships.

Network dynamics and opportunity discovery

We have argued that opportunities for discovery are influenced by cooperative as well as competitive relationships of varying strength. In this section, we combine the cooperative and the competitive dimension in order to further elaborate on the effects of interactions on the ability to discover new opportunities during technological innovation in networks. The combination of weak and strong competitive and cooperative relationships correspondingly results in the grid depicting different network characteristics in Figure 2.1. Based on these characteristics, we return to the previously claimed need for meeting places, absorptive capacity and communicative capacity, in order to enable exploration and opportunity discovery through improved leakiness.

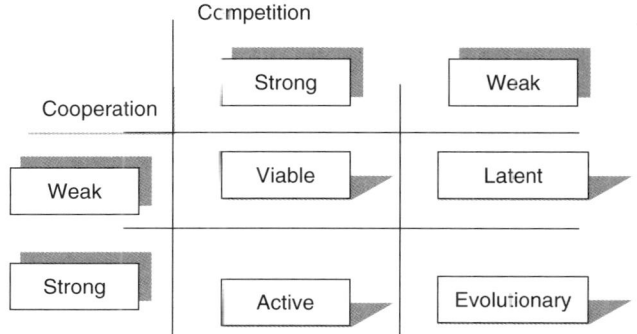

Figure 2.1 Networks characteristics and opportunity seeking patterns

from relevant business disciplines, and following conceptual developments from such integration, acquire empirical evidence into the international activities of a much wider range of organizational types.

In this chapter, we propose a simple integrative model (Figure 3.1) that positions international opportunity perception as central to the international entrepreneurial process, the outcome of which is a pattern of internationalization which we equate with international opportunity exploitation. Drawing on Shane and Eckhardt's (2003) conceptualization of the entrepreneurial process as one of perception and exploitation of opportunities, we suggest that international entrepreneurship can be viewed also with this process at its core. The stance we take is that international opportunity perception will be influenced primarily by the firm's international entrepreneurial culture, its organizational context, specifically its resource-based strategy and current dominant international *modus operandi*, and by the domestic and host-country environmental context.

Perception of international opportunities may result ultimately in the exploitation of selected opportunities through, following the internationalization as entrepreneurial behavior approach (Coviello and Jones, 2004; Jones and Coviello, 2005), the establishment of business activities in countries where opportunities present themselves at specific points in time. The result will be a pattern of international opportunity exploitation, which here we equate with its pattern of internationalization. The dominant international *modus operandi* can be represented by three generic forms. These are, following conventional internationalization approaches, venturing abroad by relying on arm's length trade in the market, on collaboration modes with foreign partners and on internal transfers within the firm, or hierarchy. For

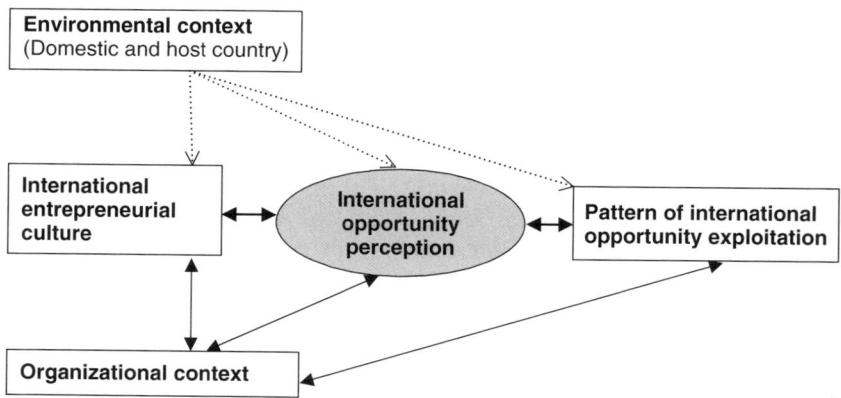

Figure 3.1 A Simple integration: international entrepreneurial culture, international opportunity perception and international opportunity exploitation

Latent networks

Networks characterized by weak cooperation and weak competition, are labeled latent networks when discussing opportunity discovery and exploration. The weak ties imply the existence of heterogeneous information and resources that could be combined in novel ways. On the other hand, the lack of competition as well as of strong cooperation between firms with similar goals also reduces the inclination to search. There is thus no strong drive from cooperation or competition towards opportunity discovery.

Since the relationships within the network tend to be rather passive, flows of information and resources are not established. There are no meeting places for random exchanges of the potentially heterogeneous information and resources, and new combinations will therefore be rare and coincidental. Following the limited interaction between firms, it will be difficult to achieve high levels of absorptive capacity (cf. Larsson et al., 1999) since firms have limited experience of each other. Similarly, firms will have limited experience of opening up to disclose information and resources, indicating that the communicative capacity is low. However, the lack of competitive pressures can mean that firms are not too careful about guarding their resources and their information, and as a result there may be some leakiness in the weak ties to other firms. The limited flows of information and resources suggest that this is a situation with network slack: there are information and resources in the network, but the firms are unaware of it. It is likely that the absence of competitive pressures within the network provides opportunities for slack to accumulate, which potentially provides resources for exploration. At the same time, however, no cooperation helps firms to access and utilize the network slack.

If firms wish to improve their potential for opportunity discovery, they need to seek active interaction with others in their network to improve their absorptive capacity. Firms therefore need to focus on arena building in order to access the heterogeneous information needed for technological innovation. Granovetter (1973) argues that bridging ties are valuable as they increase the focal actors information about opportunities that can be found. To develop bridging ties, translators that mediate knowledge and information are needed (cf. Cohen and Levinthal, 1990). Within this situation however, there are limited pressures or incentives to interact and instead there is a tendency toward inertia. The situation of weak cooperation and competition within a network does not stimulate network alertness or opportunity discovery. If discoveries are made in this situation, they are a result of individual entrepreneurial activities, rather than networking.

Evolutionary networks

Strong cooperation and weak competition within a network creates a setting labeled evolutionary. There are ample possibilities to explore opportunities within the existing relationships. The actors embedded in these networks have created an atmosphere of trust, developed common means of communication, and have a high level of commitment. The actors are willing to invest and develop the relationships. Further, the actors are well aware of the interacting counterparts' possibilities and thus they are able to deepen the cooperation by utilizing the resources and information available in the network.

The history of recurring interaction with strong commitment and high levels of trust will have established high absorptive as well as communicative capacity (Larsson et al., 1999). Firms are not anxious to hide information from each other and hence there will be a leakiness of resources and information between the firms. It follows that there are established meeting places, but only within the boundaries of existing relationships and knowledge areas.

Major steps forward in technology development will be more scarce, however, since there will be limited opportunities for the combinations of heterogeneous pieces of information and resources. Network slack develops instead through the accumulation of homogeneous resources and information, as the existing cooperation mainly follows established patterns. Therefore, there is a risk that the established relationships and exchanges within the network allow routines to develop, and that the discovery of opportunities primarily entails rationalization of existing technologies (cf. March, 1991).

Consequently, truly innovative combinations between heterogeneous pieces of information and resources will require that firms open up to other networks in order to meet with heterogeneous environments. In such new environments, firms will have much more limited communicative and absorptive capacity with their counterparts, which will hamper the leakiness of resources and information. This, coupled with a desire to be loyal to existing relationships, increases the drift towards inertia, and this lack of competitive pressure causes an accumulation of slack within the network, further contributing towards stability.

Active networks

A network characterized by strong cooperation and strong competition can be labeled "active." The strong competition forces organizations to explore and exploit new opportunities; in other words, to be alert. If the competitive interaction is dynamic (cf. D'Aveni, 1994; Oakley, 1990), this presents opportunities for new combinations of heterogeneous information and resources. On the other hand, if the competitive interaction within the network is static, it will enable exploitation, and this will subsequently constrain exploration, since static competition enforces existing patterns and means of competition (Bengtsson and Sölvell, 2004). Depending on the type of competitive interaction, the possibilities to combine heterogeneous information and resources will therefore differ.

Due to an active search for information about competitors and the well-established relationships, networks with strong cooperation and strong competition will be characterized by rather a high absorptive capacity. However, a problem when dealing with strong competition and strong cooperation is that a calculative commitment will arise as an outcome of not fully trusting the other party (cf. Hadjikhani and Thilenius, 2003). If a calculative commitment develops, firms will only give as much information as needed in order to maintain the relationship. Therefore, we argue that firms can have reduced communicative capacity, in comparison to the absorptive capacity, which in turn creates stickiness in knowledge flows from each firm.

In this type of network, there will of course be well-established meeting places through both competitive and cooperative interactions. Cooperation means that slack is continuously generated, but the resources and the information that are accumulated are homogeneous. However, if the competitive interaction is dynamic, these meeting places can be effective for the exploration and combination of incomplete and asymmetric information and resources. If the cooperating firms are able to absorb these heterogeneous pieces of information and resources, the slack is utilized. In this situation there are also competitive pressures that force firms to search for resources and information outside established relationships and to utilize slack in the network. The competitive and cooperative forces consequently interplay and contribute to the accumulation as well as the utilization of network slack.

Viable networks

Networks where competition is strong and cooperation is weak are labeled viable. As in the latent network, the weak cooperative ties lead to an accumulation of heterogeneous information and resources, and in this situation the strong competitive pressure forces firms to explore opportunities. However, as the actors involved find limited possibilities to cooperate the opportunities are realized in a "classic" manner, where the organization or entrepreneur explores and exploits opportunities that are present in the network context. If the competition is dynamic, this will stimulate exploration, but if the competition is static, the firms are locked into a competitive play with frequent moves and counter moves. This competitive play limits the firms' actions to a certain strategic logic rather than experimenting with new ideas. Hence, it depends on the type of competitive interaction whether there are good possibilities for technological innovation through novel combinations of pieces of information and resources.

This type of network contains mainly hostile meeting places. The weak cooperation means that network slack can develop, but through competitive interactions firms can utilize the available information and resources. As firms develop rather independently within this type of network, their communicative capacity is reduced (cf. Larsson *et al.*, 1999). Firms can also restrain the flows of information etcetera due to the strong competition, which further inhibits the communicative capacity. In this situation the absorptive capacity is dependent on the competitive, rather than the cooperative interaction. Firms involved in dynamic competition develop absorptive capacity within the organization that enhances their ability to utilize and explore opportunities. Organizations and individuals are pressured by competition to actively search for new opportunities in order to beat the competing actors, and the competitive pressures reduce slack, both in terms of increased leakiness through intense interaction and through the reduction of buffers.

Discussion and conclusions

This chapter has explored how different cooperative and competitive relationships in networks enable and constrain the exploration of technological innovation opportunities. We have argued that network slack is of central importance for this exploration. Two issues can be discussed related to the type of network that develops. (1) The accumulation of slack in networks, and (2) the ability to utilize slack in networks differ depending on the relationships within the network. Different patterns of accumulation and utilization develop within the four network types as illustrated in Figure 2.2.

Accumulation of slack in networks

The accumulation of slack is stimulated by weak cooperative and weak competitive relationships. The existence of weak ties in cooperative relations implies the existence of heterogeneous information and resources that could be combined in novel ways, but the firms are unaware of the potential and do not know how to search for combinations or opportunities. Similarly, as the competitive pressure is weak firms are not careful about guarding their resources and their information. On the other hand, there may be limited

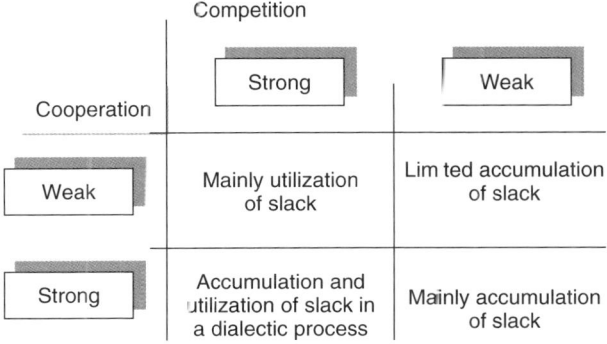

Figure 2.2 Network slack and network dynamics

incentives to innovate and thus limited consciousness and search. A low degree of intensity in competition can imply that firms are engaging in collusive behavior at the expense of customers.

Organizational slack is also more easily accumulated if competition is weak. Many organizations search for and accumulate organizational slack (Bourgeois, 1981; Cyert and March, 1963; March and Sevón, 1988). The traditional view of slack is that successful organizations store slack during good times and then use it during adverse times, such as times of fierce competition. Slack will provide the organization with resources and information needed to discover opportunities for cost reduction, and alternative strategies.

According to March and Sevón (1988) however, slack is both a source of inefficiency and a protection against the dangers of unpredictable shocks. This accordingly creates a paradox. Where there are most opportunities for exploration leading to innovation, there is also a risk that firms become lazy and inefficient. If the organizational slack is transferred to the network this risk can be avoided. Organizational slack is distributed to the network if it is used in the cooperation with other actors in the network. This is not the case in networks with weak cooperative and competitive relationships and it is therefore a risk that the network slack becomes inefficient, or in other words, unexploited.

Strong cooperative and competitive relationships also stimulate accumulation of network slack, but primarily of homogeneous resources and information. This implies that the slack can be used for exploitation rather than for exploration of new opportunities. This however holds primarily for strong static competition, but if there is dynamic competition, competing firms pressure each other to search for new opportunities through benchmarking and rivalry. The slack accumulated through dynamic competition thus consists of heterogeneous resources and information, reached through intentional search and frequent interaction.

The discussion so far has focused on networks between actors within the same area of technology. In reality however, it needs to be acknowledged that network actors, especially focal actors, are always embedded in more than one network; as Håkansson and Snehota (1989) wrote, no business is an island. Frequently, focal actors will therefore be embedded in several networks with varying characteristics as well as networks within different technological areas. These different networks can lead to the accumulation of slack with heterogeneous information and resources. This will create dynamism in the network. Similarly, Burt (1992) claims that structural holes yield both information benefits and control benefits and that firms as well as individuals purposefully work toward structuring their networks through patterns of network use. The more non-redundant contacts you have, the more efficient your network, while providing you with more benefits. We conclude that firms aiming at exploration need to be very alert in identifying structural holes in order to overcome the potentially negative effects for exploration arising within a single network.

Utilization of slack in networks

The utilization of slack in networks is dependent on leakiness in the flows of resources and information. Both strong competitive and cooperative relationships are productive in stimulating the utilization of slack in networks. Strong cooperative relationships give access to slack in networks, as strong cooperative relationships ease the flow of resources and information through high levels of absorptive and communicative capacity. Firms can benefit from stability, well-known norms, and exchanges of reliable information within the network (for similar discussions, see Galaskiewicz and Zaheer, 1999; Larsson et al., 1999) when utilizing slack. However, these flows are most marked for homogeneous pieces of information and resources as the slack accumulated through strong cooperation consists of this type of information and resources.

Strong competitive relationships also give increased access to slack in the network since there is frequent interaction that provides couplings between different pieces of information and resources. Intense competition is traditionally considered to further innovation and thus exploration and opportunity discovery (cf. Porter, 1990). In Schumpeterian models, intense competition is described as the dynamic competitive behavior that develops because of the entrepreneurial ability to act in new ways and detect new opportunities in the marketplace or in technological development (Ellig, 2001; Harari, 1999; Oakley, 1990; Shaanan and Feinberg, 1995). We argue that one important merit of intense, dynamic competition is the ability to stimulate the utilization of network slack, but that this ability is not self-evident. Strong competition stimulates absorptive capacity, but it also reduces the communicative capacity since firms try to keep information from each other.

Extensive competition has also been argued to be harmful in certain situations; intense competition reduces profitability and the long-run investments needed for exploration (cf. Brahm, 1995). We maintain that competitive pressures may also drive towards static competition and "more of the same" rather than exploration as firms can end up in "competitive inertia" (Miller and Chen, 1994). Strong static competition can thus constrain the utilization of network slack, since it will hamper the flows of heterogeneous pieces of information and resources.

Weak cooperative as well as competitive relationships hamper the utilization of network slack due to low levels of absorptive as well as communicative capacity. Weak ties, both in cooperation and competition, suggest the presence of heterogeneous resources and the existence of slack that can be used for novel combinations. However, firms are not actively searching for these resources and they lack the ability to recognize the opportunities for exploration that arise.

A strong polarization of cooperation and competition is not fruitful from a network perspective, as both are present in a business network as the firms are embedded in cooperative and competitive relationships. As we have discussed in this chapter, cooperation and competition will enable or hamper the exploration of opportunities in different ways. A combination will consequently give the best outcome.

In this chapter we have introduced the concept of slack in relationships and we feel that more research is needed to elaborate on how slack in relationships is generated in the interactions between the counterparts and how it can be utilized when exploiting innovative processes in business networks. Another interesting research area is to analyze how information is divided among the firms embedded in the business network.

References

Alvarez, S.A. and Busenitz, L.W. (2001). The Entrepreneurship of Resource-based Theory, *Journal of Management*, 27(6), 755–75.

Bengtsson, M. (1998). *Climates of Competition*, Amsterdam: Harwood Academic Publishers.

Bengtsson, M. and Eriksson, J. (2002). Stickiness and Leakiness in Inter-organizational Innovation Projects, in K. Sahlin-Andersson and A. Söderholm (Eds) *Regenerated Projects. Beyond Project Management. New Perspectives on the Temporary–Permanent Dilemma. Festschrift for Rolf A. Lundin.* Liber: Malmö.

Bengtsson, M. and Kock, S. (1999). Cooperation and Competition in Relationships among Competitors in Business Networks, *The Journal of Business and Industrial Marketing*, 14(3), 178–94.

Bengtsson, M. and Sölvell, Ö. (2004). Climates of Competition: Clusters and Innovative Performance, *Scandinavian Journal of Management*, 20(3), 225–44.

Bourgeois III, L.J. (1981). On the Measurement of Organizational Slack, *Academy of Management Review*, 6(1), 29–39.

Brahm, R. (1995). National Targeting Policies, High-Technology Industries, and Excessive Competition, *Strategic Management Journal*, 16, 71–91.

Bresman, H. and Sölvell, Ö. (1997). Local and Global Forces in The Innovation Process of The Multinational Enterprise – An Hour-Glass Model, in H. Eskelinen (Ed.) NORDREFO 1997:3. *Special Issue: Regional Specialisation and Local Environment – Learning and Competitiveness*, Stockholm, 43–64.

Brown, J.S. and Duguid, P. (2001). Knowledge and Organization: A Social-Practice Perspective, *Organization Science*, 12(2), 198–213.

Burt, B. S. (1992). *Structural Holes*, Cambridge, MA: Harvard University Press.

Busenitz, L.W., West III, G.P., Shepherd, D., Nelson, T., Chandler, G.N. and Zacharakis, A. (2003). Entrepreneurship Research in Emergence: Past Trends and Future Directions, *Journal of Management*, 29(3), 285–308.

Cohen, W. and Levinthal, D. (1990). Absorptive Capability: A New Perspective on Learning and Innovation, *Administrative Science Quarterly*, 35(1), 128–52.

Cyert, R.M. and March, J.G. (1963). *A Behavioral Theory of the Firm*, 2nd Edn. Oxford: Blackwell.

D'Aveni, R.A. (1994). *Hypercompetition: Managing The Dynamics of Strategic Maneuvering*, New York: The Free Press.

Easton, G. (1990). Relationships Among Competitors, in G. Day, B. Weitz and R. Wensley (Eds) *The Interface of Marketing and Strategy*, Greenwich, CT: JAI Press Inc., 57–100.

Eckhardt, J.T. and Shane, S.A. (2003). Opportunities and Entrepreneurship, *Journal of Management*, 29(3), 333–49.
Eisenhardt, K.M. and Schoonhoven, C.B. (1996). Resource Based View of Strategic Alliance Formation: Strategic and Social Effects in Entrepreneurial Firms, *Organization Science*, 10(2), 136–50.
Ellig, J. (2001). Introduction, in Jerry Ellig (Ed.) *Dynamic Competition and Dynamic Policy. Technology, Innovation and Antitrust Issues*, Cambridge: Cambridge University Press. 1–15.
Galaskiewicz, J. and A. Zaheer (1999). Networks of Competitive Advantage, in S. Andrews and D. Knoke (Eds) *Research in the Sociology of Organizations*. Greenwich, CT: JAI Press, 237–61.
Gnyawali, D.R. and Madhavan, R. (2001). Cooperative networks and competitive dynamics: a structural embeddedness perspective, *Academy of Management Review*, 26(3), 431–45.
Granovetter, M. (1973). The Strength of Weak Ties, *American Journal of Sociology* 78(6), 1360–80.
Hadjikhani, A. and Thilenius, P. (2004). A View on Commitment in the Industrial Long-Term Relationship, *International Business Review*; Under Review Process, (Unpublished manuscript; Uppsala University).
Håkansson, H. and Snehota, I. (1989). No Business is an Island – The Network Concept of Business Strategy, *Scandinavian Journal of Management*, 5(3), 187–200.
Hamel, G. (1991). Competition for Competence and Inter-partner Learning Within International Strategic Alliances, *Strategic Management Journal*, 12, 83–104.
Hamel, G., and Prahalad, C.K. (1994). *Competing for the Future*, Boston, MA: Harvard Business School Press.
Harari, O. (1999). Obsolete.com?, *Management Review*, 88(8), 31–4.
Hayek, F.A. (1945). The Use of Knowledge in Society, *The American Economic Review*, 35(4), 519–30.
Hite J. M. (2003). Patterns of Multidimensionality among Embedded Network Ties: A Typology of Relational Embeddedness in Emerging Entrepreneurial Firms, *Strategic Organization*, 1(1), 9–49.
Ingram, P. and Baum, J.A.C. (1997). Opportunity and Constraint: Organizations' Learning from the Operating and Competitive Experience of Industries, *Strategic Management Journal*, 18, Special Issue: Organizational and Competitive Interactions, 75–98.
Inkpen, A.C. and Crossan, M. (1996). Believing is Seeing: Joint Ventures and Organizational Learning, *Journal of Management Studies*, 32(5), 596–618.
Kirzner, I.M. (1973). *Competition and Entrepreneurship*, Chicago: University of Chicago Press.
Kirzner, I.M. (1997). Entrepreneurial Discovery and the Competitive Market Process: An Austrian Approach, *Journal of Economic Literature*, 35(1), 60–85.
Kock, S. (1991). *A Strategic Process for Gaining External Resources through Long-Lasting Relationships*. Swedish School of Economics and Business Administration, Helsinki.
Larsson, R., Bengtsson, L., Henriksson, K., and Sparks, J. (1998). The Interorganizational Learning Dilemma: Collective Knowledge Development in Strategic Alliances, *Organization Science*, 9(3), 85–305.
Larsson, R., Bengtsson, L., Henriksson, K., and Sparks, J. (1999). Barriers to Interorganizational Learning: Developing Collective Knowledge Across Corporate Boundaries, *Advances in Management Cognition and Organizational Information Processing*, 6, 115–47.

Makadok, R. (1998). Can First-Mover and Early-Mover Advantages be Sustained in An Industry with Low Barriers to Entry/Imitation?, *Strategic Management Journal*, 19, 683–96.

March, J.G. (1991). Exploration and Exploitation in Organizational Learning, *Organization Science*, 2(1), 71–87.

March, J.G. and Olsen, J.P. (1979). *Ambiguity and Choice in Organizations*, 2nd edn, Bergen: Universitetsförlaget.

March, J.G. and Sevón, G. (1988) Gossip, Information and Decision-Making, in J.G. March (ed.) *Decision and Organizations*. Oxford, Cambridge: Basil Blackwell. 429–42

Marsden, P.V. and Campbell, K.E. (1984). Measuring Tie Strength. *Social Forces*, 63, 482–501.

Miller, D. and Chen, M-J. (1994). Sources and Consequences of Competitive Inertia: A Study of the U.S. Airline Industry, *Administrative Science Quarterly*, 39, 1–23.

Nagarajan, A. and Mitchell, W. (1998). Evolutionary Diffusion: Internal and External Methods Used to Acquire Encompassing, Complementary, and Incremental Technological Changes in The Lithotripsy Industry, *Strategic Management Journal*, 5, 477–96.

Oakley, A. (1990). *Schumpeter's Theory of Capitalist Motion*, Aldershot: Edward Elgar.

Oliver, A.L (2004). On the Duality of Competition and Cooperation: Interorganizational Networks within Knowledge-intensive Industries, *Scandinavian Journal of Management*, 20(1–2), 151–72.

Porter, M.E. (1990). *The Competitive Advantage of Nations*, London: Macmillan.

Pouder, R. and St John, C. (1996). Hot Spots and Blind Spots: Geographical Clusters of Firms and Innovation, *Academy of Management Review*, 21(4), 1192–225.

Powell, W.W. (1990). Neither Market nor Hierarchy. Network Forms of Organization, *Research in Organization Behavior*, 12, 295–336.

Powell, W.W., Koput, K.W. and Smith-Doerr, L. (1996). Interorganizational Collaboration and the Locus of Innovation: Networks of Learning in Biotechnology, *Administrative Science Quarterly*, 41, 116–45.

Rice, M.P., Kelley, D., Peters, L., and O'Connor, G.C. (2001). Radical Innovation: Triggering Initiation of Opportunity Recognition and Evaluation, *R&D Management*, 31(4), 409–20.

Schumpeter, J.A. (1942). *Capitalism, Socialism and Democracy*, New York: Harper Torchbooks.

Shaanan, J. and Feinberg, R.M (1995). Dynamic Competition and Price Adjustments, *Southern Economic Journal*, 62, 460–66. Chapel Hill; Oct.

Shane, S., Locke, E.A. and Collins, C.J. (2003). Entrepreneurial Motivation, *Human Resource Management Review*, 13(2), 257–79.

Szulanski, G. (1996). Exploring Internal Stickiness: Impediments to The Transfer of Best Practice Within The Firm, *Strategic Management Journal*, 17(10), 27–43.

Teece, D. and Pisano, G. (1994). The Dynamic Capabilities of Firms: An Introduction, *Industrial and Corporate Change*, 3(3), 537–56.

Törnquist, G. (Ed.) (1986). *Svenskt näringsliv – i geografiskt perspektiv*. Stockholm: Liber.

Uzzi, B. (1997). Social Structure and Competition in Interfirm Networks: The Paradox of Embeddedness, *Administrative Science Quarterly*, 42(1), 35–67.

Van Den Bosch, F.A.J., Volberda, H.W. and De Boer, M. (1999). Coevolution of Firm Absorptive Capacity and Knowledge Environment: Organizational Forms and Combinative Capabilities, *Organization Science*, 10(5), 551–68.

3
International Entrepreneurial Culture, International Opportunity Perception and Pattern of International Exploitation: Towards an Integrated Model

Pavlos Dimitratos and Marian V. Jones

Introduction

Currently topical in international business research is the emergent field of international entrepreneurship. Interest in this topic has gained momentum in recent years, with an increasing number of articles appearing in journals and dedicated special issues (Coviello and Jones, 2004). Following the definition advanced by McDougall and Oviatt (2000) international entrepreneurship deals with the innovative, proactive and risk-seeking behavior of firms across borders. Its relevance in the modern era of globalization, wherein firms seek to achieve a competitive advantage worldwide, has escalated. It appears that Wright and Ricks (1994) could not have been more correct when they predicted that this area would become one of the most topical areas in international business.

Development of a new field of study presents challenges. Proponents of the international entrepreneurship field including McDougall and Oviatt (2000), and Thomas and Mueller (2000) have stressed that the area should be enriched with theoretical frameworks. Others (Dimitratos et al., 2004; Young et al., 2003; Zahra and George, 2002) have criticized the failure of researchers to date to expand international entrepreneurship research focus beyond the activities of international new ventures or born global firms. In particular, the latter authors suggest that international entrepreneurship should extend to the examination of entrepreneurial activities of all firms going abroad, irrespective of sector, age, size and stage of internationalization. We agree with this line of criticism and suggest that if international entrepreneurship is to develop and gain solid theoretical underpinnings, it needs to further integrate conceptual approaches and theoretical perspectives convenience, we call the first trading-based modes, the second network-based modes, and the third subsidiary-based modes. Trading modes relate to exporting, network-based modes to licensing, franchising, joint ventures and strategic alliances, and subsidiary-based modes to multinationals expanding through their subsidiaries. In this way we enable the examination of entrepreneurial activities irrespective of the firm's age, size, stage of internationalization, or state of independence.

The notion of international opportunity alertness, perception and discovery is key to our examination in this conceptual chapter. We posit that factors which influence the founder or management team's awareness, perception and discovery of value-creation opportunities in the international marketplace is the crucial determinant of the means by which international opportunities are exploited, and hence the pattern of internationalization taken by the firm. In other words, factors that influence the way the firm *perceives opportunities* abroad significantly influence subsequent action with regard to the countries selected for entry, the business modes through which entry is effected, and the products, goods, services or systems that are transferred into the selected countries. We suggest that firms with a positive international entrepreneurial culture, as moderated by organizational and environmental conditions, may differently perceive opportunities abroad, thus their patterns of internationalization will differ from those with a less positive international entrepreneurial culture (Figure 3.1).

In developing our conceptual framework we apply concepts from entrepreneurship and strategic management, namely environmental determinism, resource-based and head office assignment perspectives. We aim at analyzing how variables from these perspectives may affect international opportunity perception, which is assumed to be affected by the international entrepreneurial culture of the firm, and its internal and environmental contexts. In this parsimonious model, the emphasis is on outward internationalization, notwithstanding the significance that inward international activities can have on initiation and development of international entrepreneurship within the firm (Jones, 1999, 2001). The model that we produce here is strongly influenced by conceptualizations advancing international entrepreneurial culture (Dimitratos and Plakoyiannaki, 2003), and internationalization as a time-based entrepreneurial behavior (Jones and Coviello, 2005) as frameworks for international entrepreneurship research. Here we position international opportunity perception as the process linking the entrepreneurial mindset of the firm, to the resultant pattern of internationalization. The objective of this chapter is to present, describe and explain a model which attempts to integrate these three components.

It is generally posited that international entrepreneurship can lead to value-creation for the firm in the foreign marketplace (e.g. Dimitratos *et al.*, 2004; McDougall and Oviatt 2000; Zahra and Garvis, 2000), rendering the entrepreneurship construct instrumental to the growth and development of the firm abroad. The entrepreneurial construct is relatively under explored in the international entrepreneurship literature to date, and little is known about what effect the firm's mindset as regards international entrepreneurial attitude or organizational culture may have on its pattern of foreign market servicing. We suggest that a key mediating variable between the firm's mindset, or *international entrepreneurial culture* and its resultant pattern of foreign market servicing mode is the way in which the firm perceives opportunities abroad (international opportunity perception). Specifically the simple integrated model illustrated in Figure 3.1, shows how the firm's mindset conceptualized as its international entrepreneurial culture, is directly influenced by elements of its organizational context, and moderated by elements of the environment. This mindset enables the international opportunity perception process to take place, which subsequently influences the way in which opportunities abroad are exploited, and hence, the firm's pattern of internationalization. The process is iterative and cyclical in that the resulting pattern of internationalization determines the current *modus operandi*, which in turn influences the future mindset of the firm and future process of international opportunity recognition.

Opportunity and international opportunity perception

Entrepreneurship may be defined as the discovery, evaluation and exploitation of future goods and services (Shane and Eckhardt, 2003; Venkataraman, 1997). International entrepreneurship therefore is the same process but extended internationally, or across borders into different countries. International entrepreneurial opportunities (Casson, 1982; Schumpeter, 1934; Shane and Eckhardt, 2003; Shane and Venkataraman, 2000), are [international] situations in which new goods, services, raw materials, markets and organizing methods can be introduced through the formation of new means ends or means–ends relationships. Shane and Eckhardt (2003: 164) describe the entrepreneurial process as a directional but non-linear process involving the existence of opportunities, the discovery of opportunities and the exploitation of opportunities as illustrated in Figure 3.2a.

Figure 3.2b illustrates the way in which we extend Shane and Eckhardt's conceptualization of the entrepreneurial process to depict the international entrepreneurial process in which the existence of international opportunities leads to their perception and discovery, and ultimate exploitation. Taking

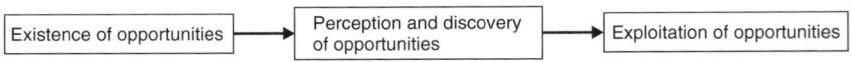

Figure 3.2a The entrepreneurial process
Source: Adapted from Shane and Eckhardt (2003: 164).

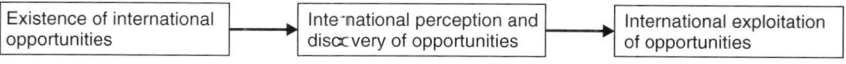

Figure 3.2b The international entrepreneurial process
Source: The authors.

the existence of international opportunities as given, the model we present in Figure 3.1 identifies factors that we see as important in enabling the firm to perceive international opportunities, but otherwise parallels the process depicted in Figures 3.2a and 3.2b.

Opportunity may emerge from changes in the value chain (Schumpeter, 1934), from changes in the firm's internal and external environment and from changes in the information relationships between players in the firm's market. Internationally, these sources of opportunity combinations may be vast and are likely to be limited by the firm's ability to perceive and discover opportunities. The existence of international opportunities is therefore likely to be limited to those to which the firm is alert and responsive, which are discernable through its entrepreneurial mindset, and therefore, in Figure 3.1, we suggest that international opportunity perception is influenced by the relationship between the firm's international entrepreneurial culture, as moderated by its environment, and its organizational context. Cohen and Levinthal (1990) suggest that firms have an absorptive capacity gained from prior knowledge, which enables them to acquire new knowledge about markets, technologies and production processes enhancing their ability to devise new means–ends frameworks in response (Shane 2003). Prior knowledge about markets, and prior knowledge of how to serve markets was found by Shane (2003) to facilitate the discovery of entrepreneurial opportunities. Firms which already have knowledge and experience of international business are likely to find that opportunity recognition is enhanced in comparison to firms with none, but will be influenced by the extent of their knowledge and experience. Therefore, we suggest that the firm's dominant international *modus operandi* will significantly influence the type of opportunities it perceives, and its ultimate means of exploiting them.

An entrepreneurial mindset, or organizational culture enables the firm to be alert and responsive to opportunities (Hisrich and O'Brien, 1982), but also, firms that are attentive to opportunities are more likely to behave entrepreneurially as regards their growth and development (Kirzner, 1973). Therefore, international entrepreneurship is strongly intertwined with the way firms become alert, search and act upon opportunities abroad (McDougall and Oviatt, 2003). Further, entrepreneurial discovery defined by Shane and Eckhardt (2003: 176) is "–the perception of a new means-ends frameworks to incorporate information neglected by prices–" and during the process of discovery individuals or groups "perceive of a previously unseen

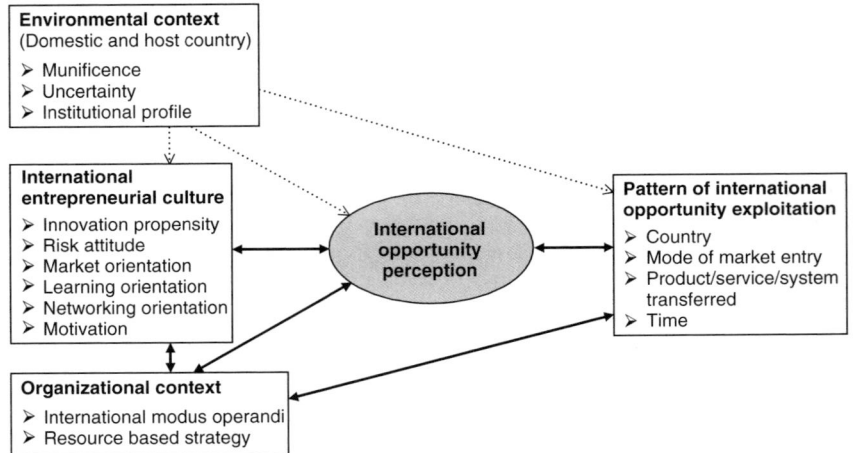

Figure 3.3 Towards a detailed integration: international entrepreneurial culture, international opportunity perception and international opportunity exploitation

or unknown way to create a new means–ends framework" (Shane and Eckhardt, 2003: 168). Perception of new opportunities requires a particular mindset, but also information from the firm's environmental context, and competencies and capabilities developed through its current organizational context. In the following sections, and in Figure 3.3, we attempt to detail the factors that we see as key influences on the process of international opportunity perception.

Environmental context

The presence of environmental context is dictated by the environmental determinism model. The population ecology perspective (Aldrich, 1979; Hannan and Freeman, 1977) would argue in favor of this model, suggesting that international behavior of the firm is affected by environmental variables in domestic and international scenes. The effect of environmental and organizational variables on the pattern of foreign market servicing mode is well documented in the international business literature (e.g. Dunning, 1988; Johanson and Vahlne, 1977). As regards the impact of environmental and organizational variables on international opportunity perception, researchers posit that cultural, institutional and political settings mold entrepreneurs' cognitive systems (Minniti, 2004; Mitchell et al., 2000). *Munificence* and *uncertainty* can be employed to capture perceptions of managers in the domestic and the host country environmental context because they are typically used in empirical studies that consider environmental effects (Keats and Hitt, 1988; Lawless and Finch, 1989). The differentiation between the two countries is important inasmuch as previous research has to a large extent ignored this distinction assuming that parameters such as high competitive intensity and technological change influence concurrently both domestic and international environmental contexts. Nevertheless, this is likely to be a simplification taking into account the dissimilar effect of environmental variables of foreign and domestic countries on international entrepreneurial activities (McDougall et al., 2003; Young et al., 2003). Further, study into trading-based international entrepreneurship can use the domestic and host country *institutional profile* measure for entrepreneurship that includes regulatory, cognitive and normative dimensions (Busenitz et al., 2000). The inclusion of this variable has significant public policy interest since it relates to the courses of action of domestic country institutions influencing entrepreneurial behavior.

The effect of domestic and international environmental variables, notably munificence, uncertainty and institutional profile will moderate the mindset of the firm, its process of international opportunity perception and pattern of international opportunity exploitation. The firm's degree of exposure to the international environment, through its current dominant *modus operandi* is likely to affect the extent to which environmental factors influence the opportunity perception process.

International entrepreneurial culture

We propose that the extent of entrepreneurship in the internationalized firm may be measured through its international entrepreneurial culture. In accordance with recent suggestions of researchers advocating a broader conceptualization of entrepreneurship (Brown et al., 2001; Lumpkin and Dess, 2001), we propose a related conceptualization that extends beyond the innovativeness, risk-seeking and proactiveness vis-à-vis competitors that are typically used to capture the international entrepreneurship construct (e.g. McDougall and Oviatt, 2000; Zahra and Garvis, 2000).

Dimitratos and Plakoyiannaki (2003) advance six elements that they suggest distinguish the entrepreneurial profile of firms venturing abroad through any market servicing mode. They are drawn from a literature review of entrepreneurship, international entrepreneurship, international business and organization theory studies, and together indicate the *international entrepreneurial culture* of an organization.

Drawing on Dimitratos and Plakoyiannaki (2003) therefore, the first element of a firm's international entrepreneurial culture, *innovation propensity* refers to the proclivity of the firm to espouse new and creative ideas, products, or processes designed to service the international market (cf. Lumpkin and Dess, 1996). The second element, *risk attitude* refers to the extent to which the firm is prepared to undertake significant and risky resource commitments in the international market (cf. Miller and Friesen, 1978). The third element, *market orientation* refers to the posture and behavior that the firm can adopt in order to create superior value for its customers in the international market (cf. Narver and Slater, 1990), and comprises the dimensions of customer orientation, interfunctional coordination and proactiveness vis-à-vis competitors. The fourth element, *learning orientation* refers to the propensity of the firm to actively obtain and use to its advantage intelligence on the international market (cf. Moorman, 1995; Slater and Narver, 1995). The fifth element, *networking orientation* refers to the extent to which the firm obtains resources from the indigenous environment through alliance creation and social embeddedness to use in its activities in the international market (cf. Granovetter, 1973; Gulati, 1998). The sixth element *motivation* refers to the process of initiation, direction and energization of human behavior of subsidiary managers and employees regarding ventures in the host market (cf. Geen and Shea, 1997).

Taken together, the six elements that comprise the firm's international entrepreneurial culture indicate the firm's mindset towards opportunity perception. A positive international entrepreneurial culture is likely to indicate that the firm is alert, open and receptive to ideas and opportunities.

Proposition 1: Firms with a positive international entrepreneurial culture, as influenced by organizational conditions, and moderated by environmental conditions, will be more alert and receptive to international opportunities; and

Proposition 2: Firms with a positive international entrepreneurial culture, as moderated by organizational and environmental conditions, may differently perceive opportunities abroad, thus their patterns of internationalization will differ from those with a less positive international entrepreneurial culture.

Differences in scores between the six elements might indicate the way opportunities are recognized and acted upon, or the types of opportunities that are recognized. For example a firm with a high score on innovation propensity but a low score on market orientation, may recognize the opportunity for product innovation in a foreign market, but lack the ability to recognize specific customer needs in that market that would enable the firm to create the superior value necessary to effectively exploit that opportunity.

Proposition 3: Firms that differ in specific elements of international entrepreneurial culture, as moderated by organizational and environmental conditions, will differ in the way, and in the type of international opportunities they perceive, and hence those they choose to exploit.

Organizational context

International modus operandi

Another set of factors that may influence the firm's mindset and ability to perceive international opportunities relates to its experiential knowledge from its past and current international business activities. Here we suggest that one of the key influences will be the firm's current dominant *modus operandi* which will indicate the nature and scope of the firm's involvement with its overseas markets.

Proposition 4: The firm's current dominant *modus operandi* will influence its international entrepreneurial culture which in turn will influence the potential scope of international opportunities it will perceive.

Trading-based international operations

As studies on international entrepreneurship tend to take a holistic approach to internationalization which embraces a range of foreign market entry modes, there are few studies in this emergent body of work that concentrate solely on trading-based international entrepreneurship (e.g. Ibeh, 2003). However, trading-based approaches to internationalization, according to traditional exporting literature are especially typical of small internationalized firms that lack resources or experience that would enable them to service foreign markets through more advanced modes. As trading tends to be conducted at arm's length, and often through domestic or foreign-based intermediaries, the firm's exposure to international opportunities may be limited to those which are revealed through the intermediary, and are likely to be limited to the product and geographical parameters stipulated in the agency agreement.

While it is conjecture at this point, we hypothesize that, for trading-based firms it is likely that environmental variables of the domestic country can have a greater moderating effect on the international entrepreneurial culture – international opportunity perception and trading arrangements – than variables of the foreign country. This statement would be backed by findings of Zahra et al. (1997), which empirically support the key influence of domestic country environmental variables on exporting ventures of young firms. Indeed many exporting firms are driven into exporting activities following competitive pressures or saturated demand at home (e.g. Liouville, 1992; Naidu and Prasad, 1994). It is likely that exporting firms screen international opportunities through the lens of their domestic market. These firms are involved in the most cautious pattern of foreign market servicing mode since they may give emphasis only to stimuli at home, and so, fail to monitor and evaluate opportunities abroad in a direct and straightforward way. We claim that for exporting firms international opportunity perception is at its most limited.

Proposition 5: Firms whose current dominant *modus operandi* is trading based will be characterized by a less positive international entrepreneurial culture than firms using network based or subsidiary based modes, and the scope of international opportunities they perceive is likely to be limited to incremental adjustments to its current international trajectory.

Network-based international operations

In this dominant *modus operandi* the entrepreneurial firm relies on contractual/collaborative arrangements including licensing, franchising, joint ventures and strategic alliances to expand in the international marketplace. Network-based international entrepreneurship seems to be that type of international entrepreneurship that has most commonly been investigated in related studies. Indeed works on international new ventures often provide evidence on firms that use extensive collaborative modes to service foreign markets (Coviello and Munro, 1997; Madsen and Servais, 1997; Oviatt and McDougall, 1995). Most empirical findings in this area are drawn from case studies, which although they provide interesting insights into this theme, seem inadequate to support generalizable results. Entrepreneurial culture and environmental context of the domestic and the host country are the same with those of the trading-based type of international entrepreneurship.

We support the idea that international opportunity perception is considerably filtered through the interaction of the international entrepreneurial firm with its foreign partner. This is related to the fact that market knowledge on foreign market conditions is acquired through joint venture and alliance agreements (Agarwal and Ramaswami, 1992; Davidson, 1982). In addition, psychic distance with a foreign market may be alleviated through the establishment of network-based arrangements (Hennart and Larimo, 1998; Kim and Hwang, 1992), rendering the joint venture collaboration key to the construal and analysis of international opportunities. It is also very likely that awareness, identification and exploitation of opportunities abroad in network-based international entrepreneurship are higher compared with the trading-based type. This is because in the latter form of *modus operandi* the exporting firm obtains relatively less information on foreign market conditions in contrast to the contractual/collaborative mode where the firm works closely with its partners to pursue common objectives. The possibilities of international opportunity perception for firms operating through-network based *modus operandi* are likely to be more extensive than for trading firms, given the arguments above, but may be limited by the extent of internationalization of the networks within which they operate

(Blankenburg-Holm, 1995). Thus, firms that operate in industry sectors that are globalized will be exposed to wider opportunity possibilities than those in relatively localized industries. The extent to which they perceive potential opportunities will be indicated by their international entrepreneurial culture which is likely to be positively influenced by their network-based operations that are characterized by cross-border interactivity between network partners.

Proposition 6: Firms whose current dominant *modus operandi* is network based will be characterized by a more positive international entrepreneurial culture than firms using trading based or subsidiary based modes, but the scope of international opportunities they perceive is likely to be indicated by the extent of internationalization of the networks in which they operate.

Subsidiary-based international operations

According to Young *et al.* (2003), entrepreneurship in multinational subsidiaries is a theme that should draw further empirical research in the future. Scholars (e.g. Birkinshaw, 2000. 2001; Birkinshaw and Hood, 2000; Hedlund, 1994) have stressed the increasingly important role of subsidiaries within multinational corporations (MNCs) bringing to light evidence on an emerging era of the MNC evolution, namely the "liberalism era" (Birkinshaw and Hood, 2001). In this period, subsidiaries are delegated substantial authority, decision-making power and responsibility. Studies in this "subsidiary focused [type of] research" (e.g. Birkinshaw, 2000; Prahalad, 1999) show that novel ideas and business approaches surface from entrepreneurial subsidiaries around the world rather than MNC headquarters.

In a recent literature review, Paterson and Brock (2002) note that entrepreneurship in subsidiaries is a theme that is likely to receive growing research attention in the subsidiary management research. As subsidiaries pursue local opportunities that can be exploited for the benefit of the MNC system worldwide (Birkinshaw, 1997), development of subsidiary entrepreneurship may be of value to the whole MNC. In addition, it can be of value to the foreign country economy since national interest of the host nation dictates that subsidiaries are given the autonomy to develop new products, processes and business practices (Edwards *et al.*, 2002), and apparently act more entrepreneurially.

Birkinshaw and his colleagues (Birkinshaw, 1997, 1999; Birkinshaw *et al.*, 1998) have offered interesting insights into the theme of multinational subsidiary-based entrepreneurship in their work on subsidiary entrepreneurial initiative. Nonetheless, we concur with observations (Birkinshaw, 1997; Wright, 1999) suggesting that the subsidiary entrepreneurship issue deserves further investigation. Increasingly attention has been given in the subsidiary-focused research to the fact that the environmental context of the host country affects entrepreneurial and innovative capabilities of the subsidiary (Birkinshaw, 1999; Frost, 2001; Zahra *et al.*, 2000). Embeddedness of the subsidiary in its local environment can also be beneficial from a public policy perspective because it is likely to be associated with aspects such as local adaptation and responsiveness, development of employee skills, resistance to downsizing, and spillovers of technological and management know-how (Birkinshaw and Hood, 1998; Graham and Krugman, 1995). Thus, incorporating the environmental determinism view in this model has considerable public policy interest since public policy decision makers can affect to some extent related environmental variables. Consequently, examining the effects of host country environmental variables has value for both researchers and public policy organizations.

As with the trading-based and network-based forms of operation, we posit that the six elements of international entrepreneurial culture can capture subsidiary entrepreneurial culture, and munificence and uncertainty may be employed to capture perceptions of foreign-owned subsidiary managers in the host country environmental context. Further, such a study can use the host country institutional profile measure for entrepreneurship that includes regulatory, cognitive and normative dimensions.

Researchers who espouse the head office assignment perspective would argue that the subsidiary is an instrument of the MNC and that management at the headquarters is responsible for defining the imperatives of subsidiaries abroad (Vernon, 1966). Studies of subsidiary-based entrepreneurship should include insights from the head office assignment perspective as this also influences the relationship between subsidiaries and headquarters. Hence, constellations of variables can incorporate parameters linked to the subsidiary–headquarters relationship. The four key variables are suggested to be: *global strategic mandate*, which relates to the influential role that the subsidiary plays in developing and marketing a product line worldwide (Roth and Morrison, 1992; Rugman and Bennett, 1982); *subsidiary autonomy*, which seemingly comprises one of the growing themes in the subsidiary literature (Paterson and Brock, 2002; Young and Tavares, 2004), and refers to the freedom that subsidiaries can have in acting and making decisions independently from the headquarters; *subsidiary credibility* with the headquarters, which may increase the level of subsidiary capabilities in the eyes of head office managers (Birkinshaw, 1999); and *headquarters–subsidiary communication*, which concerns the frequency with which management in the two countries communicate with each other (Birkinshaw *et al.*, 1998; Birkinshaw, 1999).

In relation to the international opportunity perception of the subsidiary-based type, we hypothesize that inasmuch as the MNC relies on its foreign subsidiaries for its international activities the degree of international opportunity perception is the highest among all three dominant *modus operandi*.

Many modern multinational subsidiaries function essentially as autonomous centers contributing to a "multi-centre structure" whereby organization-specific advantages are developed in different countries (Andersson and Forsgren, 2000; Forsgren et al., 1992). In spite of this, foreign-owned subsidiaries are mechanisms that help the internationalized firm to significantly monitor and identify market opportunities abroad. Neither the trading- nor the network-based type of internationalization may enable the provision of a higher degree or more immediate type of opportunity perception in foreign markets. MNCs have to find the appropriate incentive systems (O' Donnell, 2000) in order to ensure that their subsidiaries competently discover and act upon international opportunities.

Proposition 7: Firms whose current dominant *modus operandi* is subsidiary-based will be characterized by a level of international entrepreneurial culture determined by their global strategic mandate, subsidiary autonomy, subsidiary credibility and headquarters–subsidiary communication. Subsidiaries positive on all four factors are likely to perceive a wider scope of international opportunities than firms operating through trading or network-based modes. Subsidiaries negative on the same four factors are likely to exhibit a similar pattern of international opportunity recognition as trading-based firms.

The more detailed model that we advance (Figure 3.3), attempts to extend the international entrepreneurship literature into the field of subsidiary entrepreneurship by potentially testing moderating effects, which involve variables linked to host country environmental conditions and subsidiary–headquarters relationships. Providing empirical insights into these interactions is of interest in respect of both theory and practice. Researchers would gain insights from such a study that brings into the international entrepreneurship field notions from the environmental determinism, the subsidiary-focused and the head office assignment perspectives. Policy makers may better understand the potential conducive effects of environmental factors on the entrepreneurial activities of subsidiaries. Managers of subsidiaries would be interested in finding out which subsidiary–headquarters variables and what environmental conditions can enhance awareness and identification of opportunities for their affiliates.

Resource-based strategy

The existence of the organizational context is dictated by the resource-based view. This view posits that idiosyncratic resources and capabilities may render the firm competitive advantage (Barney, 1991), implying that organizational growth abroad would be influenced by core competencies of the internationalized firm. Our interest is in how the firm's resource-based strategy is likely to influence opportunity perception and exploitation in an international context.

Entrepreneurs are often described as those willing to take risks without regard to resources (Stevenson, 1983). In Stevenson's view, entrepreneurial firms are likely to be driven by an opportunistic resource orientation by which they place less regard on the ownership of resources, than on the control of them including the ability to use, exploit and extract value from resources, which are accessible but not necessarily owned by them (Brown et al., 2001; Stevenson, 1983). Entrepreneurial firms, by extension of this line of reasoning, are more likely to make use of networks in the internationalization process than firms that are less entrepreneurial (less opportunistic) in their use of externally held resources. However, if firms are to recognize resource-based opportunities, whether emerging from their own, or other externally held resources, they need to be able to identify novel combinations of resources.

Denrell et al. (2003) suggest that the alignment of resources towards new uses will only be possible if several other actors have already recognized the opportunity and acted on it. Commenting on the process of discovery of such opportunities, the latter authors suggest that it is likely to have been serendipitous. "That is, success is a consequence of effort and luck joined by alertness and flexibility" (Denrell et al., 2003: 985).

Proposition 8: Firms that are resource constrained but with a positive international entrepreneurial culture, as influenced by the current dominant *modus operandi*, and moderated by the environment, may be more alert and responsive to international opportunities, but may lack the ability to exploit them.

Additionally organizational variables such as the management characteristics, structure and systems of the firm may affect international opportunity perception (Chang and Rosenzweig, 2001; Zahra et al., 2005). In relation to variables of the organizational context for exporting entrepreneurial firms, availability of human, financial and production resources has often been cited a facilitating factor for internationalization in the relevant literature (Yang et al., 1992; Yaprak, 1985). Management systems for internationalization, such as appropriate planning and control of exporting ventures are also significant to successful international activities (Burton and Schlegelmilch, 1987; ENSR, 1996). The vision to succeed abroad also forms a variable in the organizational context inasmuch as it can guide behavior and formulate strategies of the exporting firm (Dichtl et al., 1984; Leonidou et al., 1998; Lim et al., 1993). In agreement with findings in the stages theory of internationalization (Bilkey and Tesar, 1977; Johanson and Vahlne, 1977), experiential knowledge on the foreign market under consideration is a key influential parameter in the same set.

Proposition 9: Firms that are resource enriched and with a positive international entrepreneurial culture, as influenced by the current dominant *modus operandi*, and moderated by the environment, may still be less alert and responsive to international opportunities, but have a better ability to exploit those recognized than firms that are resource constrained.

The resource-based view in the network-based *modus operandi* may pertain also to variables of the organizational/collaborative context. Positive attitude of the internationalized firm towards collaborative modes is typically found to be a factor conducive to enhanced performance (Beamish, 1984). Host country experience of the firm in the country where collaboration takes place is additionally a variable that may influence performance positively (Artisien and Buckley, 1985). Two other factors referring to the alliance likely to influence favorably performance of the collaborative arrangement (and internationalized firm) abroad are goal congruence (Simiar, 1983) and commitment (Hu and Chen, 1996) between partners.

Summary

To this point, we have attempted to explain ways in which the international mindset or international entrepreneurial culture of the firm is influenced by and related to its current international *modus operandi*, and moderated by its environment. We suggest that together, these factors render the firm alert to the perception and discovery of international opportunities. In the next section we describe the association between international opportunity perception and the pattern of international opportunity exploitation. We claim that different ways and degrees through which firms become alert, seek and discover opportunities abroad are vital to the foreign market servicing mode they subsequently employ, the countries they enter, and the products, services and resources they transfer to the foreign market. Differences between firms in perceptions of opportunities abroad lead to dissimilar strategies on how to exploit foreign opportunities as reflected by the pattern of internationalization. As posited, the association between international opportunity perception and pattern of international opportunity exploitation is iterative and cyclical, because engagement through the current dominant *modus operandi* can also dictate the way firms identify and act upon opportunities in the international marketplace, in future. As Weick (1979) puts it, firms grasp environments only through the perceptions of their managers.

Pattern of international opportunity exploitation

It is now generally accepted that firms do not necessarily follow the incremental, linear pattern of internationalization espoused by early studies of small firm internationalization (e.g. Bilkey and Tesar; 1977). Recent evidence suggests that firms may follow much more complex patterns involving a range of entry modes and countries (Jones, 1999; Jones and Coviello, 2005; Knight and Cavusgil, 1996; Oviatt and McDougall, 1995), and this may involve the transfer of a range of products, services and resources (Andersen, 1997), established over time in intense or extended periods (Hurmerinta-Peltomaki, 2003; Jones, 1999).

The Schumpeterian (1934) view of entrepreneurial opportunity posits that opportunity might emerge from changes in the value chain (Shane and Eckhardt, 2003). Thus the creation of new products, services, production systems and ways of organizing, as well as the discovery of new raw materials or sources of raw materials and new geographic markets represent opportunities for the entrepreneurial firm. Following Schumpeter, it is clear that internationalization represents a process of international opportunity exploitation; a process of innovation in which opportunity combinations of products, services and resources transferred, new country markets and new modes of operation may be perceived and assembled by the firm over variable time periods (Jones and Coviello, 2005).

Proposition 10: The types of opportunities perceived by the firm, as influenced by its international entrepreneurial culture and organizational context, and moderated by the environment, will determine its pattern of international exploitation over time.

The permutations and combinations of resource, product, mode and country opportunities are likely to be vast and to some extent subject to serendipity. The development of theory with predictive ability in respect of the pattern of opportunity exploitation is likely to be challenging to say the least. The value of the model we have produced here may lie more in its potential use as an analytical tool for retrospective data than as a predictor of likely trajectories of internationalization. However, as the few broad propositions that we have advanced suggest, while international opportunities may be infinite, the firm's alertness and ability to perceive them will be limited and tempered by its current operations, mindset, resource base, and environment. It is likely therefore that the realms of possibility for international opportunity expansion are predictable to the extent to which the firm's perceptions are limited by the factors identified in the model (Figure 3.3). For example, firms whose current *modus operandi* is network based may follow opportunities dictated by the extent of internationalization of the network, by the limits of their own resources and combinative opportunities with network partners who have identified similar opportunities.

Internationalization can be seen as a process of innovation (Andersen, 1993, 1997), and by inference following Schumpeter, is a process of opportunity exploitation. An innovation perspective on internationalization is evident in a number of recent studies (e.g. Jones, 1999; Jones and Coviello, 2004, 2005; Knight and Cavusgil, 1996, 2004; Oviatt and McDougall, 1995). Emphasis has tended to be on the pattern or process of opportunity exploitation (internationalization) rather than on its antecedent process of opportunity recognition. This latter process deserves attention in future studies on internationalization as an entrepreneurial process (Dimitratos and Plakoyiannaki, 2003), and in this chapter we have attempted to lay the foundations for further conceptual development in that respect.

Missing from our model is the process of opportunity selection and evaluation which should lie between international opportunity perception and international opportunity exploitation. Shane and Eckhardt (2003) contend that little is known about what proportions of discovered opportunities are evaluated, or what percentage of evaluated opportunities is actually exploited. While the literature on the entrepreneurial process may be silent in that respect, the literatures on foreign market entry mode choice and foreign market evaluation are well developed and future researchers might usefully integrate those findings into the international entrepreneurial process model.

Conclusions

In this chapter, we have suggested that the entrepreneurial process of opportunity perception and exploitation lies at the heart of international entrepreneurship as a field of study. Positioning the opportunity perception and exploitation process at its center, we have advanced an integrative model drawing on multidisciplinary perspectives but essentially integrative of entrepreneurship and internationalization theories on the growth and development of the firm. We suggest that the firm's ability to perceive and discover international opportunities is determined primarily by its mindset or international entrepreneurial culture, as influenced by organizational factors such as its current dominant *modus operandi* and resource-based strategy, and moderated by environmental factors such as munificence, uncertainty and institutional profile.

The model is integrative in another sense and that is how different firms, following different patterns of internationalization as manifested by their dominant foreign market servicing mode, can be studied using an integrated model of entrepreneurial behavior. Much of the classic literature on internationalization is fragmented due to the focus of different studies on separate modes of international operations. For convenience, we categorized the three different types of international expansion modes as; trading-based, network-based and subsidiary-based corresponding to ventures in the international marketplace by relying on the market, on collaboration and on hierarchy, respectively. We suggest that international entrepreneurship can be a phenomenon that is relevant to all firms irrespective of foreign market servicing mode. In order to pursue such a study, we sought to explore the same model of international entrepreneurship under different circumstances. Yet, the main idea in this chapter is that international opportunity perception is the mediating variable between international entrepreneurship and the pattern of foreign market servicing mode.

Specifically, in this chapter we propose that the international entrepreneurship – international opportunity perception and pattern of international opportunity exploitation – may be moderated by the influence of environmental and organizational sets of variables. We also support the notion that exporting firms may perceive opportunities abroad rather modestly and through the lens of their domestic market; firms that use contractual/collaborative modes may perceive opportunities abroad to a comparatively higher extent through their foreign partners; and, MNCs that employ their own hierarchy may perceive opportunities abroad to the highest possible extent through activities of their multinational subsidiaries, depending on factors associated with the headquarters–subsidiary relationship.

Our model and potential variations of it have important implications for theory. We suggest that by placing international opportunity perception at the center of this model the significant role of becoming alert, searching and evaluating opportunities abroad is accentuated in international entrepreneurship research. The way top management teams enact with and interact with their environments can influence their international opportunity exploitation patterns. Viewed in this light, we concur with the statement that future research on international entrepreneurship should focus to a greater degree on cognitive systems of firms' top management teams (Zahra et al., 2005).

In addition, studies that use this model and its variations apply notions from entrepreneurship and strategic management theories. Specifically, the model shows that notions from the environmental determinism, resource-based view and head office assignment perspectives are likely to have merit in international entrepreneurship research. In doing so, we sought to provide a holistic framework through which the international entrepreneurship study will acquire greater theoretical coherence. Also, models such as those discussed in this chapter can be applied to firms that have outward international activities through any foreign market servicing mode, and therefore, may be valid for firms of all sectors, ages and sizes. This is an important contribution as it seeks to avoid fragmentation in the field that mainly tends to examine entrepreneurial activities of international new ventures.

The model has key implications for public policy makers. Inasmuch as it stresses the key role of the environmental context of the domestic and the host environmental context, it highlights the possible courses of action that public policy makers can take in affecting environmental variables in favor of entrepreneurial activities. Indeed, to the best of our knowledge, only one study has empirically confirmed the positive role of (domestic) environment for entrepreneurial activities abroad (Dimitratos et al., 2004). Inclusion in the model of *institutional profile* will inform policy makers who have the power to affect related variables linked to regulatory dimensions. Pursuing studies applying the model advanced in this chapter will help identify how public policy can assist international entrepreneurial ventures, an area that has received scant empirical research attention.

The chapter has also important implications for managers of entrepreneurial firms. The iterative and cyclical influence of the firm's current dominant *modus operandi* on opportunity perception and subsequent pattern of international opportunity exploitation can help managers realize that if they attempt to modify their perceptions in relation to opportunities abroad, their foreign market servicing modes are subject to change in future. This in turn may enable them to become more alert and responsive to future opportunity. This opens up avenues concerning strategic change for the internationalized firm in the international marketplace. Also, research involving the investigated model can identify which organizational factors are conducive to perception of opportunities and patterns of internationalization. Identification of determining factors associated with this model will suggest to managers what combinations of organizational and environmental factors can lead to choice of patterns of internationalization, an area wherein only very few studies exist. In particular, such an analysis may reveal to managers of MNCs factors that could render subsidiaries more entrepreneurial and alert to opportunities abroad, possibly turning them into 'centers of excellence' with positive impacts for the whole multinational system.

References

Agarwal, S. and Ramaswami, S.N. 1992. Choice of Foreign Market Entry Mode: Impact of Ownership, Location and Internalization Factors, *Journal of International Business Studies*, 23, 1–27.

Aldrich, H.E. 1979. *Organizations and Environments*, Englewood Cliffs, NJ: Prentice-Hall.

Andersen, O. 1993. On The Internationalization Process of Firms: A Critical Analysis, *Journal of International Business Studies*, 24(2), 33–46.

Andersen, O. 1997. Internationalization and Market Entry Mode: A Review of Theories and Conceptual Frameworks, *Management International Review*, 37(2), 7–42.

Andersson, U. and Forsgren, M. 2000. In Search of Centre of Excellence: Network Embeddedness and Subsidiary Roles in Multinational Corporations, *Management International Review*, 40(4), 329–50.

Artisien, P.F.R. and Buckley, P.J. 1985. Joint Ventures in Yugoslavia: Opportunities and Constraints, *Journal of International Business Studies*, 16(Spring), 111–34.

Barney, J. 1991. Firm Resources and Sustained Competitive Advantage, *Journal of Management*, 17, 99–120.

Beamish, P.W. 1984. *Joint Venture Performance in Developing Countries*. Unpublished doctoral dissertation, University of Western Ontario.

Bilkey, W.J. and Tesar, G. 1977. The Export Behavior of Smaller-Sized Wisconsin Manufacturing Firms, *Journal of International Business Studies*, 8(1), 93–8.

Birkinshaw, J. 1997. Entrepreneurship in Multinational Corporations: The Characteristics of Subsidiary Initiatives, *Strategic Management Journal*, 18, 207–29.

Birkinshaw, J. 1999. The Determinants and Consequences of Subsidiary Initiative in Multinational Corporations, *Entrepreneurship Theory and Practice*, 24(1), 9–36.

Birkinshaw, J. 2000. *Entrepreneurship in the Global Firm*, London: Sage.

Birkinshaw, J. 2001. Strategy and Management in MNE Subsidiaries, in A. Rugman and T. Brewer (Eds) *Oxford Handbook of International Business*, 380–401. Oxford: Oxford University Press.

Birkinshaw, J. and Hood, N. 1998. Multinational Subsidiary Evolution: Capability and Charter Change in Foreign-Owned Subsidiary Companies, *Academy of Management Review*, 23, 773–95.

Birkinshaw, J. and Hood, N. 2000. Characteristics of Foreign Subsidiaries in Industry Clusters, *Journal of International Business Studies*, 31, 141–54.

Birkinshaw, J. and Hood, N. 2001. Unleash Innovation in Foreign Subsidiaries, *Harvard Business Review*, 79(3), 131–8.

Birkinshaw, J., Hood, N. and Jonsson, S. 1998. Building Firm-Specific Advantages in Multinational Corporations: The Role of Subsidiary Initiative, *Strategic Management Journal*, 19, 221–41.

Blankenburg-Holm, D. 1995. A Network Approach to Foreign Market Entry, in K. Moller and D. Wilson (Eds) *Business Marketing: An International and Network Perspective*, 375–405. Boston: Kluwer Academic Publishers.

Brown, T.E., Davidsson, P. and Wiklund, J. 2001. An Operationalization of Stevenson's Conceptualization of Entrepreneurship as Opportunity-Based Firm Behavior, *Strategic Management Journal*, 22, 953–68.

Burton, F.N. and Schlegelmilch, B.B. 1987. Profile Analyses of Non-exporters versus Exporters Grouped by Export Involvement, *Management International Review*, 27(1), 38–49.

Busenitz, L.W., Gömez, C. and Spencer, J.W. 2000. Country Institutional Profiles: Unlocking Entrepreneurial Phenomena, *Academy of Management Journal*, 43, 994–1003.

Casson, M. 1982. *The Entrepreneur: An Economic Theory*, Oxford: Martin Robertson.

Chang, S. and Rosenzweig, P.M. 2001. The Choice of Entry Mode in Sequential Foreign Direct Investment, *Strategic Management Journal*, 22, 747–76.

Cohen, W. and Levinthal, D. 1990. Absorptive Capacity: A New Perspective on Learning and Innovation, *Administrative Science Quarterly*, 35(1), 128–53.

Coviello, N.E. and Jones, M.V. 2004. Methodological Issues in International Entrepreneurship Research, *Journal of Business Venturing*, 19(4), 485–508.

Coviello, N.E. and Munro, H.J. 1997. Network Relationships and The Internationalisation Process of Small Software Firms, *International Business Review*, 6(4), 361–86.

Davidson, W.H. 1982. *Global Strategic Management*, New York: Wiley.

Denrell, J., Fang C. and Winter, S.G. 2003. The Economics of Strategic Opportunity, *Strategic Management Journal*, 24, 977–90.

Dichtl, E., Leibold, M., Köglmayr, H.-G. and Müller, S. 1984. The Export Decision of Small- and Medium-Sized Firms: A Review, *Management International Review*, 24(2), 49–60.

Dimitratos, P. and Plakoyiannaki, E. 2003. Theoretical Foundations of An International Entrepreneurial Culture, *Journal of International Entrepreneurship*, 1, 187–215.

Dimitratos, P., Lioukas, S. and Carter, S. 2004. The Relationship between Entrepreneurship and International Performance: The Importance of Domestic Environment, *International Business Review*, 13, 19–41.

Dunning, J.H. 1988. The Eclectic Paradigm of International Production: A Restatement and Some Possible Extensions, *Journal of International Business Studies*, 19, 1–31.

Edwards, R., Ahmad, A and Moss, S. 2002. Subsidiary Autonomy: The Case of Multinational Subsidiaries in Malaysia, *Journal of International Business Studies*, 33, 183–91.

ENSR (European Network for SME Research). 1996. *The European observatory for SMEs*. Fourth Annual Report

Forsgren, M., Holm, U. and Johanson, J. 1992. Internationalization of the Second Degree – The Emergence of European-based Centres in Swedish Firms, in S. Young and J. Hamill (Eds) *Europe and the Multinationals – Issues and Responses for the 1990s*, 235–53. London: Edward Elgar.

Frost, T.S. 2001. The Geographic Sources of Foreign Subsidiaries' Innovations, *Strategic Management Journal*, 22, 101–23

Geen, R. and Shea, J.D.C. 1997. Social Motivation and Culture, in D. Munro, J.F. Schumaker and S.C. Carr (Eds) *Motivation and Culture*, 33–48. New York: Routledge.

Graham, E.M. and Krugman, P.R. 1995. *Foreign Direct Investment in the United States*, 3rd edn. Washington, DC: Institute for International Economics.

Granovetter, M. 1973. The Strength of Weak Ties, *American Journal of Sociology*, 78, 1360–80.

Gulati, R. 1998. Alliances and Networks, *Strategic Management Journal*, 19, 293–317.

Hannan, M.T. and Freeman, J.F. 1977. The Population Ecology of Organizations, *American Journal of Sociology*, 82, 929–64.

Hedlund, G. 1994. A Model of Knowledge Management and The N-form Corporation, *Strategic Management Journal*, 15(Summer Special Issue), 73–90.

Hennart, J.-F. and Larimo, J. 1998. The Impact of Culture on The Strategy of Multinational Enterprises: Does National Origin Affect Ownership Decisions? *Journal of International Business Studies*, 29, 515–38.

Hisrich, R.D. and O'Brien, M. 1982. The Woman Entrepreneur as a Reflection of The Type of Business, in K. Vesper (Ed.) *Frontiers of Entrepreneurship Research*, 54–67. Wellesley, MA: Babson College.

Hu, M.Y. and Chen, H. 1996. An Empirical Analysis of Factors Explaining Foreign Joint Venture Performance in China, *Journal of Business Research*, 35, 165–73.

Hurmerinta-Peltomaki, L. 2003. Time and Internationalisation: Theoretical Challenges Set by Rapid Internationalisers, *Journal of International Entrepreneurship*, 1(2), 217–36.

Ibeh, K.I.N. 2003. Toward a Contingency Framework of Export Entrepreneurship: Conceptualisations and Empirical Evidence, *Small Business Economics*, 15(1), 49–68.

Johanson, J. and Vahlne, J.-E. 1977. The Internationalization Process of The Firm: A Model of Knowledge Development and Increasing Foreign Market Commitments, *Journal of International Business Studies*, 8(1), 23–32.

Jones, M.V. 1999. The Internationalisation of UK Small High-Technology Firms, *Journal of International Marketing*, 7(4), 15–41.

Jones, M.V. 2001. First Steps: An Examination of The First Cross-border Business Activities of a Sample of a UK High Technology Firms, *Journal of International Management*, 7(3) 191–210

Jones, M.V. and Coviello, N.E. 2005. Internationalization: Conceptualizing an Entrepreneurial Process of Behaviour in Time, *Journal of International Business Studies*, 36(3), 284–303.

Keats, B.W. and Hitt, M.A. 1988. A Causal Model of Linkages among Environmental Dimensions, Macro Organizational Characteristics, and Performance, *Academy of Management Journal*, 31, 570–98.

Kim, W.C. and Hwang, P. 1992. Global Strategy and Multinationals' Entry Mode Choice, *Journal of International Business Studies*, 23(1), 29–53.

Kirzner, I.M. 1973. *Competition and Entrepreneurship*, Chicago: University of Chicago Press.

Knight, G. and Cavusgil, S.T. 1996. The Born Global Firm: A Challenge to Traditional Internationalization Theory, in C.R. Taylor (Ed.) *Advances of International Marketing*, 11–26. New York: JAI Press.

Knight, G. and Cavusgil, S.T. 2004. Innovation, Organizational Capabilities, and The Born-global Firm, *Journal of International Business Studies*, 35(2): 124–41.

Lawless, M.W. and Finch, L.K. 1989. Choice and Determinism: A Test of Hrebiniak and Joyce's Framework on Strategy–Environment Fit, *Strategic Management Journal*, 10, 351–65.

Leonidou, L.C., Katsikeas, C.S. and Piercy, N.F. 1998. Identifying Managerial Influences on Exporting: Past Research and Future Directions, *Journal of International Marketing*, 6(2), 74–102.

Lim, J.-S., Sharkley, T.W. and Kim, K.I. 1993. Determinants of International Marketing Strategy, *Management International Review*, 33(2), 103–20.

Liouville, J. 1992. Under What Conditions Can Exports Exert a Positive Influence on Profitability? *Management International Review*, 32(1), 41–54.

Lumpkin, G.T. and Dess, G.G. 1996. Clarifying The Entrepreneurial Construct and Linking it to Performance, *Academy of Management Review*, 21, 135–72.

Lumpkin, G.T. and Dess, G.G. 2001. Linking Two Dimensions of Entrepreneurial Orientation to Firm Performance: The Moderating Role of Environment and Industry Life Cycle, *Journal of Business Venturing*, 16, 429–51.

Madsen, T.K. and Servais, P. 1997. The Internationalization of Born Globals: An Evolutionary Process? *International Business Review*, 6, 561–83.

McDougall, P.P. and Oviatt, B.M. 2000. International Entrepreneurship: The Intersection of Two Research Paths, *Academy of Management Journal*, 43, 902–08.

McDougall, P.P. and Oviatt, B.M. 2003. Some Fundamental Issues in International Entrepreneurship, http://www.usasbe.org/knowledge/whitepapers/index.asp

McDougall, P.P., Oviatt, B.M. and Shrader, R.C. 2003. A Comparison of International and Domestic New Ventures, *Journal of International Entrepreneurship*, 1, 59–82.

Miller, D. and Friesen, P.H. 1978. Archetypes of Strategy Formulation, *Management Science*, 24, 921–33.

Minniti, M. 2004. Entrepreneurial Alertness and Asymmetric Information in a Spin-Glass Model, *Journal of Business Venturing*, 19, 637–58.

Mitchell, R.K., Smith, B., Seawright, K.W. and Morse, E.A. 2000. Cross-cultural Cognitions and The Venture Creation Decision, *Academy of Management Journal*, 43, 974–93.

Moorman, C. 1995. Organizational Market Information Processes: Cultural Antecedents and New Product Outcomes, *Journal of Marketing Research*, 32, 318–36.

Naidu, G.M. and Prasad, V.K. 1994. Predictors of Export Strategy and Performance of Small- and Medium-Sized Firms, *Journal of Business Research*, 31, 107–15.

Narver, J.C. and Slater, S.F. 1990. The Effect of a Market Orientation on Business Profitability, *Journal of Marketing*, 54(4), 20–36.

O' Donnell, S.W. 2000. Managing Foreign Subsidiaries: Agents of Headquarters, or An Independent Network? *Strategic Management Journal*, 21, 525–48.

Oviatt, B.M. and McDougall, P.P. 1995. Global Start-ups: Entrepreneurs on a Worldwide Stage, *Academy of Management Executive*, 9(2), 30–43.

Paterson, S.L. and Brock, D.M. 2002. The Development of Subsidiary-Management Research: Review and Theoretical Analysis, *International Business Review*, 11, 139–63.

Prahalad, C.K. 1999. Transforming Internal Governance: The Challenge for Multinationals, *Sloan Management Review*, 40(3), 31–9.

Roth, K. and Morrison, A. 1992. Implementing Global Strategy: Characteristics of Global Subsidiary Mandates, *Journal of International Business Studies*, 23, 715–36.

Rugman, A.M. and Bennett, J. 1982. Technology Transfer and World Product Mandating in Canada *Columbia Journal of World Business*, 17(4), 58–62.

Schumpeter, J.A. 1934. *The Theory of Economic Development: An Enquiry into Profits, Capital, Credit, Interest, and the Business Cycle*, Cambridge, MA: Harvard University Press.

Shane, S. 2003. *A General Theory of Entrepreneurship: The Individual–Opportunity Nexus*, Cheltenham: Edward Elgar.

Shane, S. and Eckhardt, J. 2003. The Individual–Opportunity Nexus, in Z.J. Acs and D.B. Audretsch (Eds) *Handbook of Entrepreneurship Research*, 161–91. Boston: Kluwer Academic Publishers.

Shane, S. and Venkataraman. S. 2000. The Promise of Entrepreneurship as a Field of Research, *Academy of Management Review*, 25(1), 217–26.

Simiar, F. 1983. Major Causes of Joint Venture Failures in The Middle East: The Case of Iran, *Management International Review*, 23(1), 58–68.

Slater, S.F. and Narver, J.C. 1995. Market Orientation and The Learning Organization, *Journal of Marketing*, 59(3), 63–75.

Stevenson, H.H. 1983. A Perspective on Entrepreneurship, *Harvard Business School Working Paper* 9–384–131.

Thomas, A.S. and Mueller, S.L. 2000. A Case of Comparative Entrepreneurship: Assessing The Relevance of Culture, *Journal of International Business Studies*, 31(2), 287–301.

Venkataraman, S. 1997. The Distinctive Domain of Entrepreneurship Research: An Editor's Perspective, in J. Katz and R. Brockhaus (Eds) *Advances in Entrepreneurship, Firm Emergence and Growth*, 119–38. Greenwich. CT: JAI Press.

Vernon, R. 1966. International Investment and International Trade in The Product Life Cycle, *Quarterly Journal of Economics*, 80, 190–207.

Weick, K.E. 1979. *The Social Psychology of Organizing*. 2nd edn, Reading, MA: Addison-Wesley.

Wright, R.W. (Ed.) 1999. International Entrepreneurship: Globalization of Emerging Businesses, *Research in Global Strategic Management*, 7. Greenwich, CT: JAI Press.

Wright, W.R. and Ricks, A.D. 1994. Trends in International Business Research: Twenty-Five Years Later, *Journal of International Business Studies*, 25, 687–701.

Yang, Y.S., Leone, R.P. and Alden, D.L. 1992. A Market Expansion Ability Approach to Identify Potential Exporters, *Journal of Marketing*, 56(1), 84–96.

Yaprak, A. 1985. An Empirical Study of The Differences between Small Exporting and Non-exporting US Firms, *International Marketing Review*, 2(2), 72–83.

Young, S. and Tavares, A. 2004. Centralization and Autonomy: Back to The Future, *International Business Review*, 13, forthcoming.

Young, S., Dimitratos, P. and Dana, L.-P. 2003. International Entrepreneurship Research: What Scope for International Business Theories? *Journal of International Entrepreneurship*, 1, 31–42.

Zahra, S.A. and Garvis, D.M. 2000. International Corporate Entrepreneurship: The Moderating Effect of International Environmental Hostility, *Journal of Business Venturing*, 15, 469–92.

Zahra, S.A. and George, G. 2002. International Entrepreneurship: The Current Status of The Field and Future Research Agenda, in M. Hitt, D. Ireland, D. Sexton and M. Camp (Eds) *Strategic Entrepreneurship: Creating an Integrated Mindset*, 255–88. Cambridge, MA: Blackwell.

Zahra, S.A., Dharwadkar, R. and George, G. 2000. Entrepreneurship in Multinational Subsidiaries: The Effects of Corporate and Local Environmental Contexts. Working Paper Series, 9 9/00–027. Atlanta, GA: Georgia Tech CIBER, Georgia Institute of Technology.

Zahra, S.A., Korri, J.S. and Yu, J. 2005. Cognition and International Entrepreneurship: Implications for Research on International Opportunity Recognition and Exploitation, *International Business Review*, 14, forthcoming.

Zahra, S.A., Neubaum, D.O. and Huse, M. 1997. The Effect of The Environment on Export Performance among Telecommunications New Ventures, *Entrepreneurship Theory and Practice*, 22(1), 25–46.

4
Subsidiary Business Networks and Opportunity Development in Multinational Enterprises: A Comparison of the Influence of Internal and External Business Networks

Mohammad Yamin

Introduction

The multinational enterprise and 'opportunity development'

The objective of this paper is to make a contribution to understanding the nature of opportunity development within the multinational enterprise (MNEs). As explained in Chapter 1, opportunity development is broadly understood as new technological resource combinations and capability development.

Developments in the MNE literature strongly support a focus on opportunity development as a fruitful line of investigation. Thus whereas initially the literature on MNEs emphasised the exploitation of firm's existing knowledge and other 'ownership advantages' in foreign countries, there is now much greater interest in understanding the MNE's quest for *new* sources of technological development and organisational competence (Almeida et al., 2002; Buckley and Casson, 1976; Cantwell, 1989, 2000; Dunning, 1993; Florida, 1997; Hymer, 1976; Pearce, 1999). Other writers have expressed this development in terms of a shift of focus from asset exploiting towards asset augmenting activities of MNEs. In this context, Dunning (1998) has highlighted 'strategic asset seeking' as being the most important motive behind MNE investment activity and a key factor in the MNE's competitive advantage (Dunning and Lundun, 1998).

Foreign subsidiaries play a significant and, arguably, critical role in the asset augmenting activities of MNEs (Yamin, 1999). There is now a realisation amongst academic investigators that subsidiaries of many multinational firms have matured well beyond being 'miniature replicas' of their parents and have become increasingly 'creative' in a variety of directions (Birkinshaw and Hood, 1998; Ghosahl and Bartlett, 1988; Pearce, 1999). In fact a number of writers have specifically stressed the mandate-developing and entrepreneurial roles often played by MNE subsidiaries (Birkinshaw, 1996, 1997; Regnér, 2003; Yamin, 2002). Yamin (2002) has argued that the greater propensity for entrepreneurship on the part of foreign subsidiaries compared to the subunits of a national firm constitutes an important basis for the advantage of multinationality. Equally importantly, there is a similar realisation amongst MNE decision makers that foreign subsidiaries can play a role in asset augmenting activities. Thus a large survey reported that most MNE CEOs agreed that 'the primary role of our overseas units is to find out and *take advantage of opportunities* within the countries in which they operate' (Leung and Tan, 1993, table 1, emphasis added).

Study focus: subsidiary business networks and opportunity development

Perhaps the most significant development in the MNE subsidiary literature, however, is the detailed investigation of the role of business networks in the process of opportunity development in the MNE (Andersson and Phalberg, 1997; Andersson and Forsgren, 2000; Andersson and Holm, 2002; Andersson et al., 2001a; Andersson et al., 2001b; Andersson et al., 2002; Forsgren et al., 1999; Holm and Pedersen, 2000). These studies have highlighted embeddedness in business networks, indicated by mutual adaptations in general business conducts between the subsidiary and its suppliers and/or its customers, as an underlying factor in knowledge creation in MNEs. Through their business interactions with their partners, subsidiaries develop technological and organisational competencies which, when transferred to other units, help to improve the overall level and range of the competencies within the MNE. More specifically, embeddedness in business relationship gradually develops into technical embeddedness which in turn drives technological and product development capabilities in the subsidiary. The subsidiary business network literature strongly confirms prior evidence, from a more general setting, that a business relationship develops into technological interdependencies between business partners and that these enhance the technological competence and innovative performance of partners (Araujo, 1999; Lane and Labutkin, 2001; Tyre and Von Hippel, 1997; Von Hippel, 1988). The subsidiary business network literature applies and develops this insight ('learning through interacting') in the specific organisational context of the MNE. It thus bears repeating that subsidiary embeddeness is arguably the foundation of the 'opportunity development' processes within MNEs. Given that the MNE, compared to a uni-national company, has a greater *potential* for tapping into a diversity of sources of knowledge and technology, subsidiary embddedness in business networks initiates a process that turns this potential into realizable opportunities for MNE's competence development.

Whilst a subsidiary's business partners could be either sister affiliates in the MNE or external businesses, most of the attention has been paid to subsidiaries business relations with external businesses and to the impact of such relationships on the MNEs. With some exceptions (Andersson et al., 2001; Schmid and Schuring, 2003) internal business relations – that is, business relationships between affiliates of the same MNE – have not been the focus of empirical investigation. Most empirical studies only include measures/indicators of external business embeddedeness in their analyses.[1]

Thus, broadly speaking, extant studies strongly imply that it is subsidiary embeddedness in external networks that *really* matters in this respect. However, given that internal embeddedness has thus far remained largely in the background, it may be rather premature to privilege external subsidiary embeddedness as the main, let alone the only source for 'opportunity development' in the MNE. Whether subsidiary embeddedness in *internal* business relationships can have similar consequences, in qualitative and quantitative terms, to external embeddedness is still an open question.

This chapter addresses the above gap.[2] Our approach is to start from 'first principles', asking two questions: (a) whether or under what conditions is a genuinely *business* relationship between internal partners a possibility?, and (b) whether internal business relationships generate the kind of ongoing mutual technical interactions and adaptations that are usually associated with business network learning? For the purpose of the following discussion, a 'business' relationship always entails a commercial or a transactional dimension, that is, the parties (internal and external actors) to the relationship are buyers and sellers. Thus, asking whether internal business relationships are *possible* entails enquiring whether two parties that are already related to each other by virtue of being subsidiaries of the same firm can, nevertheless, also become buyers and sellers and conduct their business according to commercial rather than administrative criteria.

In section 4.2.2, we discuss this issue and conclude that, in theoretical terms, internal business relationships are certainly a possibility in the context of the federative MNE. However in section 4.2.3, we show that, again on theoretical grounds, internal embedded business relationships are less likely to generate 'deep' adaptations compared to externally embedded relationships. Thus in internal business relationship, 'learning through interacting' is a weaker process. In section 3 we develop propositions on how internal and external embdddedness of subsidiaries generate opportunities for competence development in the MNE. We focus on subsidiary 'organisational performance' by which, following Andersson *et al* (2001b), we mean the impact of the subsidiary on the rest of the MNE through its knowledge development and knowledge sharing activities.

Network analysis and inter-subunit business relationships in MNEs

Background

Although the network concept has been very influential in MNE research there are two quite distinct approaches to how the network concept is used in this research (Forsgren, 2004). In the following sub-section, we will rely on both approaches to investigate whether internal business relationships are a possibility. First, we briefly indicate the distinctive aspects of the approaches.

One stream of literature adopts a contingency theory perspective in that it views the MNE as a particularly suitable organisational arena for a networking approach to management. There is a recognition that, because the MNE is inevitably a differentiated organisation, the traditional managerial reliance on hierarchy (e.g. centralisation and formalisation) needs to be supplemented or even supplanted by a networking approach the building block of which is the essentially personal relationship that binds the management strata of the MNE into a more or less coherent team (Ghoshal and Nohira, 1997; O'Donnel, 2000; Tsai and Ghoshal, 1998). The intra-firm network drives the process of exchange and value creation between different subunits of the MNE (Tsai and Ghoshal, 1998). This consideration is relevant to the emergence of business relationship between subunits as we shall discuss below.

On the other hand there is a literature from the 'markets-as-networks' (MAN) perspective (McLoughin and Horan, 2002; Forsgren, 2004). Here the starting point is the 'ordinary' business transaction between a buyer and a seller (a 'market' phenomenon) and its evolution, via increasing interdependence, into a business relationship (i.e. the building block of the business 'network' phenomenon). When applied to the analysis of the MNE, the initial focus has been on subsidiaries rather then the organisation as a whole although it is clearly acknowledged that subsidiaries are influenced both by their business networks and by the overall strategy of the MNE as determined by headquarters (Forsgren, 2004).

Are internal business relationships possible in MNEs?

The relative neglect of internal business relationships and networks is partly explained by the fact intra-organisational interdependencies do not necessarily fit into the MAN perspective. The perspective implies *independent* organisations *voluntarily* engaging in a process entailing increasing interdependence with *selected* businesses partners (Johanson and Mattsson, 1994). Thus, strictly speaking, MAN may be inapplicable to organisational *subunits* as they lack ultimate decision authority. This, in principle, is equally true of subunits' internal and external partner interdependencies. However, in practice, a subsidiary's external partners are probably less 'visible' to the MNE headquarter (Holm *et al.*, 1995) and, more broadly, the assumption of organisational isolation between the MNE and the subsidiary has probably more substance in the case of externally embedded subsidiaries (Yamin, 2002).

A subsidiary's intra-firm interactions are more closely in the preview of the MNE decision makers and the interdependencies are less likely to develop into the sort of business relationships envisaged in the MAN perspective. There is probably a large element of 'logistic' delivery (of components or services).[3] Logistic delivery entails a high degree of standardisation and the does not suggest the privileging or prioritising of *particular* inter-subsidiary relationships. If the interdependency between subsidiaries is only administrative in nature and consists only of logistic delivery, then a business relationship between subsidiaries cannot develop. The important thing is therefore that this sort of interdependence does not lead to mutual adaptation in technological and production processes that the MAN view envisages (Belussi and Areangeli's, 2001-'steady state' network type may apply here). Consequently, in such cases, inter-subsidiary interdependencies are not associated with 'opportunity development' in the MNE.

However the are a number of considerations suggesting that the possibility of internal business relationship within MNE cannot be ruled out. For one thing the scope for subsidiary manipulation by the centre in order to exercise operational flexibility should not be exaggerated as the centre often lacks the informational and organisational pre-requisites (Kogut and Kulatilaka, 1994). Empirical evidence indicates moderate degrees of operational flexibility at best (Ragan, 1998). More generally the picture of a closely coordinated MNE is significantly at odds with reality (consider Zander and Sölvell's 'the phantom multinational'): most MNEs have experienced their recent expansion through acquisitions (Andersson *et al.*, 1997; UNCTAD, 2000; Zander and Sölvell, 2002) and by definition newly acquired subsidiaries are unlikely to be in any sense fully coordinated with the rest of the MNE system at least in the short term. However this does open up opportunities for the development of business relationship between subunits of the MNE.

From a theoretical perspective, the possibility of market or business relationships *within* hierarchies has been noted in the transaction cost/internalisation literature from Coase (1937) onwards. Buckley and Casson (1998) argue that increasing environmental volatility has generated an aversion to 'internal monopoly' within the MNE (p. 28). Headquarters bureaucracies have come under increasing attack and have been to a degree supplanted by divisional centres (see also Forsgren *et al.*, 1995) with an attendant increase in sourcing autonomy at the division (and subsidiary?) level (Buckey and Casson, 1998: 32). Recent literature indicates a significant degree of subsidiary leverage for independent initiative and mandate building and whilst these are mostly developed through business relationship with external partners in the host country, the potential for internally focussed business relationships is also acknowledged (Birkinshaw, 1996; Birkinshaw and Ridderstrale, 1999; Buckley and Casson, 1998).

This last observation is strongly linked with the 'networking' perspective in MNE. It is the recognition of the unworkability of an exclusively hierarchical and top-down approach to managing the MNE that has driven the search for an alternative approach. Ghoshal and Bartlett's (1990) advocacy of viewing the MNE as a federative rather than a unitary organisation was an important step in this direction. Since then there has been much emphasis on the value of intra-organisational network of relationships among the MNE management strata. Most recently this basic view has been articulated through the application of the 'social capital' concept to intra-MNE relationships (Kostova and Roth, 2003; Tsai, 2000; Tsai and Ghoshal, 1998). Dimensions of organisational social capital, in particular, 'social interactions'[4] and 'mutual trust' are shown to drive the process of resource (information, products, personnel and support) exchange and combinations between different subunits (Tsai and Ghoshal, 1998). Whilst such resource exchanges are a manifestation of intra-organisational solidarity rather than of ongoing business interactions (as between suppliers and customers) the former can open up opportunities for the latter. For example the exchange of personnel between subunits may help the subunits to identify mutually profitable business opportunities.

In conclusion, we believe that three factors argue for increasing opportunities for business relationships between MNE subunits:

1. The 'flattening' of MNE hierarchy and increasing scope for subunit initiatives.
2. Increasing subunit capability for mandate development focussed on internal or external business opportunities.
3. The emergence of the federative MNE and the formation of inter-subunit networks within them.

4.2.3 Features of internal and external business relationships

Even when inter-subsidiary business relationships are established they may be somewhat different from business relationships with external partners. The crucial issues, in terms of subsidiary role in the opportunity development process (with respect to technological competence in the MNE), is whether internal business relationships generate significant technical and production adaptations, as these are viewed as a key source for competence development in the subsidiary and thus its ability to contribute to competence development in the MNE as a whole. In this section we consider four factors affecting the 'productivity' of a business network for the subsidiary. Table 4.1 lists the factors and their consequences for internal and external networks.

Table 4.1 Subsidiary business network: Internal versus external business networks

Factors affecting network formation	Internal business networks	External business network	Consequences for the subsidiary
Influence of corporate context	High	Low/medium	Internal network likely to have activity focus closer to MNE 'dominant logic' than external networks
Control by HQ	High	Low	Investment in internal business networks more constrained by the MNE's 'internal capital market'
Initial (non-administrative) interdependencies generated via	Managerial networks	Market transactions	More frequent and 'deeper' adaptations in external networks
Location and geography	More likely to be cross-border	More likely to be in host country	Internal networks subject to a greater degree of 'damage of distance'

All subsidiaries have to operate within a corporate context that has been shaped by various factors. One particularly relevant aspect is the notion of managerial 'dominant logic' (Bettis and Prahalad, 1986, 1995). Dominant logic is an information filter; organisational attention is focussed on data deemed relevant by the dominant logic. 'Other data are largely ignored ... the "filtered" data are then incorporated into the strategy, systems and values' (Bettis and Prahalad, 1995). The notion of environmental filtering is also strongly present is Penrose's theory of the growth of the firm – where investment plans are largely defined by the firm's 'productive opportunity'. Productive opportunity is a 'perceptual' boundary of what firms can and cannot do successfully (Penrose, 1959). The dominant logic of the organisation clearly affects the behaviour and choices of subunits. In fact in the Bettis and Prahalad (1995) view 'behaviour reinforcement' is an important aspect of the concept. In the context of foreign subsidiaries, Birkinshaw and Ridderstarle (1999) have shown that, what they call 'corporate immune system', constrains the subsidiary initiatives.

However it is reasonable to expect that subsidiaries that have corporate or internal business ties and relationships will be more tightly constrained by the corporation dominant logic. Thus the network context of internal relationship inevitably includes other MNE subsidiaries, all connected to the parent for various business or administrative reasons. The most important player in the network context is usually the HQ itself. Because the HQ is the 'custodian' of the dominant logic of the enterprise as a whole it is bound to take a keen interest in how inter-subsidiary relations develop and would exercise its power and authority to influence these business relationship in a direction supporting or reinforcing the dominant logic.

On the other hand externally embedded subsidiaries are probably more able to develop business initiatives in new directions. This is partly due to their relatively higher degree of organisational autonomy (Yamin, 2002) and their ability to 'hide' initiatives (from the centre) until they are a *fait-accompli* (Birkinshaw and Ridderstrale, 1999). It is also partly due to externally embedded subsidiaries being more likely to adopt an 'inductive' approach to opportunity or initiative definition based more on trial and error. By comparison the HQ approach to business opportunity definition is likely to be more 'deductively' based and follow more closely existing industry 'recepies' and within the trajectory of MNE's current competencies (Regnér, 2003; Yamin, 2002).

In addition to its role as a member of the subsidiary's network context, the HQ has formal control authority that it can exercise to further reinforce subsidiary conformity. It has been argued that MNE headquarters effectively act as an internal capital market (Mudambi, 1999); a principal consideration for the MNE headquarter is control over the investment resources of the subsidiary to ensure that one subsidiary's investment does not 'crowd out' investment opportunities for other subsidiaries. However it is likely that this HQ function is more easily carried out with respect to internally embedded subsidiaries; internal network embeddedness enhances HQ control over the subsidiary (Andersson and Forsgren, 1996; Holm *et al.*, 1995). Externally embedded subsidiaries are likely to have greater degrees of strategic autonomy and enjoy greater freedom in investment decisions (Mudambi, 1999). Thus the MNE is in a stronger position to influence or even direct the development of business relationships within the internal network. Consequently, mutual adaptations that do take place in internal networks are likely to be limited in scope.

External business relationships are also shaped by the surrounding network context. Furthermore the HQ is normally an important node in this context too, but the nature of the relationship between the network context and the focal relationship is clearly fundamentally different in the two cases. The HQ is less of a pivotal influence in the externally embedded subsidiary's network. Previous studies show that the MNE HQ is not necessarily very familiar with the subsidiary's external business relationships and that this tends to weaken its control over the focal subsidiary (Andersson and Forsgren, 1996, 2000; Holm *et al.*, 1995; Medcof, 2001). In particular subsidiary investment in business relationship enjoys some effective autonomy as the subsidiary is less dependent on internal funding to develop its business relationships. Thus in comparison to internally embedded relationships, external relationship are less circumscribed or bounded by their network context. Potentially at least, mutual adaptations in external networks are likely to be more 'creative'.

Thirdly, mutual adaptations are likely to be less 'frequent' in internal relationships and networks. Adaptation in a business relationship implies (or in fact requires) *initial ignorance* of partner characteristics. Business relationships evolve from arms-length transactions with particular customers and suppliers. Therefore, at least initially, adaptation is a consequence of the *discovery* of partner characteristics (and needs) and of the investments opportunities that the accommodation to the partner opens up. Internal business relationships do not necessarily start life as transactions (see above). By virtue of their membership of the organisation they are already tied to each other by information flows of not only an administrative nature but also by some degree of knowledge flows (Gupta and Govindrajan, 1991, 2000). This is strongly reinforced by the practice of networking in the organisation. As we have already indicated, inter-subunit network relationships are associated with inter-subunit resource transfers including information, product and personnel between subunits. Thus the potential business partners are to some degree *known to each other* and quite possibly internal business partners may be selected or mutually come together *because* they are already (perceived to be) somewhat compatible and hence the required adaptation is perceived to be either absent or minor. Of course the relationship may develop in a way that will necessitate significant adaptations by the partners over time. However, if we assume that business relationships are path-dependent then internal relationships may get stuck in a low-adaptation trajectory. In particular, the enduring influence of the managerial network may encourage interactions mainly at or *through* the management strata at the subunits.

But business network adaptations are a source of value creation *because* they entail multiple and interacting functional and operational interdependencies. The interactions are not purely or even mainly 'managerial' but involve the whole organisation including operational and routine activities as well. Thus business adaptation is defined as the close coordination of inter-partner dependencies that helps to create 'an efficient *workflow* system'[5] (Blakenburg Holm et al., 1999: 47, my emphasis). We suggest that adaptations are 'deep', if they are generated through interactions at all levels of the value chain and involve the organisations as whole rather than only a small group within the organisation (see also Tasoukas, 1996: 22).

Finally, there is the issue of location. In a multinational firm, inter-subsidiary networks will almost inevitably be cross-border (if the subsidiaries are in the same country then they are likely to be highly integrated and exchanges between them will be of the 'logistic' type. Thus, for example interactions between a production subsidiary and an R&D subsidiary in the same country will be of this sort). In the context of supplier–customer relationships, the significance of location is fully indicated by Tyre and Von Hippel (1997).

They argue that adaptive learning has a 'situated' dimension – meaning that intimate knowledge of the physical context of partner value adding activity is a critical part of the process. Situated learning does not merely require 'co-presence' but specifically physical presence and close familiarity with partner activities in their location or situation. Importantly, 'communication' is a poor substitute for situated learning. Goodall and Roberts (2003) also emphasise the connection between organisational knowledge and situated action. It is the situated nature of knowledge acquisition (and knowledge maintenance) that they argue is the basis of the 'damage' of distance.

It follows from the above that inter-subsidiary relationships will be constrained by geographical distance. Considering that business relationships entail interaction (and hence frequent travel) by functional and operational personnel and not merely the top management (who, as suggested in note 4, may enjoy exclusive travel facilities), we can surmise that cross-border business relationship may be at a disadvantage. By contrast relationships between a subsidiary and external partners are more frequently (but not always) in the host country and often in the same region or locality within the host country. Thus they are more likely (than internal relationships) to benefit from proximity. This reinforces the chances of having 'deeper' adaptations in externally focussed subsidiary business relationships.

Network focus and subsidiary organisational performance in the MNE

In the previous section we have focussed on subsidiary network relationship and the considered the (possible) differential impact of internal and external networks on the subsidiary. The conclusion is that, compared to externally embedded subsidiaries, internal business relationships are (1) subject to greater control by parent and are more constrained by the corporate context; and (2) have a 'narrower' and 'shallower' pattern of business interactions. In this section we consider the implications of these for subsidiary organisational performance.

Subsidiary role in knowledge transfer to other MNE units

It follows from the above that internally embedded subsidiaries are more likely to develop knowledge and competence that is closer to the MNE current 'dominant' logic. They are closely tied to the MNE HQ is terms of the direction of the development of their activities. In particular their technological and innovative activities are likely to remain close to the parent firm technology 'trajectory' (Pearce, 1999). By contrast, externally embedded subsidiaries develop knowledge and competence that is more likely to be differentiated from that of the MNE. If we adopt Gupta and Govindrajan's (2000) terminology, we can suggest that the externally embedded subsidiaries create a higher percentage of non-duplicative knowledge, whereas the internally embedded subsidiaries create a greater percentage of duplicative knowledge (see also Frost, 2001).

However all subsidiaries have a combination of duplicative and non-duplicative knowledge. The duplicative component is generally sourced from internally coordinated activities (including subsidiary's R&D, see Foss and Pedersen, 2002) and other internally networked business relationships. Non-duplicative knowledge is sourced from the foreign location of the subsidiaries but is usually developed through business relationship with specific customers and suppliers (which could be either sister affiliates or other external businesses). Knowledge transfer requires both duplicative and non-duplicative components. The non-duplicative component gives the knowledge a value whereas the duplicative component creates absorptive capacity for the recipient. Internally embedded subsidiaries are likely to have a 'better' combination of duplicative and non-duplicative knowledge. The non-duplicative component of the knowledge is developed within internal business relationship and is therefore developed in a relatively familiar business context to the sister affiliates. It, therefore, is going to be perceived as 'relevant' new knowledge (Gupta and Govindarajan, 2000). By contrast externally embedded subsidiaries are likely to have a non-duplicative knowledge base that is shaped mainly by its business (and consequently technological) embeddedness in business relationship with external partners (Lane and Lubatkin, 1998). Thus the non-duplicative knowledge is likely to be further away (relative to that of internally embedded subsidiaries) from that of parent and the sister affiliates. Based on these considerations we put forward the following proposition.

Proposition 1: Internally embedded subsidiaries transfer knowledge to the MNE more frequently than externally embedded subsidiaries.

Subsidiary contribution to MNE production and product development

What is the outcome of such knowledge transfer likely to be? I suggest that frequent knowledge transfer will be focussed mainly on current production activities and will have a mainly 'adaptive' character (Frost, 2001) in the sense that it helps to spread 'best' practice (Szulanki, 1996) in relation to the current value chain activities of the recipients. The main focus of the knowledge transfer and development in internal business relationship is on current production activities ('programmes of exploitation', March, 1991). Externally embedded subsidiaries are less likely to be important to sister subsidiaries for the purpose of production development as they have knowledge that is likely to be less relevant in this respect. Thus we put forward the following proposition:

Proposition 2: Internally embedded subsidiaries are more important than externally embedded subsidiaries for MNE production developments.

Externally embedded subsidiaries are (relative to internally embedded) are more loosely tied to the MNE. Thus even though they are less frequently or intensively involved in knowledge transfer or development in the MNE, they are likely to be the source of somewhat more novel and possibly more strategically valuable new knowledge for the MNE. In terms of Hansen's analysis of knowledge sharing across organisational subunits, 'weak-coupling' between subunits has the advantage of offering greater 'search' opportunities for identifying novel ideas, concepts and practices useful in product development and innovative activities of the searching subunit (Hansen, 1999, 2002). This suggests that the relatively low levels of knowledge transfers that do take place between the externally embedded subsidiaries and the MNE are likely to be potentially more productive as there is significant scope for cross-unit learning. In a tightly coupled organisation, in which cross-unit contacts and knowledge flows are both frequent and intensive, subunits have full knowledge of each other's capabilities, and the chances of finding useful novelty is absent or low (see also Ahuja, 2000; Ruef, 2002). Empirical evidence suggests that internally sourced knowledge transfers are not very productive (e.g. in terms of patent citations and 'knowledge-building' (Phene and Almeida, 2003; Yamin and Otto, 2004). Therefore we suggest that knowledge transfers involving externally embedded subsidiary, although less frequent, is likely to be somehow more significant and 'eventful'. For example, externally embedded knowledge transfer is more likely to be organised on a discrete basis through a product development project team rather than take place informally (Hedlund and Ridderstrale, 1995; Subramaniam et al., 1998). Thus we put forward the following proposition:

Proposition 3: Externally embedded subsidiaries are more important than internally embedded subsidiaries for MNE product development.

Subsidiary influence on MNE strategy

If subsidiaries are perceived as 'important' for production or product development in the MNE, that, potentially is a basis for their ability to exercise influence. In this sense power to influence has a resource dependency foundation (subsidiaries have something – specifically technological and market-based competence – that the MNE values). Andersson and Phalberg (1997) define influence as 'informal attempts to affect issues and behaviour indirectly' (p. 321) and argue that while subsidiaries do not have authority (which rests exclusively with the parent) they have the ability to influence strategy. With the exception of Andersson and Phalberg's early study there has up to now been little direct focus on subsidiary influence as such. However previous studies have clearly demonstrated that the some subsidiaries possess precondition for influence. For example, a subsidiary's elevation to the status of a 'centre of excellence' is a reflection of the value that other subunits (and in particular the HQ) attach to its perceived competence and (indirectly perhaps) to its network relationships (Andersson and Forsgren, 2000).

In a recent paper, Andersson et al. (2004) point out that up till now the literature has focussed on the subsidiary's 'negative' power – its power to escape or reduce control over its activities by the HQ. They argue that in a federative MNE, whilst formal power (authority) is vested at the HQ, organisational power is in fact distributed amongst the members of the federation; the key source of power for subsidiaries is their network embeddedness, whilst the HQ sources of power are its 'legal' authority over strategic decision and to a certain degree its (independently acquired) knowledge of the subsidiaries network base.

Thus we would expect that both internally and externally embedded subsidiaries will have some influence over MNE strategy as both have resources that are important (and hence of value) to the rest of the MNE. However we would hypothesise that the externally embedded subsidiary has greater influence on MNE strategy (and specifically on technology and product development strategy). There are three reasons for this. First, we have argued in the previous section that externally embedded subsidiaries are likely to be perceived as 'important' in relation to their product development contributions. From the perspective of the MNE, and in particular from the perspective of the MNE headquarter, the externally embedded subsidiary occupies a valuable position in a 'structural hole' (Burt, 1992) indirectly linking the MNE to important sites of technological and market expertise. Second, this is reinforced by the fact that MNEs are increasingly emphasising 'strategic asset seeking' investments. Dunning highlights this as the 'most significant change in the motives for FDI over the last two decades' (Dunning, 1998: 50). Gaining strategic assets is not purely a question of locating activities in a host environment with particular business system/innovation systems characteristics but often also requires the development of close business relationship with businesses operating in that environment (Forsgren et al., 2000). Clearly externally embedded subsidiaries are a much more likely site for MNE strategic assets developments than internally embedded ones as the latter already operate in broadly a similar range of product and technology field as the parent. Finally, previous research has indicated that the network context of externally embedded subsidiaries is relatively opaque to the MNE headquarter and the MNE is dependent on the subsidiary in transferring such embedded competence to elsewhere in the MNE (Andersson and Holm, 2002).

Internally embedded subsidiaries have a somewhat different resource basis with which to negotiate for influence within the MNE. Internally embedded subsidiaries are valuable mainly because they enhance the MNE's current operational efficiency by facilitating relatively smooth transfer of 'best practice'. Influence over product development can be viewed as a *reward* for such subsidiaries. The MNE may cede a degree of influence to such subsidiaries to keep them on board. By comparison, the MNE is relatively more *dependent* on externally embedded subsidiaries as they are likely to make direct contribution to developing MNE technology in new directions. The above discussion suggests the following propositions:

Proposition 4: Externally embedded subsidiaries have a greater strategic influence on the MNE product/technology development strategy the MNE than internally embedded subsidiaries.

Proposition 5: The influence path of internally embedded subsidiaries is through knowledge transfer and MNE production development.

Proposition 6: The influence path of externally embedded subsidiaries is through MNE product and technology development.

Concluding remarks

The main conclusion of this chapter is that while intra-MNE business relationships are certainly a possibility, they are likely to have a set of distinctive characteristics. Returning to the notion of the opportunity development process, we can see from the analysis that internally embedded subsidiaries do play a distinctive role in the process. Broadly speaking internally embedded subsidiaries contribute more to the MNE programmes of exploitation rather than to programmes of exploration (March, 1991). Nevertheless these subsidiaries create significant opportunities for efficiency enhancement in the MNE mainly through the knowledge transfer process.

A broader conclusion is that the neglect of internal subsidiary embeddeness is theoretically unwarranted and thus that empirical investigation of the consequences of internal subsidiary embddedness is necessary. In the absence of such empirical evidence our knowledge regarding the role of subsidiaries in opportunity development in MNE is severely limited.

Notes

1. The findings relating to external subsidiary embddedeness are clearly robust as other studies not dependent on network analysis have also provided strong

evidence not only that subsidiary innovations are frequently sourced from the local host environments (Frost, 2001; Phene and Almeida, 2003; Yamin and Otto, 2004) but also that subsidiaries grow 'progressively closer to local host country networks both in terms of sourcing and sharing knowledge' (Phene and Almeida, 2003).

2. In this chapter we assume that a subsidiary's 'network focus' is either internal or external. A focal subsidiary has an internal (or corporate) 'network focus' if the majority of its key business partners are also subunits of the same MNE. A subsidiary's network focus is external if its key business partners are not subunits of the same MNE. A situation of 'balanced focus' – in which the key business relationships equally straddle the internal and external domains – is also a possibility. However the analysis of this chapter will assume that network focus is binary and ignores the intermediate case.

3. A related phenomenon is indicated by the notion of operational flexibility articulated by Kogut (1983, 1990). Here subsidiaries tend to duplicate similar operations in different markets, rather than developing complementary activities. This again tends to limit the scope for business (customer–supplier) relationships.

4. It is perhaps noteworthy that physical distance/proximity does not seem to be a factor in intra-organisational social interactions. Thus respondents in Tsai and Ghoshal (1998: 468) are managers of units in *different countries* who nevertheless engage in high degrees of social interactions with each other. This perhaps reflects the very narrow basis for 'social' capital in the organisation; participants are exclusively at the very zenith of the organisation who do not face the kind of inconvenience and effort that are normally involved in frequent travel (i.e. they may have access to private company jets and private airports and bypass the congestion of major airports and scheduled flights). For a different, 'damage-of-distance', view of intra-organisational social interactions see Goodall and Roberts (2003).

5. The work flow concept has usually been employed with respect to *intra*-organisational interdependencies in which a number of subunits are closely organised (Astley and Zac, 1990). Thus it seems that business relationship are productive (of value) to the extent that they mimic a closely coordinated multi-unit organisation – at least in some respects(?). One interpretation could be that intra-organisational coordination is achieved through discrete design from the centre whereas in business relationships the coordination is an emergent process accompanied by organisational learning. Thus if the MNE is actually a fully coordinated system then the prospect for internal business relationships are limited. The subsidiaries have well-adapted and coordinated roles defined and managed centrally. In this scenario we are back in the situation in which inter-subsidiary exchanges are of the logistical type (cf 'steady state' networks).

References

Ahuja, G. (2000). Collaboration Networks, Structural Holes and Innovation: a Longitudinal Study, *Administrative Science Quarterly*, 45, 425–55.

Almeida, P., Song, J. and Grant, R. (2002). Are Firms Superior to Alliances and Markets? An Analysis of Cross Border Knowledge Building, *Organisation Science*, 13(2), 147–61.

Andersson, M., Holm, U. and Holmstrom, C. (2001). Relationship Configuration and Competence Development in MNC Subsidiaries, in H. Håkansson and J. Johanson (Eds) *Business Network Learning*. London: Pergamon.

Andersson, U. and Forsgren, M.(1996). Subsidiary Embeddedness and Control in The Multinational Corporation, *International Business Review*, 5(5), 487–508.

Andersson, U., Johanson, J. and Vahlne, J-E. (1997). Organic Acquisition and The Internationalisation of The Business Firm, *Management International Review*, 37(2), 67–84.

Andersson, U. and Pahlberg, C. (1997). Subsidiary Influence and Strategic Behaviour in MNCs: An Empirical Study, *International Business Review*, 3, 319–34.

Andersson, U. and Forsgren, M. (2000). In Search of Centres of Excellence: Network Embeddedness and Subsidiary Roles in Multinational Corporations, *Management International Review*, 40(4), 329–50.

Andersson, U. and Holm, U. (2002). Managing Integration of Subsidiary Knowledge in The Multinational Corporation – A Note on The Role of Headquarters, in V. Havila, M. Forsgren and H. Håkansson (Eds) *Critical Perspectives on Internationalisation*. London: Elsevier.

Andersson, U., Forsgren, M. and Holm, U. (2001a). Subsidiary Embeddedness and Competence Development in MNCs – A Multi-Level Analysis, *Organization Studies*, 22(6), 1013–34.

Andersson, U., Forsgren, M. and Pedersen, T. (2001b). Subsidiary Performance in Multinational Corporations: The Importance of Technology Embeddedness, *International Business Review*, 10, 3–23.

Andersson, U., Forsgren, M. and Holm, U. (2002). The Strategic Impact of External Networks: Subsidiary Performance and Competence Development in The Multinational Corporation, *Strategic Management Journal*, 23, 979–96.

Andersson, U. Forsgren, M. and Holm, U. (2004). Fighting for Power: Subsidiary Influence on Strategic Decisions in The Federative MNC, Unpublished paper, Department of Business Studies, Uppsala university.

Arajuo, L. (1999). Knowing and Learning as Networking, *Management Learning*, 29(3), 317–36.

Astley, G. and Zac, J. (1990). Beyond Dyadic Exchange: Functional Interdependence and Subunit Power, *Organization Studies*, 11(4), 481–501.

Blankenburg-Holm, D., Eriksson, K. and Johanson, J. (1999). Creating Value through Mutual Commitment to Business Network Relationships, *Strategic Management Journal*, 20, 467–86.

Belussi, F. and Areangeli, F. (1998). A Typology of Networks: Flexible and Evolutionary Firms, *Research Policy*, 27, 418–28.

Bettis, R. and Prahalad, C. (1986). The Dominant Logic: A New Linkage between Diversity and Performance, *Strategic Management Review*, 7(6), 485–501.

Bettis, R. and Prahalad, C. (1995). The Dominant Logic: Retrospective and Extension, *Strategic Management Journal*, 16, 5–15.

Birkinshaw, J. (1996). How Multinational Subsidiary Mandates are Gained and Lost, *Journal of International Business Studies*, 27(3), 467–95.

Birkinshaw, J. (1997). Entrepreneurship in Multinational Corporations: The Characteristics of Subsidiary Initiatives, *Strategic Management Journal*, 3, 207–30.

Birkinshaw, J. and Hood, N. (1998). Multinational Subsidiary Evolution: Capability and Charter Change in Foreign-Owned Subsidiaries, *Academy of Management Review*, 23(4), 773–96.

Birkinshaw, J. and Ridderstrale, J. (1999). Fighting the Corporate Immune System: A Process Study of Subsidiary Initiatives in Multinational Corporations, *International Business Review*, 8, 149–80.

Buckley, P. and Casson, M. (1976). *The Future of the Multinational Firm*, London: Macmillan.

Buckley, P. and Casson, M. (1998). Models of The Multinational Enterprise, *Journal of International Business Studies*, 29(1), 21–44.
Burt, R. (1992). *Structural Holes: The Social Structure of Competition*, Cambridge, MA: Harvard University Press.
Cantwell, J. (1989). *Technological Innovations and Multinational Corporations*, Oxford: Blackwell.
Cantwell, J. (2000). Theories of International Production, in C. Pitelis and R. Sugden, (Eds), *The Nature of the Transnational Firm*, 2nd edn, London: Routledge.
Coase, R. (1937). The Nature of The Firm, *Economica*, 4, 386–405.
Dunning, J. (1993). *Multinational Enterprise and The Global Economy*, Wokingham: Addison-Wesley.
Dunning, J. (1998). Location and The Multinational Enterprise: Neglected Factor? *Journal of International Business Studies*, 29(1), 45–66.
Dunning, J. and Lundun, S. (1993). The Geographic Source of Competitiveness of Multinational Enterprise: An Econometric Analysis, *International Business Review*, 7(2), 115–34.
Florida, R. (1997). The Globalisation of R&D, *Research Policy*, 26, 85–103.
Forsgren, M., Holm, U. and Johansen, J. (1995). Division Headquarters Go abroad – A Step in The Internationalisation of The Multinational, *Journal of Management Studies*, 32(4), 475–91.
Forsgren, M., Pedersen, T. and Foss, N. (1999). Accounting for The Strength of MNC Subsidiaries: The Case of Foreign-Owned Firms in Denmark, *International Business Review*, 2, 181–96.
Forsgren, M., Johansen, J. and Sharma, D. (2000). The development of MNC Centres of Excellence, in U. Holm and T. Pedersen (Eds), *The Emergence and Impact of MNC Centres of Excellence*, London: Macmillan.
Forsgren, M. (2004). Use of Network Theory in MNC Research, in V. Mahanke and T. Pedersen (Eds), *Knowledge Flows, Governance and the Multinational Enterprise: Frontiers in International Management Research*, London: Palgrave.
Foss, N. and Pedersen, T. (2002). Transferring Knowledge in MNCs: The Role of Sourcing of Subsidiary Knowledge and The Organizational Context, *Journal of International Management*, 8, 49–57.
Frost, T. (2001). The Geographic Sources of Foreign Subsidiaries' Innovations, *Strategic Management Journal*, 22, 101–23.
Ghoshal, S. and Bartlett, C. (1990). The Multinational Corporation as an Interorganizational Network, *Academy of Management Review*, 15(4), 603–25.
Ghoshal, S. and Nohria, N. (1997). *The Differentiated MNC: Organizing Multinational Corporations for Value Creation*, San Francisco: Jossey-Bass. Publishers.
Goodall, K. and Roberts, J. (2003). Repairing Managerial Knowledge-Ability over Distance, *Organization Studies*, 24(7), 1153–75.
Gupta, A. and Govindrajan, V. (1991). Knowledge Flows and The Structure of Control within Multinational Corporations, *Academy of Management Review*, 16(4), 768–92.
Gupta, A. and Govindrajan, V. (2000). Knowledge Flows within Multinational Companies, *Strategic Management Journal*, 21, 473–96.
Hansen, M. (1999). The Search-Transfer Problem: The Role of Weak Ties in Sharing Knowledge across Organisational Subunits, *Administrative Science Quarterly*, 44, 82–111.
Hansen, M. (2002). Knowledge Networks: Explaining Effective Knowledge Sharing in Multiunit Companies, *Organization Science*, 13(3), 232–48.
Hedlund, G. and Ridderstrale, J. (1995). International Development Projects: Key to Competitiveness, Impossible or Mismanaged, *International Studies in Management and Organisation*, 25(1–2), 156–84.

Holm, U. and Pedersen, T. (Eds) (2000). *The Emergence and Impact of MNC Centres of Excellence*, London: Macmillan.

Holm, U., Johanson, J. and Thilenius, P. (1995). Headquarters Knowledge of Subsidiary Network Contexts in the Multinational Corporations, *International Studies of Management and Organisation*, 1–2, 97–120.

Hymer, S. (1976). *The International Operations of National Firms*, Cambridge, MA: MIT Press.

Johanson, J. and Mattsson, L-G. (1994). The Markets as Networks Tradition in Sweden, in G. Laurent, G. L. Lilien and B. Prass (Eds), *Research Traditions in Marketing*, Boston: Kluwer.

Kogut, B. (1983). Foreign Direct Investment as a Sequetial Process, in C. P. Kindelberger and D. Audresch (Eds), *The Multinational Corporation in the 1980s*, Cambridge, MA: MIT Press.

Kogut, B. (1990). International Sequential Advantages and Network Flexibility, in Bartlett, Doz and G. Hedlund (Eds), *Managing the Global Firm*. London: Routledge.

Kogut, B. and Kulatilaka, N. (1994). Operating Flexibility, Global Manufacturing, and The Option Value of a Multinational Network, *Management Science*, 40(1), 123–140.

Kostova, T. and Roth, K. (2003). Social Capital in Multinational Corporations and A Micro-macro Model of Its Formation, *Academy of Management Review*, 29(2), 297–317.

Lane, P. and Lubatkin, M. (1998). Relative Absorptive Capacity and Interorganisational Learning, *Strategic Management Journal*, 19(5), 461–77.

Leung, S. and Tan, C. (1993). Managing across Borders: an Empirical Test of the Bartlett and Ghoshal Organisational Typology, *Journal of International Business Studies*, 24, 3449–64.

March, J. (1991). Exploration and Exploitation in Organisational Learning, *Organisation Science*, 1, 15–28.

McLoughlin, D. and Horan, C. (2002). Markets as Networks: Notes on a Unique Understanding, *Journal of Business Research*, 55, 535–43.

Medcof, J. (2001). Resource-based Strategy and Managerial Power in Networks of Internationally Dispersed Technology Units, *Strategic Management Journal*, 22, 909–1012.

Mudambi, R. (1999). MNE Internal Capital Market and Subsidiary Independence, *International Business Review*, 8, 197–211.

O'Donnell, S. (2000). Managing Foreign Subsidiaries: Agents of The Headquarters or an Interdependent Network? *Strategic Management Journal*, 21, 525–48.

Pearce, R. (1999). The Evolution of Technology in Multinational Enterprises: The Role of Creative subsidiaries, *International Business Review,* 2, 125–48.

Penrose, E. (1959). *The Theory of the Growth of the Firm*, Oxford: OUP.

Phene, A. and Almeida, P. (2003). How do Firms Evolve? The Patterns of Technological Evolution of Semiconductor Subsidiaries, *International Business Review*, 12, 349–467.

Ragan, S. (1998). Do Multinationals Operate Flexibly? Theory and Evidence, *Journal of International Business Studies*, 29(2), 217–37.

Regnér, P. (2003). Strategy Creation at The Periphery: Inductive versus Deductive Strategy Making, *Journal of Management Studies*, 40(1), 57–82.

Ruef, M. (2002). Strong Ties, Weak Ties and Islands: Structural and Cultural Predictors of Organisational Innovation, *Industrial and Corporate Change*, 11(3), 427–49.

Schmid, S. and Schuring, A. (2003). The Development of Critical Capabilities in Foreign Subsidiaries: Disentangling The Role of The Subsidiary's Business Network, *International Business Review*, 12, 755–82.

Subramaniam, M., Rosenthal, S. and Hatten, K. (1998). Global New Product Development Processes: Preliminary Findings and Research Propositions, *Journal of Management Studies*, 35, 773–96.

Szulanki, G. (1996). exploring Internal Stickiness: Impediments to Transfer of Best Practice within The Firm, *Strategic Management Journal*, 17. 27–44.

Tasoukas, H. (1996). The Firm as a Distributed Knowledge System, *Strategic Management Journal*, 17 (special issue), 11–25.

Tsai, W. and Ghoshal, S. (1998). Social Capital and Value Creation: The Role of Intrafirm Networks, *Academy of Management Journal*, 41(4), 464–76.

Tsai, W. (2000). Social Capital, Strategic Relatedness and The Formation of Intraorganizational Linkages, *Strategic Management Journal*, 29(2), 297–317.

Tyre, M. and Von Hippel, E. (1997). The Situated Nature of Adaptive Learning, *Organization Science*, 8(1), 71–83.

UNCTAD (2000). *World Investment Report 2000: Cross-Border Mergers and Acquisitions*, New York: United Nations.

Von Hippel, E. (1988). *The Sources of Innovations*, Oxford: Oxford University Press.

Yamin, M. (1999). 'An Evolutionary Analysis of Subsidiary Innovation and Reverse Transfer in Multinational Enterprises, in F. Burton, M. Chapman and A. Cross (Eds), *Multinational Enterprises, Transaction Costs and Internal organisation*, London: Macmillan.

Yamin, M. (2002). Subsidiary Entrepreneurship and The Advantage of Multinationality, in V. Havila, H. Håkansson and M. Forsgren (Eds), *Critical Perspectives on Internationalisation*, London: Elsevier.

Yamin, M. and Otto, J. (2004). Patterns of Knowledge Flow and MNE Innovative Performance, *Journal of International Management*, 10(2).

Zander, I. and Sölvell, O. (2002). The Phantom Multinational, in V. Havila, H. Håkansson, and M. Forsgren (Eds), *Critical Perspectives on Internationalisation*. London: Elsevier.

5
Value Processes in Industrial Networks: Identifying the Creation and Realisation of Value

Martin Johanson and Torkel Strömsten

Introduction

Production of value is an important topic among business researchers (i.e. Ramirez, 1999; Kale *et al.*, 2001). In imperfect markets characterised by differentiation and heterogeneity, which often take the form of a network (Håkansson and Snehota, 1995), the ability to create value and then realise the value potentials can be the key to growth and well-being for the business firm, as this ability is imperfectly spread among the actors. However, in contrast to Barney (1986), Denrell *et al.* (2003) and Kirzner (1997), who argue that finding opportunities and producing value in relation to other actors is a result of luck, serendipity and the firm's alertness, we maintain that the industrial network has its own logic, which is understandable to those who participate in, or otherwise have experience with, the network. Taking not only the firm or the dyad into consideration but also the network of firms and relationships, we argue that the mechanism behind what produces value is better understood if we separate the value process into two parts: value creation and value realisation. Creating and realising value is not a random process experienced only by the lucky few, nor is it a process that is isolated from other actors in the network. Rather, it is a process for those who have patience, experience in relations with other actors, and knowledge about the use of complex resource constellations.

The chapter is organised as follows. First, we discuss the value concept, and after that, the creation and realisation of value from a network perspective (e.g. Håkansson and Snehota, 1995). This section advances creation and realisation of value as sequences in the temporal process, and the exchange and use of resources as levels in a network structure. This is followed by a case from the European pulp and paper industry, which is used to illustrate the creation and realisation of value in industrial networks. We end the chapter with a discussion where we also present a model for understanding value creation and value realisation.

The value concept

Contemporary value literature offers two types of definitions of value. A narrow definition of value is the total worth of the benefits received for the price paid (Anderson and Narus, 1998; Porter, 1985; Simpson *et al.*, 2001; Zeithaml, 1988), while a broader definition suggests that value is the perceived trade-off between the total benefits gained and sacrifices made through an activity (e.g. Möller and Törrönen, 2002; Walter *et al.*, 2001). This implies that value contains both direct and tangible benefits and indirect and intangible benefits. Value often goes beyond tangible and measurable resources such as product quality, price and service (Simpson *et al.*, 2001) and has dynamic elements such as innovation development and product innovations (Tsai and Ghoshal, 1998; Walter, Ritter, and Gemünden, 2001). Both Anderson and Narus (1998) and Zeithaml (1988) indicate that value is personal and idiosyncratic and is based on the actor's perceptions.

The classic value concept has two broad connotations. First, value has to do with the exchange that takes place between actors in a market. In those situations, an *exchange value* is created. Second, value is also created when resources are used, combined together in new or routine ways; here, a *use value* is created. This distinction between an exchange value and a use value goes back a long way. Smith (1776) divided value into these two components, and Ramirez (1999) shows in a literature review of the concept of value that the Latin connotation originally had these two components. The distinction between an exchange value and a use value is also used by Alderson (1965). Although these two levels or mechanisms of value have a long tradition in the literature, exchange and use of resources are seldom combined even as they are each other's prerequisites in practical reality.

The industrial network perspective incorporates both the exchange and use of resources, as the actors that are engaged in exchange with each other are dependent upon resources that are combined and used in industrial activities. This is reflected for example in both Johanson and Mattsson's (1992) and Håkansson and Waluszewski's (2002) frameworks. However, these works only implicitly bring up value as a topic, and so far there have been few attempts to explicitly investigate value from a network perspective.

Value, firms and industrial networks

Researchers from the IMP (Industrial Marketing and Purchasing Group) tradition emphasise the importance of long-term relationships that are structured like a network (Axelsson and Easton, 1992; Håkansson and Snehota, 1995). Over the last decade, several researchers have studied value creation in a relationship and network context (Barringer and Harrison, 2000; Ford and McDowell, 1999; Kothandaraman and Wilson, 2001; Tsai and Ghoshal, 1998). Gassenheimer *et al.* (1998) even maintain that the mutual economic and social values which are produced in the relationship comprise the glue that keeps the relationship together. However, even if a network perspective is taken, the main unit of analysis is often the dyadic relationship, with the network often playing the role of 'context'.

A network consists of connected actors performing interdependent activities and using heterogeneous resources (e.g. Håkansson, 1987). Firms and relationships are connected and form a structure, a network. This means that a relationship is affected by a larger exchange network, but it is also affecting the same network. Consequently, this research tradition views economic organisation as a network phenomenon, where several actors, beyond the dyadic relationship, are involved in the process (e.g. Blankenburg-Holm *et al.*, 1999; Håkansson and Waluszewski, 2002).

The network perspective bases its reasoning partly on the assumption that resources are heterogeneous, with reference to Penrose's (1959) seminal work, but also on the idea that firms are dependent on other firms' provision of resources (Cook and Emerson, 1978; Kelley and Thibaut, 1959; Pfeffer and Salancik, 1978). One important consequence of the heterogeneity of resources is that relationships tend to be long-term as learning takes place within the relationships.

Combining heterogeneous resources over firm boundaries in the network implies that the value a firm can realise depends on what resources are combined together and what counterparts it works with. Due to the heterogeneity of resources, there are always things to learn, such as how to use the resources more effectively or efficiently (Håkansson, 1993). The resources that actors use to perform their activities have interfaces to other resources, and the use of a resource at one place in a network will therefore also affect the use of another resource, controlled by an actor in a different part of the network. This means that the value of a resource often is created in one part of a network, but the realisation of that value might occur somewhere else in the network. This implies that the value created by a set of actors is only a potential opportunity until it is realised by other actors.

Knowledge about how to combine resources and manage their interfaces, as well as knowledge about how resources are used and developed by counterparts and also *their* counterparts, is crucial in the process of creating and realising value. Basically, a firm creates value for a customer so that the customer, in turn, will be able to create value for *their* customers; by doing this, value is realised. In reality, what often happens is that a firm builds features into a product that might not be used directly by the customer, but that the customer needs in order to create value for its own customer. Thus, the creation and realisation of value take place at the same time, but these are also separated spatially in the network.

Thus, with the network as a unit of analysis it is not only possible to separate the creation from the realisation of value, it is also possible to see a rather sharp line separating where the two different levels of activity take place, between the exchange of resources and the use of resources.

Opportunity and value processes in networks

In industrial networks characterised by stable and long-term relationships, seizing and exploring opportunities is not only a question of being the most effective or innovative firm, nor even of getting the most out of an exchange relationship. Instead, we argue that for a firm to be able to seize opportunities, it is essential also to be aware of the value created on the use level in the network. This awareness comes from being a network participant, and by taking part in the use and exchange of resources, firms can find new ways of combining resources and relationships in the network. This means that in industrial networks finding and exploring opportunities and creating and realising value are closely interrelated. The reason for this is that both of these concepts concern how firms combine and re-combine resources.

The knowledge that comes with patience makes it easier to understand how resources are related to each other and how they relate to the relationships in the network. Understanding these connections can give firms a new set of opportunities to act from. It is possible to add features to a product, features that can add value to related resources or firms, and thereby increase the value realised in other relationships. Thus, new opportunities can be found from using resources over time in demanding relationships. The network is neither transparent nor easily accessible to outsiders. The outsider firm, which, by definition, does not have the experiences-based insight and awareness of the network, has two broad strategies at hand.

The outsider firm can try to study and understand the network logic from the outside, in order to combine resources in new ways that both fit into the prevailing resource structure and are superior to the existing combination. When this is done, the firm can try to enter the network. This is a difficult task as it requires understanding of the complex structure; due to the complexity it is difficult, without having direct prior experience of the network, to develop resource combinations that will fit into that network.

A second option is to first get an understanding of the network by entering into it, and then develop products and resource combinations which can provide value for the network. This also a difficult path as it takes time to search for opportunities in the network without being a fully 'accepted' network participant. This process takes time, and whether one succeeds or not depends on one's ability to read and comprehend the different logics of the network in order to make it possible for key actors to create and realise value. The time this will take might also demand substantial financial resources.

This strategy also requires a 'way in' to the network, a bridge or a weak tie (Burt, 1992; Granovetter, 1973).

Thus, creating and realising value in an industrial network is usually a complex process characterised by several firms participating in and exploring the structure of tightly connected resources, which, in turn, means that present use of resources is almost always a source of new opportunities, both for the traditional network participant and for outsider firms. It is not a coincidence that industrial networks are stable structures where firms and relationships tend to remain the same over long periods of time, while the use of resources changes and new technologies and products continuously appear.

The case study

We will use the relationship between Holmen and Springer as our point of departure in order to illustrate how value is created and realised in business networks. The main part of the information comes from some 100 interviews with the firms in the network around Holmen Paper and Springer Verlag. Most of the interviews were conducted between 1996 and 2001 (Wedin, 2001). After that, additional interviews were carried out in order to further follow the development within the firms concerned in the case.

Presentation of the actors in the focal relationship

Holmen Paper (Holmen) is one of Europe's largest producers of paper, with a production capacity of some 1.3 million tons of printing paper. Axel Springer Verlag (Springer) was founded in 1946 and is one of the largest media companies in Europe; it is also one of Holmen's biggest and most important customers. Springer publishes a large number of daily papers as well as weekly and monthly magazines such as *Die Welt*, *Welt am Sonntag*, *Hamburger Abendblatt* and *Bild am Sonntag*.

Holmen and Springer have been doing business since the 1940s. Springer buys a large number of products from Holmen, among them a product called Holmen Super Bright, which is produced in one of Holmen's production units, Hallsta Paper Mill (Hallsta). In fact a specific paper machine, PM11, is used for the production of the *Bild am Sonntag*'s edition of 2.5 millions copies. Hallsta is one of four paper mills within Holmen. Hallsta has a capacity of 650,000 tons of a product, called wood-containing paper and employs about 1000 people.

Every year 30,000 tons of paper are shipped by a boat owned by Hallsta and Holmen from the little village of Hallstavik, 100 kilometres north of Stockholm to the Hamburg area, where Springer has its headquarters and one of its printing houses, in Ahrensburg. Within, the relationship contacts take place on all levels, from CEO level to the people who are responsible for production at each company. Formal meetings take place at least twice a year, while more informal ones take place at least once a month.

The negotiations regarding price and quantities take place once a year. This can be a rather extended process and an extremely important one for Holmen as the outcome in the Springer negotiation will affect the content of most other customer relationships, at least those on the same geographical market. Springer is one of Europe's largest buyers of printing paper, with some 500,000 tons of paper on its purchasing list every year. The price that is negotiated between Holmen and Springer to a large extent becomes the floor, which the other buyers have to adapt to. Smaller buyers have to accept a higher price; the question is only how much higher the price level will be.

Holmen Paper's products and production facilities

When Voith, a German supplier of various types of equipment for the paper industry, built the new paper machine PM11 in 2002 at Hallsta, it was almost 30 years since Hallsta had invested in a new paper machine. PM11 has a production capacity of about 200,000 tons per year. About 50 per cent of its production is devoted to a single product group, Holmen Super News (within this product group the paper grades differ in terms of brightness). Springer is without doubt PM11's biggest customer and purchases about 20 per cent of the paper machine's capacity. The quality that Hallsta produces for *Bild am Sonntag* is called Holmen Super Bright. In general the overall heading for PM11's products is 'improved newsprint'.

The production line supplying *Bild am Sonntag* consists of a wood line, a Thermo Mechanical Pulping (TMP3) mill and a paper machine (PM11). The supplier of this facility is Metso, one of the largest manufacturers of equipment for the paper industry. A TMP mill consists of a number of disc refiners. These are, in turn, equipped with refiner segments, which are round metal plates. In the refiners wood chips are processed between the plates into pulp. In order to meet the different, required physical properties of the paper, especially strength properties but also the more optical properties, the wood chips have to be intensively processed in the refiner and between the refiner segments. The operation is very electricity-intensive; about 3000 kWh in total is consumed in the TMP process. In total, Hallsta consumes about 1.9 TWh during a year. The supplier of electric power is Vattenfall, which has been supplying Holmen with electricity since the early 1900s.

After it has been processed in the disc refiner, the pulp is bleached with hydro peroxide. Holmen Super Bright has a higher brightness and surface weight than standard newsprint. Further, Holmen Super Bright has some other physical properties that are central for Springer. Important properties are the optical features, such as a high opacity, as well as different strength properties, such as tear strength and tensile strength.

All the suppliers mentioned, Voith, Metso and Vattenfall, consider Holmen a key customer, and the relationships have been more or less working and healthy for a long time even if there have been times of conflict as well. All three suppliers are active in research and development, and Holmen and its production facilities can reap the benefits from these efforts. For example, without the development work conducted by Metso and Voith, the different strength features that are created in the disc refiners and further enhanced in the paper machine would not be present. Further, Vattenfall has worked to lower the voltage dips that had earlier caused production breakdowns during thunderstorms throughout warm summer months.

Springer's production facility in Ahrensburg

The Ahrensburg site where *Bild am Sonntag* is produced has several printing presses, and a large number of magazines and newspapers are printed there. The most common printing technology used by Holmen's customers is the web offset technology, and this is also used at Springer's printing site in Ahrensburg. In a web offset printing machine, a printing plate transfers the printing ink to the paper web via a rubber blanket. The paper must therefore tolerate interaction with components in the printing process such as ink, printing plates and rubber blankets. Thus, there is a direct physical interface between these components in the printing press and, in order to achieve an efficient process, there are high demands on the paper's runability in the printing press. Runability has to do with how long it is possible to run the press without stops caused by the paper and is to a large degree a function of different strength features of the paper. For example, the press may have to stop because of breaks in the paper web, or due to a need to clean the printing plates and rubber blankets because wood fibres have been torn off from the paper's surface and have got stuck on the rubber blankets.

Another big customer for PM11 is Interprint, one of Scandinavia's biggest magazine producers, which produces tabloids, journals and books. What distinguishes Interprint is that it uses a somewhat different printing technology from, for example, Springer, which uses the offset technology. Interprint uses the photogravure printing method, where the ink is distributed from 'valleys' on the printing plates to the paper. This method requires a very even paper surface, and the wood fibres must therefore be well defibrated. Some years ago, Holmen's strategy for PM11 was to go for the customers with the photogravure printing technology, since this was expected to become a dominant technology within the printing industry. However, that expectation was not met. But as some products go to customers with photogravure printing presses, all the other customers of PM11 also get pulp that is processed for this printing technology, including Springer. This pulp is more processed in the disc refiners than it actually needs to be.

Springer's customers

Springer gets two major types of revenues from *Bild am Sonntag*, from sold papers and from firms advertising in the paper. Springer's five biggest customers account for 8 per cent of the total advertisement revenues in the *Bild am Sonntag* case. Pictures and advertisements are designed in relation to the type of paper that is going to be used in the printing press (Holmen Super Bright) and the type of printing press that is used (a double round, double wide web off-set press supplied by MAN Roland). Therefore, the design of advertisements and pre-press operations are also more or less adapted to input resources and the printing press. The information about what the printing press can handle in technical terms has been distributed to the different firms. An important part of the selling of advertisements is therefore to make advertisement customers and their advertisement agencies adapt their advertisements to the existing technical facilities. The adaptations can, for example, concern how many screen lines and dots per inch an image can be printed in. The more screen lines, the better the quality of the image.

Bild am Sonntag (and its advertisers) wants to make readers aware of the advertisements. An effective way to achieve this is to use lots of colours. The more colours that are used in the advertisement, the greater the possibility that a reader will pay attention to the ad and be affected by it. Therefore, a general trend in the newspaper industry is to use more and more colours in the advertisements and also in the whole newspaper. If more colour is used, a paper with higher printability is demanded, for example, a paper that can absorb ink in an efficient way that does not disturb the printing process and makes the images look nice on the paper. Moreover, in order to achieve a good 'contrast' between the advertisement and the paper, a whiter paper is needed. Therefore the paper grades that Springer has demanded have over the years changed in the direction of a whiter paper and a paper with higher printability.

As a consequence the manufacturing of printing inks has been pushed towards a larger share of colour inks as the possibilities to print with four colours have increased because of, among other things, the use of the offset method. Today 50 per cent of the inks used are colour inks. Among the suppliers of inks is Gebrüder Smith. Springer and Gebrüder Smith work together on a regular basis to improve the printing process and the printing quality.

As a result, it is not unusual that at least big printing houses work systematically to combine the different input resources in specific combinations. For example paper from paper supplier A is combined with ink from ink supplier A in one printing press, and paper from paper supplier B is combined with ink from ink supplier B in the second printing press, etc. The ink recipe may be adapted, for example in terms of viscosity, and the different printing presses must be adapted to the different combinations, for example in terms of the printing press' web tension, which also depends on how much ink and how damp the paper is. The finished newspaper is in practice a combination of printing inks, newsprint, the level of dampness, printing plates, and rubber blankets from different suppliers put together in specific combinations in the printing press. No single input works as a totally independent variable in the process, and there is more or less a constant adaptation between the different items.

Here Holmen is able to support Springer with advice, through the Technical Marketing function, an organisational unit that is the customers' helping hand when problems arise. It also happens that Technical Marketing collaborates with parallel suppliers such as printing ink suppliers, control equipment suppliers, etc. By engaging in these types of activities Holmen and Hallsta also learn a lot about the problems that Springer faces. Through its relationship with Springer, Holmen has over the years gained knowledge about the requirements that Springer and Springer's customers have for their products.

A model for creation and realisation of value in networks

From the case, we can see that the exchange between Holmen and Springer is indeed dependent upon what happens outside the dyad, as it affects the relationships that the parties have with third parties. The case also indicates that the use of resources tends to be more extensive and concerns more actors than the exchange layer. This means that the resources a firm uses, such as machines, equipment, knowledge and human resources, are adapted and committed to several other firms' use of resources, often without the firms doing business, that is, exchanging resources, with each other.

Exchange tends to be embedded in a set of use interdependencies which often concern more than two firms. This is an important observation as it makes up the frame for how firms can create and realise value from resources in industrial networks. The use dependence is a constraint for the firms in the network. On the other hand, the use dependence offers a pool of resources and expertise, which can be combined in order to produce value.

It is possible to see value creation and value realisation as sequences in place and time, but also to see one as a source and prerequisite for the other (see Figure 5.1). Creation and realisation are related not only to *where* resources are exchanged and used, but also to *when* value is created and realised. We believe that value has to be created before it can be realised and, moreover, we have identified two levels of a network, which makes possible four processes where value is produced in the network.

First, it seems that value can be created on the exchange level between two or more actors in the network. In this process, the value created can later be realised on the exchange level in other relationships in the network. However, and *second*, the value created on the exchange level between, for instance, two firms doing business with each other, can be realised on the use level in connected or even more distant relationships in the network. This type of creation is related to the resources exchanged and to the activities directly performed when exchanging the resources.

Third, on the use level, which consists of the physical resources, the technological system, resources can be combined in either new or routine ways by production people, maintenance functions, etc. In these combinations, a value potential is present due to the features created. However, the value

Creation and Realisation of Value 119

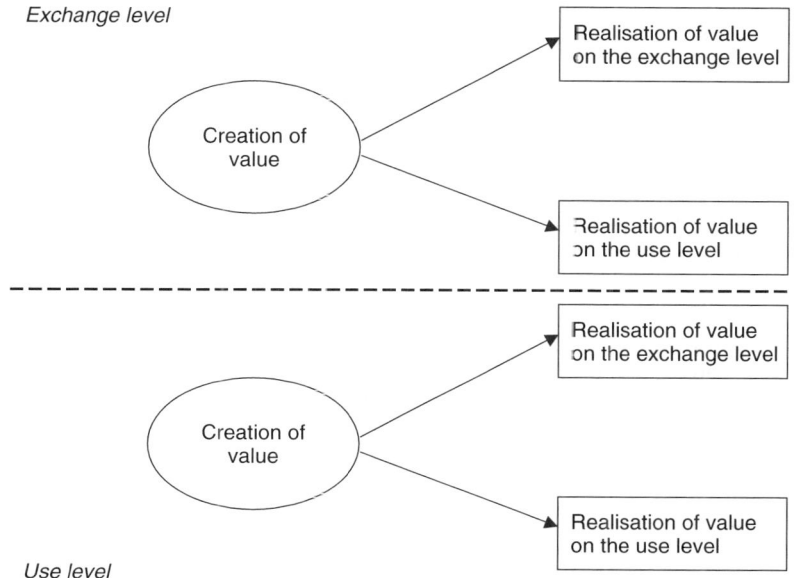

Figure 5.1 A model of the creation and realisation of value

created on the use level between several firms might be realised between other firms doing business with others on the exchange level.

The fourth and final process also starts with firms combining and re-combining resources on the use level, that is, they create a potential value, which can be realised on the same level between other firms in the network. This realisation of value can take place several tiers away from the firm that created the valuable features in the first place. However, this is not something that just happens by chance. There is a systematic coordination of the resources in the network.

By being knowledgeable and aware of how resources are used, what features are valued and by whom, directly and, more importantly, indirectly, a firm can detect opportunities on the use level to create and realise value. Managing the value process is about creating value for a customer, and, at the same time, making it possible for the customer to create value for other firms. By having knowledge about resource combinations, one and several steps away from itself, a firm may thereby be able to realise value.

By making this separation of value production from a network perspective, one gains increased understanding of the process of value production in general as well as a language to better grasp situations in which value is realised, or in fact when there are value potentials that are waiting to be unpacked and realised.

Case analysis

From the case we can pick the following example: Runability and printability are critical paper features for Springer. These features are developed in a sequence of activities back at Holmen's production unit Hallsta. The suppliers of the production facilities that create these features are Metso and Voith. Metso develops and manufactures the disc refiners, which produce the pulp, and Voith develops and manufactures paper machines. The runability and printability features are created first when the wood fibres are defibrated in the disc refiner and then made into a printing paper in the paper machine. Both the research and development work that Metso and Voith are committed to is critical for Springer to realise, as is the development work that takes place in long-term relationships with firms such as Holmen.

Figure 5.2 illustrates the firms, the relationships and the resources in the network which are involved in the different value processes. Two triads of firms – Holmen, Vattenfall and Metso, and Man Roland, Gebrüder Smith and Holmen – interact in order to create value on the use level. Their efforts in terms of value are fundamental in order for Springer and BMW to realise value on the exchange level. However, as the figure presents the exchange and use levels, it is striking not only that the network seems to contain eight firms and seven exchanges of eight resources, but also that the use dependence developed by joint activities concerns eleven relationships and many more straight-use interdependencies. For example, the production facility that Metso provides for the TMP process is indirectly used in all the resources

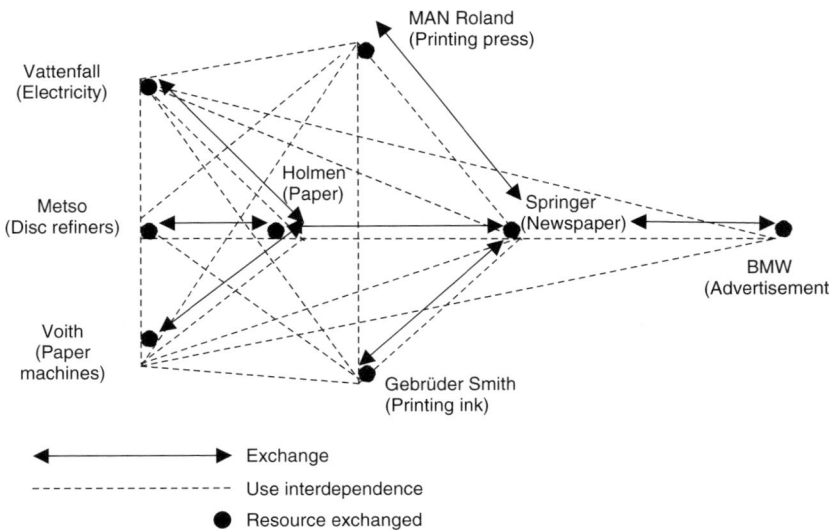

Figure 5.2 An illustration of the creation and realisation of value

presented in the figure. The interfaces can be both direct and indirect, and it is in the physical and commercial interfaces that the value is created and realised in the above-illustrated network.

A resource is part of both a selling and a buying system (Håkansson and Waluszewski, 2002), and will therefore be used by one customer or several customers. The features created in the first interface will then be activated and taken care of more or less deliberately. In this case, one can say that value has been realised, both on the exchange level and on the use level. Further, the activated features of the paper exchanged between Holmen and Springer, Holmen Super Bright, are processed with other resources and are used in creating new features. This is evident in Springer's printing process, where the paper's strength features created at Holmen's production facilities are realised and new features are re-created (e.g. printability in broad terms). These features will then be part of a realising value process in interaction with advertisers such as BMW The realisation and creation is therefore part of the same using and producing system as well as part of a common buying and selling system. It is in Holmen's interest that these features are realised. Therefore, Holmen has set up an organisational unit, Technical Marketing, which fulfils three functions: first, as a link between Holmen and Springer, second, as a support to Springer's internal us its resources, and third, as facilitator in the exchange between Springer and their customers. Thus, one can suggest that Holmen uses resources which support the customer's realisation of the features that Holmen has created in the first place.

Thus, the processes of value creation and value realisation are not linear. Instead, the creation and realisation of value are dependent upon each other. As the value of some specific resource features are realised in a production process, these features at the same time help to create value that is later on activated and hence realised in another production or development process. In addition, the features created in the first place are created for a very specific purpose, to be used, realised, by a specific counterpart. The resource features are purposefully created. The processes of value creation and value realisation are therefore intimately linked to each other. Therefore, the knowledge about resources and the effects of resource combinations and how well developed the knowledge is in relation to the resources exchanged is crucial in order to realise the full potential value at a given moment.

An example from the case might illustrate this. Advertisements are an important source of revenues for *Bild am Sonntag* and Springer. *Bild am Sonntag* is, of course, doing its best to create value in its relationships with the advertisers. The journalists try to write good articles and the photographers to take catchy photos, but what concerns the advertisers most is something that is created in another part of the network, where other firms, Holmen and their suppliers Voith and Metso, cooperate (despite the fact that the latter two are competitors when it comes to selling paper machines). This cooperation makes it possible to produce a bright and strong paper.

However, strength and brightness are not enough. A white paper does not attract the readers' attention, but a lot of sharp colours do, so ink has to be applied to the paper. Such a combination of colours and brightness is required, for instance, by one of Springer's biggest advertisers, BMW. Springer usually purchases the ink from Gebrüder Smith; the ink is tried out in combination with Holmen's paper in the printing presses in Ahrensburg. The increased use of colour ink in order to attract advertisers would not be possible without the collaborative work of these firms.

An example that illustrates how value created on the exchange level in one relationship can later be realised in several other exchanges is the price negotiation between Holmen and Springer. In fact, the case shows how the price negotiation between the two parties is indeed embedded in the other exchange relationships, as the Springer deal sets the floor for other customers, and these negotiations cannot start until Holmen has a price for Springer. Given that Holmen can get a fair price from Springer, one can start to see whether this year's budget will meet expectations or not as there is more value (higher prices) that can be realised in the other customer relationships.

In the same way that exchange and use are interdependent, a similar relationship prevails between the creation of value and realisation of the potential value created. Value cannot be realised if it has not first been created. But, a created value is not necessarily always realised. Instead, there are potentials for value that can be seen as realised or unrealised opportunities. And, at the same time, the realisation of value is part of value-creating processes. One can easily think of examples of when something has been created but has no practical value. The following example from the case might illustrate the issue of non-realised value. Experiences gained by producing paper for customers with photogravure printing technology like Interprint could be utilised by Holmen in its relationship with Springer when it was necessary. The photogravure printing technology requires an even paper surface and well-defibrated wood fibres. This very concrete value is created and realised in the relationship between Holmen and Interprint, but in the relationship with Springer this value is only a potential, that is, the paper has an even surface and is made out of well-defibrated wood fibres, value that cannot be realised by Springer or any other web-offset customer. Thus, taking away features that are not fully used, or never realised, can also be a way to create and realise value for a firm. Also, this is something that demands a specific knowledge about customers' and even customers' customers' production processes.

Concluding remarks

In this chapter we have brought forward the idea that the value processes in industrial networks for good reasons can be separated into two parts: value creation and value realisation. These processes take place in two different but interrelated network levels, an exchange level and a use level. We illustrated our idea with a case from the pulp and paper industry, looking at a long-term relationship between Holmen and Springer. This case shows how the value generated at one place is, further on, in another part of the network, realised and thereby also a part of a new creation process. At the same time, these processes are a prerequisite for the first creation process, meaning that both value processes are dependent upon each other.

We have found, by separating creation and realisation, that value is a relative concept, which can be viewed as potential opportunity for the actors in the network. Value that is created is not always realised, but makes up an opportunity for the actors in the network, and not only for those who have created the value. This, in turn, means that those who enjoy the realisation of value are not necessarily the actors that created that same value. In order to reap the full benefit from the value, it is not enough or even necessary to move outside the boundaries of the single firm and even the dyad of two firms. In order to fully capture the mechanisms that drive value creation and value realisation, firms can get a deeper understanding of the value processes by seeing what goes on beyond their business with their own customers.

References

Alderson, W. (1965). *Dynamic Marketing Behaviour*, Homewood, IL: Richard D Irwin, Inc.

Anderson, J. C. and Narus, J. A. (1998). Business Marketing: Understand What Customers Value, *Harvard Business Review*, 76(6), 53–65.

Axelsson, B. and Easton, G. (1992). *Industrial Networks – A New View of Reality*, London: Routledge.

Barney, J. B. (1986). Strategic Factor Markets: Expectations, Luck and Business Strategy, *Management Science*, 17(1), 99–120.

Barringer, B. B. and Harrison, J. S. (2000). Walking a Tightrope: Creating Value through Interorganizational Relationships, *Journal of Management*, 26(3), 367–403.

Blankenburg-Holm, D., Eriksson, K. and Johanson, J. (1999). Creating Value through Mutual Commitment to Business Network Relationships, *Strategic Management Journal*, 20(5), 467–86.

Burt, R. S. (1992). *Structural Holes: The Social Structure of Competition*, Cambridge, MA: Harvard University Press.

Cook, K. S. and Emerson, R. M. (1978). Power, Equity and Commitment in Exchange Networks, *American Sociological Review*, 43(5), 721–39.

Denrell, J., Fang, C. and Winter, S. G. (2003). The Economics of Strategic Opportunity, *Strategic Management Journal*, 24(10), 977–90.

Ford, D. and McDowell, R. (1999). Managing Business Relationships by Analysing the Effects and Value of Different Actions, *Industrial Marketing Management*, 28(5), 429–42.

Gassenheimer, J. B., Houston, F. B. and Davis, J. C. (1998). The Role of Economic Value, Social Value, and Perceptions of Fairness in Interorganizational Relationship Retention Decisions, *Journal of the Academy of Marketing Science*, 26(4), 322–37.

Granovetter, M. S. (1973). The Strength of Weak Ties, *American Journal of Sociology*, 78(6), 1360–80.

Håkansson, H. (ed.) (1987). *Industrial Technological Development; A Network Approach*, London: Croom Helm.
Håkansson, H. (1993). Networks as a Mechanism to Develop Resources, in P. Beije, J. Groenewegen, O. Nuys (eds), *Networking in Dutch Industries*, Leven-Apeldorn: Garant, 207–23.
Håkansson, H. and Snehota I. (1995). *Developing Relationships in Business Networks*, London: Routledge.
Håkansson, H. and Waluszewski, A. (2002). *Managing Technological, Development. IKEA, the Environment and Technology*, London and New York: Routledge.
Johanson J. and Mattsson L-G. (1992). Network Position and Strategic Action – An Analytical Framework, in B. Axelsson and G. Easton (eds), *Industrial Networks: A New View of Reality*, London: Routledge, 205–17.
Kale, P., Dyer, J. and Singh, H. (2001). Value Creation and Success in Strategic Alliances: Alliancing Skills and the Role of Alliance Structure and Systems, *European Management Journal*, 19(5), 463–71.
Kelley, H. H. and Thibaut, J. W. (1959). *The Social Psychology of Groups*, New York: Wiley.
Kirzner, I. M. (1997). Entrepreneurial Discovery and the Competitive Market Process: An Austrian Approach, *Journal of Economic Literature*, 35(1), 60–85.
Kothandaraman, P. and Wilson, D. T. (2001). The Future of Competition: Value-Creating Networks, *Industrial Marketing Management*, 30(4), 379–89.
Möller, K. E. K. and Törrönen, P. (2002). Business Suppliers' Value Creation Potential: A Customer-based Analysis, *Industrial Marketing Management*, 32(2), 1–10.
Porter, M. (1985). *Competitive Advantage*, New York: Free Press.
Pfeffer, J. and Salancik, G. R. (1978). *The External Control of Organizations: A Resource Dependence Perspective*. New York: Harper & Row.
Penrose, E. T. (1959). *The Theory of the Growth of the Firm*. Oxford: Basil Blackwell.
Ramirez, R. (1999). Value Co-production: Intellectual Origins and Implications for Practise and Research, *Strategic Management Journal*, 20(1), 49–65.
Simpson, P. M., Siguaw, J. A. and Baker, T. L. (2001). A Model of Value Creation: Supplier Behaviors and Their Impact on Reseller-Perceived Value, *Industrial Marketing Management*, 30(2), 119–34.
Smith, A. (1776). *An Enquiry into the Nature and the Causes of the Wealth of Nations*, London: Stratton and Cadell.
Tsai, W. and Ghoshal, S. (1998). Social Capital and Value Creation: The Role of Intrafirm Networks, *Academy of Management Journal*, 41(4), 464–76.
Walter, A., Ritter, T. and Gemünden, H. G. (2001). Value Creation in Buyer–Seller Relationships: Theoretical Considerations and Empirical Results from a Supplier's Perspective, *Industrial Marketing Management*, 30(4), 365–77.
Wedin, T. (2001). Networks and demand. Phd thesis, Dep. of Business studies, Uppsala University.
Zeithaml, V. A. (1988). Consumer Perceptions of Price, Quality, and Value: A Means-End Model and Synthesis of Evidence, *Journal of Marketing*, 52(3), 2–22.

Part II

Opportunity Development in International Business

6
Business Opportunities, Subsidiaries and Interpreneurial Activity

Cecilia Pahlberg and Magnus Persson

Introduction

Although the concept of *opportunity* is frequently used, it is still rather vague. In the introductory chapter it was suggested that *'opportunities should be studied as some kind of process in which the opportunity is found and realized'* (p. 3) and that business network theory might have something important to say about this. It was also indicated that this concept could be seen as a new and advantageous combination of resources. In this chapter we will discuss how subsidiaries within multinational companies (MNCs) may detect and exploit business opportunities. In order to detect and exploit such opportunities, two antecedent conditions are necessary: *specific market knowledge* that is novel and relevant to the subsidiary's *technological knowledge*, which include both embodied (specific technology such as innovations, production processes, and products) and un-embodied form of knowledge. When these two conditions are fulfilled, a business opportunity might be detected and subsequently exploited. Below, we will further discuss this by drawing on both entrepreneurial theories and business network theories.

Nowadays it is commonly recognized that MNCs are widely differentiated across their subunits (Ghoshal and Nohria, 1989; Nohria and Ghoshal, 1997). Different technologies will develop in different parts of the organization, as units engage in exchange activities with their business counterparts. Research in recent decades has pointed out the importance of being able to transfer and leverage knowledge and innovations across subsidiaries (Bartlett and Ghoshal, 1989; Ghoshal and Bartlett, 1988; Gupta and Govindarajan, 1994; Schlegelmilch and Chini, 2003; Zander and Kogut, 1995), to be able to source knowledge through subsidiary relations with local counterparts (Andersson *et al.*, 2001; Eriksson and Hohenthal, 2001; Pennings and Harianto, 1992), and to combine new and old knowledge (Kogut and Zander, 1992). In this implicit shift in focus, from subsidiaries as exploiters to subsidiaries in their role of exploring and innovating, that is, acting entrepreneurially, the thrust of the research has been on how to tap knowledge from a local network and diffuse this throughout the corporation to upgrade the competitive advantage. However, little attention has been brought to the actual outcome of these processes; rather, they are generally considered to enhance innovative ability or performance of subsidiaries, and subsequently of the MNC as a whole.

In this chapter we identify two distinct effects of creating and acquiring knowledge through linkages with the internal MNC network and the local, external, business network. By being embedded in an external network, subsidiaries will encounter new market knowledge that can favour the detection of opportunities. Second, the ability to transfer existing technological knowledge from within the MNC across organizational subunits facilitates the exploitation of these opportunities. In this sense, subsidiaries act as agents of opportunities, enlarging the potential scope of exploitation of new technologies developed within the corporation by linking these technologies to idiosyncratic market knowledge.

The chapter is structured as follows. In the next section, inspired by entrepreneurial theories, we develop a concept of business opportunity. This is done by explicating arguments of the importance of specific market knowledge and technological knowledge, to the detection of business opportunities. We also conclude, that subsidiaries might detect business opportunities that they themselves cannot exploit, and that they may turn to other parts of the MNC to leverage technological knowledge to do so. We find two main obstacles to this; cognitive differences across the MNC organization, and the distribution of decision-making rights.

The second section of the chapter applies the framework of business opportunities to the subsidiary network context. We show that subsidiary network embeddedness is an important determinant to subsidiary exposure to novel and relevant market knowledge. Moreover, based on our reasoning on cognitive differences and decision-making rights, we argue that subsidiary external embeddedness affects the ease with which the unit can leverage technological knowledge from other parts of the corporation to exploit detected business opportunities.

This chapter thus contributes in two different ways. First, it identifies two possible outcomes of organizational leveraging of technological knowledge in the multinational firm, and second, in doing this, it introduces elements that allow for more rapid change and dynamism in business network theory, a theory that otherwise is characterized by a focus on stability and incremental change. The arguments put forward will be summarized in three propositions and their implications discussed. In the concluding section of the chapter, the concept of *interpreneur* will be introduced to capture the meaning of the subsidiary function within MNCs which combines knowledge about the local market with knowledge about technologies in different parts of the MNC.

Characteristics of business opportunity

The following arguments in this first section of the chapter build on three preconditions: (1) the detection of opportunities is a function of prior knowledge (Shane, 2000), (2) the detection and exploitation of opportunities is related to market knowledge and technological knowledge held by the actor/subsidiary (Wiklund & Shepherd, 2003), and (3) market knowledge is dispersed and contextual in time and place (Hayek, 1945). As pointed out by the Austrian School, opportunities are unknown until they are discovered, which implies that one cannot systematically search for an opportunity (Kirzner, 1997). A fundamental question then is: How are new business opportunities recognized?

Our view is that prior knowledge that is complementary with new information is essential in order to detect opportunities. Shane (2000) formulates the importance of the combination of knowledge about technology and knowledge about the market context in the following way: 'New information about a technology might be complementary with prior information about how particular markets operate, leading the discovery of the entrepreneurial opportunity to require prior information about those markets' (p. 452). Apparently, prior market knowledge is seen as fundamental to the detection of opportunities. This market knowledge must then be complemented with relevant knowledge about new technology. To make an analogy to chemistry, changes in the knowledge about technologies act as a catalyst, which due to existing prior knowledge about how markets operate, make the actors aware of a potential situation in which they can act to create new business. The main point here is that opportunities are detected as a result of subsidiary conjecture of complementarities between market knowledge and technological knowledge (Wiklund and Shepherd, 2003).

We wish to address this problem from a different point of view. Instead of considering changes in the knowledge about existing technologies as driving the detection of opportunities, we will convey market knowledge, and subsidiary exposure to bits and pieces of novel market knowledge, as the instigator of opportunity detection. It is important to note that in doing this we wish not to imply that one perspective would be more important, or more correct, than the other – it is simply a choice relating to the focus of this chapter. This choice is based on our definition of market knowledge. *Market knowledge*, as this concept is used here, does not refer to generic knowledge that is relatively stable and can be used in different parts of the organization (such as how to market products, how to use CRM systems, etc.). Rather, the essential market knowledge for detecting opportunities is the type of knowledge Hayek (1945) referred to as contextually bound in *time* and *place*. According to Hayek, such knowledge cannot be concentrated at a centre, since it is 'the man on the spot' who possesses such particular knowledge. An essential feature is its elusive character – it is only valuable for a certain period of time, to certain actors, and under certain circumstances.

Market knowledge – novelty and relevance

Two aspects of subsidiary exposure to market knowledge are important here: the amount of *novel* and *relevant* knowledge that the subsidiary receives. Novelty relates to the very definition of opportunity as something new, previously unseen, that cannot be searched for (Kirzner, 1997). However, an extensive amount of novel market knowledge is of limited use if this knowledge is not related to the specific area in which the subsidiary operates. For instance, there is a risk that an opportunity present in the local business network will not be detected if the subsidiary is not already familiar with a technology that could be used to exploit this opportunity. Firms will be more inclined to detect such opportunities that relate to already owned resources (Denrell *et al.*, 2003). Otherwise, the opportunity will simply pass unnoticed. Thus, the technological knowledge held by the subsidiary make some pieces of market knowledge valuable. This knowledge both enables the subsidiary to detect opportunities in certain areas in which the unit is well endowed, and restrict the vicinity within which opportunities can be detected. While relevance might well include other types of criteria such as alignment to organizational goals, values, and strategy, we will here limit ourselves to the criterion of complementarity between the market knowledge and technological knowledge of the unit (see Figure 6.1).

However, there is reason to be somewhat cautious here. Several authors, including some we have cited, note that actors may detect opportunities based on very general knowledge about the existence of technologies (what we might label information), rather than on the specific technological

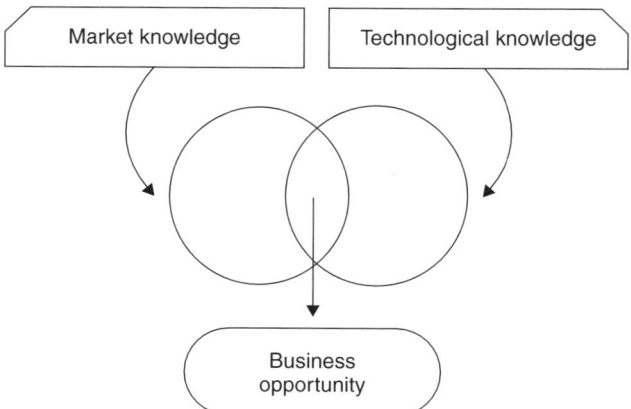

Figure 6.1 The characteristics of business opportunities

knowledge itself (see for example Kirzner, 1997; Shane, 2000). Following this line, we also suggest that subsidiaries will detect opportunities that fall outside the vicinity of what they can exploit themselves. Therefore, a key argument is that by being informed about current technological developments and technologies in use in other parts of the MNC, subsidiaries can value new market knowledge and perceive opportunities on this basis rather than only on their own technological knowledge.

Detecting a potentially valuable opportunity is thus not equal to possessing the relevant skills and resources needed to actually move forward to exploit that opportunity. Rather, subsidiaries have the important function of acting as intermediaries between local market opportunities and technological knowledge proprietary to the MNC. By accessing technological knowledge currently located elsewhere in the organization, subsidiaries can help to remedy the problems caused by organizational distance between knowledge elements; for instance, the separation of technological development from the market can potentially lead to under-identification of opportunities to exploit this technology, since central decision-makers are unlikely to identify all possible opportunities related to this technology (Shane and Venkatarman, 2000).

Access to technological knowledge

Once the subsidiary has identified an opportunity that it is unable to exploit on its own, it can either cooperate with specific counterparts in its external network to develop a technology or it can try to get access to the technology within the MNC and leverage it through intra-firm linkages. Each of these alternatives has its restrictions and possibilities. Although several researchers have pointed out the importance of the firm's external network in accessing resources (see for example Gulati et al., 2000; Lorenzoni and Lipparini, 1999; Pennings and Harianto, 1992) we incline here towards the latter alternative. In the following discussion we concentrate on the application and commitment of MNC technological knowledge to local opportunities.

Birkinshaw (1997) argued, in investigating subsidiary initiatives and entrepreneurial action in MNCs, that a fundamental challenge facing MNCs is the commitment of resources from the back end of the organization, to support subsidiary entrepreneurial undertaking in response to identified local opportunities. However, it is not merely a problem of organizing for transfer but also includes difficulties in the build-up process towards the decision to do so. Albeit subsidiaries sometimes have considerable allowance for autonomous action, the employment of resources found elsewhere in the organization would often require the approval of headquarters (HQ) prior to engagement. The distance between HQ and the subsidiary has consequences that significantly can impede this process. Examining the concept of 'truly dispersed knowledge', Foss (1999) presented a number of problems relating to this. Two of these are of particular relevance to this discussion.

First, different organizational members have different cognitive constructs; second, entrepreneurial activity leads to problems in the distribution of decision-making rights.

Cognitive differences. Cognitive constructs, that is, the way we perceive and interpret our surroundings, and the way we select, search, and value information, determine how we act and understand. Cognitive attributes are, however, not givens but are shaped through our experience (Schneider and Angelmar, 1993). In turn, the various operating environments, tasks, and contingencies across the MNC organization will shape cognition of different parts of the organization. The internal cognitive differentiation this gives rise to comes into play at two different aspects in the context of our arguments. First, as pointed out by Birkinshaw (1997), securing access to internal resources often requires a process of 'persuasion' towards decision-making authority (in this case the HQ) where holding the same world-view significantly facilitates the communication and thus likely the outcome. And second, collaborative arrangements for the leveraging of internal MNC technological knowledge to a local business context could be confronted with cognitive problems due to the needs to bridge intra-organizational barriers between different subunits (see for instance Dougherty, 1992).

Decision-making rights. The special character of market knowledge, as defined here, hinders HQ from making informed judgements about the value of specific opportunities due to information asymmetries and the context specificity of the market knowledge. In requesting resources for pursuing the exploitation of a business opportunity, problems can arise since it can be hard for HQ to *ex ante* distinguish between entrepreneurial effort and an act of opportunism. Subsidiaries with considerable local discretion over their own activities and mandates in creating new business are thus in a more favourable position to pursue opportunities. Sluggish, vertical, decision-making processes are unfeasible; the often-elusive nature of opportunities calls for swift, ready action, which implies that units with decision-making power on the usage of MNC proprietary resources will be better equipped for this task. The need to organize for combinations of different knowledge bases and resources becomes apparent in the face of the dispersion of assets that characterize many multinational operations. Contextually bound market knowledge raises doubts over the efficiency of centralized decision-making; as Hedlund (1994) noted, this might entail decisions being brought to the information, rather than vice-versa. On the other hand, while business opportunities might appear highly valuable from the subsidiary's point of view, they might not lie in the interests of the whole corporation. Distributed decision-making rights come with the risk of uncoordinated, and sometimes also opportunistic, behaviour on the part of the subunit. Consequently, while delegating decision-making rights to subsidiary level can mitigate problems related to the process of HQ 'persuasion', it might be done at the cost of internal coordination.

In the next section some propositions will be articulated. They are developed by applying business network theory to the concept of opportunity presented above. Specifically, we look at subsidiary embeddedness in local business networks, and how this affects the subsidiary's exposure to novel and relevant market knowledge, as well as the impact external embeddedness has on subsidiary access to MNC technological knowledge.

Detection and exploitation of business opportunities – a network view

So far, we have concluded that subsidiary detection and exploitation of business opportunities is dependent on the access and exposure to specific market knowledge and technological knowledge. In the following, we will examine how this is affected by subsidiary embeddedness in its local business network. By doing so, we hope to introduce elements of rapid change in a theory that often is characterized by a focus on incremental action and stability. The explicit interface between the two is (1) the network as a source of knowledge, whose properties affect the detection of business opportunities (2) and as influencing cognitive schemes and subsidiary decision-making rights, which in turn affects the access to technological knowledge from other corporate units.

A firm's network of relationships is a source of both opportunities and constraints (Gulati *et al.*, 2000). Basically, the subsidiary is embedded in a set of exchange relationships through which it performs its activities on the local market. While the concept was originally developed by sociologists to study relationships at the individual level, a number of researchers have demonstrated the strength of the embeddedness concept in application to business environments (Andersson and Forsgren, 1996; Uzzi, 1997). Subsidiary embeddedness has been defined as the general closeness of the relationship, which includes the intensity of information exchange and level of mutual adaptation of the counterparts (Andersson *et al.*, 2001). Research on business networks has shown that over time some relationships between the subsidiary and specific local actors become more important than others. Gradually the subsidiary will develop strong relationships with some actors important for this unit, while others will continue to be at armslength distance (Ford, 1990; Håkansson, 1989; Johanson and Mattsson, 1987). Subsidiary embeddedness within the business network can further be depicted as partly consisting of relationships external to the MNC, and partly consisting of relationships to other units within the same corporation with which the subsidiary has an exchange relationship. This has led researchers to make a distinction between internal and external embeddedness (Andersson and Forsgren, 1996). It can be said that the subsidiary by its membership in two different networks also is subject to two different sets of influences: one from the local network on which the unit is dependent in its daily business activities, and the other from the corporation to fulfil its role and function within the MNC. A subsidiary's embeddedness in its local network has, for instance, been shown to have implications for HQ control over the unit (Andersson and Forsgren, 1996), in the creation and acquisition of knowledge through network linkages (Forsgren *et al.*, 2000), and for the competence development of other MNC subsidiaries through internal transfer (Andersson *et al.*, 2001).

Embeddedness and detection of opportunities

The business network is the subsidiary's main source of information exchange with the environment (Andersson *et al.*, 2001). In analysing social network structures, Burt (1992) argued that while opportunities spring up everywhere, the information benefits of the network structure surrounding the actor define who knows about such opportunities. Since information is unevenly spread across a set of actors in a network, and no actor can process all available information, the network functions as a 'screening device'. Network counterparts can thus constitute important sources of information, and while such second-hand information about events and developing opportunities is often fuzzy and imprecise, it can serve to signal the rise of something important (Burt, 1992).

Granovetter (1973) suggested that the strength of a relationship might be a fundamental trait determining its value in providing new information. Distant and infrequent relationships, (*weak ties*), are important because they provide the focal actor with novel information by bridging between different, tightly knit social structures (Granovetter, 1973). In direct application to a business environment, this would imply that subsidiaries with a large number of weak ties are more likely to attain for them new information and market knowledge. However, this analogy suffers from two major weaknesses. First, the weak ties of organizations are those of arms-length distance. Arms-length relationships coordinate organizational behaviour through one key piece of information: price. In order for the concept of weak ties to be applied to the organizational level, there must be additional dimensions to the concept that explain why the mass of novel information is enabling, considering the parsimony in richness. Second, the detection of a business opportunity is not only a matter of receiving market information. Following the arguments of Shane (2000) we claim that this market knowledge needs to be relevant to the subsidiary or, in other words, complementary to the technological knowledge of the unit in order to facilitate the detection of profitable opportunities.

As stressed in our theoretical discussion, the detection of opportunities is influenced by the amount of *novel* and *relevant* market knowledge reaching the subsidiary. It can be assumed that counterparts with whom the subsidiary is more intensely interacting are more familiar with the unit than those actors with whom the subsidiary has a more distant relationship. Consequently, these closer actors will be better at screening information (Burt, 1992) and forwarding relevant notions and pieces of information to the subsidiary. But while high levels of business network embeddedness is positive for the relevance of received market knowledge, too high levels of embeddedness in a business network can also be detrimental to firm performance (Uzzi, 1997). Such *over-embeddedness* might occur because the subsidiary is relying too heavily on too few counterparts. By being over-embedded, the value of the received information is limited due to its lack of novelty. As put by Hansen (1999), strong ties will lead to a greater amount of redundant information in the relationship since 'everyone knows what the others know'. While less-embedded subsidiaries, having a great number of weak ties, can enjoy large amounts of novel market knowledge, most will be discarded as irrelevant. And while a few dense relationships might provide the unit with mostly relevant information, novelty might be insufficient to significantly impact the probability of detecting opportunities. These arguments lead us to conclude that the relationships between opportunity detection and level of external embeddedness is likely to exhibit an inverted U-shaped relationship. Accordingly, we can put forth the following proposition:

Proposition 1:   There is an inverted U-shaped relation between the level of external embeddedness and the subsidiary's probability of detecting business opportunities in the local market.

Embeddedness and exploitation of opportunities

A subsidiary will sometimes detect opportunities in the local market that it cannot exploit on its own. First, as pointed out previously, detecting an opportunity does not necessarily imply that the unit owns the resources needed to exploit this opportunity. Second, the development of technological knowledge is seen as an incremental process that builds upon what is previously known – that is, there is a steady search for improvements (Cantwell, 1991). Thus, the possibility of a subsidiary quickly responding to detected opportunities through its own technological knowledge can in many cases be considered as very limited. Subsidiary ability to access technological knowledge located elsewhere in the MNC will thus expand the vicinity within which the unit can exploit opportunities. Accordingly, on an MNC level, Doz and Prahalad (1991) suggested that the firm's ability to coordinate resources and their use across the organizational system in order to take advantage of opportunities in different parts of the world is becoming increasingly important.

We will now continue to look at how subsidiary external embeddedness affects the possible exploitation of opportunities, to which the subsidiary cannot by itself respond due to lack of appropriate technological knowledge.

As argued in the framework of business opportunities earlier, this hinges on two important aspects; cognitive differences between the subsidiary and other parts of the corporation, and the distribution of decision-making rights. Let us begin with analysing how subsidiary external embeddedness affect cognitive differences inside the firm.

Externally embedded subsidiaries will adapt to the local environment in various ways. Close relationships to local counterparts – including institutions, local government, customers, and suppliers – will affect the unit in its activities and how it perceives itself and its surroundings. For instance, Walsh (1995) argued that individuals' experiences drawn from an information environment creates a 'knowledge structure', that is, a template with which the individual organizes and interprets his/her environment. Differences in cognitive structures within the MNC can lead to differing beliefs, values, and goals among subunits. In a study of how the technology–market linkage can create problems in innovative processes, Dougherty (1992) suggested that different parts of large organizations have different 'interpretive schemes', helping actors identify relevant issues and make sense of those issues. Essential here is that cognitive structures are not stable over time, but are formed with experience and subsequently shape experience (Schneider and Angelmar, 1993). When such interpretive schemes are not aligned between subsidiary and other parts of the organization, this will present barriers to the communication and coordination of subsidiary activities.

Perhaps the most apparent example of this is the concept of *perception gaps* in the subsidiary–HQ relation (Birkinshaw et al., 2000). Perception gaps are the difference in perceived strategic importance of the subsidiary. If the subsidiary overestimates its strategic importance, it might well choose to pursue opportunities to create new business although such activities lie beyond its function as perceived by the HQ. Such perception gaps arise as a result of three different factors: first, the differing experiences among HQ and subsidiary managers, which lead them to interpret information in different ways; second, the imperfect information flows inside the MNC; and third, the decreasing subsidiary dependence on the HQ due to the accumulation and development of its own resources, which consequently leads to an increase in the possibility that it may act freely (Birkinshaw et al., 2000).

Our second proposition relates to these cognitive differences between subsidiaries and the HQ. By interacting with, learning from, and being exposed to, different environments, tasks, and problems, subsidiaries will differ from HQ in how they perceive, and what they perceive as opportunities and problems, all of which will impede the process of gaining access to MNC resources.

Proposition 2: Related to the exploitation of business opportunities, subsidiary external embeddedness will negatively influence its access to technological knowledge from other parts of the corporation.

Essential to the subsidiary's possibility to exploit business opportunities, is the extent to which it can leverage technological knowledge from other parts of the organization. This, however, is both time and resource consuming, and is very likely to be difficult if other actors do not perceive it as a legitimate activity given the formal organizational role of the subsidiary. The greater extent to which the subsidiary may make discrete decisions on the usage of corporate resources for such activities, the easier it will be to exploit opportunities. A subsidiary with the formal role of producing at a low-cost location will likely have less easy access to technological knowledge outside its specific area of responsibility since it is not the task of this unit to engage in entrepreneurial activities. Conversely, some subsidiaries have the explicit task of creating new business and searching out new venues for profit – basically, a more explorative task. Units with such roles will be in a more favourable position to access MNC technological knowledge since this is legitimized by their formal assignment, which includes such activities. However, as pointed out by many researchers, the subsidiary role is not a once-and-for-all decided feature; it evolves over time and must not be perceived equal by all actors. Birkinshaw et al. (2000) argued that the subsidiary role actually is negotiated and jointly understood by HQ and subsidiary managers. Subsidiary evolution can also be understood in terms of its capabilities; it is determined by the HQ formal assignment, interaction with the local environment, and the initiatives taken by the subsidiary itself (Birkinshaw and Hood, 1988).

The local environment of the subsidiary has been argued to significantly influence the unit's possibility to develop and assimilate new, valuable knowledge (Frost, 2001; Malmberg et al., 1996). Subsidiary technological resources are shaped by their specific context and the subsidiary's interaction within this context, giving each subsidiary its own characteristic capabilities and competencies (Ghoshal and Bartlett, 1990; Nohria and Ghoshal, 1997). The evolution of subsidiary knowledge can take different routes; some evolve into what have been referred to as Centres of Excellence (Forsgren et al., 2000), building up skills and knowledge within its internal organization and becoming internally recognized for excellence in certain areas, while others might face depletion of their knowledge. In this process, the form and extent of interaction with business counterparts is a fundamental factor. Research on technological development in firms has shown that interaction with the surrounding network of counterparts, such as some vital customers and suppliers, is essential to technological developments and learning in business relationships (Håkansson and Waluszewski, 2002; Pennings and Harianto, 1992; von Hippel, 1988).

While Birkinshaw et al. (2000) see a subsidiary's development of its own valuable knowledge and resources as something that increases perception gaps, an increasing amount of literature emphasizes the importance of MNC recognition of such peripheral knowledge creators as a potential source of competitive advantage (Bartlett and Ghoshal, 1989; Foss and Pedersen, 2002; Gupta and Govindarajan, 1991). In order to fully capture the potential of locally developed knowledge, it is highly likely that once its existence has been recognized, HQ will work for the diffusion of this knowledge to other parts of the MNC. The outflow of knowledge from the subsidiary must, however, not be a result of fiat pressures; subsidiaries can draw benefits from such activities, for instance, through gaining intra-organizational power, and thus engaging voluntarily in knowledge diffusion (Foss and Pedersen, 2002). As the subsidiary engages increasingly in exchange of experiences, knowledge, and information with other parts of the organization, the cognitive differences between the units and the counterparts over time become less apparent. Further, subsidiaries engaging in such knowledge diffusion often hold, or come to hold, a more strategic role in the MNC network. Roth and Morrison (1992) proposed that subsidiary mandate in the MNC is positively associated with the level of subsidiary competence relative to sister-units. By holding a strategically important position, the subsidiary will have more influence in strategic decisions, such as distribution of resources, and enjoy increased mandate in the creation of new business. Subsidiary mandate is particularly important in convincing other units about the value of an opportunity – something which otherwise is likely to be very difficult since its value hardly can be judged *ex ante*. The foregoing reasoning leads us to the following proposition:

Proposition 3: Related to the exploitation of business opportunities, subsidiary strategic importance is positively related to subsidiary access to MNC resources.

In the next section, we will discuss which subsidiaries are most likely to combine market and technological knowledge.

Subsidiaries as interpreneurs

A main competitive advantage of MNCs is that they have the possibility to transfer and combine knowledge among subsidiaries (Kogut and Zander, 1992; Malnight, 1996). Since this is a more rapid process than the incremental developments occurring in the local business network, it is vital for the MNC to stimulate such activity. We have earlier emphasized that subsidiaries may act as agents of technological resources dispersed within the MNC by linking these technologies to the idiosyncratic knowledge of market situations. To capture this activity, which may result in a business opportunity, we introduce the term *interpreneurial activity*, while subsidiaries performing it are called *interpreneurs*. As illustrated in Figure 6.2, the concept of interpreneur focuses on the combination of activities in the corporate and local networks and relates to both market knowledge and technological resources.

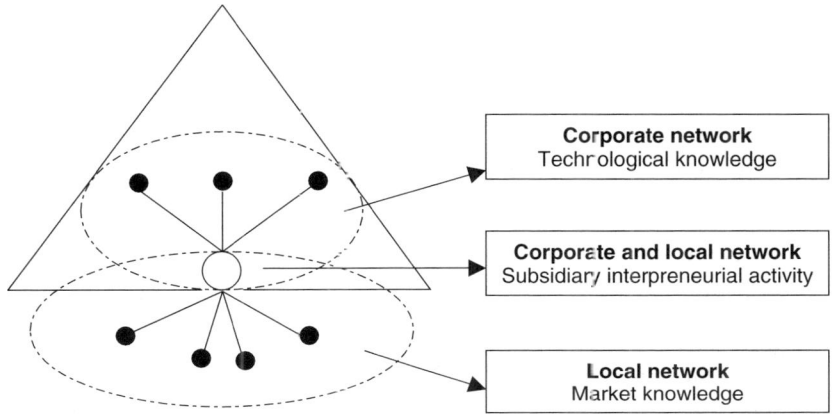

Figure 6.2 The locus of interpreneurial activity

It is likely that the further a detected opportunity falls beyond the vicinity of what can be done by the subsidiary itself, the more important it will be for the subsidiary to get access to resources from other MNC units, such as other subsidiaries, R&D units, or HQ to exploit the opportunity. Furthermore, this is also a major advantage of being part of an MNC since there is a possibility to acquire resources developed in other parts of the firm. However, we do not suggest that all subsidiaries within an MNC have these kinds of possibilities to act as interpreneurs. The question is: Which subsidiaries do?

It is nowadays generally acknowledged that subsidiaries are not satellite replicas of the HQ, exploiting home-country competences in multiple markets. Rather, they are heterogeneous, evolve over time, and have different roles (Birkinshaw and Hood, 1988). In the mid-1980s, Bartlett and Ghoshal (1987, 1989) in a number of publications suggested a transition of strategic archetypes such as the international, multidomestic, and global MNCs to what they called the transnational MNC. Another typology was introduced by Gupta and Govindarajan (1991, 1994) who made a distinction among subsidiaries in MNCs by labelling them Global Innovator, Integrated Player, Local Innovator, or Implementer, depending on the degree of inflow/outflow of knowledge. An underlying assumption in such classifications is that the different roles are *given* to the subsidiaries by HQ, based on their capabilities and the strategic importance of the local market, and that the different flows between the subsidiaries are organized by HQ. Further, the influence from external actors is not explicitly taken into consideration.

An alternative way of analysing subsidiary roles is to consider these roles to be *taken* by the subsidiaries rather than given by HQ. Birkinshaw and Hood (1988) refer to this as subsidiary choice and relate it to a network perspective. This is in line with the typology developed by Andersson and Forsgren (1995, 2002) who argue that the degree of embeddedness in the local and corporate network creates differences in knowledge and competencies among the subsidiaries. They conclude that some subsidiaries will be 'givers' while other will be 'receivers', and make a distinction between four archetypes: (1) the *external* subsidiary, which has most relationships with counterparts outside the MNC, (2) the *semi-vertical* subsidiary, in which the relationships are mainly external, but the subsidiary to some degree is corporately embedded, (3) the *vertical* subsidiary, which functions as the long arm to the parent company, and (4) the *integrated* subsidiary. According to Andersson and Forsgren, the last type, which is integrated into the MNC both on the input and the output side, is often put forward as an 'ideal'.

The typology developed by Andersson and Forsgren (2002) emphasizes that descriptions of MNCs must take both internal and external relationships into consideration. However, none of the four archetypes fully captures the main characteristic of the interpreneur – to act as a bridgehead between the corporate and local networks. The integrated subsidiary is probably too integrated into the MNC system, having close relationships with HQ and sister-units, while its external relationships are mainly 'market-like' (*ibid.*). The other three archetypes are either too externally embedded or not enough involved in the MNC.

We next discuss the consequences of local embeddedness for the interpreneurial role and assess the importance of relationships with internal counterparts.

Local embeddedness and the interpreneurial role

A subsidiary needs both novel and relevant market knowledge to detect opportunities in the local market. While a high level of external embeddedness is positively related to relevance, novelty might be insufficient if the subsidiary is over-embedded, which implies that for a subsidiary to detect market opportunities – a prerequisite for acting intrepreneurially – it must strike a balance, since too high or too low levels of external embeddedness might impede the attainment of both relevant and novel market knowledge.

However, the consequences of a too high a degree of external embeddedness can also be related to the discussion of technological resources. Several empirical studies have shown that the interaction with external actors is a key characteristic of technological development (Dosi, 1988; Håkansson, 1987; Lundvall, 1988; von Hippel, 1988). Such relationships are characterized by adaptations, stability, and incremental developments. However, while external embeddedness, with strong ties to specific actors in the local network, is advantageous for a subsidiary when it comes to technological development, this embeddedness might result in a situation where the subsidiary is 'locked-in' in its relationships with a few important counterparts. Acting on an opportunity is by definition to do something new, and if the subsidiary has many strong ties to its local network, this implies that the subsidiary is highly involved in the network and thus more constrained by this network in its actions (Hansen, 1999). So, the paradox is that while a high degree of embeddedness – with close relationships to a limited number of important counterparts – is important for the technological development in the MNC subsidiaries, too high levels of embeddedness might be counter-productive (Andersson et al., 2001; Uzzi, 1997) by isolating the subsidiaries from new influences and limiting their degrees of freedom by interlocking them into these relationships. In other words, not only is detection negatively affected (*cf.* Proposition 1) but also exploitation of new technology is constrained by the system of technological interrelatedness in which the unit exists (Cantwell, 1991). This has implications in so far as the subsidiary's possibilities of breaking into new venues of business are limited, not only by the technological competence currently within or accessible to the subsidiary, but also by the context in which it operates.

Relationships with internal counterparts

So far, we have discussed the risks of being too externally embedded. We will now turn to the importance of relationships with internal/corporate counterparts. In order for a subsidiary to be involved in interpreneurial activities, it must have access to relevant and novel market information, which can be combined with technologies dispersed in the MNC. To get access to these technologies, relationships to internal actors – HQ as well as sister-units – are important. In Proposition 3 we suggested that subsidiaries, which are of strategic importance to the MNC, are more likely to also get access to MNC resources. A main reason that some subsidiaries have a strong position within the MNC is that they have developed knowledge and resources in their local networks which other units are dependent upon (Holm and Pedersen, 2002). Since they are of vital importance for the development in the MNC, they are likely to be highly involved in relationships with several internal units.

However, it must be noted that there are often difficulties in using knowledge/technologies developed in other parts of the firm due to, for instance, stickiness (Szulanski, 1996), ambiguity (Simonin, 1999), and 'not-invented-here' syndromes (Allen, 1977). As pointed out by Forsgren *et al.* (2000), of special interest is the context-specificity of knowledge, which implies that knowledge developed in one subsidiary's local business network cannot easily be used in other business contexts of corporate units. However, it has been indicated (Andersson *et al.*, 2002) that subsidiary corporate embeddedness enhances the possibility that knowledge developed in a subsidiary through external relationships can be transferred to sister-units. As shown by them (*ibid.*, p. 992), 'the negative influence of context-specificity and the lack of motivation to participate in knowledge transfer within the MNC, which follows from being externally embedded, are counteracted by corporate embeddedness'.

To summarize, we suggest that in order for a subsidiary to be involved in interpreneurial activities and combine local market knowledge with technological resources in the MNC, it is essential to strike a balance in the degree of external embeddedness as well as a balance between external and internal embeddedness.

Concluding remarks

In the introductory chapter of this book it was put forward that the placing of opportunity development in a business network setting would shed some light on business network dynamics, that is, complement the dimensions of present and past to include a future perspective. This has been accomplished in this chapter through the discussion of the role of subsidiaries in MNCs and their importance in combining technological resources and market knowledge to detect and exploit a business opportunity. Technological development is often the result of interaction between actors in a business network, characterized by adaptations, stability, and incrementality. Market knowledge, on the other hand, is contextually bound in time and place, and this dispersed and complementary knowledge among subsidiaries, can, when combined with knowledge about technological resources, infuse change and dynamism. According to the reasoning in Chapter 1, knowledge about market and technologies, and about opportunities where the two come together, is a firm's most vital asset. Subsidiaries having access to such relevant knowledge may act as interpreneurs.

One of the implications of the arguments presented in this chapter is that opportunities cannot be systematically searched for. This is not equal to saying that the detection is a matter of luck, or chance, or that all subsidiaries will be equally likely to encounter opportunities in the course of their activities save for the factor of serendipity (Denrell *et al.*, 2003). Our arguments put the local network, and the subsidiary relationships in this network, in focus as a fundamental factor in determining subsidiary opportunity detection. When it comes to exploitation, this is a response to a certain situation in which the subsidiary finds possibilities to create new businesses and relationships. In this process, relationships with actors within the MNC are also essential, since such relationships enable subsidiaries to take advantage of resources spread throughout the MNC.

References

Allen, T. J. (1977). *Managing the Flow of Technology*, Cambridge, MA: MIT Press.
Andersson, U. and Forsgren, M. (2002). Integration in the Multinational Corporation: The Problem of Subsidiary Embeddedness, in R. McNaughton and M. Green (Eds) *Global Competition and Global Networks*, Aldershot, UK: Ashgate, 343–65.
Andersson, U. and Forsgren, M. (1996). Subsidiary Embeddedness and Control in the Multinational Corporation, *International Business Review*, 5(5), 487–508.

Andersson, U. and Forsgren, M. (1995). Using Networks to Determine Multinational Parental Control of Subsidiaries, in S. Paliwoda and J. Ryans (Eds) *International Marketing Reader*, London: Routledge, 72–87.

Andersson, U., Forsgren, M. and Holm, U. (2002). The Strategic Impact of External Networks – Subsidiary Performance and Competence Development in the Multinational Corporation, *Strategic Management Journal*, 23(11), 979–96.

Andersson, U., Forsgren, M. and Holm, U. (2001). Subsidiary Embeddedness and Competence Development in MNCs – A Multi-level Analysis, *Organization Studies*, 22(6), 1013–34.

Bartlett, C. A. and Ghoshal, S. (1987). Managing Across Borders: New Strategic Requirements, *Sloan Management Review*, 28(4), 7–16.

Bartlett, C. A. and Ghoshal, S. (1989). *Managing Across Borders: The Transnational Solution*, Boston, MA: Harvard Business School Press.

Birkinshaw, J. (1997). Entrepreneurship in Multinational Corporations: The Characteristics of Subsidiary Initiatives, *Strategic Management Journal*, 18(3), 207–29.

Birkinshaw, J., Holm, U., Thilenius, P. and Arvidsson, N. (2000). Consequences of Perception Gaps in The Headquarters–Subsidiary Relationship, *International Business Review*, 9, 321–44.

Birkinshaw, J. and Hood, N. (1988). Multinational Subsidiary Evolution: Capability and Charter Change in Foreign-Owned Subsidiary Companies, *Academy of Management Review*, 23(4), 773–95.

Burt, R. S. (1992). *Structural Holes: The Social Structure of Competition*. Cambridge, MA: Harvard University Press.

Cantwell, J. (1991). The Theory of Technological Competence and its Application to International Production, in D. G. McFetridge (Ed) *Foreign Investment, Technology and Economy Growth*, Calgary: University of Calgary Press, 33–67.

Denrell, J., Fang, C. and Winter, S. G. (2003). The Economics of Strategic Opportunity, *Strategic Management Journal*, 24(10), 977–90.

Dosi, G. (1988). The Nature of the Innovative Process, in G. Dosi, C. Freeman, R. Nelson, G. Silverberg and L. Soete (Eds) *Technical Change and Economic Theory*, London: Pinter Publishers, 221–38.

Dougherty, D. (1992). Interpretive Barriers to Successful Product Innovation in Large Firms, *Organization Science*, 3(2), 179–202.

Doz, Y. and Prahalad, C. K. (1991) Managing DMNC's: A Search for a New Paradigm, *Strategic Management Journal*, 12/Special Issue: Global Strategy (Summer, 1991), 145–64.

Eriksson, K. and Hohenthal, J. (2001). The Transferability of Knowledge in Business Network Relationships, in H. Håkansson and J. Johanson (Eds) *Business Network Learning*, Oxford: Pergamon, 91–106.

Ford, D. (1990). *Understanding Business Markets*, San Diego: Academic Press Limited.

Forsgren, M., Johanson, J. and Sharma, D. (2000). Development of MNC Centers of Excellence, in U. Holm and T. Pedersen (Eds) *The Emergence and Impact of MNC Centers of Excellence – a Subsidiary Pespective*, London: McMillan, 45–67.

Foss, N. J. (1999). The Use of Knowledge in Firms, *Journal of Institutional and Theoretical Economics*, 155(3), 458–86.

Foss, N. J. and Pedersen, T. (2002). Transferring Knowledge in MNC's: The Role of Sources of Subsidiary Knowledge and Organizational Context, *Journal of International Management*, 8(1), 49–67.

Frost, T. S. (2001). The Geographic Sources of Foreign Subsidiaries' Innovations, *Strategic Management Journal*, 22, 101–23.

Ghoshal, S. and Bartlett, C. A. (1988). Creation, Adoption, and Diffusion of Innovation of Subsidiaries of Multinational Corporations, *Journal of International Business Studies*, 19(3), 365–88.

Ghoshal, S. and Bartlett, C. A. (1990). The Multinational Corporation as an Interorganizational Network, *Academy of Management Review*, 15(4), 603–25.

Ghoshal, S. and Nohria, N. (1989). Internal Differentiation Within Multinational Corporations, *Strategic Management Journal*, 10(4), 323–37.

Granovetter, M. S. (1973). The Strength of Weak Ties, *American Journal of Sociology*, 78(6), 1360–80.

Gulati, R., Nohria, N. and Zaheer, A. (2000). Strategic Networks, *Strategic Management Journal*, 21, 203–15.

Gupta, A. K. and Govindarajan, V. (1991). Knowledge Flows and the Structure of Control within Multinational Corporations, *Academy of Management Review*, 16(4), 768–92.

Gupta, A. K. and Govindarajan, V. (1994). Organizing for Knowledge Flows within MNCs, *International Business Review*, 3(4), 443–57.

Håkansson, H. (1987). *Industrial Technological Development*, London: Routledge.

Håkansson, H. (1989). *Corporate Technological Behaviour*, London: Routledge.

Håkansson, H. and Waluszewski, A. (2002). *Managing Technological Development*, London: Routledge.

Hansen, M. T. (1999). The Search–Transfer Problem: The Role of Weak Ties in Sharing Knowledge across Organization Subunits, *Administrative Science Quarterly*, 44, 82–111.

Hayek, F. A. (1945). The Use of Knowledge in Society, *The American Economic Review*, 45(4), 519–30.

Hedlund, G. (1994). A Model of Knowledge Management and the N-Form Corporation, *Strategic Management Journal*, 15/Special Issue: Strategy: Search for New Paradigms, 73–90.

Holm, U. and Pedersen, T. (2002). *The Emergence and Impact of MNC Centres of Excellence. A Subsidiary Perspective*, London: Macmillan Press.

Johanson, J. and Mattsson, L.-G. (1987). Interorganizational Relations in Industrial Systems: A Network Approach Compared with the Transaction-cost Approach, *International Studies of Management and Organization*, 17(1), 64–74.

Kirzner, I. M. (1997). Entrepreneurial Discovery and the Competitive Market Process: An Austrian Approach, *The Journal of Economic Literature*, 35(1), 60–85.

Kogut, B. and Zander, U. (1992). Knowledge of the Firm, Combinative Capabilities, and the Replication of Technology, *Organization Science*, 3/Focused Issue: Management of Technology, 383–97.

Lorenzoni, G. and Lipparini, A. (1999). The Leveraging of Inter-Firm Relationships as a Distinctive Organizational Capability: A Longitudinal Study, *Strategic Management Journal*, 20, 317–38.

Lundvall, B.-Å. (1988). Innovation as an Interactive Process: From User–Producer Interaction to the National System of Innovation, in G. Dosi, C. Freeman, R. Nelson, G. Silverberg and L. Soete (Eds) *Technical Change and Economic Theory*, London: Pinter.

Malmberg, A., Sölvell, Ö. and Zander, I. (1996). Spatial Clustering, Local Accumulation of Knowledge and Firm Competitiveness, *Geografiska Annaler. Series B. Human Geography*, 78(2), 85–97.

Malnight, T. W. (1996). The Transition from Decentralized to Network-Based MNC Structures: An Evolutionary Perspective, *Journal of International Business Studies*, 27(1), 43–65.

Nohria, N. and Ghoshal, S. (1997). *The Differentiated Network*, San Francisco: Jossey-Bass.

Pennings, J. M. and Harianto, F. (1992). Technological Networking and Innovation Implementation, *Organization Science*, 3(3), Focused Issue: Management of Technology, 356–82.

Roth, K. and Morrison, A. J. (1992). Implementing Global Strategy: Characteristics of Global Subsidiary Mandates, *Journal of International Business Studies*, 23(4), 715–35.

Schlegelmilch, B. B. and Chini, T. C. (2003). Knowledge Transfer between Marketing Functions in Multinational Companies: A Conceptual Model, *International Business Review*, 12(2), 215–32.

Schneider, S. C. and Angelmar, R. (1993). Cognition in Organizational Analysis: Who's Minding the Store? *Organization Studies*, 14(3), 347–74.

Shane, S. (2000). Prior Knowledge and the Discovery of Entrepreneurial Opportunities, *Organization Science*, 11(4), 448–69.

Shane, S. and Venkatarman, S. (2000). The Promise of Entrepreneurship as a Field of Research, *Academy of Management Journal*, 25(1).

Simonin, B. L. (1999). Transfer of Marketing Know-How in International Strategic Alliances: An Empirical Investigation of the Role and Antecedents of Knowledge Ambiguity, *Journal of International Business Studies*, 30(3), 463–90.

Szulanski, G. (1996). Exploring Internal Stickiness: Impediments to the Transfer of Best Practice Within the Firm, *Strategic Management Journal*, 17/Special Issue: Knowledge and the Firm, 27–43

Uzzi, B. (1997). Social Structure and Competition in Interfirm Networks: The Paradox of Embeddedness, *Administrative Science Quarterly*, 42(1), 35–67.

von Hippel, E. (1988). *Sources of Innovation*, Oxford: Oxford University Press.

Walsh, J. P. (1995). Managerial and Organizational Cognition: Notes from a Trip Down Memory Lane, *Organization Science*, 6(3), 280–321.

Wiklund, J. and Shepherd, D. (2003). Knowledge-based Resources, Entrepreneurial Orientation, and the Performance of Small and Medium-sized Business, *Strategic Management Journal*, 24(13), 1307–14.

Zander, U. and Kogut, B. (1995). Knowledge and the Speed of the Transfer and Imitation of Organizational Capabilities: An Empirical Test. *Organization Science*, 6/Focused Issue: European Perspective on Organization Theory, 76–92.

7
International Experience and the Recognition of Business Opportunities in Foreign Markets – A Study of SME's International Experiences and Choice of Location

Jukka Hohenthal and Jessica Lindbergh

Introduction

International expansion of business firms has often been seen as a choice among various international investment opportunities (e.g. Young, 1989). These investment opportunities are characterised by different probability distributions of returns that are initially unknown. As the firm acts, more information about returns is gathered and the firm gains a clearer picture of the alternatives (Arrow, 1974; Radner, 1979; Radner and Rotschild, 1975). The decision maker is supposed to choose the investment opportunity with the highest expected return, unless that opportunity poses a higher risk. Risk is a variation in outcome that can be calculated and considered when deciding. There are, however, several problems with this view of optimal decision-making behaviour. For example, managers do not consider all alternatives; they tend to search in the vicinity of the current problem (Cyert and March, 1963). Moreover, people assess the same situation differently which means that risk is in the eye of the beholder.

In the internationalisation process model, Johanson and Vahlne (1977) suggest that a firm's accumulated experiential knowledge will influence its recognition of foreign business opportunities. However, detection of opportunities is hampered by the firm's initial lack of market knowledge. This perceived lack of knowledge is greater in markets that are more culturally different than the expanding firm's home market. Consequently, firms tend to enter countries they see as similar to their home market. As they gain experience they move into markets that are more culturally different.

Additionally, several authors (e.g. Eriksson *et al.*, 1997; Barkema and Vermeulen, 1998) argue that firms with international experience develop a vast stock of knowledge that the firm can utilise in subsequent operations in other foreign markets. It is suggested that internationally diversified firms create a general knowledge of how to conduct international business. Thus, these firms will have developed more relevant prior knowledge about both foreign markets and internationalisation.

There is still much disagreement about the concepts of cultural and psychic distance. Several studies claim that the concepts have lost their relevance with increasing globalisation (Nordström and Vahlne, 1992; Stöttinger and Schlegemilch, 1998). These claims require further investigation, since they fail to take into account the firm's capacity to learn to handle foreign cultures. We shall therefore divide the process into two steps, early internationalisation and further internationalisation by experienced firms. In previous studies the level of international presence has often been used as a proxy for international business knowledge (Delios and Beamish, 1999). To account for the results of experience, we shall introduce a new concept: managerial experiential knowledge. Managerial experiential knowledge is the result of both the firm's and the manager's international experience. A firm's entry into a foreign market is contingent upon identifying and acting on specific business opportunities in that market. We shall argue that a firm sees more opportunities and acts on them when it has more relevant managerial experiential knowledge. In this chapter, we regard acting on business opportunities as resource commitment within business relationships (Håkansson, 1982; Turnball and Valla, 1986; Ford, 1990) and thus, disregard temporary market transactions.

All of the above arguments suggest that experience plays an important role in the recognition of business opportunities in foreign markets. Using a sample of 494 firms from New Zealand, Denmark and Sweden, this study aims to fill a gap in the literature concerning the effect of international experience on a firm's location choice. The study attempts to clarify the relationship between international presence, managerial experiential knowledge and international business opportunities. We look at cultural differences to see if they have an impact on a firm's market selection and if a variety of international presence leads to entry into markets that are culturally different. The study is of relevance because it clarifies a number of issues in the internationalisation literature. First, it develops the cultural distance concept by testing whether cultural distance is more important during the first step abroad. Second, it introduces the concept of managerial experiential knowledge to avoid the common usage of crude experience measures as a proxy for knowledge about internationalisation. Finally, it will offer an explanation of how managerial experiential knowledge influences the discovery of new international business opportunities. We accomplish this by first discussing the first step into a new market and how a firm's international presence and development of managerial knowledge influences further steps. This is followed by development and tests of hypotheses and finally we suggest further research.

International business opportunities and cultural differences

Internationalisation can be viewed as an act of entrepreneurship (Lu and Beamish, 2001) since the firm is searching for growth opportunities by entering new markets (Lumpkin and Dess, 1996; Zahra *et al.*, 1999). To find opportunities in a foreign market the firm must have prior experience with that market. The firm would usually have more knowledge about markets that are culturally similar to its home market (Johanson and Vahlne, 1977), meaning that a firm would normally see new business opportunities in culturally similar markets first. The firm's experience is a result of prior business that often takes place within networks of long-term business relationships (Anderson and Narus, 1990; Håkansson and Johanson, 1992). Thus the experiential knowledge of the firm is a result of prior business activities conducted within a network of relatively stable business relationships.

Adding a new link to the network through a new business relationship in a new market will open up a new set of opportunities within that market for the internationalising firm. Once it has entered the new market, conducting business will reveal other potential customers (Johanson and Vahlne, 1990) while making the firm visible to other firms in that market. Before entering a new market, the firm must identify potential buyers to whom it stands a reasonable chance of making sales. To function in the foreign market the firm must transform information into knowledge through experience. The firm can thus only gain knowledge as a result of market entry. All things being equal, it is easier for a firm to enter a similar market about which it has no knowledge than a dissimilar market. Thus we must be able to categorise markets into relatively similar markets.

In international business literature the concepts of psychic distance and cultural distance are widely used to define cultural differences between countries (Shenkar, 2001). A group of researchers at Uppsala University played a crucial role in developing the concepts, and their work is usually seen as the starting point for the discussion of psychic distance (Johanson and Vahlne, 1977; Johanson and Wiedersheim-Paul, 1975; Hörnell *et al.*, 1973), though the term has been used in prior research (Beckermann, 1956; Linneman, 1966). The early articles about psychic distance (Johanson and Vahlne, 1977; Johanson and Wiedersheim-Paul, 1975; Hörnell *et al.*, 1973) focus on the firm and its knowledge of foreign countries, where a lack of such knowledge illustrates a large psychic distance. The assumption is that psychic distance influences the uncertainty in the decision-making process concerning international activities. Psychic distance is defined as 'the sum of factors preventing the flow of information from and to the market' (Johanson and Vahlne, 1977).

In the internationalisation process model (Johanson and Vahlne, 1977), psychic distance is an important variable in understanding the incremental procedure of a firm's internationalisation process. Psychic distance illustrates the problems a firm might encounter early in its entry into a foreign market. The factors preventing a firm from receiving information about a new market, that is, psychic distance, increase the uncertainty of the outcome of a firm's action. It also inhibits the firm from recognising opportunities in the foreign market due to lack of market-specific knowledge. Psychic distance is assumed to correlate with geographic distance. It is also acknowledged that two geographically close countries can differ completely from each other due to such things as political systems.

Another widespread concept in the international business literature is cultural distance. It is commonly referred to as an index composed by Kogut and Singh (1988) based on Hofstede's (1980) four cultural dimensions, 'Individualism versus Collectivism', 'Power Distance', 'Uncertainty Avoidance', and 'Masculinity versus Femininity'. By categorising countries into these dimensions, based on differences in degree of people's approach to any of the above dimensions, Hofstede presents a map where it is possible to compare countries with each other, since they reveal problems that are common to different countries but solved with different solutions (Hofstede, 1991). Hofstede defines culture as 'collective mental programming' (1980: 13), suggesting that we are conditioned by our surroundings. Culture is what we share with other members of our nation and what separates us from others. Nationality is important to individuals since it gives us a feeling of togetherness and culture is constantly reinforced in our way of acting, on both a social and a private level (Hofstede, 1983). The collective mental programming is difficult to change since people are programmed together with their fellow countrymen. Culture in itself is not constant, but since it is a collective phenomenon, which is institutionalised and reinforced over and over in our society it can only change slowly.

Ronen and Shenkar (1985) show that countries can be clustered together in more homogeneous groups and that the differences between cultural clusters are of more interest than differences between specific countries (Barkema et al., 1996; Erramilli, 1991). Using the national border as a unit of analysis assumes a national uniformity, which may ignore cultural similarities in countries with contiguous borders (Shenkar, 2001; Mariotti and Piscitello, 1994).

Despite what can be assessed as a general approval of the influence of cultural differences on a firm's behaviour, empirical results vary in international business literature concerning a firm's choice of location. Some have argued that a concept such as psychic distance is no longer relevant due to globalisation (Nordström, 1991; Stöttinger and Schlegelmilch, 1998). A number of studies failed to find support for sequentially entering into culturally distant countries (Benito and Gripsrud, 1992; Engwall and Wallenstål, 1988; Sullivan and Bauerschmidt, 1990).

When internationalising, some studies support the concept of 'cultural learning'. Erramilli (1991) found that as a firm's experience increases it becomes more geographically diversified and tends to enter countries at a greater distance from its home market. Barkema, Bell and Pennings (1996) also report that an expansion pattern, where the firm gradually enters distant cultures, is more successful due to the firm's experiential learning while internationalising. Thus, experience is argued to have an impact on the firm's location choice. This appears to be relevant at the firm level (e.g. Erramilli, 1991; Barkema *et al.*, 1996) and at the individual level, that is, management's international experience (Oviatt and McDougall, 1994; Reuber and Fischer, 1997). This suggests that experience matters and therefore we assume that the first step abroad differs from the following steps.

The first step abroad

In the firm's internationalisation process, knowledge is required about both the market and the firm (Johanson and Vahlne, 1977; Madhok, 1996, 1997). Eriksson *et al.* (1997) divided the necessary knowledge into three different types. To operate internationally the firm must have knowledge of its capability as well as resources. This is labelled internationalisation knowledge and is embedded in the routines and structure of the firm. There is also a need for market knowledge – both foreign business knowledge and foreign institutional knowledge. Foreign business knowledge is gained from experience within the business network of customers, while foreign institutional knowledge is gained from the experience of government, institutional framework, rules, norms and values. In the initial stage of internationalisation the firm's knowledge is minimal, since each type of knowledge requires an activity geared towards a foreign market (Johanson and Vahlne, 1977). Firms that are about to take their first step abroad tend to be small. Along with lacking international experience, they also lack resources to handle possible problems (Yip *et al.*, 2000). Thus, the first entry differs in nature from consecutive entries (Cavusgil, 1980; Dow, 2000; Yip *et al.*, 2000).

When firms operate in their domestic market they can rely on their lifelong experience, which is then embedded into the firms' routines (Johanson and Wiedersheim-Paul, 1975; Johanson and Vahlne, 1977). However, when firms seek new markets, they are entering unknown territory. They will encounter considerable uncertainty due to a lack of market knowledge. Therefore, it is argued, firms choose a market that appears to be similar in order to lower the perceived risk of entering the unknown market (Johanson and Vahlne, 1977; Davidson, 1980).

Following the notion of cultural learning, Barkema, Bell and Pennings (1996) found that cultural barriers impact a firm's internationalisation and that it learns from previous experience when incrementally entering cultural clusters that are different. In line with this reasoning, the empirical studies of Davidson (1980) and Erramilli (1996) show that in the initial process of internationalisation, market dissimilarity has a larger impact on a firm's market selections. We therefore claim that in the beginning of their internationalisation, firms enter markets that appear to be similar.

Hypothesis 1: The firm's first market entry is made in a market culturally similar to the home-market.

Further international expansion

Once a firm has taken the first step into a foreign market, we should expect a different path of foreign expansion. Two processes can now begin: the firm can start creating knowledge by evaluating its initial beliefs and other firms in the market see a new player. As the firm establishes a new business relationship in that market it will start to acquire experience needed to see further opportunities (Barkema *et al.*, 1996). Through business relationships, the firm will also be able to access its counterpart's business network, thus making it possible to find additional opportunities. This process is also described in the internationalisation process model, where experiential knowledge is considered a primary driving force for the growth of the firm (Penrose, 1959; Johanson and Vahlne, 1977). Shane (2000) suggests that firms need prior knowledge of markets, prior knowledge of ways to serve markets, and prior knowledge of customer problems to discover certain business opportunities. In this chapter we define this type of knowledge as managerial experiential knowledge.

Managerial experiential knowledge is the result of past experience. We learn from experience to make decisions, but learning is dependent on accurate and immediate feedback about the relationship between situational conditions and the appropriate responses. This feedback is often lacking because outcomes are commonly delayed and not easily attributable to a particular action. Most important decisions are also unique and therefore provide little opportunity for learning (Kahneman and Tversky, 1986). This means that neither length of exposure to a certain situation nor the number of situations encountered can accurately capture management's perception about how well they know something. It is not until we develop more realistic expectations through repeated exposure to relevant situations that behaviour is influenced by consequences. But when a person acts on an erroneous belief, it can also alter how others behave, thus shaping the social reality in the direction of the initially mistaken belief (Bandura, 1986: 13). The expectations the actors hold about a situation will shape their behaviour (Penrose, 1959: 41). This behaviour will lead to new encounters that make it possible to form more accurate expectations and thus better results. Thus, past experiences contribute to the development of knowledge structures and self-functions that influence current perceptions, thoughts and actions.

Managerial experiential knowledge is thus influenced by both the length of time the firm and the manager have been active in international business and the number of countries the firm has been active in. We therefore have to distinguish between firms' international presence and perceptions of that experience if we are to understand how managers act.

When a firm enters a market it will not only be able to see new opportunities, it will also be seen by other actors in that market. This increases the chances of someone else seeing the market entry as an opportunity. Within a network of business relationships firms can develop norms for acceptable behaviour and diffusion of information about behaviour (Coleman, 1990; Walker *et al.*, 1997). Once a firm has become embedded into a country, information about the firm begins to diffuse throughout that network (Granovetter, 1985). The entrant firm can benefit from its network connections, making it easier to realise opportunities as well as making it easier for other actors to see and act on perceived opportunities connected to the entrant firm.

The learning that occurs from being internationally diversified increases the firm's organisational knowledge (Madhok, 1996; Eriksson *et al.*, 1997). Routines are developed as a result of past experience (Penrose, 1959; Nelson and Winter, 1982) and experience from more situations is expected to increase knowledge (Bandura, 1986) and lead to better work performance (Levinthal and March, 1993). Firms with a greater diversity of experiences have a better ability to understand and acknowledge opportunities presented to them (Penrose, 1959). Once the firm has discovered that there is a market in the new location, much of the initial uncertainty disappears. The process of internationalisation can be viewed as a learning process (Johanson and Vahlne, 1977), where firms with international experience in several countries develop a rich stock of knowledge (Ghoshal, 1987; Barkema and Vermeulen, 1998) and learn how to handle a variety of different issues when conducting business in foreign markets (Eriksson *et al.*, 2000). In Lu and Beamish's (2001) study on prior experience of foreign direct investments and performance, the results illustrate the initial difficulties firms have with minor experiences of foreign direct investments. However, these disadvantages of foreignness (Hymer, 1976) decrease when the firms' experiences of operating in diverse countries increase. In line with the above reasoning we claim that international presence will increase managerial experiential knowledge.

Hypothesis 2: Firms with international presence have more managerial experiential knowledge.

The claim that firms learn from their own experience in international expansion is common, but tests supporting that claim are rare (cf. Barkema *et al.*, 1996; Eriksson *et al.*, 1997; Kogut and Chang, 1996). The claim that managerial experiential knowledge leads to better knowledge in dealing with foreign cultures is also common (Davidson, 1980), but to the best of our knowledge this has never been tested. We shall therefore test the claim that managerial experiential knowledge makes it easier to engage in business in culturally distant markets.

Hypothesis 3:   Firms with more managerial experiential knowledge will enter markets that are more culturally different.

The greater the level of an organisation's global business experience, the more likely its CEO will interpret the issue of foreign investment as an opportunity (Denison et al., 1996). An alternative way to regard opportunities is to see them as a chance to use the firm's knowledge and resources in a new setting (Kirzner, 1973; Schumpeter, 1949; Shane, 2000). According to Shane (2000), prior knowledge of markets, prior knowledge of ways to serve markets, and prior knowledge of customer problems will determine if a firm will discover a certain business opportunity. Seeing an opportunity is thus contingent upon having prior experience that will enable the firm to perceive something as a business opportunity. The reason for dividing it into two steps is that we need to understand the path from international presence to managerial experiential knowledge. We also need to understand whether an increase in managerial experiential knowledge leads to a firm entering culturally more different countries. If firms are to see new opportunities in foreign markets with increasing experience the whole chain is secure. International presence has to lead to more managerial experiential knowledge and more managerial experiential knowledge has to lead to entry into more distant markets. The final hypothesis is:

Hypothesis 4:   Discovery of new international business opportunities is contingent on the development of managerial experiential knowledge and managerial experiential knowledge is the result of international presence of the firm.

Sample and tests

The tests are based on a sample of 494 CEOs or managers in charge of international operations in small- and medium-sized Swedish, Danish and New Zealand firms. Firms were selected from the business directories of the three countries based on two criteria: they should have an export share of at least 10 per cent and they should have between 50 and 200 employees. The net response rate for New Zealand was 19.5 per cent, for Denmark it was 27 per cent and for Sweden 35 per cent. The average age of the firms was 55 years for the Swedish firms, 30 for the New Zealand firms, and 35 for the Danish firms. The firms had been involved in international business on an average of 35 years in Sweden, 16 years in New Zealand, and 21 years in Denmark. The average size of the firms was 110 employees in Sweden, 88 in New Zealand, and 94 in Denmark.

To study managerial experiential knowledge within a network setting, we frame knowledge development within one specific ongoing relationship, because we rely on the notion that firms internationalise by incremental expansion in specific relationships (Blankenburg-Holm *et al.*, 1996, Coviello and Munro, 1995; Chen and Chen, 1998). An ongoing customer relationship, in this context, could mean a relationship with an agent, distributor, or customer in the entry country. The term 'ongoing' indicates that the relationship is not a discreet event, but rather a part of the firm's continued and incremental market expansion in a country. We thus test the firm's real encounters with problems in a cultural setting.

Measures

Cultural distance. To capture the firms' international operations, an index similar to Ronen and Shenkar's (1985) socio-cultural clustering of countries (countries displaying similarity in religion, language and geography) was used but adapted to the context of the Danish, New Zealand and Swedish firms. The index contains 11 cultural clusters; Nordic, Germanic (including Holland), Anglo Saxon (including South Africa), Latin European (including Belgium), Eastern European, Independent (Brazil, Japan, India, Israel), Latin America, Far Eastern, Arab, Middle Eastern (Turkey, Iran, Greece), Africa. Denmark, New Zealand and Sweden respectively were excluded from the index depending on the origin of respondent. Like Barkema *et al.* (1996), we created a cultural similarity/dissimilarity scale, or a 'cultural distance' measurement according to the Ronen and Shenkar (1985) index where the focal firm's home cultural cluster receives a value of one and the cluster farthest away receives a value of 12.[1] The advantage of this measure is that it does not assume that the four factors identified by Hofstede accurately portray national culture, nor does it assume linearity, additivity or normal distribution of the factors' scores.

The cultural clustering of countries is a useful map of similarities and dissimilarities when discussing the firms' abilities to learn about institutional issues and to use this knowledge in another country. It allows us to generalise a firm's knowledge about one country to another country if they belong to the same cultural cluster (Ronen and Shenkar, 1985). As for the firms, this implies that more diversified learning occurs if the firms conduct business in countries that belong to different cultural clusters rather than operating in a number of countries that are similar to each other (Erramilli, 1991; Barkema *et al.*, 1996).

International presence. This construct contains three variables describing different types of international presence within the firm: the number of years the firm has been involved in international business, the number of countries the firm is selling to and number of years the person in charge of international activities has been conducting international business. By including both firm and individual international presence, we capture two types of international exposures that, some argue, influence a firm's internationalisation (Johanson and Vahlne, 1977; Oviatt and McDougall, 1994).

Managerial experiential knowledge. This construct captures the firm's experiential knowledge of how to manage international business and – its managerial experiential knowledge. The construct contains four variables concerning the respondents' assessment of the firm's experience with management and support of personnel abroad, development and adaptation of products, doing business with new customers and cooperation with other firms. A 7-point Likert scale was used where 1 represented low international experience and 7 represented high international experience in the various categories. Managerial experiential knowledge is measuring the actual results of the rather crude measures of international presence.

To test hypothesis 1 we looked at how many of the first international business ventures went to countries that are culturally similar to the home market. As we can see in Figure 7.1 there is a slow development towards entering markets outside the firm's own cultural cluster. But almost 70 per cent of the firms still began their internationalisation in the same cultural cluster as their home market in the last period of 1991–98 (see Figure 7.1). Countries belonging to the same cultural cluster are: for Sweden, the Nordic countries

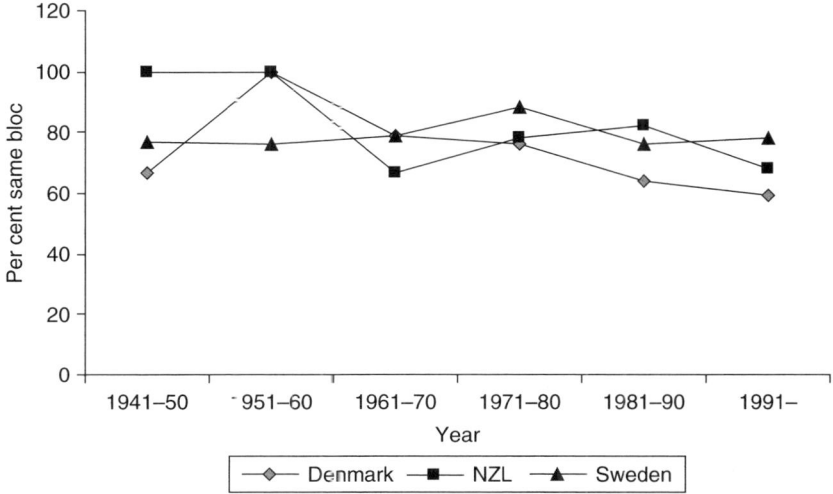

Figure 7.1 Percentage of first entries in the same cultural block as the home market

(Finland, Denmark, Norway); for Denmark, the Nordic countries and Germany; and for New Zealand, the English-speaking countries (Australia, the UK, Ireland, the USA and South Africa). So, we find support for hypothesis 1: The firm's first step abroad is in a culturally similar market to the home-market. The firm will thus experience less uncertainty in culturally similar countries and probably also discover more opportunities in these markets.

To test the second and third hypotheses we must understand the interaction between international presence, managerial experiential knowledge and cultural differences and their influence on location choice. Thus we need to understand how international presence influences the firms' managerial experiential knowledge and how managerial experiential knowledge influences the choice of cultural cluster into which the firms enter. This is done using a statistical analysis technique known as structural equations modelling. It is particularly suitable for relationships where the dependent variable in one relationship becomes the independent variable in the next relationship (Jöreskog and Sörbom, 1993). The statistical package used is LISREL. LISREL models are evaluated through two types of validity considerations: the validity of the whole model and the validity of the separate relationships in the model. The three measures used in this chapter are: (1) the GFI, which checks for sample size effect, and which should be above 0.90; (2) the RMSEA, which measures population discrepancy per degree of freedom and should be below 0.08; and (3) the CFI, checking for non-normal distributions and should exceed 0.90. To check the separate relationships we use t-values, R-square values and factor loadings. As for the separate relationships, all factor loadings are above 0.38, all t-values are above 6.24 indicating significance at the 5 per cent level and all R-square values but one are above 0.25 (see Table 7.1). The one below 0.2, a value often proposed as a cut-off (Hair et al., 2000, Sharma, 1996), is personal international presence with a loading of 0.13. Even though this value is rather low, and excluding it would make a better overall fit, we chose to retain it since it is an important part of the theory. The results in Figure 7.2 show that prior international presence affects managerial experiential knowledge (co-efficient is 0.48 and t-value is 5.76), supporting hypothesis 2. Firms with more managerial experiential knowledge enter countries that are more culturally distant, thus supporting hypothesis 3. The complete model is valid since the RMSEA is 0.074, the GFI is 0.96 and the CFI is 0.91. Thus, hypothesis 4, stating that acting on international business opportunities is contingent on the development of managerial experiential knowledge and managerial experiential knowledge is the result of international presence, is also supported. The strong results show that they hold for all three countries individually as well as for the whole group. We also tested whether firms with more international presence would enter markets that are more culturally distant without the intermediate effect of managerial experiential knowledge. We did, however, not find any significant direct effects of international presence on entry into more culturally distant markets.

Table 7.1 The indicators

Indicator	Abbreviation	Factor loading	t-value	R^2 value
Approximately which year did the firm start doing international business?	YEARAB	0.61	8.98	0.50
To approximately how many countries do you sell?	VARIAT	0.71	9.78	0.37
For how long have you been working in international business?	PERSIN	0.38	6.24	0.14
What is your firm's international experience in management and support of personnel abroad	MANEXP	0.50	n.a.	0.25
What is your firm's international experience in development and adaptation of products?	PRODEX	0.60	7.63	0.36
What is your firm's international experience in doing business with new customers?	BUSEXP	0.77	6.87	0.60
What is your firm's international experience in cooperation with other firms?	COOPEX	0.58	11.63	0.34
What country is your assignment in?	CULTDIS	1.0	n.a.	1.0

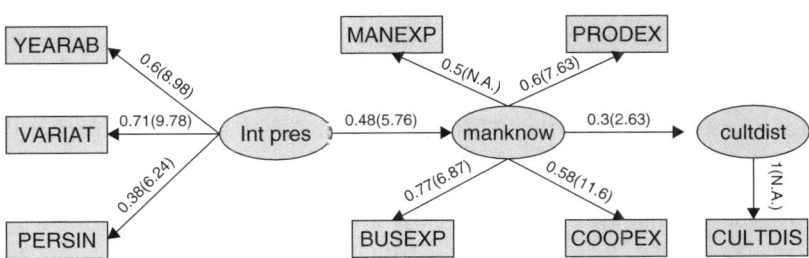

Chi-square 64.36, df = 19, RMSEA = 0.076, GFI = 0.96, AGFI = 0.93

Figure 7.2 The relationship between international presence, managerial experiential knowledge and choice of location

Results and conclusion

In this chapter, hypotheses concerning choice of location and the importance of international presence for managerial experiential knowledge development were tested using a process view on internationalisation. The study was carried out with 494 firms from Denmark, Sweden and New Zealand. Our findings support some of the basic assumptions of the Uppsala internationalisation process model, that: firms without prior international experience face uncertainty and therefore recognise and realise business opportunities in markets that are similar; international presence enhances the firms' managerial experiential knowledge; and managerial experiential knowledge impacts the firms' progress into new cultural arenas.

The results support hypothesis 1, showing that the first international business activity takes place in the same cultural cluster as the home market. Over nearly six decades more than 70 per cent of the firms had their first foreign involvement in countries similar to their home-market. Contrary to what several authors claim (e.g. Nordström and Vahlne, 1992; Stöttinger and Schlegemilch, 1998; Sullivan and Bauerschmidt, 1990) this longitudinal illustration shows that the firms' internationalisation pattern is not time bound. It also suggests that it is not specific to the Scandinavian context. In general, studies on experience and location choice focused on firms from one country (Barkema *et al.*, 1996; Erramilli, 1996; Yip *et al.*, 2000) whilst our study is based on firms from three different countries, giving us the opportunity to determine if differences in country of origin rather than experience impacts location choice.

Our results further support the idea that suitable market selection is not always based on a systematic appraisal. It is an endeavour to minimise uncertainty, as argued by the internationalisation process model, which shapes firms' behaviour. This is consistent with Yip, Biscarri and Monti's (2000) findings that firms behave in an ad hoc mode when internationalising. However, some caution is needed, since all three countries have small home markets and this may suggest that the firms have limited resources, at least in the initial stage of internationalisation. This does not undermine the fact that all the firms from the different countries display similar patterns when choosing their first international engagement. Therefore, we feel confident that concepts such as psychic distance are not out-dated (*cf.* Stöttinger and Schlegelmilch, 1998).

We also studied the relationship between international presence, managerial experiential knowledge and location choice. Firms with more international presence have more managerial experiential knowledge, and are thus capable of engaging in business that takes place in more culturally different markets than firms with little or no international presence. The results suggest that firms with international presence learn how to deal with the various management aspects required by international business relationships. Managerial experiential knowledge makes it possible to see and act on opportunities that would be considered too risky without that knowledge. The managerial experiential knowledge gained by conducting international business illustrates that firms engage in a process of cultural learning (Johanson and Vahlne, 1977; Barkema *et al.*, 1996). The results also support Penrose's (1959) argument that firms with diversified experience, in this case more international experience, benefit from prior activities as their assessment of opportunities becomes more realistic. They also have a better capability of developing their international business.

One reason why researchers have found conflicting results for the relation between experience and psychic distance (e.g. Benito and Gripsrud, 1992; Sullivan and Bauerschmidt, 1990) might very well be that these authors have failed to separate crude experience measures like international presence from the actual perception of the involved actors as to what they have experienced. The results of the overall model show that length and width of international presence does influence the perceptions of what the managers have actually experienced, but there is no perfect fit between the two. We might therefore be better off if we were to ask directly about the actors perceptions about their experience rather than to check on other crude experience measures if we are to understand firm behaviour.

We can safely conclude that firms working within a domestic network of business relationships will see opportunities first in culturally similar countries. Cultural similarity will both reduce uncertainty and make it easier to perceive business opportunities. Once the firm has established its presence in a new market, experience carrying out business in that market will make it see further opportunities while reducing uncertainty, thus making the firm act on those opportunities. Presence in a market will also presumably make it possible for local actors to see the entrant firm as an opportunity. An entrant into a new network will bring something new to that network and this idiosyncratic capability will give it a chance to expand within that new setting. Presence in several cultural settings will also increase the firm's managerial experiential knowledge in handling international business, making it possible to enter culturally dissimilar countries.

The results also show that the impact of cultural similarities/dissimilarities on firm behaviour is related to both firm experience and individual experience. Individual experience, however, is of less influence, suggesting that the formation of routines of international business activities is important for a firm's continued internationalisation. Another explanation for the internationalisation process model that does find support in this chapter is that a firm stepping into a new market connects to a new network and that this connection can be used to enhance further expansion. The firm not only increases its managerial experiential knowledge, but also its capacity to see and act on business opportunities in other countries.

Entering a new international business network will start a number of processes in the firm. First, the firm's managerial experiential knowledge will increase as it acts to realise a new international business opportunity. This action will lead to encounters with strange cultures and institutions and the possibility of learning how to adapt the firm's way of working to new situations. It will also enhance the firm's position relative to firms connected to the network. This makes it easier to realise future business opportunities. Stepping into a new market will also make the firm visible to other actors, enabling them to see new business opportunities with the entrant. A firm that is predominantly involved in domestic networks will lack managerial experiential knowledge and visibility in other countries. Beginning internationalisation in a nearby culture is often the only feasible option.

To better understand how a network can influence the choice of location, we must examine how the network in which the firm is involved enhances managerial experiential knowledge. We also need to know what types of knowledge and social capital the firm can acquire through the business network. Furthermore, we need to understand whether the personal network of the involved actors will influence knowledge flow and social capital within a network. Answering these questions would make it possible to develop a better understanding of the internationalisation process.

Note

1. We also used a condensed scale where the countries furthest away (blocs 7–12) got the same value to reflect that relatively few business engagements were carried out in these blocs and that it is difficult for the firms to distinguish between distant blocs. This did not lead to any significant changes in the resulting model.

References

Anderson, J. C., and Narus, J. A. (1990). A Model of Distributor Firm and Manufacturer Firm Working Partnerships. *Journal of Marketing*, 54, 42–58.

Arrow, K. J. (1974). *The Limits of Organization*, New York: Norton.

Bandura, A. (1986). *Social Foundations of Thought and Action*, Englewood Cliffs, NJ: Prentice-Hall.

Barkema, H. G., and Vermeulen, F. (1998). International Expansion through Start-up or Acquisition: A Learning Perspective, *Academy of Management Journal*, 41(1), 7–26.

Barkema, H. G., Bell, J. H. J., and Pennings, J. M. (1996). Foreign Entry, Cultural Barriers and Learning *Strategic Management Journal*, 17(2), 151–66.

Beckermann, W. (1956). Distance and the Pattern of Intra-European Trade, *Review of Economics and Statistics*, 38, February, 31–40.

Benito, G. R. G. and Gripsrud, G. (1992). The Expansion of Foreign Direct Investments: Discrete Rational Location Choices or a Cultural Learning Process? *Journal of International Business Studies*, 23, 461–76.

Blankenburg Holm, D., Eriksson, K. and Johanson, J. (1996). Business Networks and Cooperation in International Business Relationships, *Journal of International Business Studies*, 27(5), 1033–53.

Cavusgil, S.T. (1980). On the Internationalization Process of Firms, *European Research*, 8, 273–81.

Chen, H. and Chen, T-J. (1998). Network Linkages and Location Choice in Foreign Direct Investment, *Journal of International Business Studies*, 29(3), 445–68.
Coleman, J. (1990). Social Capital in the Creation of Human Capital, *American Journal of Sociology*, 96, S95–S120.
Coviello, N. E. and Munro, H. J. (1995). Growing the Entrepreneurial Firm. Networking for International Market Development, *European Journal of Marketing*, 29(7), 49–61.
Cyert, R. M. and March, J. G. (1963). *A Behavioural Theory of the Firm*, Englewood Cliffs, NJ: Prentice-Hall.
Davidson, W. H. (1980). The Location of Foreign Direct Investment Activity: Country Characteristics and Experience Effects, *Journal of International Business Studies*, 12(Fall), 9–22.
Delios, A. and Beamish, P. (1999). Ownership Strategy of Japanese Firms, Transactional, Institutional and Experience Influences, *Strategic Management Journal*, 20(10), 915–933.
Denison, D. R., Dutton, J. E., Kahn J. A. and Hart, S. L. (1996). Organizational Context and the Interpretation of Strategic Issues: A Note on CEOs' Interpretations of Foreign Investment, *Journal of Management Studies*, 3(4), 453–74.
Dow, D. (2000). A Note on Psychological Distance and Export Market Selection, *Journal of International Marketing*, 8(1), 51–64.
Engwall, L. and Wallenstål, M. (1988). Tit for Tat in Small Steps: The Internationalization of Swedish Banks, *Scandinavian Journal of Management*, 4(3/4), 147–55.
Eriksson, K., Johanson, J., Majkgård, A. and Sharma, D. D. (1997). Experiential Knowledge and Cost in the Internationalization Process, *Journal of International Business Studies*, 28(2), 337–60.
Eriksson, K., Johanson, J., Majkgård, A. and Sharma, D. D. (2000). Effect of Variation on Knowledge Accumulation in the Internationalization Process, *International Studies of Management and Organizations*, 30, 26–44.
Erramilli, K. M. (1991). The Experience Factor in Foreign Market Entry Behaviour of Service Firms, *Journal of International Business Studies*, 22(3), 479–501.
Erramilli, K. M. (1996). Nationality and Subsidiary Ownership Patterns in Multinational Corporations, *Journal of International Business Studies*, 26, 225–48.
Ford, D. (1990). *Understanding Business Markets: Interaction, Relationships and Networks*, San Diego: Academic Press.
Ghoshal, S. (1987). Global Strategy: An Organizing Framework, *Strategic Management Journal*, 8, 425–40.
Granovetter, M. (1985). Economic Action and Social Structure: The Problem of Embeddedness, *American Journal of Sociology*, 78, 1360–80.
Hair, J. F., Anderson, R. E., Tatham, R. L. Black, W. C. (2000). *Multivariate Data Analysis*, New York: Macmillan.
Håkansson, H. (1982). *International Marketing and Purchasing of Industrial Goods: An Interaction Approach*, Chichester: Wiley.
Håkansson, H. and Johanson, J. (1992). The Network as a Governance Structure: Interfirm Cooperation beyond Markets and Hierarchies, in G. Grabher (Ed.) *The Embedded Firm*, London: Routledge, 35–51.
Hofstede, G. (1980). *Cultures Consequences: International Differences in Work-related Values*, Beverly Hills, CA: Sage
Hofstede, G. (1983). The Cultural Relativity of Organizational Practices and Theories, *Journal of International Business Studies*, 2, 75–89.

Hofstede, G. (1991). *Cultures and Organizations: Software of the Mind*, Berkshire, England: McGraw-Hill.
Hörnell, E., Vahlne, J-E. and Wiedersheim-Paul, F. (1973). *Export and Foreign Establishments* (Export och utlandsetableringar), Stockholm: Almqvist & Wiksell.
Hymer, S. (1976). *The International Operations of National Firms: A Study of Direct Investment*, Cambridge, MA: MIT Press.
Johanson, J. and Vahlne, J-E. (1977). The Internationalization Process of the Firm – A Model of Knowledge Development and Increasing Foreign Market Commitments, *Journal of International Business Studies*, 8(1), 23–32.
Johanson, J. and Vahlne, J-E. (1990). The Mechanism of Internationalisation, *International Marketing Review*, 7(4), 11–24.
Johanson, J. and Wiedersheim-Paul, F. (1975). The Internationalization Process of the Firm – Four Swedish Cases, *Journal of Management Studies*, 12(3), 305–22.
Jöreskog, K-G. and Sörbom, D. (1993). *LISREL 8: Structural Equation Modelling with the SIMPLIS Command Language*, Hillsdale, NJ, Lawrence Erlbaum Associates Publishers.
Kirzner, I. M. (1973). *Competition and Entrepreneurship*, Chicago: University of Chicago Press.
Kogut, B. and Chang, S. J. (1996). Platform Investments and Volatile Exchange Rates: Direct Investment in the U.S. by Japanese Electronic Companies, *The Review of Economics and Statistics*, 78, 221–31.
Kogut, B. and Singh, H. (1988). The Effect of National Culture on the Choice of Entry Mode, *Journal of International Business Studies*, 19(3), 411–32.
Levinthal, D. A. and March, J. G. (1993). The Myopia of Learning, *Strategic Management Journal*, 14(8), 95–112.
Linneman, H. (1966). *An Econometric Study of International Trade Flows*, Amsterdam: North-Holland.
Lu, J. W. and Beamish, P. W. (2001). The Internationalization and Performance of SME's, *Strategic Management Journal*, 22, 565–86.
Lumpkin, G. T. and Dess, G. G. (1996). Clarifying the Entrepreneurial Orientation Construct and Linking it to Performance, *Academy of Management Review*, 21, 135–72.
Madhok, A. (1996). Know-how-, Experience- and Competition-related Considerations in Foreign Market Entry: An Exploratory Investigation, *International Business Review*, 5(4), 339–66.
Madhok, A. (1997). Cost, Value and Foreign Market Entry Mode: The Transaction and the Firm, *Strategic Management Journal*, 18(1), 39–61.
Mariotti, S. and Piscitello, L. (1994). Information Costs and Location of FDIs within the Host-country: Empirical Evidence from Italy, *Journal of International Business Studies*, 26(4), 815–41.
Nelson, R. R. and Winter, S. G. (1982). *An Evolutionary Theory of Economic Change*, Cambridge, MA: Harvard University Press.
Nordström, K. A. (1991). *The Internationalization Process of the Firm – Searching for New Patterns and Explanations*. Dissertation, Institute of International Business (IBB), Stockholm School of Economics.
Nordström, K. A. and Vahlne, J-E. (1992). Is the Globe Shrinking? Psychic Distance and the Establishment of Swedish Sales Subsidiaries during the Last 100 Years, Conference paper presented at the International Trade and Finance Association's Annual Conference, April 22–25, Laredo, Texas.
Oviatt, B. M. and McDougall, P. P. (1994). Toward a Theory of International New Ventures, *Journal of International Business Studies*, 25, 45–64.

Penrose, E. T. (1959). *The Theory of the Growth of the Firm*, Oxford: Basil Blackwell.
Radner. R. (1979). Rational Expectations Equilibrium: Generic Existence and the Information Revealed by Prices, *Econometrica*, 47, 655–78.
Radner, R. and Rotschild, M. (1975). On the Allocation Effort, *Journal of Economic Theory*, 10, 358–76.
Reuber, A. R., Fischer, E. (1997). The Influence of the Management Team's International Experience on the Internationalization Behaviours of SMEs, *Journal of International Business Studies*, 28, 807–25.
Ronen, S. and Shenkar, O. (1985). Clustering Countries on Attitudinal Dimensions: A Review and Synthesis, *Academy of Management Review*, 10, 435–54.
Schumpeter, J. A. (1949). *Change and the Entrepreneur*, Cambridge, MA: Harvard University Press.
Shane, S. (2000). Prior Knowledge and the Discovery of Entrepreneurial Opportunities, *Organization Science*, 11(4), 448–69.
Sharma, S. (1996). *Applied Multivariate Techniques*, New York: John Wiley & Son.
Shenkar, O. (2001). Cultural Distance Revisited: Towards a More Rigorous Conceptualization and Measurement of Cultural differences, *Journal of International Business Studies*, 32(3), 519–35.
Stöttinger, B. and Schlegemilch, B. B. (1998). Explaining Export Development through Psychic Distance: Enlightening or Elusive? *International Marketing Review*, 15(5), 357–72.
Sullivan, D. and Bauerschmidt, A. (1990). Incremental Internationalization: A Test of Johanson and Vahlne's Thesis, *Management International Review*, 30(1), 19–30.
Turnbull, P. W. and Valla, J.-P. (1986). *Strategies for International Industrial Marketing: The Management of Customer Relationships in European Industrial Markets*, London: Croom-Helm.
Walker, G., Kogut, B. and Shan, W. (1997). Formation of An Industry Network, *Organization Science*, 8(2), 109–25.
Yip, G. S., Biscarri, J. G. Monti J. A. (2000). The Role of the Internationalization Process in the Performance of Newly Internationalizing Firms, *Journal of International Marketing*, 8(3), 10–35.
Young, S. (1989). *International Market Entry and Development: Strategies and Management*, Hemel Hempstead: Harvester Wheatsheaf.
Zahra, S. A., Kuratko, D. F. and Jennings, D. F. (1999). Guest Editorial: Entrepreneurship and the Acquisition of Dynamic Organizational Capabilities, *Entrepreneurship Theory and Practice*, 23(3), 5–10.

8
Opportunities of Being Multinational: A Study of Organizational Rejuvenation, Relationships and Knowledge

Maria Adenfelt and Katarina Lagerström

Introduction

In the global environment of this century, numerous multinational enterprises (MNEs) across practically all industries consider the pursuit of entrepreneurial opportunities by taking entrepreneurial actions as the critical means of competitive advantage (Kuratko *et al.*, 2001). When taking place within large established enterprises, these actions are labelled *corporate entrepreneurship* (Covin and Miles, 1999; Dess *et al.*, 2003; Sharma and Chrisman, 1999).

Corporate entrepreneurship is the driving force of development of business opportunity in terms of accumulating, converting and levering resources for new product and process ventures, as well as for organizational change (Dess *et al.*, 2003). The most important resource in this context is claimed to be knowledge (Grant, 1996; Kuratko *et al.*, 2001) and consequently, management of knowledge across borders becomes an increasingly important feature.

Corporate entrepreneurship expresses itself in different forms, one of which is *organizational rejuvenation* and, in this chapter, the focus is on the outcome of such rejuvenation within an MNE. Dess *et al.* (2003) argue that research on corporate entrepreneurship can benefit from drawing upon prior network research in that MNEs' involvement in different relationships may serve as means of accessing knowledge which, in turn, is imperative in pursuing new initiatives. This suggestion is also in line with the inquiry addressed in this book, namely that business network theory might contribute to an understanding of opportunity development, as business units forming close relationships are likely to have the complementary knowledge needed for developing and exploiting future opportunities. Furthermore, we agree with Dess *et al.* (2003) that these types of inquiries benefit from the application of methodologies making it possible to identify unfolding and emergent processes.

Following the presented arguments, the purpose of this chapter is to unfold how – by its rejuvenation – the Information Systems Unit (IS-unit) at the MNC Heitz seizes the opportunities of combining and using locally developed knowledge across units. Throughout the article, we draw upon research within the rapidly growing field of corporate entrepreneurship and we integrate research on business network theory and the knowledge-based view. The theoretical section is followed by a methodology section. Then, the case study is elaborated, focusing on the rejuvenation of the IS-unit and the use of the different sub-organizational forms for spurring opportunity development. Finally, findings and implications from the study are presented.

Corporate entrepreneurship and Opportunity Development

Entrepreneurship is based on recognizing opportunities and using diverse resources to develop these for improved performance (e.g. Ardichvili *et al.*, 2003; Ventkatamaran, 1997). Eckhardt and Shane (2003: 336) define entrepreneurial opportunities as 'situations in which new goods, services, raw material, market and organizing methods can be introduced through the formation of new means, ends or means–ends relationships'. One important and complicating issue in relation to the process of opportunity recognition and development which has most likely never been done before is how to quantify and measure the outcome of the activities. Therefore, in line with Shane *et al.* (2003: 262), we propose that it is feasible to view opportunities as potentialities for profit making. However, as these potentialities have not yet been realized, measuring outcomes is neither relevant nor possible.

Before proceeding to the discussion of corporate entrepreneurship, we briefly turn to the conditions used to define entrepreneurship for the sake of clarity: 'Entrepreneurship encompasses acts of organizational creation, renewal, or innovation that occur within or outside an existing organization' (cf. Schumpeter, 1934; Sharma and Chrisman, 1999: 17; Zahra, 1993). This definition does not only reveal the importance of newness in strategy and structure, but also, and most importantly, the possible existence of entrepreneurial abilities within established enterprises. In recent years, the entrepreneurial abilities of enterprises have even become a major subject and corporate entrepreneurship is viewed as the sum of enterprise innovation, renewal and venturing beyond the ordinary activities (Sharma and Chrisman, 1999).

In the literature, four different forms of corporate entrepreneurship are discussed as opportunities for innovation and change – sustained regeneration, domain redefinition, strategic renewal and organizational rejuvenation (Covin and Miles, 1999; Dess *et al.*, 2003; Sharma and Chrisman, 1999).

Sustained regeneration is the form of corporate entrepreneurship concerned with continuous innovation, that is, a constant introduction of new products and services or entrance into new markets to capitalize on market opportunities (Covin and Miles, 1999; Dess *et al.*, 2003). The focal point of *strategic renewal* is the enterprise interaction with the external environment. The enterprise seeks to redefine its relationships with its markets or competitors by fundamentally altering how it competes (Covin and Miles, 1999). *Domain redefinition* refers to proactively creating new product market positions neither recognized nor actively sought out by competitors (Dess *et al.*, 2003).

The last corporate entrepreneurship form and the focus of this paper is *organizational rejuvenation*, which refers to efforts by the enterprise to sustain or improve its competitive position by altering internal processes, structures and capabilities. The focal point is then on the organization *per se*, which frequently entails actions for redefining operations, changing the value chain activities, or improving the possibility of implementing the enterprise strategy (Covin and Miles, 1999). Dess *et al.* (2003) argue that organizational rejuvenation today is becoming more focused on support activities such as procurement and human resource management. However, it is important to acknowledge that the four different forms often exist concurrently and that often, it is not possible to determine beforehand the outcome of entrepreneurial actions taken to recognize and develop opportunities (e.g. Covin and Miles, 1999; Shane *et al.*, 2003).

Knowledge and corporate entrepreneurship

Corporate entrepreneurship leading to the development of opportunities within established MNEs is exceptionally challenging. The challenges reside in the contradictory conditions for opportunity development. Enterprises ought to take advantage of their existing knowledge by not pursuing opportunities extending beyond their core competencies, while the pursuit of new business activities and/or renewal of strategy, which by default implies venturing beyond core competencies, is inherent in opportunity development (Floyd and Wooldridge, 1999). Nevertheless, the four forms of corporate entrepreneurship provide a foundation for the creation of different types of new knowledge which, in turn, creates the opportunity to produce new goods, new methods for production and support and for entering new markets (Eckhardt and Shane, 2003; Kuratko *et al.*, 2001). This might then lead to improved performance and/or additional corporate entrepreneurship activities. Zahra *et al.* (1999) thus claim the necessity of integrating the new knowledge, that is, making it useful throughout the organization for value-creation.

Given the importance of taking advantage of the knowledge throughout the enterprise, today's MNEs benefit from coordinating activities supporting and facilitating the creation and the sharing of knowledge from several sources, that is, both individuals and business units (Ireland *et al.*, 2001).

Furthermore, creating processes and structures within the MNE that can support the exploitation of relevant new knowledge across multiple countries has become an important competitive concern (Cohendet *et al.*, 1999).

Relationships, knowledge and corporate entrepreneurship

As an organization, the MNE consists of geographically dispersed units involved in their own sets of inter and intra-organizational relationships (Andersson *et al.*, 2002), making them differentiated and heterogeneous (Nohria and Ghoshal, 1997). Intra-organizationally, the units are linked to each other by different activities and thereto-related resource flows, thereby creating a complex and evolving system of interdependent relations (Forsgren and Johanson, 1992). Consequently, coordinating the activities and flows within the MNE is the key task for management (Gupta and Govindarajan, 1994). As mentioned above, the flow of knowledge across units is viewed as the most important one (e.g. Madhok and Phene, 2001).

A business unit in the MNE is assumed to undertake certain activities and is allocated resources accordingly. The gap between what resources a unit controls and the initiatives pursued beyond those resources is identified as opportunities (Stevenson and Jarillo, 1990). In other words, business unit initiatives can be seen as discrete, proactive undertakings that advance a new way for the enterprise of using or expanding its resources (Kanter, 1982; Miller, 1983). In turn, these initiatives are the outcome of unit-specific characteristics, shaped from interacting with different counterparts (Penrose, 1980). The networks of market- and enterprise-relationships thus serve as drivers of opportunity recognition and development (Ardichvili *et al.*, 2003). In line with Jack and Anderson (2002), we therefore argue opportunities to be contextual and that there is a need for understanding the local structures in order to understand and recognize the potential of the opportunity. Understanding and taking advantage of the overall network of relationship is even identified as the key for managers in supporting change (*cf.* McGrath and Krackhardt, 2003).

To summarize the theoretical part, corporate entrepreneurship serves as driving force of business opportunities. One form of corporate entrepreneurship is organizational rejuvenation, implying the alteration of processes, structures and capabilities to improve the competitive positions of already established MNEs. Knowledge is a key resource in achieving an advantageous position and therefore, understanding how organizational rejuvenation can improve the possibilities of exploiting knowledge across business units in the MNE becomes vital.

Research method

Considering the lack of empirical studies on corporate entrepreneurship – especially with a network approach on strategic initiatives, such as organizational rejuvenations (Covin and Miles 1999; Dess *et al.*, 2003) – a case study approach was chosen.

The MNE identified as a suitable company to study – Heitz Ltd.[1] – was conducting a reorganization with the objective of increasing the coordination among its business units. The role of information technology (IT) is important in achieving these objectives and based on that criterion, the IS-unit handling IT was considered to be appropriate. The study presented here is limited to the process of organizational rejuvenation relating to IT-activities; a limitation motivated by the fact that what is realized is often determined during the process (*cf.* Mintzberg, 1978).

Case study research can make use of different means of data collection. In the present study, the most important means was semi-structured and open-ended interviews. The data was collected through in-depth interviews lasting for two to three hours with rather broad questions that gradually became more focused as more knowledge was gained about the phenomenon studied.

The interviewees were initially selected in cooperation with the top management of the IS-unit, but later, other interviewees were contacted on our own initiative. At the time of the announcement of the reorganization, nine interviews were conducted at the IS-unit and five at IT-departments at business units in different countries. A year after the new organization had formally been implemented, there were five follow-up interviews.

In order to increase the credibility and trustworthiness of the study, the interviews were supplemented by written material. The data collection was concluded with a preliminary analysis compiled in an oral presentation at the company studied. It served as a way of establishing trustworthiness, that is, to ensure that the relevant topics had been addressed and that our results were of relevance for the study.

Organizational rejuvenation at Heitz Ltd

Heitz and IT

Heitz has developed from a traditional industrial manufacturing enterprise established in the mid-nineteenth century to an international high-technology engineering enterprise with advanced products and a world-leading position in selected areas. Already at the outset, the enterprise was active on an international basis and since then, it has steadily increased its international engagement and is today represented in more than 130 countries. Heitz claims that the explanation for its endurance is close cooperation with and adaptation to customers throughout the world and a continuous product renewal.

The enterprise is divided into three business areas and several corporate support units. Over the years, the business areas have become rather independent and self-governed with only limited inter-connections and cooperation. The support units handle finance, human resource management, and information technology (IT). The support unit handling IT – the IS-unit – is considered as particularly important, since progression within the high-technology engineering area cannot be achieved without continuous IT development and support.

Until a few years ago, there was no common policy within the enterprise concerning the choice and use of IT-solutions. The choice of IT-system and refinements and developments of existing systems were largely delegated to each business unit. Three main reasons for this policy were stated by several of the interviewees: (1) the operations of the different business units diverge and therefore, different IT-systems are necessary, (2) merged or acquired business units are given the permission to continue to use their own systems, and (3) the decentralization of the enterprise, giving the business units quite extensive decision-making rights concerning their activities. This predetermines rather large differences between the business units in the choice of IT-solutions.

Seizing opportunities by organizational rejuvenation

At Heitz, headquarters has recognized that the decentralized structure leads to the duplication of efforts in different activities such as production and development but also to large differences in working and business processes in the business units. In the last few years, headquarters has therefore expressed an increased demand on the business units to increase their coordination and take advantage of critical resources and knowledge geographically dispersed in the enterprise, just as in many other MNEs. The IS-unit is expected to play a vital role in this changing process as the possible developer of common IT-systems that can support the coordination of activities across business units. However, the duplication of efforts and differences is also evident when it comes to IT-activities in the enterprise, which implies that there is also a need for rejuvenating the organization of the IT-activities for the IS-unit to be able to develop common IT-systems.

Many of the larger business units have their own IT-department that does not only work with IT-support, but also with refinements and developments of IT-systems. In the last ten years, business units have tailored their IT-systems to suit their specific needs and demands. As described by one business unit manager: 'Our business process and our IT-system, they fit together like two pieces in a jigsaw puzzle as they have evolved slowly over time. Structure and system have been aligned with the demands of our customers.' Consequently, from an intra-organizational perspective, there are difficulties in coordinating the operations of business units and utilizing shared systems and services across borders.

The overall demand of headquarters on business units to start benefiting from the advantage of global synergies across local markets has therefore spread to the IS-unit, as articulated by one of the mangers at the unit: 'Within Heitz, there is a lot of talk about having common IT-systems as a means of using competencies across borders and thus achieving economies of scale and synergies in different activities.' Within the IS-unit, the development and implementation of common IT-systems is viewed as an opportunity and, in the longer run, as an opportunity for the whole enterprise, since it is perceived as a primary key for taking advantage of local knowledge on a global basis. Therefore, demands have been put forward to make the business units agree and unite on one common IT-system for each support process, such as sales, order-to-delivery, supply, inventory, statistics and finance. One manager at the IS-unit expresses this as: 'We have now decided to put some efforts into developing common IT-systems for the business units that are built on common business concepts, which in turn are built on common business processes. We know we need to take advantage of what has been done and used at the different business units, we have to integrate their knowledge into the common IT-system.'

The measures taken by the IS-unit to organize and handle some parts of the process relating to the development and implementation of common IT-systems across units are thus not a completely 'new' solution at Heitz. The IS-unit realized that it could actually use the experiences of prior action in the same direction within the enterprise. One manager at the IS-unit even said: 'We can learn a lot from how our worldwide-supply-system team functions. We need more competence and we need to work in a global manner; the use of organizational forms that can support this is a chance for us to be more successful when it comes to developing common IT-systems.'

The above mentioned supply team has succeeded in creating a common standard that is now in use on a worldwide basis. It thus serves as an exception from the prevailing differentiation of systems within the MNE. The especially appointed supply team, located at a business unit, performs development and maintenance of a particular IT-system. The objective of the supply team is to develop a common system and make the business units accept it. At the time of the formation of the team, each and every unit used different supply systems, which complicated their coordination. In the subsequent years, the supply team as well as the IT system have evolved. The development of the system was quite extensive at the beginning, as the business units worked differently which, in turn, affected what had to be incorporated in the system. By now, the system has become a fairly standardized product, which can be used by all units. Today, the supply team is perceived as a competence centre as it has specialized knowledge of what the system is capable of doing and an ability to approximate the needs of different business units.

Rejuvenating enterprise IT-activities

The initiative of rejuvenating the IT-activities in the enterprise with the intention of minimizing the duplication of activities and increasing coordination and knowledge sharing across business units implied a need to change the IT-activities at an overall level in the enterprise, as well as at the IS-unit. The outcome is manifested in different changes such as the use of different mechanisms and sub-organizational forms at all levels in the enterprise. One of the goals of Heitz is namely to stay at the top of the line concerning IT-activities, as that is where the business opportunities within high-technology engineering are perceived to be.

At the enterprise level, a group staff team called 'Corporate Business Development and IT' is established. The group staff consists of the CEOs of the business areas and the CEO of the IS-unit and it outlines the overall strategy for IT-activities in the enterprise and the organizational agenda for carrying it out. The agenda encompasses an outline of the strategic level in the enterprise, as well as at the operational level in the IS-unit *per se*.

Another cornerstone in the new organizational agenda is the idea of working with a global task force. The global task force – consisting of mangers from the IS-unit and managers in charge of IT at the business units – is responsible for investigating the possibilities of increased coordination and cooperation in IT-activities across business units. One of the members of the global task force perceives the role of the force as creating a more global organization: 'We know that the future is not local. It is by incorporating experiences of local units that we can develop IT- systems which enhance our competitiveness globally.' Management is thus still striving at getting a business unit perspective on how to manage enterprise IT-activities which, to some extent, is achieved by appointing managers from the business units to the global task force.

One of the main areas assigned to the global task force is to investigate how common IT-systems can be developed and used within Heitz. A related area is to locate helpdesks worldwide for providing support to the business units using the IT-systems. Previously, the general helpdesk support has been provided from one country, which is not feasible for business units located in other time zones.

However, there seems to be conflicting views between business units and headquarters on how to realize a more global organization and what the desired outcomes should be. One of the mangers at a business unit says: 'Some people at headquarters at Heitz think that globalization means centralization.' Employees at the business units are, on the other hand, perceived as trying to keep as much influence as they can by preserving as much of their own IT-solutions as possible. One of the members of the global task force tries to have a 'wider' perspective on the different views on the opportunities and implications created by the new organization for IT-activities: 'Globalization may imply to lose in some areas and win competence in other areas. Our role is to persuade, convey and mediate the essence of a global organization to the different units and how this is achieved.'

Organizational rejuvenation and knowledge utilization at the IS-unit

The organizational rejuvenation at the IS-unit largely encompasses two major changes; the merger of IT-departments into the IS-unit, and the use of sub-organizational forms for developing and maintaining common IT-systems. The decision to merge the IS-unit worldwide with the IT-departments of the largest and most progressive business units was taken by headquarters, but agreed to be an acceptable change by business units and the IS-unit. The merger is carried out by incorporating employees from the IT-departments into the IS-unit. Those employees encompassed by the merger, are still geographically located at the business units even if they, after the rejuvenation, organizationally belong to the IS-unit. The reason for this change is that this is expected to increase the potential for tapping into local knowledge sources. This, in turn, makes it possible for the IS-unit to pursue new working procedures and development activities better sensing the needs of the whole enterprise. One of the managers for example says: 'By cooperating across borders, we learn from each other and this is something we wish to emphasize more. We will hopefully in the end, as a result of us sharing our knowledge, perform our tasks in a better way and, of course, develop common IT-systems that we can all use. This in turn serves as a means of facilitating cooperation across units.'

The merger has lead to new working procedures in that the operations of the IS-unit have changed from being strictly function-oriented to becoming more competence-oriented. In the former organization, employees were assigned to operate as the direct link to different business units and handled the requests from the units independent of whether the requests were within their competence area or whether similar request were put forward by other units. This resulted in each request being treated as a unique event with a low degree of integration between them or what was going on in other business units. The competence-oriented organizational structure serves as a means of gaining synergies and increasing the likelihood of knowledge sharing. Contacts with business units are now driven by the type of IT-problem in the specific activity of a unit. This solution serves as a means of matching appropriate competencies at the IS-unit, with the needs of the business units. One top manager at the IS-unit says on this subject: 'To think in processes relating to competence is a way for us to integrate the different business units into one unity.' The main reason why this can be achieved is that the employees formerly belonging to the IT-departments at business units have a more business-related knowledge of IT-activities than those employees who have been working in the IS-unit for a long time. On the other hand, they have more technology-related knowledge of IT-activities. Many of the interviewees mention these differences, and often in a positive sense, for example, 'At the IS-unit, our strength resides in having technical knowledge but we do not know enough about the business. Those from the IT-departments, on the other hand, make a large contribution in that sense as they have in-depth knowledge of their respective business processes', or 'We from the business units can contribute with our broad business understanding on a general level. We have strong connections to those who use IT, while they have technical knowledge. This makes a good combination.' The mix of differentiated knowledge has become an important key in the IS-unit's possibility to offer the business units appropriate and coordinated IT-support.

The other major change in the IS-unit, implemented to make use of the full potentials of all employees – new and old – within the unit, but also of employees at the business units, is the use of sub-organizational forms. The management team at the IS-unit considers the use of these organizational forms, for example global IT-teams and competence centres, as an opportunity for developing common IT-systems that can be used by business units worldwide. As expressed by one manager at the IS-unit: 'For us, the reorganization has resulted in opportunities for achieving knowledge flows in new and different directions.' He continues by saying: 'The reorganization also serves as a way of developing IT-systems that can contribute to the competitiveness of the whole firm.'

The establishment of a global IT-team handling the development and implementation of an IT-system for order-and delivery serves as an example of initiatives taken in line with creating a more global organization. This team shares many similarities with the earlier mentioned IT-team responsible for developing the IT-supply system, several of the interviewees even mentioned that team as a role model.

The challenging task for the order-to-delivery global IT-team, just like for the supply team, is the development of a common IT-system that all units are willing to accept and use. Until now, the units have used their internally developed systems for handling the order-to-delivery processes. The team has members from both the IS-unit and the larger business units that are first to implement the systems, in order to create a team of members with different views and different sets of knowledge. The team members from the business units have knowledge of the system presently used at their unit, the demands of their unit's users on the new system as well as business knowledge. On the other hand, the team members from the IS-unit have a more global perspective and technical knowledge.

The management at the IS- unit also mentions that one pressing reason for using global IT- teams is that they are a means of utilizing global synergies and scale effects, as they make it possible to take advantage and combine the knowledge of different units in the enterprise. In the future, the management also considers some of the teams of employees – after the initial development and implementation of the IT-systems has been carried out – as having the potential of becoming competence centres, which is another sub-organizational form viewed as essential in the new organizational structure of the IS-unit. The intention is that these competence centres will be made responsible for further development and upgrading of the IT-systems. However, the team members themselves express doubts about the aims of their future roles. For example, one of them says: 'I really do not know where I will go on from here, or after this project, what my role is going to be in one of those competence centres.'

Thus, just as in the case of the employees at the IT-departments, the rejuvenation of the IS-unit leads to some of the global IT-team members now organizationally belonging to the IS-unit, even if they are still also located at the business units in different countries. This alteration has resulted in abundant administration for these team members in that they report their time, vacation and sick leave both to their former business unit and the IS-unit. It has also resulted in some problems in making their new roles and responsibilities known to other employees at their 'former' workplace.

The outcome of the organizational rejuvenation

The organizational rejuvenation materializing at Heitz – in particular in the IS-unit – comprises a larger and more uniform organization of IT-activities as compared to the prior outline.

The previous organization of the IT-activities between the IS-unit and individual IT-departments at large business units was due to a conviction at the business units that 'IT-activities must be closely linked to business activities ...' as expressed by one of the mangers at the IS-unit, even if the IS-unit and the IT-departments shared similar competencies and performed similar tasks. One manger with long experience of IT-activities at one of the largest business units emphasizes the significance of the enlarged mandate of the 'new' IS-unit: 'Our focus is to deliver the best solutions in IT. Although we have to have the first and last call concerning the business units' IT-strategy and choice of IT-systems and processes, we have no reason to subsist if we can't meet expectations and can do it together at a global level.'

The new competence-oriented way of working at the IS-unit enables it to re-use already developed solutions, for example in the growing area of E-business, and to capitalize on interdependencies. Solutions developed – both in the past and the present – for particular business units are adapted and used in other business units. This way of working – with the most important elements of the IT being standardized and assembled in one place – gives the IS-unit the opportunity '... to work smarter ...' as expressed by one of its managers.

'In such a large MNC as Heitz ... , there are complex causalities that have to be take into consideration' as stated by a person at the management level when describing the role of the IS-unit after the organizational rejuvenation within the MNE. It is a support unit, with no direct contacts with the external market, but to serve the business units in an efficient manner, there is a need for that particular knowledge and experience. 'Up until now, we have exclusively been reliant on business units in conveying us the business knowledge needed in performing our assignments. The reorganization serves as a possibility for us to be a step a head of the users of the IT-systems at the business units, simply by tapping into what the IT-departments worldwide know' as expressed by one of the managers at the IS-unit. This is partly accomplished in the new outline with employing people from the IT-departments at the units, and partly by the increased use of different sub-organizational forms.

One of the potential problems anticipated by the management team at the IS-units was a confusion concerning roles and responsibilities in the new organization and the understanding of these at the business units. However, in that respect, the transition has gone smoothly as concerns the business operations and the fixing of responsibility for tasks. In general, at the business units, the interviewees express opinions such as: 'We still know whom to contact at the IS-unit.' On the other hand, those employees who used to be part of the IT-departments at the business units, but who now after the rejuvenation belong to the IS-unit, have expressed concerns about the relationship between their former business units and the IS-unit. One of them says: 'I do not know what word to use to describe it … It is like a wall between us and the business unit. It is strange because the relationship used to be like a friendship, but now it is so professional and business like.' The activities performed are the same but they now belong elsewhere in the organization. This change apparently seems to have affected some intra-organizational relationships at Heitz.

To unite business units around the use of common IT-systems by implementing new common IT-systems and modifying existing IT-systems in line with the same prerequisites is another implication of the organizational rejuvenation. An important feature in developing viable common IT-systems is the ability to incorporate local needs into the solution for the final system. The possibility of being able to incorporate the individual business units' needs into the common IT-systems is built on knowledge of what their needs are. This way of trying to incorporate a major part of the needs from the outset is fairly different from how the IS-unit has previously worked.

At business units, the fear of loss of competitiveness is expressed when talking about the common IT-system instead of a continuous use of their often internally developed system: 'We lose flexibility to customers as the time for developing specific solutions will be longer with the new system.' This fear was manifested at the early stages of developing the now implemented IT-systems, when the employees working with IT at the business units tried to adapt the system to their specific beliefs of a good system, which were often in line with the system previously used. The steps away from the agreed upon solution that should be common to all business units were, however, stalled by former IT-department employees from those units who became part of the IS-unit after the rejuvenation. However, the management at the IS-unit treated the issue with somewhat more sensitivity than usual: 'How are we to encourage the spread of local ideas on how to perform business and align our business systems accordingly if we do not let local initiatives flourish?' Another manager expresses the same view: 'We can try to convince them that the new IT-systems are better for the company and therefore better for them.' A manager at one of the business units says on the same topic: 'There has been a lot of pressure on us to accept the new systems, but we have insisted on keeping our own solution. Finally, we have been convinced that the common systems will work now when our needs are incorporated at least to some extent. But to be honest I do not think we really had much choice in the end.'

The most important evidence of the organizational rejuvenation, even if doubts and concerns are expressed by both employees at the IS-unit and at business units, is that the developed common IT-systems are being implemented and used in a continuously increasing number of business units. There are even indications that they have the intended outcome, namely supporting the business units in more efficiently coordinating their activities across borders and thus, more easily meeting customer demand.

Discussion and findings

How are we to better understand organizational rejuvenation as a form of corporate entrepreneurship? What – if any – entrepreneurial opportunities do emerge in an MNE context? These questions came up in the case study on how Heitz rejuvenated by changing its internal structures and processes for IT-activities.

The overall aim at Heitz for an organizational rejuvenation was to achieve increased coordination and synergies across business units in development, production and marketing. Within the enterprise, IT is viewed as an imperative tool for realizing this as the coordination among different units as well as coherence in development processes are supported by common IT-systems. It was thus evident that the IS-unit also had to rejuvenate its organization quite drastically to be able to develop IT-systems that would be accepted and possible to use by all business units concerned. The aim of the rejuvenation at the IS-unit was partly to incorporate employees from different business units' IT-departments who possessed a different kind of knowledge than the employees at the IS-unit, partly to make it possible to use different sub-organizational forms spanning across geographical borders to tap into the local business units' knowledge. So far, the result of the 'new' organizational structure at the IS-unit is that it has managed to develop and begin the implementation of a couple of common IT-systems in business units worldwide.

The findings from the case study show that opportunity development, in this study in the form of a potential to take advantage of dispersed knowledge and use it on a global level for developing common IT-systems through acquiring employees from business units and the use of sub-organizational forms, is based on two interrelated factors.

The first factor is related to the existing *relationships* among the units in the enterprise. The direct and indirect relationships turned out to be crucial during the organizational rejuvenation processes when new ways of organizing the activities were being developed, since the new structure is the result of knowing which units and, in some cases, even which employees it was essential to incorporate to reach the intended outcome. Naturally, this process was not unproblematic either from the units' or the individuals' perspective, but it still seems as if it is slowly leading to the intended outcome.

The second factor, *knowledge combinations*, is equally important as an explicable factor for the outcome, since the relationships among units made it possible to identify that the units had different types of knowledge that needed to be combined and used for reaching the desired outcome. In this particular case, the differences in knowledge were of two different types, that is, technical knowledge and business knowledge on the one hand and local unit-specific knowledge and global common enterprise knowledge on the other. The organizational rejuvenation made it possible to integrate individuals possessing the essential business- and unit knowledge from business units into the unit possessing technical- and enterprise knowledge.

To summarize the findings of the case study, we consider that there is support for opportunity development in MNEs being dependent on relationships among business units as it makes it possible to identify the existence of different types of knowledge, which can be leveraged and combined to the benefit of numerous units for increased competitiveness of the whole enterprise. This finding is in line with the Zahra *et al.*'s (1999) argument that one of the major contributions of corporate entrepreneurship activities is the possibility to drive a knowledge creation that later becomes the foundation of the competencies from which new corporate entrepreneurial activities can emerge.

Note

1. The enterprise is anonymous at its own request.

References

Andersson, U., Forsgren, M. and Holm, U. (2002). The Strategic Impact of External Networks: Subsidiary Performance and Competence Development in the Multinational Corporation, *Strategic Management Journal*, 23(11), 979–96.

Ardichvili, A., Cardozo, R. and Ray, S. (2003). A Theory of Entrepreneurial Opportunity Identification and Development, *Journal of Business Venturing*, 18(1), 105–23.

Cohendet, P., Kern, F., Mehmanpazir, B. and Munier, F. (1999). Knowledge Coordination, Competence Creation and Integrated Networks in Globalised Firms, *Cambridge Journal of Economics*, 23(3), 225–41.
Covin, J.G. and Miles, M.P. (1999). Corporate Entrepreneurship and the Pursuit of Competitive Advantage, *Entrepreneurship Theory and Practice*, 23(3), 47–63.
Dess, G., Ireland, R., Zahra, S., Floyd, S., Janney, J. and Lane, P. (2003). Emerging Issues in Corporate Entrepreneurship, *Journal of Management*, 29(3), 351–78.
Eckhardt, J.T. and Shane, S.A. (2003). Opportunities and Entrepreneurship, *Journal of Management*, 29(3), 333–49.
Floyd, S.W. and Wooldridge, B. (1999). Knowledge Creation and Social Networks in Corporate Entrepreneurship: The Renewal of Organizational Capability, *Entrepreneurship Theory and Practice*, 23(3), 123–43.
Forsgren, M. och Johanson, J. (1992). *Managing Networks in International Business*, Philadelphia: Gordon & Breach.
Grant, R. (1996). Toward a Knowledge-Based Theory of the Firm, *Strategic Management Journal*, 17(2), 109–22.
Gupta, A.K. and Govindarajan, V. (1994). Organizing for Knowledge Flows within MNCs, *International Business Review*, 3(4), 443–57.
Ireland, R.D., Hitt, M.A., Camp, S.M. and Sexton, D.L. (2001). Integrating Entrepreneurship and Strategic Management Action to Create Firm Wealth, *Academy of Management Executive*, 15(1), 49–63.
Jack, S.L. and Anderson, A.R. (2002). The Effects of Embeddedness on the Entrepreneurial Process, *Journal of Business Venturing*, 17(5), 467–87.
Kanter, R.M. (1982). The Middle Manager as Innovator, *Harvard Business Review*, July–August, 95–105.
Kuratko D.F., Ireland, R.D. and Hornsby, J.S. (2001). Improving Performance through Entrepreneurial Actions: Acordia's Corporate Entrepreneurship Strategy, *Academy of Management Executive*, 15(4), 60–71.
Madhok, A. and Phene, A. (2001). The Co-evolution Advantage: Strategic Management Theory and the Eclectic Paradigm, *International Journal of Economics of Business*, 8(2), 243–56.
McGrath, C. and Krackhardt, D. (2003). Network Conditions for Organizational Change, *The Journal of Applied Behavioral Science*, 39(3), 324–36.
Miller, D. (1983). The Correlates of entrepreneurship in 'Three Types of Firms', *Management Science*, 29(7), 770–91.
Mintzberg, H. (1978). Patterns in Strategy Formulation, *Management Science*, 24(9), 934–48.
Nohria, N. and Ghoshal, S. (1997). *The Differentiated Network: Organizing Multinational Corporations for Value-Creation*, San Fransisco: Jossey-Bass Inc. Publishers.
Penrose, E.T. (1980). *The Theory of the Growth of the Firm*, Oxford: Basil Blackwell.
Schumpeter, J. (1934). *Capitalism, Socialism and Democracy*, New York: Harper & Row.
Shane, S., Locke, E. and Collins, C. (2003). Entrepreneurial Motivation, *Human Resources Management Review*, 13, 257–79.
Sharma, P. and Chrisman, J.J. (1999). Toward a Reconciliation of the Definitional Issues in the Field of Corporate Entrepreneurship, *Entrepreneurship Theory and Practice*, 23(3), 11–27.
Stevenson, H.H and Jarillo, J.C. (1990). A Paradigm of Entrepreneurship: Entrepreneurial Management, *Strategic Management Journal*, 11/Special Issue, 17–27.

Venkataraman, S. (1997). The Distinctive Domain of Entrepreneurship Research: An Editor's Perspective, in J. Katz and R. Brockhaus (Eds) *Advances in Entrepreneurship, Firm Emergence and Growth*, Greenwich, CT: JAI Press.

Zahra, S.A. (1993). A Conceptual Model of Entrepreneurship as Firm Behaviour: A Critique and Extension, *Entrepreneurship Theory and Practice*, 16(1), 5–21.

Zahra, S.A., Nielsen, A.P. and Bogner, W.C. (1999). Corporate Entrepreneurship, Knowledge and Competence Development, *Entrepreneurship Theory and Practice*, 23(3), 169–89.

9
Learning across the Border? Innovations, Knowledge Sharing, and Business Opportunities in MNCs

Fang Lee Cooke

Introduction

Much has been written on the importance, benefits and pitfalls of inter-organisational learning and knowledge management (KM) among networked organisations that aim to enhance their competitive advantage through complementary inter-organisational relationships and activities. These networked organisations typically include suppliers, clients and competitors who are related to each other through their involvement, often at different stages, in a certain product, service, or business process. By comparison, little attention has been given to issues related to knowledge transfer and intra/inter-organisational learning among multinational corporations (MNCs) as a specific networked organisational form. This is despite the fact that MNCs, be they in the manufacturing or service sectors, make up an increasingly large proportion of business forms in today's globalising economy. There is insufficient understanding on, for example, what MNCs do to plug into local centres of technological competence; what strategies and processes they use to co-ordinate and manage their dispersed subsidiaries across both national and organisational borders for the globalisation of locally held knowledge; and the extent to which establishment managers display corporate entrepreneurship by exploiting innovations taken place elsewhere in the MNC and turn them into business opportunities for their own establishment.

This chapter explores the strategies for identifying business opportunities and activities of knowledge sharing on innovations of product and production technology in MNCs through the in-depth case study of two plants of two multinational manufacturing firms that are based in the UK. It examines not only the formal mechanisms in place (e.g. project team, task force, steering committee) to oversee the generation and integration of corporate innovations, but also the informal organisational processes (e.g. methods and the intensity of communication) that influence the level of knowledge sharing among subsidiaries. The chapter begins by a review of literature on innovation, knowledge management and corporate entrepreneurship in MNCs. This is followed by a brief description of the study carried out and the background information of the case-study MNCs. The Finding and Discussion section provides a detailed analysis of strategies and activities of innovation and knowledge management in the two MNCs both at the corporate and plant level. It identifies a range of factors that may affect the level of knowledge sharing among different groups of workers within and between establishments in MNCs. The chapter argues that strategic knowledge management and inter-organisational learning is an important mechanism for identifying business opportunities in MNCs. The chapter concludes that a clear strategic alignment at the corporate and plant level, a high level of communication fluidity, a high level of employee involvement, and a strategic alignment of the human resource policy are necessary to enable the sharing of (tacit) knowledge and innovations held locally and turn them into wider business opportunities for the corporation.

Business innovation, knowledge management, and corporate entrepreneurship in MNCs

Two increasingly important themes have emerged in the strategic management literature: that of the knowledge-based view and that of networks and alliances for knowledge sharing. There is a general consensus in the strategic thinking that the ability for an organisation to develop and exploit knowledge faster than its competitors is a key component of its competitive advantage (Leonard-Barton, 1995; Nonaka and Takeuchi, 1995; Nonaka and Teece, 2001; Porter, 1980; Prahalad and Hamel, 1990; Teece *et al.*, 1997; Utterback, 1994). Tsang (1997) further suggests that an organisation which is quick to correct its errors and reacts quickly to environmental changes should, on average, outperform one which seldom learns from past mistakes. In addition, lessons learned in the past, if properly stored in the organisational memory, are an important source of knowledge for members of the organisation to draw upon.

Increasingly, it has been argued, innovative capacity is dependent upon building linkages through collaborative relationships (Coombs *et al.*, 1996). Writers on strategic management have accentuated the importance of embracing and exploiting externally held knowledge through organisational networks and inter-firm relationship (e.g. alliance, partnership), in a context of accelerating global competition (Castells, 1996; Child and Faulkner, 1998; Colombo, 1998; Powell *et al.*, 1996; Pucik, 1988). A network, according to Powell *et al.* (1996), 'serves as a locus of innovation because it provides timely access to knowledge and resources that are otherwise unavailable, while also testing internal expertise and learning capabilities' (p. 120). In an industrial setting of rapid technological and organisational development, the locus of innovation is often found within the networks of inter-organisational relationships that sustain a fluid and evolving community. Learning occurs within the context of membership in a community and access to a particular community may require the kinds of organisations and organisational practices that are perceived to be beneficial to that community. In a similar vein, an MNC's ability to leverage its accumulated experience to exploit geographically dispersed and idiosyncratic technological capabilities is an important dimension in its competitiveness. A fundamental challenge for MNCs is therefore how to identify and leverage capabilities that develop within their global network of subsidiaries and affiliate companies.

Gupta and Govindarajan (1991) propose that an MNC can be viewed as a three-dimensional network: that of capital flows; that of product flows; and that of knowledge flows. They suggest that an MNC can be located in one of the four positions in terms of their role in knowledge sharing (Gupta and Govindarajan, 1994). These are: global innovator (high outflow – low inflow); integrated player (high outflow – high inflow); implementor (low outflow – high inflow); and local innovator (low outflow – low inflow). It has been noted that the motivations of individual managers and units for undertaking and/or supporting knowledge flows, as well as the incentives required to underpin such actions are important to the high level of knowledge flow across organisational boundaries in the MNC.

It has also been noted that the concept of 'centre of excellence' is one mechanism that MNCs are increasingly using as 'a means of identifying and leveraging pockets of expertise found within their corporate networks' (Frost et al., 2002: 997). Lyle and Zawacki (1997: 26) define 'centres of excellence' as 'horizontal units based on related skills or disciplines' that are used to 'foster competitive competencies'. According to Frost et al. (2002: 999–1000), 'a centre of excellence is an organisational unit that embodies a set of capabilities that has been explicitly recognised by the firm as an important source of value creation, with the intention that these capabilities be leveraged by and/or disseminated to other parts of the firm'. Similarly, Moore and Birkinshaw (1998: 1) see centres of excellence as 'the focal points for knowledge development and dissemination'. In other words, the centre of excellence is seen as a form of best practice that is then disseminated throughout the firm. There is now a growing body of research evidence that suggests that the centre of excellence phenomenon is increasing among the world's major multinationals. Meanwhile, this body of evidence also suggests that many firms are struggling with the managerial issues that are related to it. Nonetheless, it is believed that more and more MNCs will adopt the centre of excellence structure as a new way of managing the corporate resources to gain competitive advantage (Frost et al., 2002).

However, this strand of literature which sees the ability to manage dispersed capabilities effectively as a key source of competitive advantage for

MNCs often ignores the difficulties in managing the knowledge transfer process across organisational boundaries. Undoubtedly, cross-boundary knowledge sharing is emerging as an important organisational feature with accelerating momentum. But this 'social progress' is not achieved in the vacuum of power and politics (Gherardi et al., 1998; Hislop et al., 2000). Furthermore, many of the studies on competitiveness tend to focus on the potential outcome of organisational learning, that is, strategic partnership for functional (e.g. core competence) and technological (e.g. R&D) complementarity at firm or industry level. They rarely get down to the micro level and behind the scene to explore how individuals in the communities shape each other's learning opportunity and outcome (Richter, 1998).

As such, there remain insufficient studies on specific organisational and managerial mechanisms through which knowledge is appropriated in MNCs. In particular, there are relatively few in-depth case studies of the ways in which people involved in knowledge transfer ventures behave, how they perceive these ventures, and whether these factors are connected to the level of knowledge transfer. The increasing popularity of the notion of knowledge management has yet failed to bring management's attention to the skills and knowledge of wider groups of workforce rather than the professional groups. For example, there is insufficient understanding of how different groups of workers involved in a given type of production technology may interact with each other for the improvisation of the production technology. If it has been noted that learning between different firms are difficult, then the sharing of knowledge can be equally as difficult in a multinational organisational setting where different establishments may belong to the same corporation but may have independent and different approach to management and cultural characteristics. As Lawrence and Lorsch (1967) observe, management practices are not universal, but dependent upon the context or environment of the firm. Contextual factors may contribute to an organisation's need or desire to utilise particular development methods and emphasis on the production technology. This is because cognitive, social, cultural, economic, and political architectures shape the perceived meanings and preferred actions at workplaces that will ultimately define performance, both at individual and organisation level. There are therefore a number of organisational and inter-organisational factors which may influence the level of knowledge sharing that can take place between organisations in an MNC network.

If knowledge sharing is an important mechanism for identifying new business opportunities in a networked business environment such as that of MNCs, then achieving a high level of communication is important for disseminating innovative ideas. In addition, it has been recognised that technological innovation and improvisation is a continuous and cross-functional process involving and integrating a growing number of different competencies inside and outside the organisational boundaries (Burns and

Stalker, 1973; Cooke, 2002; Fleck, 1987). This makes strategic knowledge management even more essential and requires a high level of corporate entrepreneurship in an MNC setting.

According to Dess et al. (2003), corporate entrepreneurship 'is concerned with various forms of newness (e.g. organisational renewal, innovation, and establishing new ventures) and has its consequences for organisational survival, growth, and performance' (p. 353). Dess et al. (2003) argue that there has been increasing evidence which suggests that corporate entrepreneurship does have an impact on organisational performance. 'From a resource-based perspective, corporate entrepreneurship is a key means of accumulating, converting, and leveraging resources for competitive purposes such as developing and using product, process, and administrative innovations to rejuvenate and redefine the firm and its markets or industries' (Dess et al. 2003: 353). In a similar vein, Stevenson and Jarillo (1990) argue that entrepreneurship should be seen as a 'mode of management' (p. 25) in large organisations that differ from traditional management. They define entrepreneurship as the pursuit of opportunity irrespective of organisational context, a focus that is akin to the classical definitions in which entrepreneurship is measured by the level of 'alertness to opportunity' (Kirzner, 1973).

Kirzner (1997) argues that entrepreneurial boldness and imagination is an important driving force in the market process and 'what constitutes that process is the series of discoveries generated by that entrepreneurial boldness and alertness' (p. 73). In other words, entrepreneurship is about opportunity discovery. As Shane (2000) argues, before technological innovations result in the process of entrepreneurial exploitation, entrepreneurs must discover opportunities in which to use the new technologies. Therefore, one of the most important consequences of corporate entrepreneurship is learning that enables the firm to develop new knowledge that renews its skills and capabilities. Entrepreneurial cognition provides important insights for understanding why entrepreneurs often see and act on opportunities that others fail to recognise. In the context of large organisations, the ability of managers to demonstrate a high level of entrepreneurship and innovativeness is a crucial factor for the success of their organisation. This is because a firm's absorptive capacity, defined by Cohen and Levinthal (1990: 128) as 'the ability to recognise external information, assimilate this information, and apply it to commercial ends', determines how successful the firm will be in obtaining entrepreneurial rents (Alvarez and Busenitz, 2001).

However, it has been pointed out that corporate entrepreneurship often fails because large organisations present environments non-conducive to creative ideas (Dess et al., 2003). Innovative proposals are often suppressed by financial control systems and other formalities that are typical of large bureaucratic organisations (Kanter, 1983). These problems may be worsened

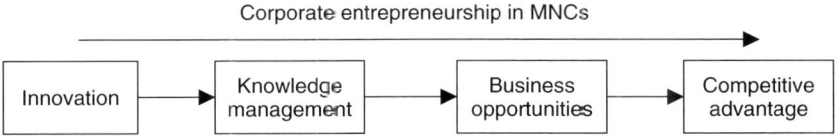

Figure 9.1 Corporate entrepreneurship: the link between innovations and business opportunities

in an MNC in which physical dispersion tends to present practical problems in learning across MNC establishments because of their heterogeneous learning needs and their heterogeneous inputs to the learning process. This creates a challenging matching problem because each establishment must commit resources to select and diffuse the right information to other establishment and avoid information congestion, since not all of their experience is applicable to other MNC establishments.

In nutshell, it is now widely recognised that strategic alliances among organisations is an important way for firms to tap into innovative ideas and turn them into business opportunities for competitive advantage. However, the achievement of this requires, among other factors, corporate entrepreneurship or managerial cognition (see Figure 9.1). The aim of this chapter is to, through the case study of two MNCs in the manufacturing industry, explore the dynamics of network relationships among establishments or subsidiaries of the MNCs and the extent to which they share knowledge and experience on similar production technology. Knowledge sharing of the innovation and improvisation of production technology in these establishments/ organisations may be a complex process, which typically involves not only individuals from different organisational positions and across organisational boundary, but also different departments and organisations related to the production technology. Thus the purpose of this chapter is to provide some insight into how knowledge transfers are perceived and managed by those involved, and the potential implications of these perceptions for innovations and business opportunities in the MNCs. It is to the case study that we now turn.

The case studies

The two MNCs (anonymised as MNC1 and MNC2 here) selected for discussion in this chapter form part of a larger study on user involvement in innovations of production technology. Empirical data were collected through a mixture of methods including semi-structured interviews with managers (both senior and middle ranking), HR personnel, supervisors and shopfloor workers, questionnaire surveys on both managers and workers, observations during site visits and analysis of company document obtained from various sources. However, it is the in-depth interviews that provide the bulk of the information drawn for the discussion in this chapter. Due to constraints of access and resources, only one plant of each MNC was studied and a small number of telephone interviews were conducted with key personnel on other plants where possible. Therefore, the discussion in this chapter draws heavily on data collected from the two plants which are both based in the UK.

The two MNCs selected here share considerable broad similarities in terms of their company history, nature of products and product markets, production processes, and global geographical spread of plants. By comparison, MNC1 is a much smaller corporation (employing approximately 4000 employees with about $1.5 billion annual turnover) than MNC2 (employing over 25,000 employees with about $5 billion annual turnover), measured by workforce size and annual turnover. Both companies have a history of over 100 years. MNC1 produces specialty chemical products that are used as ingredients for final products whereas MNC2 produces glass products for the construction and automobile industries. The nature of the products of these two MNCs are relatively simple, produced by highly automatic production technology. A dual-product market strategy is adopted by both MNCs, that is, producing both low cost products in mass volume and high quality differentiated products. Each MNC has plants in over 20 countries in the world. Each subsidiary plant of the MNC adopts relatively similar production technology and produces relatively similar products for the markets in their geographical locations. Both production processes and products are mature in these two MNCs, although both MNCs have been updating their production technology and creating new product ranges in line with innovations in their customer industries, while at the same time developing new customer bases. Both MNCs have enjoyed strong positions in the global product markets for a relatively long period of time but have encountered increasing competition in recent years. Both MNCs have had to undergo major organisational changes in recent years to adapt to the increasingly competitive global business environment. Downsizing of the workforce at the plant level and synergy integration at the corporate level have been two major initiatives adopted by both MNCs. However, trying to break away from established company traditions to meet new demands may be a tough challenge for management.

Findings and discussion

A wide range of management issues were studied in each plant in order to establish a general overview of their corporate strategies and local practices in technology management, operations management, knowledge management, and human resource management. The findings are analysed here at two levels: the strategic focus at the corporate level and the management of knowledge sharing process at the plant level (see Table 9.1).

Table 9.1 Strategies for creating business opportunities and activities of knowledge management in the case study MNCs

MNC1	MNC2
Strategies for creating business opportunities at corporate level • Alliance with customers in new business and/or product development • Website forum to harness suggestions and ideas from the public and stakeholders • Project teams at corporate level to create synergy • Internal communication forum to share best practice • Top-down approach to implementing improvement initiatives	**Strategies for creating business opportunities at corporate level** • Alliance with other producers to develop new technology and new markets • Alliance with customers in new business and/or product development • Website forum to harness suggestions and ideas from the public and stakeholders • Project teams at corporate level to create synergy • Internal communication forum to share best practice • Standardisation of production processes and benchmark plant performance across all plants • Top-down approach to implementing improvement initiatives
Management of knowledge sharing process at plant level • Senior managers adopting a pragmatic approach to knowledge transfer • Little formal communication between the management, R&D engineers and the shopfloor • Lack of awareness of shopfloor workers of channels of knowledge sharing beyond shopfloor level • Informal communications between managers and shopfloor workers on innovative ideas	**Management of knowledge sharing process at plant level** • Senior managers adopting a pragmatic approach to knowledge transfer • Top-down approach to improvement initiatives • Little formal communication between the management, R&D engineers and the shopfloor • Lack of awareness of shopfloor workers of channels of knowledge sharing beyond shopfloor level • Formal employee suggestion scheme in place to harness ideas

Strategies for creating business opportunities at corporate level

Both MNCs are found to have a clear and outward looking corporate R&D strategy. There is a strong external focus that aims to establish direct communication links between the corporation and its (potential) corporate customers and final product consumers for new business and/or product development. In other words, they use customers as innovators as a new way to create value (Thomke and von Hippel, 2002). For example, website forum is set up to tap into innovative ideas on existing products and new product range from the public and stakeholders. For MNC2, strategic technical alliance is also formed with other producers in order to promote and develop specific technology and/or gain access to new markets. The practice of creating an external network, often by taking advantage of the ICT, to harness externally held knowledge has been noted by academic writers. For example, Carlsson (2003) observes that an inter-network is a network that is designed and governed by the firm with open participation, usually facilitated by internet. It is used to gather customers' ideas and feedback on product design and innovation. Its aim is to use the external environment to create new knowledge, assimilate it and apply it to commercial ends.

Both MNCs have designated project teams at corporate level to create synergy through problem solving and/or searching for new solutions in both products and production processes. Activities of these teams also include the assessment of new and emerging technologies, which may have a longer term impact on the corporation's business or provide novel solutions to established problems connected with products or processes. These project teams, often consisting of members of different disciplinary backgrounds, are called in various names but with functions akin to that of a 'centre of excellence' as reviewed in the literature section above. Their primary objectives are twofold: developing new business opportunities through the development of new products/product markets and driving production costs down. However, more attention tends to be paid to the former than the latter, in part because the production process of both MNCs are relatively mature through constant improvisations over the decades and in part because efficiency gain may be achieved in ways that may affect workplace morale negatively. As an operations manager of MNC2 said,

> New ideas of driving production costs down invariably affect people and often in a somewhat negative way, at least for those who may be affected. For example, we have been downsizing for a number of years; we have changed the way people work to make them work more efficiently. People don't always like the changes and we have to be very careful when we introduce one. We don't do it unless we have to, and that is often driven down from the top.

Both MNCs have various internal communication channels in place to facilitate the sharing of best practices across plants. For example, an intranet forum exists in MNC1 for individual plants to publicise their innovations and for managers to look for likely solutions from sister plants to their problems (see further discussion later).

In addition, both MNCs have programmes in place to enhance plant performance. For example, MNC1 has a 'Continuous Improvement' programme, which, an operations supervisor described:

> The Continuous Improvement programme covers many areas of the business, not just around the engineering, but manufacturing and admin.

We have defined objectives, which are set by the organisation, and those objectives cascade down to achieve them, objectives. So the corporation may say, for example, we want to reduce dust in the work environment to below 1 milligram per meter cube or 3 milligram per meter cube, that will come down from the organisation to the site, the plant and the plant will build up the strategy for the next year, which is a fiscal year, they will say, in this year, we want to achieve reduction in dust, reduction in head count, improvements on down time, and so they will be objectives, and they will be cascaded down to the departmental managers and supervisors. They also further cascade down in the performance development reviews to the individuals on the ground floor.

MNC2 also standardises its production processes and benchmark plant performance across all plants on different continents. This is in addition to the constant search for synergy between the two product lines (building construction and automobile) to reduce costs. The company claims that its technical and manufacturing resources are well integrated into global programmes that identify and respond to market needs and increase the efficiency of production.

As we can see here, both MNCs are very customer oriented in an attempt to maintain and expand market share. They also tend to have a top-down approach to knowledge sharing within the corporation in order to identify new business opportunities and create synergies. Strategic focus is generally outward looking rather than inward looking that taps into employees' innovative ideas. Whereas it is crucial for firms to learn from their customers' innovative ideas and turn them into business opportunities, it is equally as important to harness that of their own employees to gain competitive advantages. However, this proves a more challenging task at the operational level.

Management of the knowledge sharing process at plant level

As discussed earlier, knowledge sharing is an important step towards identifying business opportunities in networked organisations such as MNCs. In this section, the management of knowledge sharing process at the operational (plant) level is discussed from two dimensions: (1) knowledge transfer between plants (horizontal link); and (2) knowledge management at different levels within the plant (vertical link). While there is often a clear and formal link from the corporate level to the plant level as a result of the often top-down strategic initiatives, the link between plants and between different departments within the plant appear to be much weaker and less evident (see Figure 9.2).

1. *Knowledge transfer between plants.* At the plant level, while there is a certain amount of knowledge sharing between plants, the management of knowledge sharing on innovative ideas and/or dissemination of 'best practices'

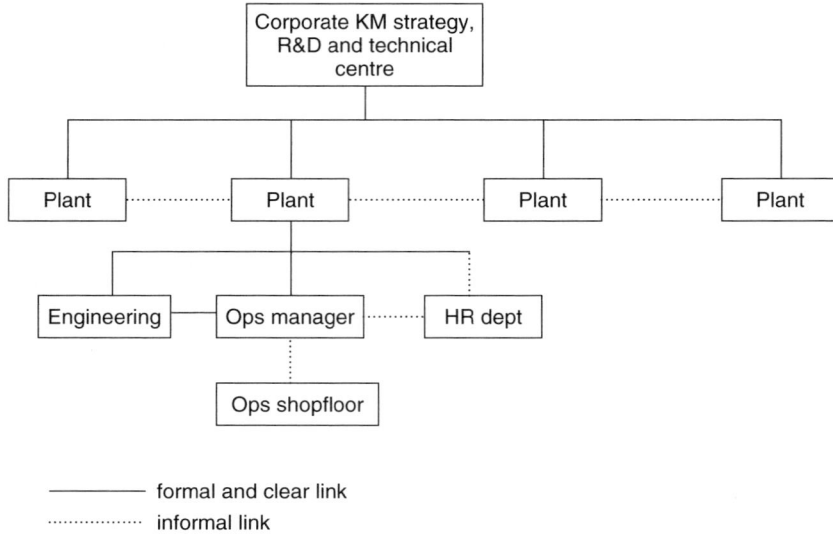

Figure 9.2 Communication links in knowledge sharing in the MNCs

appears to have taken a much more pragmatic approach by the senior managers and plant engineers. For example, the Operations Director of the plant we visited for the MNC1 case admitted that he only used the corporation's intranet forum perhaps once a month to browse through news (on innovations) and tended to look into it for solutions if there was a problem on site that he wanted to solve. However, he did not always publicise the achievement in his plant on the intranet in part because he was too busy and in part because of the difficulties in the articulation of knowledge necessary for its transfer. Instead, he might just send a brief email to the group and those who were interested could then get in touch for more information through email and/or telephone conversations and even site visits. This appears to be the practice shared by many plant managers who are the people who have access to the forum.

However, this cross-plant knowledge sharing appears to be more confined to the European plants, that is, geographically (and culturally) close plants, rather than at a global level. As an operations supervisor commented on a dust reduction project carried out site as an example of innovation and dissemination:

> [Interview question: 'Can you give me some examples about the shopfloor people coming up with ideas to improve the performance of the production equipment?']

Yeah. We have an activity in our area, which is a bulk loading activity. One of these areas where most amount of dust is reduced, so with being a directive from the organisation, they want to reduce dust, and we put a team together, and included on the team, was lads who do the bulk loading activity, and they developed a bulk loading inlay, which reduced the dust considerably, thereby, they achieved the objective of the organisation and the prototypes, all the trial work and the core idea came from the lads that do the operation.

['Was this good practice shared by the whole company?']
Yeah. What I would say is we shared it with several our sister plants in Europe, who have similar issues. Because you don't have consistency of operation in all plants, it's not applicable in all plants.

['Were they on the website or the company?']
No. I interacted it by emails. When the communication was that our plant had achieved this area in dust reduction, all the plants saw the email and they said 'we want to understand what it is' and then we started to email all the information. We didn't go on the website and say 'we have done that'. No, because the gains we make, it brings other problems also. What we don't do is to say we have got a completed solution. What we do is to say we have made a step improvement. That's what we try to do.

['Did you try to get help from other sister plants by saying, "we have the additional problem"? Have they got another step forward?']
What I did was that we had problems with magnetic protection, which picked up on metallic particles, I visited 3 of our sister plants in Europe, and looked at what issues they have, and what protection they have and when I came back, I looked at what we had and what we could do to resolve the issue. That was done by site visits.

['So this site visit enables you to improve the equipment further?']
Certainly. Improve, more understanding of what happens, because the issues I have here are not the same as we have in Spain, or Italy or Holland, they are different, because we don't have exactly the same thing, this plant is not identical to another plant. There are little differences, so you need to be tolerant of the differences that do exist, not just say that system will work in every plant because it won't.

['But you adapt the idea?']
Yes. We adapt the idea by looking at what other plants use, and say that we could use that. That will help our problem. We can't use that, because we don't do this or we do do that. It's picking up the best practice around our sister plants.

['But that's within the Europe?']
Yes. At the front end of the business, I believe it is more global than that.

The above example confirms that, as Lam (2000) argues, knowledge in MNCs is locally developed and unevenly distributed across the border and therefore, spatial proximity is important in the development and diffusion of knowledge. In addition, the similarity of the partners' basic knowledge bases, managerial commitment and interest in learning and the ability of the recipient unit to value and apply new knowledge is critical for successful knowledge transfer (Lane and Lubatkin, 1998; Szulanski, 1996) and the development of new business solutions. In this case, certain organisational context, such as the perceived geographical closeness, cultural similarity, and similarity of production technology appears to strengthen communication links between key individuals in different subsidiaries.

2. Knowledge management at different levels within the plant. In spite of the fact that both MNCs have an espoused corporate strategy of harnessing their employees' innovativeness as part of their corporate intellectual resources, for example, MNC1's corporate core values are: integrity, respect, innovation, and competitiveness, this value has not really been cascaded down to the very bottom of the organisation – the shopfloor, which may be a cradle of many innovative ideas.

Both management and shopfloor people in the two plants generally agreed that there was little formal communication between the management, R&D engineers and the shopfloor employees on knowledge management and innovations of production technology. As the Operations Director of the MNC1 plant said, 'we are a small company and it is very difficult to make everything formal. We are all on the first name terms'. Instead, most communications appear to take place on an informal basis between managers and shopfloor workers to exchange innovative ideas. As a result, there appears to be a lack of awareness, or what they called 'a lack of global view', from the shopfloor workers of channels of knowledge sharing beyond the shopfloor level, even though management tends to believe that good ideas often come from the shopfloor. In addition, there are some discrepancies between the management's perception and that of the shopfloor on what is happening, which is not unusual in most workplaces, as the interview clips with various people in the two plants reveal here.

Interview with the Deputy Operations Manager of the MNC1 plant:

['Do you think the shopfloor people have ideas that can improve the performance of the production equipment?']

Yes. The shopfloor tend to come up with ideas to make equipment easier to operate. The maintenance guys are more interested in its reliability. They all come up with little things. Something is small, and something is big. Some things are not practical. They are very expensive to implement, not worth it. Other things are very good return for a very small investment.

['Do you have any formal mechanism to harness this kind of innovative ideas?']
No.

Interview with an operations supervisor of MNC1:

['The lads, do they come up with ideas?']
Always. One of the frustrations from the lads is they don't see the speed of change quick enough. But perhaps that is because they don't have a wider understanding of the business constraints [some suggestions were not adopted because of wider cost concern].

['How involved are the shopfloor people in the innovation of production technology?']
Very. They [innovative ideas] are coming from the shopfloor, and moving up to the management hierarchy. Most of the solutions are in the heads of people, who are doing the job on the floor. It is just a way of communicating and building strategies to resolve it.

['Do you think the company has a strategy to harness this?']
We have quality teams, and we have brainstorming sessions. They are called different things, but we use different tools to bring people who can influence and have more input into solving the problems.

When a maintenance technician from MNC1 was asked,

[If you have made an improvement or innovation on the production equipment on the site, how do you make sure your sister plants know about it, or do you care, or does the company try to harness that kind of information?]

he replied:

Yeah. The company will try and harness it. Personally on the plant, we wouldn't care, I don't think, whether we tell them or not. It is not for us. So it is always the same, isn't it? Like innovation that another company's got, or another partner's got, you want that, but whether or not you try to pass it on somebody else is another thing. But as far as I am concerned, the whole of the company now shares everything they want. All new innovation comes here.

His view was shared by an operator from the same plant:

We don't have any involvement when we pass on information like that. But from what I can gather, everything now is on the database. Any improvement we have here, it is an email away. I mean you can get hold of all the information. If somebody has done one thing, then it has been put down in a database. They have done this. It has a knock-on effect on all the plants.

['So it is mainly with management?']
Yeah. It is nothing to do with us. It is the management structure that does things like that.
['But you don't have active roles, or you don't care either?']
Not really, no. Our first thoughts are for the plant. Although we know there are other parts of the company out there, as far as we are concerned, it is this plant.

Similar situation is found in MNC2.

['This kind of information is shared in this plant. Do you know what is going on on the other sites?']
No, I don't know what is happening in other plants. It is just shared in our plant. Whether the management has passed the information around different plants, I don't know. ... We just pass our information on to the groups in the warehouse. Whether the management in the warehouse come down and tell this site management and they pass on to a different area [in this plant], I have no idea (an operator of MNC2).

It becomes evident here that there is a lack of formal employee involvement other than the involvement of a few key individuals through project teams. While who are responsible for knowledge sharing is often less than clear to the shopfloor employees, there appears to be a lack of incentive for them, and to a certain extent, the management, for knowledge transfer in that barriers to knowledge sharing across plants are taken for granted and tolerated. This ambiguity, indifference, and lack of involvement is not conducive to knowledge sharing, because 'the relative network centrality of the recipient, defined as the number of communication linkages the unit has, is positively associated with transfer' (Tsai, 2001: 1002). It has also been argued that intensive integrative practices, such as cross-functional meetings and broad participation from multiple functions, further increase the chances of successful transfer (Hoopes and Postrel, 1999). The richness of communication channels has been identified as yet another factor (Gupta and Govindarajan, 2000), as is the pre-existence of social networks (Kalling, 2003) beneficial to knowledge sharing essential for creating new business opportunities.

Based on the empirical evidence, there is a need for both MNCs to strengthen their communication links both between and within the organisational boundaries, if they are to further harness the valuable knowledge held locally and tacitly on the shopfloor. As Newell *et al.* (2002) point out, knowledge is rooted in practice, action, and social relationships; knowledge exists through the interplay between the individual and the collective level. While cross-functional team working within organisation is often seen as the key to creativity and success for firms (Newell *et al.*, 2002), knowledge is produced locally in the context of application and disseminated through communities of practice and informal network. Many writers (e.g. Manwaring and Wood, 1985) have pointed out that even the most routinised jobs still demand tacit knowledge from employees. In particular, maintenance staff have been found to have more scope in contributing ideas for innovation and improvisation because of the nature of the job and the relative high level of autonomy they have in performing their tasks (Axtell *et al.*, 2000; Cooke, 2002).

In both firms, members of the project teams (centres of excellence) typically consist of individuals with high levels of education and specialist skills and with the ability to apply these skills to identify and solve problems. They are usually classified as the 'knowledge workers' at the strategic level. By contrast, the shopfloor workers are not considered as 'knowledge workers' because it is implicitly believed that their knowledge level is relatively low and not necessarily the direct innovative force of the firm. These top-down driven formal project teams stop at the engineering and managerial level with little direct involvement from the shopfloor. MNC2's maintenance technicians were particularly adamant about the need for them to be consulted when introducing technological change on the plant in order to optimise the investment. As a maintenance technician complained:

> There is a lack of communication between R&D and the maintenance function. ... We have various committees in the company. When they buy equipment, they are supposed to involve site people. But in reality, it does not happen. They just go on to buy anything they fancy. Usually we end up with a piece of kit which is not user-friendly to either the production or the maintenance. So we have to spend a lot of time ironing the problems out.

His view was supported by a production manager from the same plant:

> Maintenance people were not consulted enough. They are the ones who know the plant. They should be the first people R&D speak to.

There is a general consensus among writers on human resource management and organisational change that a bottom-up approach tends to work better when implementing management initiatives that aim to enhance employees' motivation, commitment, and innovativeness, such as quality schemes and other employee involvement schemes. However, neither of the MNCs appears to have been able to use these human resource management initiatives effectively. Instead, both MNCs have been through downsizing (MNC2 has completed it while MNC1 was still going through the process at the time of the fieldwork in the end of 2003). Both MNCs recognise that low costs are fundamental to the success in their business and their strategy is to seize every opportunity to reduce its cost base. As a result, downsizing has been the option to achieve tangible cost saving. This policy is to a certain extent incompatible with that of employee involvement and knowledge sharing. MNC2 also removed an incentive scheme which had been in place for many years in which individual employees were financially rewarded for their innovative ideas if the suggestion were adopted and achieved tangible benefits. This has acted as a demotivating factor on the shopfloor, as a maintenance technician observed,

> The company does not want to pay any more. They want to save the money. So some of the lads are not that bothered now. It was a shame. Some of the ideas were brilliant. They saved the company thousands of pounds.

As Pucik (1988) points out, with little or no reward given for contributions to the accumulation of invisible assets, learning and knowledge sharing becomes a 'hobby', not a prerequisite of the job. In a similar vein, other writers (e.g. Kanter, 1989; Nonaka, 1994; Stevenson and Jarillo, 1990) argue that creative individuals need to be supported in their endeavours and management needs to provide the necessary context for such individuals to share and create knowledge.

While MNC1's managers are doing the right thing in 'walking the floor' to communicate with the shopfloor people to listen to problems and suggestions for solutions, this practice can be applied more extensively. As Eckert (2000) observes, face-to-face interaction and close network relationships is especially important where technological innovations are incremental and where 'learning' and 'innovation' are often indistinguishable from 'normal operations'. The weakest link of MNC1, and to some extent MNC2, is the senior managers' ad hoc and pragmatic approach to the sharing of innovations across plants. A negative effect of this approach is the suppression of the propagation of business opportunities across the wider MNC corporation to generate competitive advantages.

Conclusions

This chapter has reported on the activities related to innovations and knowledge sharing as a process of developing business opportunities in two MNCs, the subjects of the case study. The study was part of a wider study on innovations in production technology that was on-going at the time when the chapter was written. The study found that both MNCs appear to have a relatively strong strategic focus on product and production innovations at the corporate level. Formal mechanisms are in place to harness innovative ideas held external to the MNCs and turn them into business opportunities.

This strategic focus, however, tends to be weakened at the plant level. In particular, communication links are not always evident between plants. Senior managers in each subsidiaries/establishment make use of the 'best practice sharing' forum on a voluntary and non-routine basis. Adoption of 'best practices' or innovations from other plants is carried out on a need-to-adopt basis, usually when there is an identified problem/area for improvement. There is less incentive (mainly because of the time constraint) for them to put their innovations and 'best practices' onto the corporate network for sharing. This suggests that learning and knowledge sharing may be a relatively low priority of local management. Similarly, communications tend to be informal between management and shopfloor level and the shopfloor workers generally lack a global view of what goes on in the corporation in terms of business innovations and best practice sharing.

In many ways, the knowledge flow, both vertical and horizontal, in these two MNCs appears to be informal rather than strategic, driven more by the specific need of problem solving in each plant than by the desire of knowledge dissemination of plant managers. There is a low level of interdependence between the subsidiaries in the two MNCs studied. There is in addition a level of conservatism or a prudent attitude among managers in adopting innovations initiated in other plants which is located in a different environment because of the perceived dissimilarities and the fear of unknown, both culturally and technically. As Shane (2000) observes, any given entrepreneur will discover only those opportunities related to his or her prior knowledge. As such, communications and knowledge sharing among subsidiary firms within an MNC may be more difficult than that among firms in a supplier-chain network involving customer and client firms, for example. This is in part because some parts of the MNCs may be geographically and culturally more distanced from each other than from external network partners (Bower, 1993), as a result of the lack of need for collaboration in their business operation. Close communications between managers of different plants in the MNC are thus necessary for transferring knowledge from one subsidiary to another to create business opportunities. As Subramaniam and Venkatraman (2001: 364) point out, 'intensive communication enables individuals to build strong ties and share their beliefs and experiences so as to transfer tacit information more effectively (Madhavan and Grover, 1998; Nonaka, 1994)'.

More broadly, the finding of this study suggests that the transfer of innovations in production technology is influenced by a number of corporate characteristics. These include the extent to which the corporate strategy can be cascaded down to the operational level; the MNC's stage of growth and level of maturity in its production technology; whether the technology is invented in-house or externally supplied; the level of interdependence between subsidiaries; the degree of communications in the network; and the perception and role of key individual players, such as the senior managers of subsidiaries.

Knowledge acquisition is a process involving various organisational levels and actors. A challenge for future empirical research is to conduct studies of knowledge management that span multiple organisational levels. The outcome of learning processes depends on the interaction of learning processes at different levels (Levinthal, 1991). To fully understand how knowledge spirals its way upward in an organisation (Nonaka, 1994), researchers need to adopt an in-depth and more nuanced approach to study the learning and knowledge sharing activities within the organisation and across organisational boundaries (Inkpen, 2000). And the study reported in this chapter is one step towards this knowledge building process. Future research also needs to examine how the processes deployed to institutionalise corporate entrepreneurship in a firm's international operations may contribute to the acquisition of new knowledge and the discovery of new business opportunities. Corporate entrepreneurship institutionalisation demands sensitivity to a number of organisational, political, and strategic issues. It also requires capturing, sharing, and integrating the knowledge the firm might have gained in its international corporate entrepreneurship activities.

It must be pointed out, however, that the two cases discussed here may not be broadly representative, since only one plant was studied in each MNC which are both based in the UK. The findings may, for example, reflect the national characteristics of the UK more than that of other countries. Furthermore, while new MNCs in the start up and early period of growth with new production technology and process may have more scope for learning and improvisation, that is when the high degree of involvement of users will yield significant benefits, the perceived need for and benefits from user involvement and knowledge sharing may be reduced as the technology approaches its maturity. Such may be the case in these two MNCs. However, it can be argued that it is equally as important, if not more so, for mature businesses to identify and develop new business opportunities in order to maintain their growth. The finding discussed in this chapter does support the wider consensus in the literature on learning and knowledge transfer in MNCs that cross-border knowledge sharing between globally dispersed MNCs seems to be limited (Yamin and Otto, 2003; Zander and Sorvell, 2000). If knowledge sharing is an important step towards developing corporate business opportunities in MNCs, then those who do not actively engage in knowledge sharing activities will miss out important opportunities. It is hoped that this chapter will make a contribution to the study and management of business innovations and knowledge sharing across organisational borders in MNCs as part of corporate entrepreneurship.

Acknowledgement

The author would like to acknowledge the Engineering and Physical Science Research Council (EPSRC) for funding the two-year research project (grant

No: GR96569) on user involvement and innovations of production technology, from which this chapter has derived.

References

Alvarez, S. and Busenitz, L. (2001). The Entrepreneurship of Resource-based Theory, *Journal of Management*, 27, 755–75.
Axtell, C., Holman, D., Unsworth, K. Wall, T., Waterson, P. and Harrington, E. (2000). Shopfloor Innovation: Facilitating the Suggestion and Implementation of Ideas, *Journal of Occupational and Organisational Psychology*, 73, 265–85.
Bower, D. (1993). New Technology Supply Networks in the Global Pharmaceutical Industry, *International Business Review*, 2(1), 83–95.
Burns, T. and Stalker, G. (1994). *The Management of Innovation*, Revised edition, Oxford: Oxford University Press.
Carlsson, S. (2003). Knowledge Managing and Knowledge Management Systems in Inter-organisational Networks, *Knowledge and Process Management*, 10,(3), 194–206.
Castells, M. (1996). *The Rise of the Network Society*, Oxford: Blackwell.
Child, J. and Faulkner, D. (1998). *Strategies of Co-operation: Managing Alliances, Networks, and Joint Ventures*, Oxford: Oxford University Press.
Cohen, W. and Levinthal, D. (1990). Absorptive Capacity: A New Perspective on Learning and Innovation, *Administrative Science Quarterly*, 35, 128–52.
Colombo, M. (1998). *The Changing Boundaries of the Firm*, New York: Routledge.
Cooke, F. L. (2002). The Important Role of Maintenance Workforce in Technological Change: A Much Neglected Aspect, *Human Relations*, 55(8), 963–88.
Coombs, R., Richards, A., Saviotti P. and Walsh V. (1996). Introduction: Technological Collaboration and Networks of Alliances in the Innovation Process, in R. Coombs, A. Richards, P. Saviotti, and V. Walsh (Eds), *Technological Collaboration: The Dynamics of Co-operation in Industrial Innovation*, Cheltenham: Edward Elgar, 1–17.
Dess, G., Ireland, R., Zahra, S., Floyd, S., Janney, J. and Lane, P. (2003). Emerging Issues in Corporate Entrepreneurship, *Journal of Management*, 39(3), 351–78.
Eckert, C. (2000). Managing Effective Communication in Knitwear Design, *The Design Journal*, 2(3), 29–42.
Fleck, J. (1987). Innofusion or Diffusation: The Nature of Technological Development in Robotics, *Department of Business Studies Working Paper*, No. 9, Edinburgh University.
Frost, T., Birkinshaw, J. and Ensign, P. (2002). Centres of Excellence in Multinational corporations, *Strategic Management Journal*, 23, 997–1018.
Gherardi, S., Nicolini, D. and Odella, F. (1998). Towards a Social Understanding of How People Learn in Organisations: The Notion of Situated Curriculum, *Management Learning*, 29(3), 273–97.
Gupta, A. and Govindarajan, V. (1991). Knowledge Flows and The Structure of Control within Multinational Corporations, *Academy of Management Review*, 16, 768–92.
Gupta, A. and Govindarajan, V. (1994). Organising for Knowledge Flows within MNCs, *International Business Review*, 3(4), 443–57.
Gupta, A. and Govindarajan, V. (2000). Knowledge Flows within Multinational Corporations, *Strategic Management Journal*, 21, 473–96.
Hislop, D., Newell, S., Scarbrough, H. and Swan, J. (2000). Networks, Knowledge and Power: Decision making, Politics and the Process of Innovation, *Technology Analysis and Strategic Management*, 12(3), 399–411.

Hoopes, D. and Postrel, S. (1999). Shared Knowledge, 'Glitches', and Product Development Performance, *Strategic Management Journal*, 20, 837–65.

Inkpen, A. (2000). Learning through Joint Ventures: A Framework of Knowledge Acquisition, *Journal of Management Studies*, 37(7), 1019–43.

Kalling, T. (2003). Organisation – Internal Transfer of Knowledge and the Role of Motivation: A Qualitative Case Study, *Knowledge and Process Management*, 10(2), 115–26.

Kanter, R. (1983). *The Change Masters*, New York: Simon and Schuster.

Kanter, R. (1989). The New Managerial Work, *Harvard Business Review*, November-December, 85–92.

Kirzner, I. (1973). *Competition and Entrepreneurship*, Chicago, IL: University of Chicago Press.

Kirzner, I. (1997). Entrepreneurial Discovery and The Competitive Market Process: An Austrian Approach, *Journal of Economic Literature*, 35(1), 60–85.

Lam, A. (2000). Tacit Knowledge, Organisational Learning and Societal Institutions: An Integrated Framework, *Organisation Studies*, 21(3), 487–513.

Lane, P. and Lubatkin, M. (1998). Relative Absorptive Capacity and Interorganisational Learning, *Strategic Management Journal*, 19, 461–77.

Lawrence, P. and Lorsch, J. (1967). *Organisation and Environment*, Boston: Harvard.

Leonard-Barton, D. (1995). *Wellsprings of Knowledge: Building and Sustaining Sources of Innovation*. Boston, MA: Harvard University Press.

Levinthal, D. (1991). Organisational Adaptation and Environmental Selection – Inter-related Processes of Change, *Organisation Science*, 2, 140–5.

Lyle, S. W. and Zawacki, R. A. (1997). Centre of Excellence: Empowering People to Manage Change, *Information Systems Management*, Winter, 26–9.

Madhavan, R. and Grover, R. (1998). From Embedded Knowledge to Embodied Knowledge: New Product Development as Knowledge Management, *Journal of Marketing*, 62(4), 1–12.

Manwaring, T. and Wood, S. (1985). The Ghost in the Labour Process, in D. Knights, H. Willmott and D. Collinson (Eds), *Job Redesign: Critical Perspectives on the Labour Process*, Farnborough: Gower.

Moore, K. and Birkinshaw, J. (1998). Managing Knowledge in Global Service Firms: Centres of Excellence, *Academy of Management Executive*, 12(4), 81–92.

Newell, S., Robertson, M., Scarbrough, H. and Swan, J. (2002). *Managing Knowledge Work*, Basingstoke: Palgrave.

Nonaka, I. (1994). A Dynamic Theory of Organisational Knowledge Creation, *Organisation Science*, 5(1), 14–37.

Nonaka, I. and Takeuchi, H. (1995). *The Knowledge-Creating Company*, New York: Oxford University Press.

Nonaka, I. and Teece, D. (Eds) (2001). *Managing Industrial Knowledge: Creation, Transfer and Utilisation*, London: Sage Publications.

Porter, M. (1980). *Competitive Strategy*, US: Free Press.

Powell, W., Koput, K. and Smith-Doerr, L. (1996). Interorganizational Collaboration and the Locus of Innovation: Networks of Learning in Biotechnology, *Administrative Science Quarterly*, 41(1), 116–45.

Prahalad, C. K. and Hamel, G. (1990). The Core Competence of the Corporation, *Harvard Business Review*, May-June, 79–91.

Pucik, V. (1988). Strategic Alliances with Japanese: Implications for Human Resource Management, in F. J. Contractor and P. Lorange (Eds), *Co-operative Strategies in International Business*, New York: Lexington Books, 487–98.

Richter, I. (1998). Individual and Organizational Learning at the Executive Level: Towards A Research Agenda, *Management Learning*, 29(3), 299–316.
Shane, S. (2000). Prior Knowledge and the Discovery of Entrepreneurial Opportunities, *Organisation Science*, 11(4), 448–69.
Stevenson, H. and Jarillo, J. (1990). A Paradigm of Entrepreneurship: Entrepreneurial Management, *Strategic Management Journal*, Summer Special Issue, 11, 17–27.
Subramaniam, M. and Venkatraman, N. (2001). Determinants of Transnational New Product Development Capability: Testing the Influence of Transferring and Deploying Tacit Overseas Knowledge, *Strategic Management Journal*, 22, 359–78.
Szulanski, G. (1996). Exploring Internal Stickiness: Impediments to the Transfer of Best Practice within the Firm, *Strategic Management Journal*, 17, 27–43.
Teece, D. J., Pisano, G. and Shuen, A. (1997). Dynamic Capabilities and Strategic Management, *Strategic Management Journal*, 18, 509–33.
Thomke, S. and von Hippel, E. (2002). Customers as Innovators: A New Way to Create Value, *Harvard Business Review*, April, 5–11.
Tsai, W. (2001). Knowledge Transfer in Intraorganisational Networks: Effects of Network Position and Absorptive Capacity on Business Unit Innovation and Performance, *Academy of Management Journal*, 44(5), 996–1004.
Tsang, E. (1997). Organizational Learning and the Learning Organization: A Dichotomy between Descriptive and Prescriptive Research, *Human Relations*, 50(1), 73–89.
Utterback, J. M. (1994). *Mastering the Dynamics of Innovation: How Companies Can Seize Opportunities in the Face of Technological Change*, Boston, MA: Harvard Business School Press.
Yamin, M. and Otto, J. (2003). Patterns of Knowledge Flows and MNE Innovative Performance, a paper presented in the International Business Research Centre seminar workshop series, Manchester School of Management, UMIST, UK.
Zander, I. and Sorvell, O. (2000). Cross-border Innovation in the Multinational Corporation, *International Studies of Management and Organisation*, 30, 44–67.

10
Network Opportunities and Obstacles in Mergers and Acquisitions: The Role of Resource Embeddedness

Enrico Baraldi and Torkel Strömsten

Introduction

Firms engage in mergers and acquisitions (M&As) in order to exploit and realise profit opportunities (Kirzner, 1997). According to the literature on M&As, these opportunities can implicitly be divided into *firm-related* opportunities and *industry-related* opportunities. Firm-related opportunities are concerned with exploiting managerial synergies, such as redundant functions or activities once two firms have merged (Sudarsanam et al., 1996). Industry-related opportunities concern the positive effects that a firm can obtain by changing or stabilising the structure of its industry: for example, taking over a firm producing a hostile substitute product (Porter, 1980, 1985).

A problem for many merging firms is that the *value* that the merger is supposed to create is seldom realised (e.g. Bild, 1998). But, in spite of this, M&As are a common strategic path for many firms (Caves, 1989; Goldberg, 1983; Larsson and Finkelstein, 1999). The reasons for the failure to create value can be searched within the merging firms, or in the structures of the industries in which they operate. But there are certainly other types of explanations of why M&As fail to deliver value. An issue that has been largely ignored within the M&A research is the merging firms' *business network* context (Anderson et al., 1994; Anderson et al., 2003; Havila and Salmi, 2002). The business network can in fact hide risks and obstacles that can impede the realisation of the M&A opportunities expected at the firm or industry level. But more important perhaps, in the network there are opportunities that the bidding firm might be able to take advantage of only if it has an ability to 'read' the network of the target firm and the heterogeneous resources that are included in this network.

Accordingly, the interaction among heterogeneous resources in the target's business network can create both obstacles and opportunities for a bidder. Resource heterogeneity (Penrose, 1959) suggests that the value of a resource varies depending on which specific other resources it is combined with across a whole network of firms. This view clearly differs from the idea that the resources involved in an M&A are made more or less valuable by their exposure to generalised 'competitive forces' in an industry (Porter, 1980) or by knowing more about a firm's internal 'complex resources' (Denrell et al., 2003). As knowledge about resources is sketchy due to their heterogeneity, there are always features and interfaces to discover, across the whole network, not only within the single firm. Thus, we argue that behind successful cases of M&As there are actors with specific knowledge about how to combine resources (business units, relationships, production facilities and products) across the network. These resource combinations should not only be planned for in advance, but there should also be resource combinations that can be contingently activated if some third parties do not act according to plan. These actors also know that the *firm-related* and *industry-related* opportunities must be in accordance with the *network* for them to be realised. Thus, the network can be used as a resource in order to reap the benefits from the identified firm-related and industry-related opportunities, which still must be present to motivate an actor to accomplish an M&A.

The chapter is organised as follows. First, we present three types of opportunities associated with an M&A: firm-internal, industry-related and network-related. Then, three empirical observations follow. We proceed then with our analysis of the case illustrations and conclude the paper with a discussion and concluding remarks.

Three types of opportunities in mergers and acquisitions

The M&A literature (e.g., Larsson and Finkelstein, 1999; Walter and Barney, 1990) stresses numerous rationales or motives to explain a merger or an acquisition. Walter and Barney (1990) listed 20 reasons or objectives behind an M&A (Howell, 1970; Kitching, 1967; Steiner, 1975; Walter and Barney, 1990). These reasons include financial issues and market positioning. Other motives concern the target's expertise in product development. From the 20 listed reasons it is possible to distinguish two broad types of opportunities associated with an M&A. The first category of opportunities concerns internal factors within the firms that merge. The second deals with the sector or industry where the firms operate. We suggest here a third type of opportunities, to a large extent unexplored and only very implicitly included in Walter and Barney's list: this third type emphasises the network context of the merging firms, and especially of the target firm.

Firm-related opportunities are the first important rationale behind an M&A. M&As are expected to lead to increased economies of scale, deriving from the opportunity to allocate larger production volumes to at least some of the facilities within the merged firms, leading to the so-called operational synergies (Chatterjee, 1986; Larsson and Finkelstein, 1999; Lubatkin, 1983; Walter and Barney, 1990). Economies of scope are also viewed as important drives: the M&A offers in fact the opportunity of having more and varied resources, including knowledge about resources that can be potentially better combined inside the merging firms (Foss, 1997; Penrose, 1959; Peteraf, 1993; Teece *et al.*, 1997). Size matters both for scale and scope economies. But taking advantage of the synergies created from an M&A often implies the need of internal changes and recombinations. Key issues in relation to firm-related opportunities are the possibilities to reduce overlapping functional units, such as R&D departments and sales offices, highlighting what Sudarsanam, Holl and Salami (1996) call value creation through exploiting 'Managerial Synergies' (*Ibid.*, p. 674).

The *industry-related opportunities* offered by the M&A concern the expected positive effects deriving from changing the industry structure, as inspired by an industrial organisation analysis (see Porter, 1980, 1985). In this case it is a matter of changing the power structures in an industry by increasing the bargaining power through an acquisition or a merger (Caves and Porter, 1977; Chatterjee, 1986; Larsson and Finkelstein, 1999; Scherer, 1980). Thus, an M&A offers opportunities if it allows the merging firms to achieve a strong position in one or more industries: the bidder can, for instance, acquire a competitor (a firm active within the same industry), a customer or a supplier (engaging thus in vertical integration). For example, if the firm needed to control a critical resource currently controlled by a supplier, it would perform an acquisition leading to a backward integration. If, on the other hand, a distribution channel is considered as strategic for a firm, forward integration is an option. If the structure of an industry is threatened by a *substitute* product, incumbent firms may react through some M&A activities (Larsson and Finkelstein, 1999; Walter and Barney, 1990). Increasing market share or position is considered crucial in industry-related opportunities. Size gives scale-related benefits to a firm, at the same time as the firm with increased size improves the bargaining position in relation to suppliers and customers.

The *network-related opportunities* offered by an M&A are of different types than those we reviewed above: network-related opportunities cut across the two previous levels of analysis and types of opportunities. The network view (Anderson *et al.*, 1994; Håkansson and Snehota, 1995) covers the level of specific inter-firm interactions, as opposed to the other two types of opportunities, which are either restricted to the single firm or generalised as forces in whole industries.

The network view on the opportunities offered by M&As stresses that these opportunities are 'combinatorial' and, implicitly, that they are complex and hence very hard to identify in advance of an M&A, especially in the absence of a very detailed analysis of the networks of both merging firms, *before* and *after* the M&A. We suggest, in fact, that in order to possibly identify network-related effects, opportunities and obstacles, a network view on M&As needs to be complemented by a dynamic view (even more so than in the two other perspectives, the internal and the industry-related ones). More precisely, one needs to analyse the pre-M&A and post-M&A network around each of the two firms that merge. A central aspect for an actor is to be able to identify dynamic processes in order to be able to use and exploit opportunities that emerge in the network, during and after the merging process.

Network-related opportunities in M&As are certainly also related to power, scale and scope economies (as also the firm- and the industry-related opportunities are), but they emerge at a more fine-grained level of interaction among individually identified firms, belonging to different industries and related by complex interplays or even business relationships (see e.g., Håkansson and Snehota, 1989, 1995). A merger or a takeover changes, not only the industry or the firm's internal structure, but also the network structure (Anderson et al., 2000; Havila and Salmi, 2002). A problem for firms engaged in an M&A is that the effects deriving from the alteration of the network structure caused by the M&A are very hard to anticipate. But certainly, these unexpected network effects are even harder to anticipate if an explicit network view is not taken on the M&A process and on its outcome. Since, networks not only consist of social actors, such as organisations/firms and the relationships between them, but also of physical artefacts, such as products and production facilities (Håkansson and Waluszewski, 2002), the interactions between these physical resources have to be taken into consideration. For example, a product sold by a target firm, might be part of a technological system that a competitor to the bidder controls. The discussion on the three different types of opportunities we identified is summarised in Table 10.1.

Empirical illustrations

In order to illustrate the importance of the networks of both the target and the bidder in a merger or a takeover, we use three short case illustrations. The first case concerns Ericsson's attempt in the early 1980s to create, by means of two acquisitions, a powerhouse in the IT business. The second case concerns the Swedish brewery Spendrup's acquisition of another brewery to gain access to distribution channels. The third case covers the merger between two American bioscience firms aimed at obtaining a more complete range of offerings for customers. Each of the empirical illustrations presents the drivers and the expectations behind the M&A. These drivers help to identify the envisaged opportunities (or the threats the firms tried to avoid with the M&A), especially at the internal and industry level. The cases show that each M&A had outcomes not only on the firm and the industry level, but also on

Table 10.1 Three types of opportunities driving mergers and acquistions

	Levels of analysis for identifying opportunities in M&As		
	Internal opportunities	Industry-related opportunities	Network-related opportunities
Unit of analysis	The fit between the *internal structures* of the firms in the acquisition process	The fit between the target's and the bidder's respective *industry indicators* (market shares, growth rates, etc.)	The fit between the target's and the bidder's *networks*
Main drive behind the M&A	Efficiency through exploiting synergies. Scale or scope-related opportunities. Knowledge sharing between target and bidder. Cash flows from the target	Improve position in the industry in relation to competitors. Improve bargain position in relation to customers and suppliers. Scale and scope-related opportunities. Cash flows from the target	Improve position in the network, in relation to suppliers and customers (including their other suppliers). Reap benefits from resource heterogeneity. Combining new and old relationships at network level
The view of the target's resources	Internally focused. Capacity of production facilities important, but also skills of personnel	Capacity a central aspect in order to gain size. The respective products are valued in terms of market share and sector-level growth rates	Resources controlled by other firms, both the target and others, a crucial aspect. Heterogeneity of resources might lead to unexpected network effects
The role of the target's relationships	Not considered	Target's relationships to competitors. Relationships to customers collapsed into market shares and those to suppliers into bargaining power	The role of specific customer and of specific supplier relationships is crucial. Also target's *indirect* relationships are considered

the network level, with unexpected effects involving third parties or resources not directly connected to the deal. These 'network effects' were never part of the official picture of the deals because this picture often only contained explanations on the firm or the industry level. And even in the interviews conducted, the interviewees were more likely to refer to intra-firm or industry related factors to explain the opportunities and expectations before the deal. The same units of analysis were used by the actor to explain unexpected outcomes from the M&As. It was only thanks to the specific theoretical and analytical tools of, for instance, Håkansson and Waluszewski (2002) that the network effects identified and presented here were recognised. By using these tools to understand the expectations and outcomes of the M&A, the empirical illustrations and our analysis could be enriched by adding a network perspective to the other two perspectives.

Ericsson Information Systems: merging into the IT Industry[1]

On 1 January 1982 Ericsson, the Swedish telecom firm, made its official entrance in the computer industry, with a company named 'Ericsson Information System AB' (EIS, henceforth). Ericsson entered the IT sector with the goal of becoming a technology integrator capable of providing complete solutions for the 'paperless' office. Ericsson had identified important technical and industrial opportunities: Ericsson envisioned a major development opportunity in the growing need for computerised information systems and in the technical convergence between telecom equipment and computers (the so-called 'datacom'). Not only was the IT sector expected to have a higher growth rate than the telecom sector, but Ericsson feared that such IT giants as IBM could rapidly enter into telecom by exploiting the technical convergence of telecom with IT.

Ericsson saw itself well positioned to seize such opportunity, thanks to its technical competence base. In fact, Ericsson had already made inroads into IT with its new digital phone switch AXE and the computer system UAC 1601. Moreover, in the mid-1970s Ericsson launched the large project MD110, a digital switch for private organisations, such as large firms: this could open for a completely new type of customers, compared to the state-owned telcos that Ericsson had been supplying for 80 years. This technical competence was consolidated within two of Ericsson's business units.

But the above competence and product range alone were not sufficient for Ericsson successfully entering the IT sector. Ericsson was missing complementary products to create the envisaged complete solutions for office automation (computer terminals, advanced servers, etc.), contacts with customers and an established sales network, and, last but not least, experience of the computer industry. Ericsson took therefore the opportunity to rapidly obtain these necessary resources by acquiring Datasaab, a large Swedish computer manufacturer, with sales of SEK1.2 billion and 3400 employees. Datasaab's three core divisions, *Alfaskop terminals* (SEK400 million), *banking systems* (SEK400 million) and *business systems* (SEK300 million) were merged with Ericsson's 'G' and 'S' divisions into EIS. At its birth in 1982, EIS had 3900 employees and budgeted sales of SEK3 billion, making it one of Scandinavia's largest IT producer, second only to IBM.

EIS faced the challenge to integrate the diverse products, technologies and customers addressed by the business units involved in the M&A. In Ericsson's vision, Alfaskop terminals, minicomputers for banking and industrial applications and data networks should be technically integrated around a central hub, the digital switch MD110. This would be the ground in EIS's offerings for the paperless office. But meanwhile, at least until 1985, no step was taken to integrate EIS's international sales units: MD110 and telex were still sold by the Ericsson Group's subsidiaries, whereas computers by the former Datasaab's subsidiaries. Still, sales dramatically increased in 1982 for all products, and especially for the Alfaskop terminals. Important sales contracts were signed even for the not yet fully developed MD110 with such key customers as Volvo and several telecom operators. Despite the lack of product and organisational integration, the enthusiasm was at a peak in 1983 when EIS announced another major step: the acquisition of Facit AB. Facit contributed to EIS 4300 employees (of which 1800 outside Sweden) and a turnover of SEK1.3 billion, obtained from four main product areas, *computer terminals*, *peripherals* (printers, etc.) *calculators* and *office furniture*.

Besides the apparent product complementarities, the acquisition was driven by the opportunity to reach the mass market offered by Facit's large retail organisation (6000 points of sales in 120 countries). So, all the potential integration problems of a new back-to-back M&A were set aside in front of EIS's next commercial move: the launch of Ericsson's PC in April 1983. This product being aimed at small businesses and individual consumers, Facit's 6000 points of sales were a key resource to insure capillary coverage of the mass market.

The year 1983 was a very positive one for EIS: break-even was reached and sales rocketed to SEK4 billion. However, more and more clouds started appearing on EIS's horizon. Sales on the US market were not going according to plan and severe quality problems were identified (e.g., MD110 had more than 3000 bugs). EIS tackled these problems with four major reorganisations in four years, whereby the various products and facilities were assigned each time to different business units. In 1983, attempts were also made to solve problems in the US: first, a joint venture with Honeywell was created to sell and adapt MD110. Moreover, to conquer the US, EIS decided to build from scratch a large distribution network with 50 regional offices, since Facit had no retail presence in the US. This investment would cost EIS SEK500 million. But after a 40 per cent sale increase in 1984, EIS and all PC producers were hit by a major overproduction crisis in July 1985. EIS, which had oriented its efforts towards PCs (and even refurbished existing products into PCs), had to make heavy disinvestments and personnel cut. The US market was abandoned, along with the idea to develop and sell totally integrated office solutions. When demand for PCs recovered in 1986, Ericsson deemed as too high the R&D investments necessary for wholly new PCs and decided to abandon the PC and IT race. Thus, EIS was dismantled: its computer division was sold to Nokia Data in 1987, while digital switches and telecom terminals were kept inside Ericsson in a newly created division.

The Spendrups–Wårby merger[2]

Spendrups, founded in 1897, is one of the major players in the Swedish beer industry with a turnover of SEK3000 million and 1200 employees. The firm is a family business, run by Jens and Ulf Spendrups, the sons of the founder. Spendrups has production facilities in Stockholm, Grängesberg and in Kristiansand (Norway). The firm has its roots in the northern part of the country, in Dalarna and the town Grängesberg. Today, however, the headquarters are located in Stockholm.

Until 1955, the Swedish beer market had been regulated by law and divided into 'brewery districts', within which every brewery had to keep itself. One effect of this law was that it conserved an industry structure based on many small and local breweries. But following the abolishment of this law, after 1955, breweries were allowed to sell their products anywhere in the country. At this time some breweries started to expand their operations: one of these was Pripps, another Swedish, but state-owned brewery. Pripps purchased smaller breweries, one after the other, then laid off their production and centralised it to one of their own production units.

Spendrups, on the other hand, grew slowly and internally during the 1980s, reaching a 10 per cent share of the Swedish beer market. During these years, Spendrups assumed the identity of being in opposition to the much larger and state-owned Pripps. Indeed, they used this identity calling themselves 'the private alternative'. Everyone knew who 'the private alternative' was and it was common knowledge who 'the state-owned alternative' was. It was a Goliath against David situation, Pripps against Spendrups.

Even if Spendrups could be satisfied with its performance in the 1980s, the competition from Pripps and other breweries was growing stiffer every year. In 1989 Spendrups had reached its capacity ceiling and the firm's profit margins were decreasing each year. In addition, the 10 per cent market share that the company held was not considered enough. Moreover, it was very costly to transport beer from Dalarna, where the firm had its production facility, down to Stockholm, where most customers could be found. Spendrups needed therefore a production facility in the Stockholm area. At this time, it just happened to be that Wårby Bryggeri, a brewery owned by KF (the Union of the Swedish Cooperatives) was out for sale, with one production facility in Stockholm and one in the northern part of the country, Sollefteå. With the acquisition, Spendrups would gain access to Wårby's close relationship with KF, one of Sweden's main food retailers. With the volume that Wårby sold to KF, Spendrups would be on the safe side and reach a market share of 20 per cent. The two companies would also reap the benefits from synergies that the acquisition would create amounting to SEK 30–40 million, mainly on the distribution side. Wårby also had a production facility in the northern part of Sweden, Sollefteå, which was an important, but also local, and therefore expensive market to transport to. Another positive effect expected from the merger was the opportunity to attract foreign breweries as licensing partners. Having a 20 per cent market share would make Spendrups a much more attractive partner than if the company only had 10 per cent. The firm's bargain power would therefore increase.

In 1989, Spendrups announced that it would take over Wårby from KF for SEK400 million. This was an important day as the company now figured that they had safe ground under their feet. However, some opponents had early on warned the Spendrups brothers that the good relationships between KF and Wårby was related to the fact that Wårby was owned by KF and that they had therefore a common understanding based on 'cooperative' values. Even if the Spendrups brothers were not portrayed in the media as cold-hearted capitalists, KF had no intention of doing business with 'the private alternative'. When the ownership connection between KF and Wårby disappeared, the loyalty between the store managers and their old suppliers, Wårby, also disappeared. This might also have to do with the fact that Spendrups, rather insensitively, changed the entire assortment in a short time and asked the KF stores to purchase only Spendrups products. Instead of keeping Spendrups as the sole supplier of beer and soda, KF invited Pripps to increase their deliveries all over the country. Only now, did Spendrups realise that they had paid a price for Wårby that included the relationship with Wårby's customers, but now they found themselves with production facilities that they could not fill with orders, people on the payroll and a lost face. Just two years after the acquisition, Spendrups had to close down the facility in Sollefteå, right after KF announced that four cooperatives in Northern Sweden decided to have Pripps or Falcon, another Swedish brewery, as their main supplier.

Spendrups was losing money in 1990 and the firm had to lay off people both in Stockholm and in Grängesberg, due to the acquisition. Wårby lost 10 per cent market share within KF in a very short time. But it got worse. In early 1993 Pripps signed an exclusive contract with KF, whereby KF promised to purchase 80 per cent of their entire drinking assortment from Pripps. Single stores had the formal right to buy from other suppliers, but would then be punished with a fee of SEK20 per crate that did not come from Pripps. With this contract between Pripps and KF, the effects on Spendrups of the acquisition seemed to have come to an end and Spendrups could only but consider the deal as no less than catastrophic.

However, there were more actors on the scene. ICA, the other big food retailer in Sweden, then reacted strongly. ICA is a retail chain owned by a private association of store owners. The individual retail managers own their own stores, but use a central purchasing organisation. Facing the KF–Pripps contract, ICA feared that Pripps' position would be too dominant and that they would find themselves with only one possible beer supplier in the future. This scenario had to be stopped because ICA wanted to have several available alternatives and some competition in the national brewery industry. When the central purchasers at ICA saw what happened in the Spendrups–Wårby–Pripps triad, they decided to intervene. ICA started to increase their share of purchased beer and soda from Spendrups heavily in 1993. In absolute numbers, that meant going from 30 million litres to 75 million litres. In total ICA promised to let the three remaining major breweries in Sweden, Spendrups, Falcon and Åbro to take 70 per cent of their total volume of 220 million litres.

During 1993, Spendrups managed to reach a 25 per cent market share on a market that did not grow. In the end, the acquisition of Wårby gave

Spendrups the market share the firm wanted, but in a very different way from what they expected. In fact, despite being totally rejected by KF, Spendrups managed to reach the market share that the Wårby acquisition promised in the first place, but only after the intervention of ICA.

Toro Bioscience: acquiring customers via an M&A[3]

Founded in 1995, TORO is a leading provider of services and products for genetic testing and DNA comparisons. TORO addresses distinct markets such as forensic and paternity DNA testing, and pharmacogenetics-based personalised healthcare. TORO's strategy was based on exploiting its leading technologies and its expertise in genetic analysis across its customers' network of accredited laboratories, hospitals, pharmaceutical firms, physicians, health management organisations, and government agencies. In the face of a tremendous growth since its inception, with a three digit compounded annual growth rate and total revenues of over US$41 million a year, TORO posted in 2001 a net loss of US$110 million.

Nonetheless, in the end of 2001, TORO announced it would acquire Bee for US$19 million, in order to strengthen its market position, while increasing sales and cost efficiency. Founded in 1982, Bee was an established provider of public and private paternity testing services and of DNA forensics services. Bee was a respected player in the DNA forensics field, with several scientific awards. Bee's customers included law enforcement agencies involved in high profile criminal cases. Bee owned a number of ISO and CLIA-accredited laboratories. It also had a profitable business selling diagnostic testing kits and reagents to clinical laboratories for HLA[4] tissue typing for organ and bone marrow transplantation. Bee had organised its business into four operating divisions: Paternity Testing Services, Forensic Testing Services, HLA and HLA Software. HLA Software grouped all kinds of HLA-related products, HLA-analysis software, probe sets, and so on.

This acquisition not only aimed to take over a competitor, but also to position TORO as a leading company in identity genomics, now with eight accredited laboratories of its own, the largest revenue base and the highest throughput capacity in the industry. TORO also saw the opportunity to achieve operating efficiencies and improve pricing dynamics in the sectors of paternity and forensic testing. TORO aimed to reduce overall costs by applying its technologies to replace Bee's labour-intensive DNA analysis methods. TORO believed that the merged company was very well positioned to thrive in both the established and the high-growth segments of the genetic diversity market. TORO also envisaged the opportunity to combine its customers' network of accredited labs with Bee's network of owned labs, in order to increase revenues and support its clinical Life Sciences and pharmacogenetics businesses. Here, TORO expected to have stable sales of proprietary high-margin consumables. TORO planned to fold Bee's HLA units into a new TORO Diagnostics unit that could increase sales by more than US$16 million in a year by adding Bee's DNA diagnostic products to its portfolio.

The acquisition, however, entailed significant risks, a major one being that many of Bee's products were early in their lifecycle. A strong market for these products would take a few years to materialise. Bee also had a limited direct sales force and TORO would need to increase significantly sales and marketing efforts after the acquisition. TORO analysed in detail the customer network of Bee's four divisions and identified the following opportunities, to be seized through the M&A, but also a series of obstacles:

- *Forensic Testing Services*: Despite a 40 per cent growth, an analysis showed that, among the Forensic division's 18 customers, 6 key customers (accounting for 50 per cent of this unit's revenues) were benefiting from old contracts and were unprofitable because of prices between 20 and 50 per cent lower than the other customers with recent contracts.
- *Paternity Testing Services*: As in the Forensic unit, all Paternity's customers were paying to Bee unsystematic fees and had contracts that they could cancel at will.
- *HLA*: HLA being the major source of Bee's revenues and completely dependent on three major customers, these three relationships deserved special caution. The declining margin at the end of 2001 reflected non-renewal of the high-margin contract with the key customer NMDP, a non-profit organisation that facilitated blood transfusions. The NMPD contract was not renewed in April 2001, right before finalising the acquisition, due to quality and timeliness issues.
- *HLA Software*: Even if this unit contributed the strongest and most stable margins (50–60 per cent), some of its products were in decline due to changing technologies at some of its customers. Another threat to HLA Software was its dependency on the HLA unit: 80–90 per cent of their products were complementary, and HLA's revenues were declining.

Bee's management was confident about retaining their strong relationships, but they were concerned about potential synergies with TORO. Problems would emerge in the attempts to transfer capacity across the newly merged units, due to regulatory approvals, even if this was an urgent need. A further investment of US$1.5–4 million would be necessary to finance expansion. Bee's and TORO's technologies were different, but integrating their systems was seen as an opportunity.

The merging of the two companies was not without problems. TORO had to eliminate 184 staff positions, or about 20 per cent of total head count. What was perhaps more troublesome was the fact that TORO also decided to exit two business segments that were lacking the expected growth and where they were not strong enough to withstand the competition. What had once been considered as a future cash-cow, the Bee-owned HLA units, was one of those. This also caused a decline in software services, whose sales were closely complementary to HLA's.

But there was some positive things going on as well. Quite interestingly, 85 per cent of TORO's revenue growth was attributable to the high-growth Bee-related units: the revenues of Forensic Testing Services and Paternity Integration Services jumped from US$12 million (before the acquisition) to 27 million in 2002. Those units profited by reorganising their customer relationships and renewing outdated fees and, especially, from approaching old and new customers through the former TORO's much stronger sales force. In addition, TORO integrated its cost-effective technology into Bee's operations, and kept R&D expenses in 2001 on the same level as the year before.

In December 2002, the new group presented its annual results: it had managed to increase revenues by 54 per cent, while cost only grew by 3 per cent in comparison to the previous year.

Analysing the three cases: Eis, Spendrups and Toro

In this section we analyse the three cases, pointing at (1) how the opportunities originally identified by the firms affected their behavior in the M&A and (2) the M&A's actual outcome.

Ericsson's two M&As were driven by the opportunity to enter a new dynamic industry: acquiring Datasaab and Facit aimed at rapidly gaining market shares, retail presence, products and technical expertise. EIS faced however big problems in learning the new rules of the game in the IT industry, giving up even some of Ericsson's heritage (close interplay with major customers) in the pursuit of technological dreams. Aiming too high, too fast and too broadly dissipated product development energy and reduced the reliability of EIS's products, with negative effects on some key customers. Much of the industry-related opportunities failed to materialise: sector-wide issues play certainly a role (e.g., microchip scarcity, the PC crisis and IBM's fierce price competition), but other issues are related to the business network around EIS and to resource embeddedness. First, EIS was never really able to combine the network of customer relationships it inherited from Facit and Datasaab with each other, with its selling units and with adequate products. No matter how 'valuable' these relationships were before the M&A, EIS did not do much to increase their value. For instance, EIS never interacted with customers through unified sales interfaces capable to handle all EIS range, but separate product divisions (inherited from before the M&A) continued to handle customers separately from each other. Interestingly, some profitable customers for a unit were actually fierce competitors for another one: for instance, IBM purchased peripherals from a former Facit unit, but competed with EIS on the PC segment.

An obstacle to EIS's providing complete solutions was that most customers were embedded in their installed bases of IT systems and terminals and hence, in deeper relationships to other providers than EIS. Indirect network effects further conjured against EIS's ambition to be the preferred and sole IT provider of complete solutions: customers required explicitly to have more than one IT provider to avoid over-dependence. Too much focus on technology and on industry-related opportunities distracted EIS from the network-related ones: how about EIS's strong bet on the PC market in the US, where Facit's retail network had no value? Instead, EIS extensively mobilised Facit's points of sales in Sweden, which turned Televerket (with all its retail outlets) from a good customer into a competitor in the PC and private switch markets. Also here, EIS did certainly not seize any network opportunity, but rather nullified them or created a network obstacle.

The case of the Spendrups brewery highlights the original search for the opportunity to attain scale advantages by means of the larger volumes permitted by larger market shares. This should allow better exploiting production facilities, such as production plants and transport means. On the other hand, the M&A set into motion a series of unexpected effects on the distributor relationships of Spendrup and Wårby. This case also points out the way identities of all the units in the network change in relation to the M&A. For example, being 'the private alternative' was not positive in relation to KF managers. Missing to see how Wårby, as an organisational unit, was deeply embedded in the KF culture was a major mistake by Spendrups, leading to KF more or less abandoning Spendrups after its acquisition of Wårby. However, to their rescue came a third party that had an indirect interest in Spendrups' acquisition of Wårby: ICA, the dominant food retailer, could use its size and purchasing power to create a new structure in the brewing industry and thereby 'punish' Pripps for their attempt to become the sole beer and soda supplier. As Spendrups realised this, they took the opportunity to increase their deliveries to ICA at the expense of Pripps.

The acquisition of Wårby did cost Spendrups some SEK400 million; and despite this, the direct result from the takeover was a total failure. If Spendrups had been able to 'read' the network, including ICA's and Pripps' network intentions, before concluding the M&A, they would certainly have acted differently. In fact, the best thing to do would have been just to sit and wait for Pripps to take over Wårby. In that case ICA's actions would have been more or less the same, because they feared a too-strong Pripps. In that scenario Spendrups would have had the market shares that they desired, but without the need to spend SEK400 millions. What Spendrups would have lacked in that case would have been the production facility in the Stockholm area, which was seen as strategic for the company due to distribution economy. However, the M&A obliged Spendrups to pay not only for this facility, but also for customer relationships (with KF's retail outlets) that Spendrups never could generate any revenues from.

The case of the two bioscience companies TORO and Bee shows the difficulty to assess the value of a target only in terms of its physical resources, its financial structure or its product range or served markets. A large part of Bee's value derives from the evolving pattern of its customer relationships and how these would be affected in the M&A. All three types of opportunities described earlier in the chapter appear in this case. At industry level, Bee's acquisition aimed to take over a competitor in order to strengthen TORO's position in its sector. Internal synergies were also addressed: Bee's products would benefit from TORO's strong direct sales force and marketing efforts, Bee's excellent scientific skills could be better complemented with TORO's stronger middle-management. In addition, TORO aimed to achieve operating efficiencies by applying its technologies to replace Bee's current labour-intensive methods. However, the case shows that those internal synergies are not easy to achieve, also because of the lack of supporting R&D investments after the transaction.

From a network perspective, this acquisition opened the opportunity to access Bee's business relationships, mostly to customers. TORO's explicit expectation was to buy and profit from Bee's network. Two underlying assumptions were (1) that TORO would be able to maintain the relationships with key customers and (2) that Bee's inefficient relationships could be either terminated or transformed into profitable ones. The first assumption proved wrong: when TORO was ready to fold Bee's HLA business into the new TORO Diagnostics unit, the HLA division had already lost its major customers. Also the second assumption proved wrong because TORO was unable to 'rescue' the remaining relationships of HLA. TORO had therefore to exit the HLA business, which had a domino effect on the HLA Software, whose sales volume depended on HLA's customers. HLA's customer relationships were too weak to survive the transaction. Instead, the outcome was positive for others among Bee's relationships: TORO managed to double the performance of the inefficient relationships of Forensic Testing Services and Paternity Testing Services, while getting some new customers. Even if this M&A entailed industry benefits and internal synergies (as well as unexpected negative effects, such as exiting HLA), all those are eclipsed by the impact of changes in customer relationships.

Discussion and concluding remarks

This chapter highlighted the role of a firm's network context for the business opportunities related to M&As. We argued that the M&A literature's emphasis on firm-related and industry-related types of opportunities should be complemented with a third type of opportunities, network-related ones. The undertaking of an M&A happens after a firm (or rather its management) has identified a profit opportunity (Kirzner, 1997). We presented three illustrations showing that such opportunities are often based either on a *firm-related rationale*, which emphasises the exploitation of synergies, or on *industry rationale*, which aims to improve such sector indicators as the strategic position towards competitors and the bargaining power towards suppliers or customers. However, even if M&As are undertaken with these two 'mindsets', they inevitably lead to effects on the *network level*. That is, third parties will react, positively or negatively to the M&A, and the firm has to deal with it, in one way or the other. In order to reap the profit opportunities at the firm and the industry level, care should be taken to see that the three levels, including the network one, do not contradict each other, as they sometimes follow different logics. A main conclusion of this chapter is that it is not enough to recognise a profit opportunity and the chance to seize it through, for instance, internal synergies with a merging firm: all this must be in accordance with what happens at the network level. In fact, the network might prevent from exploiting synergies at the firm or the industry level: a sales office might be harder to close down than one expects, for example due to relationships that the sales office has worked up during a long time, or a competitor might be harder to fight due to a close relationship to a third party.

Thus, a firm engaging in an M&A should look a bit *farther*, that is, not only at its own 'complex resources' (Denrell *et al.*, 2003), and a bit *deeper*, that is, not only at its industry structure: looking farther and deeper means taking into account the complex and heterogeneous resources of specific other firms in the surrounding network. Consequently, the network-related opportunities are more complex to both anticipate and to take advantage of: reading what will happen in a network if two previously independent firms become one is not an easy task. Still, we strongly argue that this is what managers need to do to reduce the risk of negative effects and value destruction after an M&A.

Acknowledgements

The authors would like to thank Hernán Camps, KPMG Financial Services, for providing one of the empirical cases presented in this chapter. Financial support was provided by Svenska Handelsbanken and Jan Wallander's Foundation.

Notes

1. The empirical sources for this case are (1) EIS's and of Datasaab's internal reports, (2) in-depth interviews with two EIS managers, (3) the 1982–85 issues of EIS's newsletter (ERINFO), (4) Ericsson's scientific review (Ericsson Review) and (5) secondary sources such as news from the daily business press.
2. The case is based on five in-depth interviews with people working for Spendrups and ICA at the time of the merger between Spendrups and Wårby. The interviews have been complemented with secondary sources such as a company biography and articles from the Swedish business press that covered the brewery industry during those years.
3. This case was originally written by Hernán Camps, KPMG Financial Services. The case is based on (1) three interviews with the Senior Consultant that supervised

the Due Diligence analysis made by KPMG Transaction Services on behalf of its customer TORO, (2) the extensive documentations on this M&A produced by KPMG (including transcripts of over 20 interviews with the merging firms) and (3) a dozen press releases about this M&A. Detailed sources are omitted for confidentiality reasons. TORO and all other company names (along with some of their features) were modified to protect the identities of the involved firms.
4. HLA stands for 'human leukocyte antigens', the genetic information encoded on white blood cells.

References

Anderson, J., Håkansson, H. and Johanson, J. (1994). Dyadic Business Relationships within a Business Network Context, *Journal of Marketing*, 58(4), 1–15.
Anderson, H., Havila, V. and Holmström, J. (2003). *Are Customers and Suppliers part(icipants) of a Merger or an Acquisition?* – A literature review, Proceedings of the 19th IMP Conference, Lugano.
Anderson, H., Andersson, P., Havila, V. and Salmi, A. (2000). *Business Network Dynamics and M&As: Structural and Processual Connectedness*, Proceedings of the 16th IMP Conference, Bath.
Bild, M. (1998). *Valuation of Takeovers*, Doctoral Thesis, Stockholm School of Economics.
Caves, R. E. (1989). Mergers, Takeovers and Economic Efficiency: Foresight vs Hindsight, *International Journal of Industrial Organisation*, 7(1), 151–74.
Caves, R. E. and Porter, M. E. (1977). Entry Barriers to Mobility Barriers: Conjectural Decisions and Contrived Deterrence to New Competition, *Quarterly Journal of Economics*, 91(2), 241–61.
Chatterjee, S. (1986). Types of Synergy and Economic Value. The Impact of Acquisitions on Merging and Rival Firms, *Strategic Management Journal*, 7(2), 119–39.
Denrell, J., Fang, C. and Winter, S. G. (2003). The Economics of Strategic Opportunity, *Strategic Management Journal*, 24(10), 977–90.
Foss, N., (Ed.) (1997). *Resources, Firms and Strategies: A Reader in the Resource-based Perspective*, Oxford: Oxford University Press.
Goldberg, W. H. (1983). *Mergers, Motives, Methods*, Aldershot, England: Gower.
Håkansson, H. and Snehota, I. (1989). No Business is an Island: the Network Concept of Business Strategy, *Scandinavian Journal of Management*, 5(3), 187–200.
Håkansson, H. and Snehota, I. (Eds) (1995). *Developing Relationships in Business Networks*, London: Routledge.
Håkansson, H. and Waluszewski, A. (2002). *Managing Technological Development. IKEA, the Environment and Technology*, London and New York: Routledge.
Havila, V. and Salmi, A. (2002). Network Perspective on International Mergers and Acquisitions: What More Do We See?, in. V. Havila, M. Forsgren and H. Håkansson, (Eds), *Critical Perspectives on Internationalisation*, London: Pergamon; Elsevier Science Ltd., 457–72.
Howell, R. A. (1970). Plan to Integrate your Acquisitions, *Harvard Business Review*, 48(6), 66–76.
Kirzner, I. M. (1997). Entrepreneurial Discovery and the Competitive Market Process: An Austrian Approach, *Journal of Economic Literature*, 35(1), 60–85.
Kitching, J. (1967). Why do Mergers Miscarry, *Harvard Business Review*, 45(6), 84–101.
Larsson, R. and Finkelstein, S. (1999). Integrating Strategic, Organizational and Human Resource Perspectives on Mergers and Acquisitions: A Case Survey of Synergy Realization, *Organization Science*, 10(1), 1–26.

Lubatkin, P. (1983). Mergers and Performance of the Acquiring Firm, *Academy of Management Review*, 8(2), 281–25.

Penrose, E. (1959, 1995). *The Theory of the Growth of the Firm*, New York: Oxford University Press.

Peteraf, M. A. (1993). The Cornerstones of Competitive Advantage. A Resource Based View, *Strategic Management Journal*, 14(3), 179–91.

Porter, M. E. (1980). *Competitive Strategy*, New York: Free Press.

Porter, M. E. (1985). *Competitive Advantage*, Glenwood, IL: Free Press.

Scherer, F. M. (1980). *Industrial Market Structure and Economic Performance*, 2nd edn, Chicago, IL: Rand McNally.

Steiner, P. O. (1975). *Mergers, Motives, Effects, Policies*, Ann Arbor, ML: University of Michigan Press.

Sudarsanam, S., Holl, P. and Salami, A. (1996). Shareholder Wealth Gains in Mergers: Effect of Synergy and Ownership Structure, *Journal of Business Finance & Accounting*, 23(5&6), 673–699.

Teece, D. J., Pisano, G. and Shuen, A. (1997). Dynamic capabilities and strategic management, *Strategic Management Journal*, 18(7), 509–53.

Walter, G. A. and Barney, J. B. (1990). Management Objectives in Mergers and Acquisitions, *Strategic Management Journal*, 11(1), 79–86.

11
Reputation as Opportunity and Risk

Carin Eriksson and Jan Lindvall

Introduction

For years, Enron was the peacock of Wall Street. In the era of deregulation, Enron was transformed from a boring pipeline operator to a risk-taking, worldwide trader of many different products. Enron was hailed as the business model of the future and Arthur Andersen was its auditors and supporters. On 16 October 2001, Enron released its disastrous third-quarter financial report, revealing more than $600 million in losses and a $1.2 billion reduction in shareholder equity. When the market learned that Enron made great losses and top managers had been profited for years at the company's expense, Enron's stock price and credit rating spiraled downward. Enron was soon filed for bankruptcy.

Exactly one year after Enron began its free fall into bankruptcy, its former auditing firm Arthur Andersen was sentenced for altering evidence of its work with the company. Prosecutors charged both a former partner and the company itself with obstruction of justice. Enron's collapse was partly blamed on questionable accounting that kept hundreds of millions of dollars in debt off its books. What was even worse – the employees at Andersen had illegally destroyed thousands of documents and computer records relating to its scandal-hit client. When the jury in the United States did find accountancy firm Arthur Andersen guilty of obstructing justice by shredding documents it was just one more step into the fall of the firm. The verdict could be seen as the death knell for the 89-year old company, once one of the world's top five accountants. The remarkable decline of the firm, from its announcement that it had discovered improper shredding of documents related to its audit of Enron, to the verdict, occurred in less than nine months. The remaining tasks of the once-proud firm were now to deal with obligations and shut itself down. Of its roughly 28,000 employees, fewer than 3000 were left a year later; of more than 1200 public-company audit clients, none remained.

The Arthur Andersen case is a spectacular case on a firm risking – and loosing – its reputation. The case also illustrates how quickly a knowledge-based service firm almost disappears as an effect of the loss of reputation. The Arthur Andersen case is in many ways more interesting than Enron when it comes to an analysis of reputations, opportunities and risks. Andersen has been seen as the auditing industry's leader for 89 years and yet the Arthur Andersen brand now finds itself on the brink of extinction.

This highlights the importance of reputations and the great risks of not having one or having a bad one. Most firms are aware of the importance of a good reputation to be able to function well. It can be argued that reputations are among the most important intangible strategic assets for the firm. For a consultancy firm, a good reputation is the key to survival; no opportunities can be found or realized with a weak or bad reputation. Most big consultancy firms seem to be very aware of this and they actively do manage their corporate reputations. But how do they do it? The purpose of this chapter is to illustrate the role of the management consultancy firms' network – with focus on their clients – in the process of building a reputation to gain opportunities.

Opportunities and risks

Opportunities are aspects of the environment viewed from a certain perspective. We follow Shane *et al.* (2003) to define opportunities as potentialities for profit making. An important element, which determines to a large degree the potentials for profit making, is the firm's reputation. A central tenet is that a firm's reputation within a network of business relations is the key to the opportunity to sell services. Following a network perspective, the value of reputations are embedded in relationships as actors are performing interdependent activities (Håkansson and Snehota, 1995; Johansson and Matsson, 1988). What one actor does affects other parts of the network. Taking the network of firms and relationships into consideration, we argue that reputation is a resource created in a network. This means that a reputation is influenced by a larger exchange network, but has also impact on the same network. We emphasize the need to better understand the process in which opportunities are found and realized.

Management consulting is not a legally or institutionally protected profession, which opens the market potentially to any individual or organization. The sector has low barriers of entry and both high birth and mortality rates. Uncertainty about the sustainability of the consulting firm, their professional background and the qualification of its staff leads to a reduction in market transparency (Gluckler and Armbruster, 2003). Important aspects of management consultancy services are immateriality, heterogeneity and interaction (Clark and Salaman, 1998). This refers to the fact that a buyer cannot pre-purchase a guaranteed level of service and the production of consultancy services necessitates interaction between the consultant and the buyer (Clark, 1995). The service is sold on a promise that a certain value will be delivered. Management consultancy work is one of the most intangible works one can think of which makes it difficult for clients to choose a consulting firm for an assignment. There are many relational risks (Das and Teng, 2001) in the use of consultancies. The consultants may have access to confidential information within client organization. As part of the consultancy firm's knowledge management systems, client data may be collected, shared and used. Project reports may be saved in internal databases and downloaded when similar projects come up. The job mobility of management consultants implies risk for the client, as a consultant may work for a competitor in the foreseeable future (Gluckler and Armbruster, 2003). As the client purchases an intangible service in subsequent cooperation, the matter of choosing a consultant assumes significance. As Gluckler and Armbruster (2003) point out, standard strategies for competing tend to be inadequate in the management consulting market. Standard theory offers two ways of competing: quality and price. The quality of the services is difficult to measure – the service is generated in co-production and after the agreement is signed. Success is contingent on a large variety of variables, which make quality hard to assess even after the consultancy project has been finished. The price is not an adequate way of competing either. Price does not resolve the uncertainty the clients perceive and service firms hardly ever pursue cost-leadership strategies (Lindahl and Beyers, 1999). Not only clients take risks. As management consulting is a two-way interaction, consultants depend on a collaborative and consent-based client attitude. An assignment depends on the goal, strategies and skills of both parties and their ability to cooperate (Sturdy, 1997). There are hardly any institutional means of reducing the risks; so if price and quality are not proper strategies for competing, how can a consultancy firm become the obvious provider of services and shape opportunities for profit making?

Creating opportunities through reputation

As discussed in chapter one, business opportunities are the fundamental market strategy tool. Reputation exists in the mind of each stakeholder and is impossible to manage directly. According to Balmer (1998: 971) image concerns the public's latest beliefs about an organization, whereas reputation represents a value judgement about the organization's qualities built up 'over a period and focusing on what it does and how it behaves'. Dowling (2001) states that corporate image is the total impression an entity makes and corporate reputation is the esteem in which the organization's image is held. Reputation makes processing of new images dependent on retained past images (Gioia, 1986). The two terms, image and reputation, are closely connected elements and both are dependent on the other to be developed. They are also allied to the term 'identity' which refers to an organization's unique characteristics, which are rooted in the behaviour of members of the organization. It answers the questions 'Who are we and where are we going?' (Albert and Whetten, 1985). Different stakeholders' perceptions of the way an organization presents itself, either deliberately or accidentally, forms the image of the organization. Since every organization of size and importance has many different identities and stakeholders, each with a variety of interests, it cannot be expected that there will be one uniform and consistent reputation. Organizations are complex phenomena and they can be expected to display different identities and images, adjustable and appropriate for a given audience. Different clusters of people, stakeholders, are likely to form different evaluations of the organization. To every organization it is of great importance to find an approach to segmenting stakeholders into groups, and understanding the basis for their different impressions (Dowling, 2001). Stakeholders are linked to the organization in different ways, either as an effect of the different needs that the organization can help to fulfil or the organization being subject to surveillance. The importance of stakeholders differs with each organization but to most service organizations the employees and the buyers the two most important groups. With management consultancy firms this is absolutely the case. Management consultancy firms produce services through people. This means that the personnel are the most important production factor. All services are produced in interaction with the client, which indicate that the client is of great importance to the management consultancy firm. The customer capital – the ongoing relationships with the people or the organizations to which it sells – is of great value for every knowledge firm such as the management consultancies.

It is often mentioned that a firm's competitive advantage depends on its knowledge, 'what it knows, how it uses what it knows, and how fast it can know something new'. One way to become more knowing is through the clients. It is not only important what the firm learns about its clients (as in traditional relationship marketing), but also what the clients know. The choices of clients are of strategic significance. The clients contribute with money (revenues), knowledge (experience) or reputation (the esteem of images). As the consultants are more involved in the implementations of their recommendations and the boundaries between consultants and clients are becoming increasingly blurred, we may put a greater emphasis on the importance of the clients. The interdependence is an important aspect of the consultant–client relationship, which may take many forms (Fincham, 1999). Through co-operation with their clients, firms are expected to handle market changes better (Nonaka and Takeuchi, 1995), be more innovative (von Hippel, 1994), better respond to clients needs (Leonard and Rayport, 1997), and to build stronger relationships.

Reputations take a long time to form and if they are good they become an asset and if they are bad, a crushing liability. The potential loss associated with a damaged reputation in addition with the inability to manipulate one's own reputation assures that an organization (or individual) with a positive reputation will continue to act reputably (Barney and Hansen 1994). The ability of the firm to manipulate its own reputation is limited by the willingness of parties external to the firm to include these attempts in their overall assessment. The values of good reputations are many. According to Dowling (2001) these are, among many, some of the reasons to actively strengthen the reputation:

- It adds extra psychological value – trust – to the products and services.
- It reduces the risk the buyer perceives when buying the product or service. Dowling (2001: 12) says: 'managers seldom get fired for buying the market leader'.
- It helps buyers choose between products and services.
- It increases job satisfaction.

Method

The purpose of this chapter is to discuss the role of the clients for reputation building. In order to do so, we have chosen to study the top-ten management consultancy firms in Sweden. The choice on Sweden is of course primarily a result of the nationality of the two authors. However, there are reasons to believe that they could be of more general interest as all of the studied firms could be characterized as 'global' and they all emphasize their international culture and work style.

As we look at the consulting field we can note that it is an industry with many different types of actors. The industry includes well-known management consultants such as McKinsey & Co, Boston Consulting Group etc. but also firms working with accounting, out-placement, temporary staffing, PR/communication, marketing, education, IT and technical consultation. In the present chapter we will limit the analysis primarily to the big management consultancy firms.

We have identified the most important consultancy firms on the basis of their sales. This method of identifying different types of firms is used in the annual book *Konsultguiden*, which is based on a yearly questionnaire conducted by the prominent Swedish business magazine *Affärsvärlden*. *Konsultguiden* has defined management consultancy firms as those having more than 50 per cent of their sales inside management consulting. At the time of the study the top ten consulting firms included Andersen (Accenture) Consulting, McKinsey & Co., PriceWaterhouseCoopers (PWC) Management Consultants, Boston Consulting Group Carta Corporate Advisors, Ernst & Young Management Consultants, KPMG Management Consultants, Arthur D. Little, Gemini Consulting, and Arthur Andersen Management Consulting. Since then major changes in the field of consultancy firms have occurred. During the time of the study Cap Gemini and Ernst & Young Management Consultants merged. Carta Corporate Advisors, the only domestic consultancy firm at that time is now a part of the US owned Booz, Allen & Hamilton. Arthur Andersen has disappeared from the market. Andersen Consulting is now called Accenture. All the firms of the study are of foreign origin, most often with headquarters in the United States, only Gemini Consulting has its headquarters in Europe (France).

Top Management is considered to be very important in the process of creating images and reputation (Whetten and Godfrey, 1998). In the selected firms the CEOs were interviewed. The interviews lasted around two hours each and have focused on the perceptions of the interviewees. Which clients do they want and why? Extensive notes were taken during the interviews and transcribed immediately following the visit. The interviews may also be seen in the context of an earlier study of the ten biggest firms and their use of consultancies (Engvall and Eriksson, 1999). Other sources of data were collected and analysed in order to gain a greater insight into the consultancy firms. These sources included internal informants (people working as consultants), internal magazines, booklets and web-presentations.

Risky business

Having the right client is essential for many reasons. The most obvious reason is of course the financial matters. But more often mentioned by the interviewees is the importance of the client for the transfer of knowledge and reputation building. Through the right kind of client you can learn more – and before the competitors – and the reputation of the firm will be improved. A bad client relationship means a lack of trust and reputation, which could take the firm down in a quick spiral. Choosing a client is an issue of strategic significance and emphasized by all interviewed CEOs. This selection of clients can be problematic and a risky process and all CEOs can give examples from experiences with clients that have cost them more than they have brought into the consultancy firms. In the words of a consultancy CEO,

> It is sometimes a risky business to choose between clients – which client should we invest in and which client should we avoid? Sometimes you make a mistake and put in time, resources and people into something that ends up like big black hole. No one wants to be in it.

When asked which firms they want to have as their client, all ten interviewed CEOs answered – 'big global firms' and they gave this answer without any hesitation at all. The big global firm is the first choice client.
As one CEO says,

> Yes, some clients are certainly better than others. All consultancies want to say that they are working with the big global firms. And some of those firms are better than others.

All top-ten consultancy firms in Sweden can themselves be considered 'global' with offices in several countries. In marketing and in proposals from the consultancies the facts often stressed are that they are themselves global and therefore well suited for the global clients which need consultancy firms able to work in a global network. The big global firms are often highly valued since they are considered to lead the development and be role models for others. Among the practices of the large companies the employment of consultants is substantial, and can therefore be expected to spread to other companies (Engwall and Eriksson, 1999). A central actor may act as a sort of evangelist influencing the development of the whole community (Lorenzoni and Baden-Fuller, 1995; Sawhney and Prandelli, 2000). Through their size the global firms become visible and they have through their sheer dominance a superior possibility to attract attention. In a world of uncertainty regarding appropriate actions to take it may appear out of date for a company not to adapt the methods applied by the largest companies. In the words of one top consultant CEO,

> Of course, there are some firms that have a better reputation than others. Some firms are considered to be ahead of others and if you work with them you are better off – you are at the front of the development and other firms get interested in you.

Firms that are often mentioned are ABB and Ericsson. ABB, working in the electrotechnical industry with headquarters in Switzerland, can hardly be considered as Swedish anymore but is still seen as a role model for Swedish companies. ABB has, in good times, been of great interest to many firms, media and the management literature. Its approach to the challenges of international management, and for the way it worked with a global strategic thrust combined with the autonomy of local operating units, has interested many (e.g. Ghoshal and Bartlett, 1997). A series of global change programmes inside ABB, did focus on developing standardized products and processes, improving quality, rationalizing supplier relations, reducing 'throughput time' and comparing plant performance through different kinds of systems, measuring indices of quality, efficiency and productivity and customer satisfaction (Belanger, 1999). The former CEO of ABB, Percy Barnevik has himself attracted much attention (De Vries, 1996). His leadership style was considered as a role model supposed to 'embody modern leadership qualities as being personal and direct'. Barnevik, was voted 'CEO of Europe's most respected company' in the Financial Times/Price Waterhouse survey of top executives and was widely regarded as one of the most successful business leaders of the 1990s (De Vries, 1996). And ABB was a top-ranked client by the consultancy firms, as one of the CEOs says,

> For a couple of years ago everyone wanted to work with ABB – we certainly did. They had a famous CEO, many interesting projects and they

were always on some business magazine's front page. They are still considered as a good client. Everyone wants to have them in their client files, because they still attract attention.

Ericsson was another top-ranked firm. The telecom giant was considered as a source of knowledge. Some of the consultancy firms did put in extra resources and created knowledge centres in the Stockholm area to be able to better keep up with the pace of the telecom industry. Ericsson was considered as an asset to the consultancy firms:

> If you work with an interesting project in a company like Ericsson other firms become interested. They want to know what's going on. We can sell new projects through the fact that they know we are working with well-known clients.

Interesting projects in firms that get attention, helps the consultancy firms to attract new clients. Through their work in companies they can fill up the open management concepts with content, with knowledge. A common concept – like the Balanced Score Card – is of little value until the consultancy firm has experience in highly valued firms to refer to. The intangible character of the management service causes a need to signal what has been done and with whom. When a client to be, asks for references, a well-known firm is the way to attract new clients:

> The big global firms are our most important clients. But some of these firms are leaders and some are followers and we want to work with the leaders. Through them we get better and attract new clients.

Long ongoing relations are important for the consultancies. On an average, 65 per cent of the consultancy firms' invoicing to clients is to firms they have had relationships with for more than three years. Small risks are connected to the long-term clients as they already enjoy trust because of previous experience. They know each other and 'speak the same language, they don't need to have everything explained over again', as one of the interviewees said. Trust is a culturally dependent phenomenon, to a large extent dependent on an overlap between the consultant's and the client's values and norms (Bergholz, 1999). Long-term clients also tend, according to the interviewees, to make more purchases and be less price-sensitive than newcomers. They may also bring in additional business through referrals.

> How do we get clients? The best way is to keep the old ones and let the word of us be spread around. Clients come to us because they know we have done interesting and important things in interesting firms.

The importance of the client is well recognized by the consultancy firms studied. They all survey their brand equity and customer loyalty. The cost to acquire a new client can be very high and can sometimes not be billed. It is a risky and sometimes very expensive operation to start new client relations. Retaining earlier clients is not as expensive and less risky.

> We have an on-going relationship and we don't need to start from the beginning every time. We have already made the tough investments in the relation. With new clients nothing is for certain.

Totally opposite to the first choice client is their next choice, the 'hot' small fast-growing business company. At the time of the study firms working with information technology in any aspect were very popular. The reasons for the willingness to work with e-business companies were according to the CEOs purely knowledge transfers – 'to be able to talk the e-talk, it's needed to walk the e-walk'. This is also an indication of how consultants need to work to give a currently new and hot concept (in this case e-strategy) content. At the time of the study the development in the e-strategy field was attracting much attention and new firms and solutions were introduced to the market at great speed.

> To learn we have to be where it is happening. Our consultants want to be there. And we keep on learning through our experiences with these new start-ups. This kind of knowledge is important to attract firms from the old economy and when we attract these traditional companies, we can do more prestigious projects and more money.

The small, fast-growing business firms have sometimes not enough money to spend on consultancies, but since they stand for some kind of new knowledge they get attention and become attractive to the consultancy firms. The more traditional mid-sized firm has too little money to spend on consulting and is seldom considered as a leading company. The mid-sized firm is considered as less visible, and in other words not an attractive client. Even less valued are the organizations in the public sector. A CEO says,

> Really, I wish that it were easier to work with the public sector. It is a lot of things that need to be done. But it is too complex, too slow, too little money and too many wills. The only time public sector gets any attention in media or among people in general, is when it's in trouble.

Some of the management consultancy firms have projects going on in the public sector, but others have decided to do as little as possible in this area. The public sector seems to attract only negative attention. In the word of one of the interviewees,

> We have decided to give up the public sector. First of all they don't want to pay for the services. Secondly many of our consultants consider the public sector as a dead-end. They don't want to work in it.

The problems with financing management consultancy projects in the public sector are one point. Another point is the internal lack of interest for working with these kinds of organizations:

> Working with organizations in the public sector makes nothing for you. It doesn't impress anyone, neither other clients nor other consultants. The only thing you meet as a consultant is pity – 'poor you' – a lot of work, stinginess and trouble is what you meet as a consultant in a public organization.

As consultancy work could be characterized as immaterial and heterogeneous it may be even more important to gather the scattered personnel around an image of the firm. It is often considered as very important to reflect a positive identity and to have a good reputation as a way to make the consultants more committed. A positive organizational identity makes the employees more willing to identify with the firm and more motivated to work hard (Dutton *et al.*, 1994). A positive identity and a good reputation can work as 'glue' for the organization – 'this is who we are and how outsiders see us and we stick together'. But it can also indicate in what aspects the members of the organization believe they are different or special. The experiences consultants have made are important for the consultancy firms since they depend on it in relation to the clients, and use it for references and reputation building. To different degrees are the consultants' knowledge is codified and stored in databases. Some consultancy firms emphasize the codification in databases for knowledge transfers, some use it more for combining the right kind of teams, but all use databases as a tool for knowledge transfers. The consultants need to codify their results into common concepts and combinations of topics. The consultants always need to have some kind of curriculum vitae on the intranet or in some knowledge base and earlier experiences with important clients is a way to do a career in the consulting firms. Or as one of the interviewees, a senior consultant, says,

> You got to have the right kind of projects – the hot ones – and put it down on your CV. With the right experiences you become someone to count on.

Consultants acquire respect and value as a knowledge worker primarily from knowledge acquired in earlier experiences with prestigious clients. This is a known fact in the consultancy firms and some of them even have an openly expressed value that says 'up or out'. As a consultant you need to prove yourself in the internal competition, where the clients are the ultimate judges. And a good result from a valued client is a way to get attention:

> Some firms and some projects are not what the consultants want to do. Consultants want to work with the more prestigious projects. It is the way to do a career in the consulting business.

This process of reputation building, the talk about all interesting projects that are done in the firm may create problems. Discontent may be the consequence, when the image of what the work would be like, differs from the reality of the consulting life:

> As a young consultant you have to realize that you can't start with boardroom consulting. Much of the consultants' work is much less glamorous. It is hard work far from glamour.

Concluding comments

The purpose of this chapter has been to discuss the role of the client in the eye of the management consultancy firms. We have in this study identified the importance of the client for the creation of positive reputation of the firm in the eyes of clients. Which client do the consultancies want and why? In what way do the clients contribute to the reputation of the consultancies? The networked reputation is the key to find and realize business opportunities. We believe that opportunities are found in the process of building and maintaining a reputation within a network. It has been concluded that management consultancy work is intangible – the service is sold on a promise that a certain value will be delivered. This highlights the importance of building the right kind of reputation. To be able to attract new clients and keep the old ones it is necessary that the consultancies have a good reputation so that clients or clients-to-be can distinguish the specific firm from others but still connect it to a certain type of firms. The reputation of the firm is dependent on retained past image and the awareness of the importance of this is high in all the firms studied. Reputation is very hard to change and can, if good, be a buffer in bad times or, if bad, a hindrance to accomplish anything good as it influences the interpretation of actions. The importance of having the right kind of client cannot be exaggerated as identity, image and reputation are built up through the interaction between clients and consultants. Clients play an active role in this process of knowledge creation and reputation building, but different clients may be able to contribute to learning processes and reputation to different degrees.

As we have discussed, working with the right kinds of clients is essential for all knowledge firms and may be even more important for management consultancies as the clients are used to learn more, through training, experiences of implementation of offered services and image building. The right kind of client has to be visible because only a visible client can get attention from the outside world and since visibility is closely connected to size and reach the right client is often a big, global firm. All top-ten consultancies prefer to be associated with these big, global firms as they characterize themselves as big and global. The visibility is important because it has the possibility of attracting the attention of other clients and other consultants. Without attention you don't have a reputation and without reputation you have no identity of success. But smaller firms also can be important clients. At the time of the study the small dot.com firms and new management concepts such as e-business or e-strategy were attracting much attention. To be able to sell services in this area the management consultancy firms believed that the e-business firms were valued clients. Through these clients the management consultancy firms infused value in rather new and unclear concepts as 'e-strategy' or 'e-commerce'. Even though this kind of phenomenon – the dot.com trend – could be considered as rather time-specific it is of interest as it might explain how consultancies work with management concepts and image building and how important the management of attention is in this process. It is also important to notice that choosing clients can be a risky business; it is not always easy to predict which firms will attract positive attention and how it will be considered later on. Some firms attract little or only negative attention and these firms are considered as 'less wanted clients'. This kind of clients cannot be used in the process of image building externally and identity shaping internally. Many mature middle-sized firms or the public sector firms are most often characterized as unattractive clients.

Attention seems to be the keyword in the creation of building reputation. A way to get attention is to work with 'new hot things'. But this kind of general attention is not enough. The best way to create opportunities in the management consulting industry is to keep the old client as trust is built through experience. To attract new clients the firm has to build a reputation in the network – a networked reputation. A client may recognize a need only after learning about a certain consultant and its services through someone in the business network. Reputation is built through references and recommendations from a known informant – a firm that attracts attention.

References

Albert, S. and Whetten, D. A. (1985). Organizational Identity, in L. L. Cummings and B. M. Staw (Eds), *Research in Organizational Behavior*, 7, Greenwich, CT: JAI Press: 263–95.

Balmer, J. M. T. (1998). Corporate Identity and the Advent of Corporation Marketing, *Journal of Marketing Management*, 14, 963–96.
Barney, J. and Hansen, M. (1994). Trustworthiness as a Source of Competitive Advantage, *Strategic Management Journal*, 15, 175–90.
Belanger, J. (Ed.) (1999). *Being Local Worldwide: ABB and the Challenge of Global Management*, New York: Cornell University Press.
Bergholz, H. (1999). Do More Than Fix my Company, *Journal of Management Consulting*, 10 (4), 29–33.
Clark, T. (1995). *Managing Consultants. Consultancy and the Management of Impressions*, Buckingham: Open University Press.
Clark, T. and Salaman. G. (1998). Telling Tales: Management Gurus Narratives and the Construction of Managerial Identity, *Journal of Management Studies*, 35 (2), 137–61.
Das, T. K. and Teng, B. S. (2001). Trust, Control and Risk in Strategic Alliances: An Integrated Framework. *Organization Studies*, 22 (2), 251–83.
De Vries, M. (1996). Leaders Who Make a Difference, *European Management Journal*, 14 (5), 486–94.
Dowling, G. R. (2001). *Creating Corporate Reputations. Identity, Image and Performance*, Oxford: Oxford University Press.
Dutton, J. E., Dukerich, J. M. and Harquail, C. (1994). Organizational Images and Member Identification, *Administrative Science Quarterly*, 39 (2), 239–64.
Engwall, L. and Eriksson, C. (1999). Advising Corporate Superstars. CEOs and Consultancies in Top Swedish Corporations. Paper presented at the 15th EGOS colloquium, Warwick University, 4–6 July.
Fincham, R. (1999). The Consultant–Client Relationship: Critical Perspective on the Management of Organizational Change, *Journal of Management Studies*, 36 (3), 335–51.
Ghoshal, S. and Bartlett, C. (1999). *The Individualized Corporation: A Fundamentally New Approach to Management*, New York: Harper business.
Gioia, D. A. (1986). Symbols, Scripts, and Sensemaking: Creating Meaning in the Organizational Experience, in H. P. Sims, Jr. and D. A. Gioia (Eds) *The Thinking Organization*, San Francisco: Jossey-Bass: 49–74.
Gluckler, J. and Armbruster, T. (2003). Bridging Uncertainty in Management Consulting: The Mechanisms of Trust and Networked Reputation. *Organization Studies*, 24 (2), 269–97.
Håkansson, H. and Snehota, I. (1995). *Developing Relationships in Business Networks*, London: Routledge.
von Hippel, E. (1994). Sticky Information and the Locus of Problem Solving: Implications for Innovation, *Management Science*, 40 (4), 429–440.
Johansson, J. and Matsson, L-G. (1988). Internationalisation in Industrial Systems – A Network Approach, in N Hood and J-E. Vahlne (Eds), *Strategies in Global Competition*, New York: Croom Helm, 287–314.
Leonard D. and Rayport, J. F. (1997). Spark Innovation through Empathic Design, *Harvard Business Review*, November–December, 103–13.
Lindahl, D. P. and Beyers, W. B. (1999). The Creation of Competitive Advantage by Producer Service Establishments, *Economic Geography*, 75 (1), 1–20.
Lorenzoni, G. and Baden-Fuller, C. (1995). Creating a Strategic Center to Manage a Web of Partners, *California Management Review*, 37 (3), 146–64.
Nonaka, I. and Takeuchi, H. (1995). *The Knowledge-Creating Company*, Oxford: Oxford University Press.

Sawhney, M. and Prandelli, E. (2000). Beyond Customer Knowledge Management: Customers as Knowledge Co-creators, in Y. Malhotra (Ed.), *Knowledge Management and Virtual Organizations*, London: Idea group Publishing.

Shane, S., Locke, E. A. and Collins, C. J. (2003). Entrepreneurial Motivation, *Human Resource Management Review*, 13 (2), 257–79.

Sturdy, A. (1997). The Consultancy Process – an Insecure Business, *Journal of Management Studies*, 34 (3), 389–413.

Whetten, D. and Godfrey, P. (Eds) (1998). *Identity in Organizations: Developing Theory through Conversations*, Thousand Oaks: Sage.

Part III

Opportunity Development and Networks

12
The Role of Business Opportunity Mediators in the Entrepreneurial Process

Björn Berggren and Lars Silver

Introduction

The dynamics of economic development in society stems from the actions of entrepreneurs starting new firms or make existing firms grow. Entrepreneurs are often depicted as strong individualists with an exceptional vision for profitable ventures or business opportunities (Baron, 1998; Stewart et al., 1998). As omnipotent observers, entrepreneurs are seen as choosing wisely from amongst various business proposals and proceeding to exploit clearly defined business opportunities from the most promising ventures. Even when the entrepreneur deviates from the original plan, they adjust to changes in the environment (Das and Teng, 1997). The classic idea of the entrepreneur is that of the self-made man, who started doing business at a young age and, by taking calculated risks, is able to turn almost any venture deemed worth pursuing into a winner (Smilor, 1997). However, this image is a myth, in stark contrast with how business opportunities are identified and exploited in real life.

In this chapter our aim is to present an alternative view of the entrepreneurial process and to introduce the concept of the business opportunity mediator. The mediator provides business opportunities in the form of established customer relationships that can be further exploited by an entrepreneur. We examine several cases where highly successful entrepreneurs emerge from a background where they do not perceive themselves as entrepreneurs. In these cases they are presented with the business opportunity from other individuals – the business opportunity mediators. By taking on these opportunities they gradually grow into their role as entrepreneurs over time. Thus, their entrepreneurial ability is partly dependent on their personality, but also heavily influenced by other individuals and knowledge gained from interactions with other parties. In many cases the choice of becoming an entrepreneur is not as clear-cut as traditional analyses would suggest. This view is in line with the theoretical discussion in Chapter 1, in that development of opportunities is not a product of entrepreneurs alone. Entrepreneurial development is significantly dependent on interactions within the surrounding social network.

Theoretical points of departure

Typically, the entrepreneur is portrayed as someone who creates a new venture in trying to meet the needs of the market. Exploiting new opportunities, new markets or new innovations are seen as the core of successful entrepreneurship (Kirzner, 1973; McClelland, 1961, Schumpeter, 1934). The popular image of the atomistic, all-seeing entrepreneur is further reinforced by the success stories of well-known high-flying entrepreneurs like Bill Gates and Richard Branson. These invariably portray the entrepreneur as personally overcoming obstacles in order to claim fame and success. However, psychological and sociological research does not support this generalisation, with the entrepreneur typically acting within a network of people (Aldrich, 1999; Hansen, 1995). Despite this, the image of the entrepreneur as a focused individual, with a state-of-the-art business plan, ready to exploit the opportunities of an emerging market, is prevalent in the literature on entrepreneurship (e.g. Fagenson, 1993; McGrath, *et al.*, 1992).

The role of chance events influencing the success of the entrepreneur and growth within firms has been suggested as an important factor frequently ignored in analyses of entrepreneurship (Bouchikhi, 1993). From this perspective, simply being motivated, having the relevant background and personality traits usually attributed to the successful entrepreneur is not always sufficient to explain the entrepreneurial process. An entrepreneur becomes successful by interacting with others (Birley, 1985), and thus is often dependent on chance and the goodwill of other people. From this we can assume that some entrepreneurs, while lacking many of the skills usually deemed necessary for success, are still successful, whereas others, who have the skills and motivation of the stereotypical entrepreneur, fail, simply through the consequences of these chance events or the actions of other people.

Evolving entrepreneurship

Entrepreneurs are commonly described in terms of: (1) their alertness to opportunities and propensity to take risks (Ardichvili *et al.*, 2003; Kirzner, 1973), (2) their impact on the surrounding economic system in relation to new markets, products, innovations or co-ordination of limited resources (Casson, 1982; Schumpeter, 1934), or (3) their characteristics or personality traits (Kets de Vries, 1977; McClelland, 1961). Authors suggest the existence of two types of entrepreneurs – the craftsman and the opportunist: these two categories sit on opposing ends of a continuum. The opportunist exhibits traits of the textbook entrepreneur: growth-oriented, well-educated, focused on the future, a wide social network and in constant pursuit of new opportunities. This is in contrast to the craftsman entrepreneur, who is viewed as the traditional small business manager, lacking the traits of the opportunistic entrepreneur. While this appears to be a rather crude distinction, nevertheless, it has gained support from other researchers who have used this typology (Das and Teng, 1997; Haynes et al., 1999).

Despite the focus on the entrepreneur as an individual who creates new firms, in most cases several other people, or teams of entrepreneurs, are involved in this process. This is particularly evident in the high-technology sector (Roberts, 1991). Even in situations where a single entrepreneur is directly responsible for creating a new venture, he or she is often assisted by one or more actors who are providing advice and support (Aldrich, 1999). Thus, the traditional view of entrepreneurship and entrepreneurs needs to be revised because it becomes increasingly difficult to discuss endogenous and exogenous proprieties of entrepreneurship, as we currently understand it, if this entrepreneurship is not located in a single person, 'the entrepreneur'. Indeed, this idea of the entrepreneur is further eroded if vital elements of the entrepreneurial activity originate from individuals who are not even a part of the entrepreneurial team. We support the idea that entrepreneurship in business should include elements of innovation (Schumpeter, 1934), alertness (Kirzner, 1973), the creation or growth of a new venture (Gartner, 1989) and a temporal element, in that when the new venture creation ends, the entrepreneurship also ends (Gartner, 1989); however, we propose that the entrepreneur is merely the actor who initiates and directs the entrepreneurship process. Under this definition, people other than the 'entrepreneur' may have had the vision or discovered the business opportunity, but it was the entrepreneur who implemented the ideas or followed up on the opportunity.

Business opportunity

The notion of chance implies that there is something unintended in a process that, by definition, cannot be anticipated and planned for. Chance has been seen as synonymous with opportunity; these chance events are fortuitous in that they provide the opportunities on which the entrepreneur may act (Bouchikhi, 1993). However, the role of chance as a vital part of entrepreneurial success is rarely highlighted; rather, entrepreneurs are said to 'seize business opportunities', as if they always go out and create them. Chance events are out of the control of the entrepreneur, but they are one of the factors that create potential opportunities for the entrepreneur: opportunities that now fall within the realm of control, in that they can be identified, evaluated and acted upon. Thus, while chance may often be linked to the creation of entrepreneurial opportunity, it is not the same thing. Entrepreneurs are by definition someone who chooses to pursue business opportunities; however, they are not necessarily the discoverers of the opportunity itself (Shane, 2000). By chance an entrepreneur may stumble upon a business opportunity but more often he/she will be introduced to the business opportunity by other people through a social network (Ardichvili *et al.*, 2003; Smilor, 1997).

The discovery of a business opportunity is usually domain-specific, that is, an entrepreneur is more likely to encounter an opportunity in his or her area of expertise (Ardichvili *et al.*, 2003; Shane, 2000). Experience and prior knowledge are important in recognising opportunities and might explain the phenomenon of serial entrepreneurs (Storey, 1994). Entrepreneurship evolves as the discovery leads to the start of a new business venture (Aldrich, 1999). The entrepreneur is born at the same time; however, the entrepreneur may be limited to only acting in specific domains, depending on aid received by other individuals. Business opportunities are customer-driven in that the entrepreneur meets a real need in the marketplace within a reasonable time (Smilor, 1997). But entrepreneurship is facilitated or constrained by the embeddedness of social relations of the entrepreneur; the more complex and larger the web surrounding the entrepreneur, the more support and opportunities will be at his or her disposal.

Business opportunity mediator

Kirzner (1973) defines entrepreneurship as alertness to information gaps in the market and the process of taking advantage of these. However, defining entrepreneurship in this way does not necessarily lead to the conclusion that it is the entrepreneur who initially perceives the market opportunity. In some cases it is a second person who alerts the entrepreneur to the opportunity, a business opportunity mediator, by providing critical resources to enable them to develop their ideas more efficiently, or by directly providing advice as to where to find the gaps in the market (Shane, 2003). This view challenges the traditional idea of the entrepreneur by suggesting that 'the entrepreneur' is in fact two people working together; one providing the, so-called, 'entrepreneurial traits' or cognitive mechanisms of the entrepreneur, while the other provides the resources or access to an advantageous position in the market. This is not the same as a new-venture team, because the person providing the resources to the entrepreneur is not doing so from an ownership motive. Because market- and customer-related issues are more problematic in the start-up phase than production-related issues (Aldrich, 1999; Birley, 1985), we predict that effective business opportunity mediators would primarily provide resources pertaining to these two areas of need.

Besides being alert to opportunities, many theorists argue that entrepreneurs are motivated by high risks and high returns (Busenitz and Barney, 1997; Stewart et al., 1998). However, recent empirical findings do not support this hypothesis, with entrepreneurs being no more inclined to take higher risks than other individuals (Wiklund, 1998; Winborg, 2000). Instead, entrepreneurs take better-calculated risks: that is, they are better informed and, hence, are better able to appreciate the risks inherent in a new venture (Baron, 1998; Paldich and Bagby, 1995). The role of the business opportunity mediator in supplying information regarding potential business opportunities provides the entrepreneur with the knowledge that allows him/her to take the next step: to determine which opportunities to pursue, and develop these into viable enterprises.

By examining real-world cases, this chapter aims to illustrate several aspects of evolving entrepreneurship that are rarely acknowledged: (1) the role of business opportunity mediators, (2) the role of chance events, and (3) how these two factors affect the creation and success of the entrepreneur. By tracing the history and development of these people as they became entrepreneurs, we hope to illustrate that entrepreneurship evolves, and that people do not necessarily enter the business world with their entrepreneurial skills fully developed.

Methodology

The four case studies presented below were part of a preliminary study to a larger survey of small- and medium-sized firms conducted in the following year. The four cases are based on interviews with entrepreneurs from the Norrtälje region of Sweden in the spring of 2003. These interviews were conducted at the firms' premises, and were taped and later transcribed. Interview length ranged from 90 to 120 minutes and during this time the interviewees spoke freely about the development of their firm as well as their own background. The interviews were generally unstructured, but certain aspects of interest were explored in-depth, such as the start-up phase of the firm. The interviewees were selected through a snowball-sampling technique, meaning that the first entrepreneur was asked to suggest other entrepreneurs that they believed had an interesting company and history. The only criteria for selection after this point was that the firm must have been established for a number of years to enable the entrepreneur to reflect upon the history of the company; hence, start-ups were not included in this sample.

Since we are in the exploratory part of the research project the fit between the research problem and method chosen seemed to be reasonable. Results from case studies have often been criticised for lacking possibilities for generalising (Scapens, 1990). In part this could be explained by the erroneous notion of the case as a sample of one (Bryman, 1989). The cases in this chapter illustrate the genesis of the business opportunity as perceived by the actors surrounding the firms and the notion of generalisation seems therefore to be of minor importance.

Four case studies of entrepreneurial opportunities

The following four cases share a common feature in that the entrepreneur in each firm was extended the opportunity to join or take over the firm by an external actor.

Case 1: Rolf Fredriksson – Norrtälje maskiner

Rolf Fredriksson, the current CEO of Norrtälje maskiner AB, started work in the 1970s as an assistant in a construction firm after graduating as a mechanical engineer. After several years he moved to the manufacturing firm Bahco in Enköping, where he worked for ten years as a truck driver. He was then promoted to head the department of maintenance and stayed with Bahco until 1986.

During his time as a manager he was required to travel extensively, so much so that it impacted on his personal life. At this time his neighbour, seeing that Rolf was looking to change career path, offered him a job at his own firm, Norrtälje Maskinuthyrning. This was a small firm that rented machines and tools for construction work, with Rolf's neighbour its only employee. While the new job was located in Norrtälje where Rolf lived, leaving a secure position in a large company was a difficult decision. Rolf was offered the firm for a relatively small sum of money and after some initial hesitation he went into business for himself.

It was two years before Rolf took on staff, with him hiring two employees in 1989. With the exception of the recession in the early 1990s, the firm has grown steadily and diversified. The core business still focuses on renting machinery to construction sites, but with an additional product range including consumable articles such as nails and hammers, and a change of focus away from retail customers.

Despite the success of these changes and the positive growth of the company, Rolf saw a prospect to further expand and diversify when he was presented with the opportunity of acquiring Norrtälje maskiner AB in 2000. This firm's primary business was retail products such as lawn mowers, chain saws and other type of gardening tools. It was founded in the 1950s and had a well-known and respected trademark in the Norrtälje region. The owner was considering retirement and offered to sell Rolf the firm. Realising the opportunities of the expanding market for gardening tools, Rolf acquired the new business. The two firms complemented each other well, with the gardening division of the firm rapidly expanding to now become more profitable than the original, machine rental division. Customers are primarily local residents and companies, with the firm now employing eleven people, and are in the process of consolidating after the acquisition of Norrtälje maskiner. Realising the importance of local networks for business opportunities, Rolf has expanded his networking activities and is part of a number of formal networks such as the freemasons and the local bowling club.

Case 2: Tommy Liljedahl – Roslagens kabel

Olle Hedlund, worked as a technical engineer in the construction industry, and was also a part-time inventor. He had established a small technical consulting firm and in 1961 was contracted by Alfa Laval, Sweden's largest manufacturer of dairy equipment, to develop the signalling system in their dishwashers. Specifically, he was to developing harnesses, the system of small cables through which signals are sent between different sub-parts of the dishwashers. Over time the signalling system, using cables attached to the separate parts of the machinery was developed. Olle conducted his research and development and eventually the harness system production in the kitchen of his Stockholm flat during his spare time. At this time, harness system manufacturing was in its infancy, and production was conducted by manually fitting the separate parts together. Only four or five small firms specialised in harnesses production.

Tommy Liljedahl was Olle Hedlund's grandnephew who began working with Olle during his vacations in the early 1970s. In his early twenties, Tommy had few ideas as to what he wanted to pursue as a career. During this time, the firm entered into a relationship with Tyco, one of the largest manufacturers of cables worldwide and gradually changed from technical consultancy to trading and assembling harness products. As the firm began to generate more business, Tommy quit school and began working full time. With the unexpected death of Olle in 1973, Tommy suddenly found himself in a position to take over the business because Alfa Laval had the blueprints for the inventions and wanted to continue working with Tommy. Together with a partner, he bought the business and completed its transformation into a harnesses assembling firm. Thus, he came into a business with an established large customer who wanted to continue doing business, as well as a good working relationship with a large manufacturer. Tommy recognised the value in automated assembly of harnesses to minimise costs, but one problem he faced was that it is difficult to find standardised solutions in the harness manufacturing industry, as the cables need to be fitted according to the specific dimensions of the machines in which they are used; thus, the output for a specific assembly will be relatively small.

In 1976 Tommy took over as general manager, and in 1978 the expanding firm moved to new premises in the small town of Norrtälje. This enabled the firm to acquire a stable and loyal workforce, with staff turnover considerably reduced. During this period the firm worked hard to establish new customer relationships, a move that paid off when their biggest customer, Alfa Laval, began harness assembly themselves. During the 1980s the firm slowly grew and started to attract business throughout the country. Today there are approximately 80 firms working in the industry, with half of these being very small. Roslagens kabel has shown a steady profit since Tommy took over and they currently have a workforce of 31 employees. The industry has not dramatically changed, as each system still needs to be custom-made for each machine in which they are used, thus, there are few large firms in the industry. One thing that has changed in Roslagens kabel during the last couple of years is the introduction of a professional board of directors. Tommy considers himself to be quite cautious as an entrepreneur, and this is evident through the slow but steady growth of the firm over the years, while having maintained a relatively even level of profits.

Case 3: Jens Marklund – Swetech

Jens Marklund is an entrepreneur who believes that anyone with good ideas can succeed. He started working in 1985, in the firm that eventually became Swetech. At 24 years old, he had recently graduated as an engineer and moved to Norrtälje where his wife had begun working. Despite Norrtälje being small and seemingly offering little chance of him quickly finding employment in his chosen profession, he was soon offered an engineering position in Safab, a company led by entrepreneur Dan Larsson (see the next case study). Safab's two major businesses were manufacturing transformers and electronics; Jens was hired for the electronics division. The intention was that the electronics division was to develop a simple and efficient production process for the assembly of electronic products for their clients.

At this time Dan Larsson began looking abroad in order to start production outside Sweden, partly because he felt that Swedish laws and attitudes were unfavourable towards the type of standardised production Safab engaged in. A production facility was started in England, and in 1990 this led to Dan Larsson persuading Jens Marklund and two other employees to take over the electronics department in Norrtälje as their own venture. Almost immediately the company was on the brink of bankruptcy when their largest customer reallocated their production purchase to Singapore. Rather than changing the emphasis of the firm away from simple production processes as had been Dan Larsson's intention, Jens elected to expand this section of the business. New customers were found and soon this decision proved its worth; it coincided with many manufacturing firms outsourcing their production. This trend enabled an astonishing growth in the firm over the last ten years. Also important was an internal reorganisation in 1992 where the customary hierarchical structure was abandoned in favour of an organisation of teams that dealt directly with the customers' needs and developed their own set of competencies amongst their members.

During the recession of the early 1990s the firm bought machinery from competitors that were leaving the market. While risky, this strategy paid off and allowed rapid expansion of the business. In 2000 one of the owners left the firm, and the majority of shares were sold to new investors, including the staff. The company changed name to Swetech and acquired a number of production facilities in Sweden, Poland and Lithuania. Currently the company's turnover amounts to 1 billion SEK, and employs over 600 people. Swetech has shown a consistent profit since 1992 and prides itself on its highly advanced logistics system and the team concept, which is spread out through the firm.

Case 4: Dan Larsson – Safab

Dan Larsson's career as an entrepreneur began in 1968, while still a student at the Royal Institute of Technology. Because his father worked in a small firm, Dan wanted to explore the possibility of developing and growing his own firm despite the trend for students at that time to want to work in larger established businesses. His firm began modestly in the field of electronic components, the same field his father worked in. Dan's father soon relocated and began working in Dan's firm after the firm he was working for was sold. Because of this, Dan inherited not only his father's skills in electronics manufacture, but more importantly, an established set of customers and valuable knowledge of the industry. Thus, the new firm was unusual in that it had the advantage of established and well-maintained customer relationships. Because of this, Dan did not have to aggressively market the company to new customers, and instead could concentrate on improving production processes. The firm quickly grew to employ ten people.

In 1980, the firm now called Safab, relocated to Norrtälje. This resulted in an almost complete turnover of staff; however, the new company was able to employ a more stable workforce in this area. The firm gradually grew to a size of 50 employees, but in 1986 Dan found that hiring employees for industrial purposes was becoming more difficult, especially in a relatively well-to-do part of Sweden. Because of this he opened a new production facility in the north of England, where unemployment was high and a willing workforce was available. While the late 1980s were a good growth period for the company, managing both the English and Swedish operations were difficult and so he decided to involve three key workers in the Norrtälje production facility. By separating the electronics department in Norrtälje this allowed him to concentrate on the more promising business in England.

In the early 1990s, with the recession and disagreements with the partners of the newly formed electronics company, Dan sold his remaining stake in the Norrtälje electronics business. His main production facility was now in England, and by selling transformers and inductors, designing inductors for specific customers and providing surface mount assembly services, the future of Safab resided on a traditional line of production. However, the early years in England were difficult, with expansion of the company slowing due to lack of capital. Safab also opened another production facility in Northern France because of specific customer relationships, but this is a relatively small part of Safab today. Safab is currently faced with finding a partner to finance the development of new ideas or to expand its presence in its traditional market.

Discussion

The four case studies provide examples of how entrepreneurship evolves over time, as well as the potential importance of business opportunity mediators. Rolf Fredriksson's decision to become an entrepreneur is typical of the fledgling entrepreneur. Having no immediate vision to start a new company, he was quite unprepared for life as an entrepreneur. Fortunately the company he acquired was small at the time, which provided the opportunity to begin slowly and learn on the job. Rolf's first encounter with the original owner was a chance event, and the timing served well to initiate business opportunity mediation. In having the former owner as his neighbour that he was on good terms with, Rolf saw that there would be few hidden risks in the venture while also benefiting from advice from the former owner during the critical first stages. The original idea remains as the core business of the firm, despite the significant expansion in product range offered by the firm. This has enabled him to maintain a solid market share from day one. The strategy of an established core business and slow steady growth has enabled Rolf to live a relatively secure life as an entrepreneur.

Tommy Liljedahl of Roslagens kabel represents another entrepreneur who has chosen slow growth out of an initial market share, and has experienced a similar and relatively uneventful success story. Tommy received considerable aid when starting his firm, as his grand uncle had already established business with a large customer and developed the initial product. As with Rolf, Tommy's decision to become an entrepreneur was initiated through the chance event of having a relative employing his services and training the young acolyte in the harness production business. As before, timing was important as Tommy was at an age where he was undecided about his future career-choice. Also, he started his company with few resources and was able to slowly assimilate knowledge over time. Despite the sudden loss of his business opportunity mediator, the established customer relationship developed by his mentor enabled the firm to continue and eventually thrive.

The third case is unusual in that Jens Marklund's firm has grown dramatically in a relatively short time span. While Jens' future in a big corporation was there for the taking, chance intervened, with him looking through the local paper at the appropriate moment and resulting in him joining a relatively small firm instead. The combination of the firm's owner wanting to focus elsewhere and him being regarded as a prospective entrepreneur and being offered part-ownership of his division has resulted in a remarkable success story. As before, a solid business idea and established customer and supplier relationships have been the platform on which Jens Marklund's leadership and strategy have led to entrepreneurial success. By choosing to focus on employee–customer relationships and perfecting logistics, Jens' entrepreneurship provided a solid foundation for growth. Without the established business to build on and his associates' support to help him, Jens' success story may not have been. Dan Larsson's role as a business opportunity mediator should not be overlooked, even though they ultimately differed in opinion.

Dan Larsson, the very man who persuaded Jens into taking over part of his old firm, is another example of business opportunity mediation; he inherited much of his father's knowledge of the transformer industry as well as some key customer relationships. In this way Dan was able to combine the enthusiasm and knowledge of the young academic with the skills of a craftsman in the industry. Dan grew into the entrepreneurship role over time, with his experiences in the 1980s demonstrating that he was the type of entrepreneur who was able to reinvent his business, and was willing to change in face of a perceived change in environment. The remarkable parallel development of Swetech and Safab illustrate an interesting case of strategic decision-making, influenced by both luck and the unforeseen developments in the environment.

These four cases are vivid examples of entrepreneurship, with the men considered to be some of the prime entrepreneurial minds in Norrtälje. Swetech in particular has been heralded as a fantastic achievement, and Jens Marklund is widely renowned for his skill as an entrepreneur – a man who never imagined himself as an entrepreneur to begin with. Indeed, all four cases were examples of fledgling entrepreneurs, in that, regardless of how experienced and successful they are today, when they started out they lacked the developed entrepreneurial skills that are often considered necessary for success. In all cases they were able to grow into their entrepreneurial careers because they had support from a business opportunity mediator with a solid business idea and established customer relationships. We see this as highlighting an element often essential to successful entrepreneurship that is currently lacking in standard definitions. Theories of entrepreneurship cannot only focus on the single entrepreneur or entrepreneur teams, but needs to incorporate the wider scope of the social environment. In Table 12.1 the contributions provided by mediators and entrepreneurs in these cases are summarised. Each of the four cases is unique, with differing variables leading to a successful entrepreneurial process.

Theoretical contributions of opportunities in business networks

The concepts arising from our study that require emphasis are that of evolving entrepreneurship and the important role of business opportunity mediation. We posit that entrepreneurship is often a process to be learnt, rather than the traditional view that it is a trait inherent in the entrepreneur. Thus, it remains an empirical question as to the direction of causality for acquiring

Table 12.1 The role and contribution of the business opportunity mediator in the four cases

Case characteristics	Norrtälje maskiner	Roslagens kabel	Swetech	Safab
Relationship of mediator to entrepreneur	Neighbour	Uncle	Employer	Father
Mediator's contribution	Transfer of going concern	Specific customer relationship	Transfer of going concern	Specific customer relationship
Entrepreneur's contribution	Marketing	Marketing	Marketing and organisation	Marketing and organisation
Mediator's exit date	Instant transfer	Several years	One year	Several years
Type of exit	Neutral	Positive	Negative	Positive

entrepreneurial skills and becoming a successful entrepreneur. Too often, research assumes that the traits of a successful entrepreneur were responsible for that success, rather than considering the possibility that the path to success helped create the skills and traits of the entrepreneur.

We also see that this process of learning is dependent on the availability of a social network of actors capable of teaching the fledgling entrepreneur; thus, knowledge transfer from the business opportunity mediator is of vital importance in many cases. While it is the entrepreneur who utilises business opportunities, and thus is recognised for doing so, it is often the business mediator who uncovered the potential avenue to approach a certain business opportunity in a network. These mediators tend to heavily influence how fledgling entrepreneurs develop their main business ideas, especially since the mediator usually knows more about the actors in the business network than the entrepreneur in the early stages of entrepreneurship. Business opportunity mediators also heavily influence what the fledgling entrepreneur will concentrate on in the early start-up phase; if the mediator offers market connections, the fledgling entrepreneur will focus on the set up of the company; if the mediator provides production methods or facilities, then the fledgling entrepreneur will focus on the marketing of products.

As seen in our cases, highly successful entrepreneurs may become entrepreneurs by chance rather than by design, usually when the person is shown a way towards a viable business position by a business opportunity mediator. A person may choose to become an entrepreneur, either as a way to escape the tedious work as an unempowered employee, or as a way for a university graduate to find an alternative to working for a big corporation. In either case the fledgling entrepreneur is seldom equipped to find business opportunities and succeed without outside intervention. Thus, the element of chance, in which the fledgling entrepreneur encounters the business opportunity mediator, needs to be more fully recognised. The traditional view of entrepreneurs as larger-than-life figures predestined to a successful future is simplistic and inaccurate. Entrepreneurship research would be better served by focusing on social contexts rather than traditional psychological profiling, especially since research in the field has been heavily biased towards psychological motives rather than the influences of the social environment. We also encourage research into the ontogeny or skill-development of the entrepreneur to better determine which traits attributed to entrepreneurship are commonly inherent in the fledgling entrepreneur and which skills are learnt or imported from the social network.

Summary

The aim of this chapter is to present evidence that various external factors may influence entrepreneurship and the development of the entrepreneur. Traditional views of entrepreneurship imply that entrepreneurs instinctively arrive at fortuitous opportunities or somehow manufacture these opportunities through skill, cunning and guile. In practice, entrepreneurs are rarely likely to posses all of the talents that are usually attributed to entrepreneurship when they start the venture. In the cases presented, it is evident that the entrepreneurs are uncertain as to which path to follow, and indeed, whether to begin the business venture in the first place. By using concepts such as chance and business opportunity mediators our study focuses on the aid entrepreneurs are given by other actors in their social network as they start their enterprise. Different characters such as neighbours, relatives and employers, intervene and provide crucial assistance to the would-be entrepreneur. These business mediators help by either transferring business ideas or crucial customer relationships in the early stages. In all cases these entrepreneurs are considered in the sense of the self-made man by the social network; in reality, they have started from a platform partially built for them and used their entrepreneurial ability in either finding new markets or new organisational structures for their ventures. The providers of aid, the business opportunity mediators, gradually reduce their role in the firm and eventually disappear, thus remaining out of sight for most observers. In all cases chance played a key role in the entrepreneurs finding their business ideas, often through a chance relationship with the person who would become their business opportunity mediator. Thus, this chapter provides some evidence that entrepreneurs also rely on chance and opportunity to stake out their careers, a concept often ignored in the research on entrepreneurial success. Also, while the entrepreneurs highlighted here began with some entrepreneurial traits, not all of these were fully established; thus, without connections in their social network to help them develop these skills, they would not have become the entrepreneurs they are today.

References

Aldrich, H. (1999). *Organizations Evolving*, London: SAGE.
Ardichvili, A., Cardozo, R. and Ray, S. (2003). A Theory of Entrepreneurial Opportunity Identification and Development, *Journal of Business Venturing*, 18, 105–23.
Baron, R. A. (1998). Cognitive Mechanisms in Entrepreneurship: Why and When Entrepreneurs Think Differently than Other People, *Journal of Business Venturing*, 13, 275–94.
Birley, S. (1985). The Role of Networks in the Entrepreneurial Process, *Journal of Business Venturing*, 1, 107–17.
Bouchikhi, H. (1993). A Constructivist Framework for Understanding Entrepreneurship Performance, *Organization Studies*, 14, 549–70.
Bryman, A. (1989). *Research Methods and Organisation Studies*, New York: Irwin.
Busenitz, L. W. and Barney, J. B. (1997). Differences between Entrepreneurs and Managers in Large Organizations: Biases and Heuristics in Strategic Decision-Making, *Journal of Business Venturing*, 12, 9–30.
Casson, M. (1982). *The Entrepreneur – An Economic Theory*, Oxford: Martin Robertson.
Das, T. K. and Teng, B. S. (1997). Time and Entrepreneurial Risk Behaviour, *Entrepreneurship, Theory & Practice*, 22, 69–88.
Fagenson, R. (1993). Personal Value Systems of Men and Women Entrepreneurs versus Managers, *Journal of Business Venturing*, 8, 409–30.
Gartner, W. B. (1989). Who is An Entrepreneur? Is the Wrong Question, *Entrepreneurship, Theory & Practice*, 13, 47–68.
Hansen, E. L. (1995). Entrepreneurial Networks and New Organization Growth. *Entrepreneurship, Theory & Practice*, 20, 7–19.
Haynes, P. J., Becherer, R. C., Helms, M. M. and Jones, M. A. (1999). The Accidental Entrepreneur: When Dissatisfaction Is the Primary Motivation for Entrepreneurship, *Journal of Business and Entrepreneurship*, 11, 89–103.
Kets de Vries, M. F. R. (1977). The Entrepreneurial Personality: A Person at the Crossroads, *Journal of Management Studies*, 14, 34–57.
Kirzner, I. (1973). *Competition and Entrepreneurship*, Chicago: The University of Chicago Press.
McClelland, D. (1961). *The Achieving Society*, Princeton: Van Nostrand.
McGrath, R. G., MacMillan, I. C. and Scheinberg, S. (1992). Elitists, Risk-takers and Rugged individualists? An Exploratory Analysis of Cultural Differences between Entrepreneurs and Non-entrepreneurs, *Journal of Business Venturing*, 7, 115–35.
Paldich, L. E. and Bagby, D. R. (1995). Using Cognitive Theory to Explain Entrepreneurial Risk-taking: challenging Conventional Wisdom, *Journal of Business Venturing*, 10, 425–38.
Roberts, E. B. (1991). *Entrepreneurs in High Technology: Lessons from MIT and beyond*, New York: Oxford University Press.
Scapens, R. (1990). Researching Management Accounting Practice: the Role of Case Study Methods, *British Accounting Review*, 22, 259–81.
Schumpeter, J. (1934). *The Theory of Economic Development*, Cambridge, MA: Harvard University Press.
Shane, S. (2000). Prior Knowledge and the Discovery of Entrepreneurial Opportunities, *Organization Science*, 11, 448–69.
Smilor, R. W. (1997). Entrepreneurship – Reflections on a Subversive Activity, *Journal of Business Venturing*, 12, 341–46.

Stewart, W. H., Watson, W. E., Carland, J. C. and Carland, J. W. (1998). A Proclivity for Entrepreneurship: A Comparison of Entrepreneurs, Small Business Owners, and Corporate Managers, *Journal of Business Venturing*, 14, 189–214.
Storey, D. J. (1994). *Understanding the Small Business Sector*, London: Routledge.
Wiklund, J. (1998). *Small Firm Growth and Perfomance – Entrepreneurship and Beyond*, Ph D. Thesis. Jönköping: Jönköping International Business School.
Winborg, J. (2000). *Financing Small Businesses – Developing our Understanding of Financial Bootstrapping Behaviour*. PhD. Thesis. School of Economics and Management. Lund: Lund University.

13
Opportunity Development for Ongoing Business Relationships

Cecilia Pahlberg and Peter Thilenius

Introduction

Seizing the opportunity often takes the key role in innovation, change and long-term success in business. The opportunity is, in that respect, something valuable occurring in the market which can be discovered and put to use by a company with the capability to do so. For a company, this means being active in the market and employing the entrepreneurial function to realize the opportunity and to change its operations accordingly. We argue that certain opportunity development can only be achieved through ongoing business relationships. Opportunity development means change in business relationships. Continuous change in ongoing business relationships is thus fundamental for opportunity development. But opportunity development is also contingent on input from the wider network of business relationships. Without change induced by the network connection, the ongoing business relationship risks stagnation and becoming routine, making opportunity development impossible. Against this background, the purpose of this chapter is to expand on the continuous opportunity development process in ongoing business relationships. More specifically, the aim is to explore the links between connection and change that provide the basis for opportunity development for the ongoing business relationship.

Opportunity development

In her seminal work "The Theory of the Growth of the Firm," Edith Penrose (1959) states that the growth of firms can mainly be explained by their search for opportunities to make money (p. 17). Hence, it can be assumed that successful companies are the ones that see opportunities and take advantage of them in a profitable way. But what do we mean by "opportunities" and how do firms see/find them? In dictionaries, various rather general definitions are given, and usually the concept is related to "chance," which implies that it cannot be planned in advance. This is in line with

Kirzner (1997), who emphasizes that one cannot systematically search for an opportunity. It is also often pointed out that the concept involves some kind of "advantageous combination" and, specifically, this focus on "combinations" is a recurrent theme throughout this book.

When it comes to research on opportunities, it is commonly stressed that specific knowledge is a most vital factor. While traditional studies emphasize the role of the individual and his/her specific knowledge, more recent research has focused on the importance of experiential knowledge. Hence, for authors such as Shane (2000) and Venkataraman (1997), prior knowledge and idiosyncratic experiences are vital for opportunities to occur. This is also in line with the arguments put forward in this book where, in the introductory chapter, it is argued that opportunity development consists of components of specific knowledge and resources, possessed by actors in a network which, when combined in new ways increase their value. This indicates that opportunities do not evolve in a vacuum but, rather, are the result of interactions. Such a perspective differs from traditional views on "opportunities" which are common in literature on entrepreneurship and where it is assumed that the heterogeneous resources (a prerequisite for opportunities to occur) develop *within* the firm. Our perspective, though, implies that knowledge and resources are dispersed among actors in a wider network consisting also of a firm's relationships with specific actors outside the firm. These actors possess their own unique knowledge and resources, and it is the interaction between them and their connected counterparts that leads to new combinations, that is the change that is essential for opportunities to occur.

In other words, it is essential to study this interaction in a business network in order to understand how opportunities occur. As noted in Chapter 1, it is still unclear by whom and how the opportunity process is initiated. Shane and Venkataraman (2000) argue that a problem with the traditional research is that the focus has mainly been on who the individual entrepreneur is and what he/she does. Exceptions are Eckhardt and Shane (2003: 344–5) and Klevorick *et al.* (1995), who refer to research on technological development and indicate that the study of industrial firms, including suppliers and customers, would increase the understanding of factors that affect the occurrence of opportunities. Studies of industrial firms have attracted much interest during the last two decades, and specifically business relationships and business networks have gained much attention (Håkansson, 1987; Håkansson and Waluszewski, 2002). In such a business relationship perspective, technological development is often seen as an incremental process among specific actors who learn through their daily activities. As knowledge is often tacit, learning-by-doing is essential, that is, the actors involved in the relationship gain experience and knowledge by working together, and step-by-step they modify their activities. The exchange with such a counterpart leads to increasing commitment and interdependence and, with time, a business relationship develops. This relationship is continuously strengthened and the parties involved adapt their ways of doing business to suit each other.

When adopting this perspective, the earlier experiences of the actors involved become central. When co-operating, these experiences are incrementally complemented with new knowledge. In Chapter 1, the three concepts of specific knowledge, specific commitment and surpass value are introduced, and it is argued that the level of imbalance between knowledge and commitment is correlated with uncertainty and surpass value. A low imbalanced situation is related to low uncertainty and positive surpass value, while high imbalance is likely to result in unnoticed opportunities or failures. The reasoning in Chapter 1 is summarized in a matrix, in which the consequences of high/low degrees of specific knowledge and specific commitment are illustrated. One main conclusion is that opportunity development requires more knowledge, which leads to higher imbalance, that is risk and uncertainty, and in order to reduce this, an incremental approach could be employed.

One problem, though, is that an incremental approach puts emphasis on continuous adaptations and improvements with one specific counterpart. In most studies on development activities, the primary focus is on a dyadic relationship, mostly between a buyer and a seller, while the surrounding network is not explicitly taken into consideration. In this chapter, we will argue that it is not sufficient to study changes in a dyadic relationship in order to understand where opportunities are likely to occur. In other words, all changes within a relationship are not *per se* opportunities, since they lack the dynamic component which characterizes opportunities.

Studies focusing on dyads emphasize stability, and can explain how an actor develops knowledge in a relationship with a specific counterpart. But they do not provide explanations on how new opportunities occur. As indicated above, a prerequisite for opportunities to occur is that new information and knowledge complement existing prior knowledge and experiences in the business relationship. Thus, change and dynamism are vital for opportunity development. The point is that, in order to understand how this affects a specific business relationship, connected relationships must be taken into consideration. The focus in this chapter will therefore be on how connections to other relationships in the business network relate to change and opportunity development for the ongoing business relationship. By doing this, we hope to shed some light on business network dynamics, that is, complement the dimensions of present and past to include a future perspective, which is one of the main purposes of this book (cf. Chapter 1).

Business relationships and change

As noted by Penrose (1959), learning processes in interactions are frequent, and several later empirical studies have also shown that interaction between buyer and seller is a key characteristic of innovation and technological development (see e.g. Dosi, 1988; Håkansson, 1987; Lundvall, 1988; von Hippel, 1988). Interaction often leads to the coordination of activities and resources between two firms (Håkansson and Snehota, 1995), which implies that interdependent production, development and administrative activities are modified and adapted to the two firms' way of doing business (Hallén, et al., 1987). Empirical data have shown that through exchanges of economic, technological, social and informational matters, the interactions take place within long-lasting relationships with specific counterparts, and "perhaps hidden under a surface of stability, these relationships are the sources for a large number of technological changes" (Håkansson and Waluszewski, 2002: 14). Most often these changes have to do with relatively small improvements of already existing solutions and thus they are perhaps best described as incremental innovations. The incremental changes allow the business relationship to evolve in such ways that its efficiency, continuity and long-time survival is ensured. The incremental changes of business relationships may however at the same time pose a threat to the business relationship. The threat lies in the risk of not being able to see opportunities for the business relationship. This might be the result if the parties' efforts to change the business relationship are too narrowly focused on small improvements of the existing situation.

But what changes of ongoing business relationships carry the transformation of the interaction beyond the small improvement associated with incremental innovation? What changes of an ongoing business relationship may rather be the result of some opportunity for that business relationship? With reference to Casson (1982) and Venkataraman (1997), Eckhardt and Shane (2003) define entrepreneurial opportunities as "situations in which new goods, services, raw materials, markets and organizing methods can be introduced through the formation of new means, ends or means–ends relationships" (p. 336). This implies that opportunities may be the result of changes in different parts of the value chain. This is in line with Schumpeter (1934) and his discussion about the five "loci of change" relating to entrepreneurship and innovation. In a business relationship setting, these areas of change are, after 70 years, still of great relevance and a current focus for research. The first locus of change defined by Schumpeter concerns the creation of new products or services which constitute a fundamental outcome of all innovativeness and the opportunities attached thereto. The discovery of new geographical markets is the second area of change clearly relating to entrepreneurial actions and opportunities. This area is still very valid today, albeit the research focuses, rather, on market-specific knowledge (see e.g. Hohentahl, 2001) and market entry processes (Blankenburg Holm, 1996). The third area relates to the creation or discovery of new raw materials, which was probably of greater importance in the 1930s than today. Nonetheless, the essence of Schumpeter's argument concerning this area can be interpreted as the impact of fundamentally new landmarks creating completely new possibilities. Today, this area of change may be interpreted instead as a question of awareness of innovations and technological breakthroughs. The fourth locus of change concerns new methods of production which in a business relationship perspective have been discussed by, for example, Waluszewski (1989), in her study of the development of new technology for the production of pulp. The last area of change relates to new ways of organizing which is a basic aspect of adapting business operations to the demands of potential customers and desired suppliers.

But change in itself, although essential for the evolution and survival of a business relationship, does not constitute the opportunity development process. Change is a fundamental and continuous process in an ongoing business relationship. This change may sometimes be due to either party's efforts to increase the integration of the business operations, thereby leading to an incremental strengthening of the relationship. Sometimes this change is a response to the advent of a competitor slowly or drastically causing a weakening of the business relationship. Occasionally, though, the change is the result of an opportunity for that relationship. This implies that not all change in an ongoing business relationship has to do with opportunity development. Following the five areas of change outlined above, one presumption that can be made is that if we want to explore opportunity development in ongoing business relationships, these are some essential areas of change to focus upon. Accordingly, changes of a business relationship in these areas may be the result of an opportunity for that ongoing business relationship. But, as indicated earlier, opportunity development for business relationships depends on the input of information from outside the business relationship. Therefore, we argue that the impact of connections in the business network has to be taken into consideration when exploring opportunity development for business relationships. The following discussion will address how different connections in the network relate to change in ongoing business relationships.

Business networks' connections

In the reasoning above, it is implied that it is insufficient to focus narrowly only on the interaction between the customer and the supplier when trying to understand opportunity development for ongoing business relationships. Instead, it is necessary to include aspects emanating from the context formed by the network of relationships surrounding the focal business relationship (Granovetter, 1973). This network context contains connections to various other relationships having an impact on the past, present and future direction and content of the interaction in the focal business relationship (Andersson et al., 1994; Blankenburg Holm, 1996). As pointed out by Håkansson and Snehota (1989: 192) "an organization's performance is conditioned by the totality of the network as a context, that is even by interdependencies among third parties." The connected relationships can thus in many respects be seen as dynamic driving forces in the evolution of the focal business relationship. This is evident in situations of, for instance, changes in production due to changes in consumer preferences introduced into the focal business relationship through its customers' and customers' customers' connections, by alterations in the supply or composition of certain fundamental input materials produced by some supplier's supplier. This reasoning lays the basis for a presumption on the importance of infusion of information from the connections in the network as a prerequisite for opportunity development for the ongoing business relationship. Opportunity development is contingent on the input of information from the wider network into the ongoing business relationship. The infusion of relevant information, not from any commonly available source, but from specific connections related to the ongoing interaction in the business relationship, creates the foundation for the idiosyncrasy necessary for opportunity development. Without this infusion of inputs from the connections in the network, some actions will certainly not be taken by the parties, the interaction in the relationships then runs the risk of becoming standardized and routine and the opportunity development is jeopardized.

Studies of business networks though are often focused on the relationships between suppliers and customers, following the value-adding activities in the chain of production from raw materials to consumers. The perspective thereby links to views relating to aspects of vertical integration, supply-chains, and distribution channels in explaining how the development of businesses occur. The basis for the reasoning in a business network perspective lies in the notion that businesses are being interlinked by technological and social interaction between the parties of the relationships, rather than by formal contractual arrangements and legal obligations. This means that, to the customer and supplier in the focal business relationship, complementary suppliers, suppliers' suppliers, customers and customers' customers, are examples of relevant connections to be included in this vertically oriented dimension of the network. The impact from these vertical connections is of course most relevant when looking at opportunity development for ongoing business relationships. Large amounts of information on the evolution of businesses, relevant for opportunity development, are introduced through the vertical connections and incorporated into the focal business relationship.

But to gain more insight into the opportunity development for business relationships, there is a risk in focusing solely on the vertical dimension. There exists a vast variety of other connections in the network which also might have an impact on the evolution of businesses. These connections include, for instance, important actors such as competitors (Bengtsson and Kock, 1999; Gomes-Casseres, 1996), governments and other non-commercial actors (see, e.g. Boddewyn, 1988; Ring et al., 1990). Unlike in the vertical connection, connections in this dimension follow a horizontal orientation thus including all connections, in addition to those relating to the vertical dimension, but yet relevant for the function and evolution of the ongoing business relationship. The argument for including this horizontal connection is based on the indirect interdependencies that exist between the relationships among actors like these and their impact on the focal business relationship. Many business network studies do not include the fact that companies' businesses are influenced/influence relationships with actors in the horizontal context. Certainly, concerning opportunity development for ongoing business relationships, the information channelled to the parties in the relationship through the horizontal connection is of utmost importance as it can be seen as an addition of exogenous information necessary to avoid synchronicity in the information content of the relationship.

Above, we have indicated that in business relationship theory, the analysis of relationships mostly relies on the behavior of the two interdependent actors forming that relationship. But, for discussions on opportunity development this would mean that there is a certain risk of synchronicity in information content leading to standardization of the interaction and allowing routines to dominate. In business network theory, though, the relationship between supplier and customer is embedded in a vertical dimension. The changes of a business relationship are thus not only an antecedent to the focal actors' activities, but also to the acts of connected suppliers' suppliers or customers' customers. It is evident that the impact of the vertical connection will relate to some areas of changes in the ongoing business relationship. However, these changes can not be based only on the parties' activities in the vertical dimension, but also on the actions of actors in the horizontal dimension. Thus, a dyadic relationship that is studied from the network perspective recognizes interdependency between several types of actors. The changes of an ongoing business relationship are thus determined first by the character of the interactions between two dyadic business partners, second by the impact of the vertically connected business actors, and third by the impact of the horizontally connected relationships. Changes of a business relationship are, thus, influenced by the support or impediment from both horizontally and vertically connected relationships. Some changes are the result of input from the vertical connection; some changes are in response to input from the horizontal connection. This means essentially that both dimensions of the connections can be considered to be important for input of information relating to opportunity development for the ongoing business relationship. While the vertical connection is relying on certain information from the perspective of, among others, the suppliers' suppliers and customers' customers, the horizontal connection provides information from other sources. Based on the notion of the importance of idiosyncratic information for opportunity development, we will in the next section discuss how the connections and change are interrelated.

Opportunity development for ongoing business relationships

In the previous sections we have discussed business relationships and the change that occurs as a result of the ongoing exchanges of economic, technological, social and informational character that take place as business is conducted. We have stressed that these changes are essential for the survival of business relationships, but they also constitute a threat to the business relationship if the business relationship becomes too self-contained. Self-containment in this situation means basing the changes of the business relationship on the confined setting of the business relationship itself. Such a focus may very well imply that the business relationship evolves, but it is more likely to be a building up of routines and thereby lack innovation and ability to develop opportunities. To avoid this, the parties in the business relationship have to take into consideration information on actions taken by other parties and activities going on in other relationships in the surrounding network. This addition, of what could be denoted idiosyncratic information from a focal business relationships' perspective, assures the possibility of changing the ongoing business relationship in such ways that opportunity development is feasible.

Opportunity development for ongoing business relationships thus means allowing input from connections in the network. This means that various bits of information introduced through both the vertical connection and the horizontal connection are to be considered as part of the opportunity development for the ongoing business relationship. The phenomenon is illustrated in Figure 13.1. The changes of the relationship are subjected to input of information from the connections in the network through some process of infusion while at the same time diffusing information about the happenings in the relationship through the connections to the wider network. This process of infusion and diffusion of information from/to the business relationship ensuring idiosyncrasy in information, is essentially what opportunity development for ongoing business relationship is all about. Without the input from the connections in the network, opportunity development for the ongoing business relationship is rendered impossible.

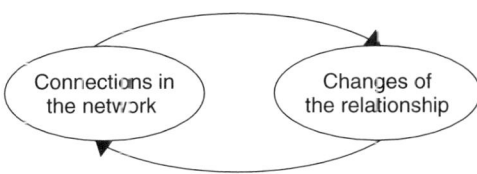

Figure 13.1 Opportunity development for ongoing business relationships

But, as indicated above, not all areas of change in the business relationship and not all input of information from the network connections relate to opportunity development. To illustrate and further investigate how network connections and business relationship changes are linked, the model of opportunity development for ongoing business relationships will be used as the starting-point for the following exploratory analysis. Using information on 279 international business relationships, the links between network connections and relationship change will be studied.

Exploring opportunity development for ongoing business relationships

The aim of the analysis in this chapter is to illustrate some aspects of opportunity development for ongoing business relationships. This will be accomplished by exploring how various areas of changes of ongoing business relationships relate to the impact of connections with other relationships. The basic assumption is that those areas of changes of ongoing business relationships that can be linked to impact from connections to other relationships in network constitute the foundation for opportunity development in the very same business relationship. Changes of ongoing business relationships which are not subjected to influence from connections may be very important for the continuity and efficiency of that business relationship, but do not provide the necessary grounds for opportunity development. In the following analysis, broad areas of changes of business relationships are thus investigated for their importance in opportunity development, by examining the varying impact of connections with other relationships. To the extent to which this impact can be found, we argue that opportunity development exists through the changes of the ongoing business relationship.

The data used in the analysis of opportunity development consist of a sub-set of extensive data – material collected within the MIN-project. The MIN-project focuses on the international operations of large Swedish multinational corporations. The multinational corporations represent a wide range of industries (metals, paper, power, retailing, transportation services and telecommunication). In this chapter, information about 279 ongoing international business relationships between a supplier and a customer provides the basis for the analysis. The information was gathered through personal interviews with the marketing managers, who were instructed to select the most important customer relationships to be included in the study. To guide the interviews and collect a large amount of the information, standardized questionnaires were used.

The changes of ongoing business relationships encompass a vast amount of activities performed through the economic, technological, informational and social exchanges taking place between the two parties. To focus the scope of changes in the ongoing business relationship to situations pertaining to areas where the entrepreneur may seize an opportunity, by identifying new and innovative combinations, Schumpeter's (1934) five areas of change relating to innovations were set as a starting-point. The first area of change relating to innovation and opportunity for the business relationships concerns the creation of new products or services. In a business relationship, this relates to ongoing product development as a foundation for innovativeness and opportunity development. Two statements, measuring how important the supplier and customer are for each other when it comes to product development, provide the necessary information for the analysis. Furthermore, a high level of adaptation concerning product technology reflects the changes made in the products subjected to exchange in the business relationship. The ability to change products in line with the requirements of the market must be seen as a driver of innovation and a fundamental aspect of opportunity development. In this analysis, two statements concerning the supplier and the customer levels of adaptation are used, together with two concerning product development, as indicators for the creation of new product/services.

The second area of innovation and change concerns the discovery of new geographical markets. In a business relationship setting, this relates to the information exchange between the supplier and customer about activities in their respective markets and also the introduction of contacts with new, important business counterparts. In the analysis, four indicators concerning the importance in these areas of the supplier for the customer and vice versa were used. The area of innovation discussed by Schumpeter, pertaining to the discovery of new raw materials and the change involved, is perhaps not as relevant today as in the 1930s when plastics and silicon-based electronics beckoned in the near future. But for ongoing business relationships, information about new materials and the opportunities they carry with them are still of great relevance to the ability to change and opportunity development. In the current analysis, therefore, the importance of the supplier for the customer and importance of the customer for the supplier, in terms of receiving technological information, are used as indicators of this area of change.

The fourth area of innovation and change discussed by Schumpeter links the development of new production methods to opportunity development. Similar to product development, this area of change concerns the importance of the supplier and customer to each other as well as the ability to change, reflected by the levels of adaptation. Following this, four indicators are used in the analysis, relating to the suppliers' and the customers' respective importance for production development and the level of adaptation concerning production technology. The fifth and last area of innovation and change relates to new ways of organizing business for possible opportunity development. For ongoing business relationships implementing new ways of organizing the exchange between supplier and customer, this means stepping away from the threat of standardization and routine leading to the inability to make certain changes, and making opportunity development impossible. In this field, the analysis also uses four indicators, all concerning the supplier's and customer's ability to change through adaptations made. Following this, the first area of change focuses on the capability for change of the customers and suppliers in their respective organizational structures, while the second area concerns the level of adaptations relating to business conduct. Change in business conduct mirrors, in a broad sense, the capability to adjust and enhance the way business is performed in the ongoing business relationship which, in combination with the ability to change the organization, lays the foundation for opportunity development. Table 13.1 below provides a summary of all indicators used for measuring innovations and changes, relating to opportunity development in the analysis.

Table 13.1 Indicators of areas of change in the business relationship

Creation of new product/services
Supplier is important concerning product development
Customer is important concerning product development
Supplier has caused adaptation for the customer concerning product technology
Customer has caused adaptation for the supplier concerning product technology

New geographical markets
Supplier is important concerning information about market activities
Customer is important concerning information about market activities
Supplier is important concerning information about new, important business contacts
Customer is important concerning information about new, important business contacts

New raw materials
Supplier is important concerning technological information
Customer is important concerning technological information

New production methods
Supplier is important concerning production development
Customer is important concerning production development
Supplier has caused adaptation by the customer concerning production technology
Customer has caused adaptation by the supplier concerning production technology

New ways of organizing
Supplier has caused adaptation by the customer concerning organizational structure
Customer has caused adaptation by the supplier concerning organizational structure
Supplier has caused adaptation by the customer concerning business conduct
Customer has caused adaptation by the supplier concerning business conduct

As discussed above, innovations and changes on their own do not mean opportunity development for the ongoing business relationship. The addition of the impact of idiosyncratic information and impulses from connected relationships in the wider network are needed. Without this, changes made in the ongoing business relationship may lead to standardization and routine, rendering opportunity development impossible. The network of all connected relationships can, as discussed above, essentially be divided into a vertical and a horizontal dimension. The vertical dimension incorporates a connected relationship that links to the value-adding aspects of the ongoing business relationship, and in aggregate forms the vertical connection. The vertical connection in this analysis is indicated by the impact of relationships with three categories of counterparts on the ongoing business relationship between the supplier and customer. The first concerns the impact of other customers on the supplier, the second captures the impact of the customer's customer, and the third the impact of any other supplier to the customer in the ongoing business relationship. The horizontal dimension of the network of relationships connected to the ongoing business relationship between the supplier and customer includes essentially all other relationships besides those value-adding connected relationships incorporated in the vertical connection. The horizontal dimension includes the impact on the ongoing business relationship of many different categories of connected relationships which, when aggregated, form the horizontal connection. The three categories of connected relationships selected to be used in this analysis are connected relationships with competitors, relationships with governmental organizations and relationships with non-commercial organizations. Table 13.2 provides a summary of all indicators used in the analysis for measuring the impact of connections relating to opportunity development in ongoing business relationships.

Table 13.2 Indicators of connections in the business network

Vertical connection
To what extent does any other customer influence the relationship?
To what extent do any of the customer's customers influence the relationship?
To what extent does any other supplier influence the relationship?

Horizontal connection
To what extent does any competitor influence the relationship?
To what extent does any governmental organization influence the relationship?
To what extent does any non-commercial organization influence the relationship?

Analysis

The aim of the analysis in this chapter is to examine how and in what situations opportunity development is possible in ongoing business relationships. The examination is based on five areas of change of the ongoing business relationship, in combination with two dimensions of connection in the surrounding network. The underlying assumption for the analysis is that when both changes and impact from connection occur in the ongoing business relationship, opportunity development is possible. In order to carry out the analysis, it is necessary to combine the indicators of each group of indicators into constructs. This was accomplished by employing each group of indicators in confirmatory factor analyses forming seven constructs representing the underlying latent variable. The individual factor loadings for all constructs are displayed in Appendix 1. As the aim of the investigation is to link changes of ongoing business relationships to the impact of connection in the network, a correlation analysis was selected as the appropriate method to provide the necessary information. The correlations between the five areas of changes of the ongoing business relationship and the two dimensions of connections in the network were therefore calculated. The resulting correlations are displayed in Table 13.3.

Looking at the results displayed in Table 13.3, six out of ten possible correlations show significant values. The vertical connection, that is connections relating to value-adding relationships, displays links to four out of five areas of change of the ongoing business relationship, revealing good possibilities for opportunity development. Only new production development seems to be without the necessary impact from the vertical connection to facilitate opportunity development. Among the four areas of change, associating the vertical connection to the area of change and innovation relating to new geographical markets seems to be the one most promoting opportunity development. Opportunity development for ongoing business relationships as new ways of organizing and through creation of new products and/or services, also seem to be relevant areas in conjunction with the vertical connection.

Turning to the horizontal connection, the results reveal links to two areas of change of the ongoing business relationship, that is, the areas of change

Table 13.3 Areas of changes and connections as opportunity development

Areas of changes / Connections	Creation of new products/ services	New geographical markets	New raw materials	New production methods	New ways of organizing
Vertical	0.37**	0.96***	0.69**	0.18	0.53**
Horizontal	0.25**	0.17*	0.39	0.15	0.09

Notes: *$p < 0.05$; **$p < 0.01$; ***$p < 0.001$.

and innovation pertaining to the creation of new products and/or services and new geographical markets. Both these areas, in combination with the effect of the horizontal connection, provide the grounds for opportunity development. As mentioned above, the vertical connection also links to these areas, meaning that for the creation of new products/services and also new geographical markets, connections to both, for example, customers and suppliers as well as to governmental or non-commercial organizations, are of importance for opportunity development. The correlations between horizontal connection and change in the ongoing business relationship are, however, clearly lower than for the same areas of change and vertical connection, indicating that vertical connection is of greater importance for facilitating opportunity development in the ongoing business relationship. This is also supported by the fact that vertical connections relate to four areas of change in the ongoing business relationship while horizontal connections relate to only two.

Interestingly, change relating to new production methods is linked neither to the horizontal connection nor to the vertical connection. New production methods are, in this line of argument, thus not the grounds for opportunity development. Change in this area is, rather, driven by some other circumstances within the ongoing business relationship, and may pose a hazard of standardization and the creation of routine, rendering opportunity development impossible.

Conclusions

In the introductory discussion we referred to definitions of opportunity, and indicated that the concept is normally related to chance. In this chapter, we have suggested that opportunity is not only a matter of chance but rather, it is dependent upon the business setting. Furthermore, we argue that the setting for opportunity in many business situations is the ongoing business relationship. Our discussion and analysis was therefore focused on linking changes of ongoing business relationship to the connections in the network. The analysis revealed that both vertical and horizontal connections are interlinked with relevant areas of change in the ongoing business relationship thereby forming the basis for opportunity development.

But a fundamental obstacle in further exploring the links between changes and connections and more clearly relating this process to opportunity is that opportunity is usually considered to be unpredictable. It is commonly agreed that it lies in the nature of an opportunity that it is almost certainly impossible to foresee. If an opportunity is possible to foresee, it is rather the result of an incremental process than the really advantageous new innovation or combination that is focused on by many researchers. Furthermore, there is really no way of telling that the opportunity is an opportunity other than in retrospect. This means that it is not the opportunity itself that usually becomes the focus of attention for studies of the phenomenon, but what is accomplished as the result of it by some party or parties with the ability to do so. It is also frequently this aftermath of the opportunity that is used as a way of telling that the opportunity happened. So, opportunity is perhaps, in a business relationships' perspective, better understood as the start of a development process for the ongoing business relationship, rather than a more or less stochastic advantageous occurrence at some point in time. Opportunity is, in this perspective, one among several forces driving the evolution of the business relationship forward. This also implies that it does not really matter for the ongoing business relationship when, where or by whom the opportunity is discovered, it is the changes of the ongoing business relationship that are valuable. It is the changes of the ongoing business relationships that are driven by opportunity, irrespective of whether the opportunity has occurred or not, that keeps the business relationship alert, ready to adapt to an always changing business situation.

This still leads us to the question of whether opportunity *can* be nurtured through these ongoing processes of changes of dynamic business relationships or is it inevitably to be considered a matter of pure chance? If opportunity can be nurtured through changing the ongoing business relationship in line with inputs from the vertical and horizontal connections in the network, surely some managerial implications are to be found. For the managements in the respective companies enjoying the relationship, insight into and knowledge of various aspects of these connections is the key to opportunity for the ongoing business relationship.

Penrose (1959) defined the opportunity as a productive opportunity if it was found in the market through the entrepreneurial function of the firm and put into operations by the managerial function of the firm, based on the actual availability of the resources needed to perform the operations the opportunity provided. In the same manner, the opportunity development for an ongoing business relationship means discovering the productive opportunity by processing information received through the connections in the network and putting it into operation by changing the operations in certain areas of the ongoing relationship. Opportunity may strike the ongoing business relationship quite frequently, but if the relationship is not in the "mode" of developing the opportunity, nothing will happen as a result of the opportunity. Our analysis indicated that certain areas of changes were closely related to innovations of products and services and finding new markets. If applying a network perspective, in order to seize an opportunity in these areas, it has by necessity to be realized through the interaction in at least one business relationship. But establishing a "new" business relationship means devoting time and efforts to evolve the business and make the interactions efficient. Perhaps it is the case that even if an opportunity is found through establishing a "new" relationship, it is more efficient and profitable to employ it in some of the already existing, active business relationships, where the interaction is recognized and changes made swiftly.

We have stressed that opportunity development for the business relationship is the ongoing process of those changes that are interlinked with some connection in the surrounding network. But can the connections be looked upon simply as driving forces enabling opportunity to occur, or can they, at the same time, be a hindrance for opportunity development? In our analysis, we have provided evidence that links exist between vertical and horizontal connections and several areas of changes in the ongoing business relationship. But it is not possible to conclude whether the actual impact of the connection on the business relationship is positive, that is supporting the ongoing business, or negative, that is suppressing the business, without more extensive studies. In the horizontal connection, competitors as well as governments may have both types of effects, and both types of effects may lead to changes for the ongoing business relationship. But whether these changes are opportunities is a question of their outcome. In the vertical connection, a common assumption is that reciprocity in actions and interdependencies reinforces the chains of relationships, providing strength and longevity for the networks. But, extensive and opportunistic opportunity-seeking by some parties in the network may cause uncertainty and negative impact from the connection on the ongoing business relationship. Clearly, this calls for a deeper understanding of the necessary balance between opportunity-driven changes and changes providing stability and long-term orientation.

Thus, not all change comes from opportunity, but rather from alterations relating to new combinations of or use of resources driven by other forces in the ongoing business relationship. One important task to be further explored is therefore to decide on how to determine some dividing line between the ordinary changes always going on in the business relationships and changes that relate to some opportunity for that business relationship. This task becomes even more challenging when taking into account the fact that an opportunity, as stated above, rarely or never can be foreseen and only identified in retrospect. There is a certain risk that when studying opportunity, happenings that leads to "good things" are seen as the result of opportunity while happenings that at a certain time are considered advantageous and perhaps give rise to "opportunity," but which in the end lead to "bad things," are excluded from the analysis. This undoubtedly calls for more systematic studies of changes of ongoing business relationships in conjunction with opportunity before clear answers can be provided.

Appendix

Construct indicator	Mean	SD	Factor-loading	t-value	R²
Creation of new product/services					
Supplier is important concerning product development	1.96	0.82	0.79	15.32	0.63
Customer is important concerning product development	2.84	1.46	0.63	11.14	0.39
Supplier has caused adaptation for the customer concerning product technology	3.05	1.38	0.89	18.44	0.80
Customer has caused adaptation for the supplier concerning product technology	2.21	1.39	0.67	12.20	0.45
New production methods					
Supplier is important concerning production development	2.43	1.18	0.43	7.23	0.19
Customer is important concerning production development	2.56	1.36	0.93	19.10	0.87
Supplier has caused adaptation by the customer concerning production technology	2.43	1.37	0.82	15.87	0.67
Customer has caused adaptation by the supplier concerning production technology	2.24	1.40	0.47	7.91	0.22
New raw materials					
Supplier is important concerning technological information	2.64	1.15	0.71	11.99	0.51
Customer is important concerning technological information	2.88	1.18	0.68	11.44	0.46
New geographical markets					
Supplier is important concerning information about market activities	2.74	1.18	0.56	9.44	0.31
Customer is important concerning information about market activities	2.36	1.17	0.60	10.27	0.36
Supplier is important concerning information about new, important business contacts	2.66	1.21	0.71	12.71	0.50
Customer is important concerning information about new, important business contacts	1.90	1.18	0.83	15.56	0.68
New ways of organizing					
Supplier has caused adaptation by the customer concerning organizational structure	2.43	1.37	0.74	13.16	0.55
Customer has caused adaptation by the supplier concerning organizational structure	2.09	1.39	0.65	11.17	0.43
Supplier has caused adaptation by the customer concerning business conduct	2.50	1.39	0.66	11.24	0.43
Customer has caused adaptation by the supplier concerning business conduct	1.76	1.16	0.58	9.69	0.34
Vertical connection					
To what extent does any other customer influence the relationship?	1.68	1.16	0.51	7.76	0.26
To what extent do any of the customer's customers influence the relationship?	3.58	1.21	0.55	8.24	0.30
To what extent does any other supplier influence the relationship?	2.32	1.29	0.14	2.44	0.19
Horizontal connection					
To what extent does any competitor influence the relationship?	1.63	2.21	0.64	10.31	0.41
To what extent does any governmental organization influence the relationship?	1.16	1.32	0.92	14.33	0.84
To what extent does any non-commercial organization influence the relationship?	1.47	0.96	0.16	2.48	0.25

References

Andersson, J., Håkansson, H. and Johanson, J. (1994). Dyadic Business Relationships Within a Business Network Context, *Journal of Marketing*, 58 (October), 1–15.
Bengtsson, M. and Kock, S. (1999). Cooperation and Competition in Relationships between Competitors in Business Networks, *Journal of Business and Industrial Marketing*, 14(3), 178–93.
Blankenburg Holm, D. (1996). *Business Network Connections and International Business Relationships*, Uppsala: Department of Business Studies.
Boddewyn, J.J. (1988). Political Aspects of MNE Theory, *Journal of International Business Studies*, 19(3), 341–62.
Casson, M. (1982). *The Entrepreneur*, Totowa, NJ: Barnes and Noble Books.
Dosi, G. (1988). The Nature of the Innovative Process, in G. Dosi, C. Freeman, R. Nelson, G. Silverberg and L. Soete (Eds) *Technical Change and Economic Theory*, London: Pinter.
Eckhardt, J. and Shane, S. (2003). Opportunities and Entrepreneurship, *Journal of Management*, 29(3), 333–49.
Gomes-Casseres, B. (1996). *The Alliance Revolution: The New Shape of Business Rivalry*, London, Cambridge, MA: Harvard University Press.
Granovetter, M. (1973). The Strength of Weak Ties, *American Journal of Sociology*, 78(6), 1360–80.
Håkansson, H. (1987). *Industrial Technological Development*, London: Routledge.
Håkansson, H. and Snehota, I. (1989). No Business is an Island, *Scandinavian Journal of Management*, 5(3), 187–200.
Håkansson, H. and Snehota, I. (1995). *Developing Relationships in Business Networks*, London: Routledge.
Håkansson, H. and Waluszewski, A. (2002). *Managing Technological Development. IKEA, the Environment and Technology*, London: Routledge.
Hallén, L., Johanson, J. and Seyed-Mohamed, N. (1987). Relationship Strength and Stability in International and Domestic Industrial Marketing, *Industrial Marketing and Purchasing*, 2(3), 22–37.
Hohenthal, J. (2001). *The Emergence of International Business Relationships. Experience and Performance in the Internationalization Process of SMEs*, Uppsala: Department of Business Studies.
Kirzner, I. (1997). Entrepreneurial Discovery and the Competitive Market Process: An Austrian Approach, *Journal of Economic Literature*, XXXV(March), 60–85.
Klevorick, A., Levin, R., Nelson, R. and Winter, S. (1995). On the Sources and Significance of Interindustry Differences in Technological Opportunities, *Research Policy*, 24, 185–205.
Lundvall, B-Å. (1988). Innovation as an Interactive Process: from User–producer Interaction to the National System of innovation, in G. Dosi, C. Freeman, R. Nelson, G. Silverberg and L. Soete (Eds) *Technical Change and Economic Theory*, London: Pinter.
Penrose, E. (1959). *The Theory of the Growth of the Firm*, Oxford: Basil Blackwell.
Ring, P.S., Lenway, S.A. and Govekar, M. (1990). Management of the Political Imperative in International Business, *Strategic Management Journal*, 11(2), 141–51.
Schumpeter, J. (1934). *Capitalism, Socialism, and Democracy*, New York: Harper & Row.
Shane, S. (2000). Prior Knowledge and the Discovery of Entrepreneurial Opportunities, *Organization Science*, 11(4), August, 448–69.

Shane, S. and Venkataraman, S. (2000). The Promise of Entrepreneurship as a Field of Research, *Academy of Management Review*, 25(1), 217–26.

Venkataraman, S. (1997). The Distinctive Domain of Entrepreneurship Research: An Editor's Perspective, in J. Katz and R. Brockhaus (Eds) *Advances in Entrepreneurship, firm Emergence and Growth*, Greenwich, CT: JAI Press.

Von Hippel, E. (1988). *The Sources of Innovation*, New York: Oxford University Press.

Waluszewski, A. (1989). *Framväxten av en ny mekanisk massateknik*. Uppsala: Acta Universitatis Upsaliensis, Studia Oeconomiae Negotiorum nr 31.

14
Opportunities and Obstacles in Using IT Systems: Embedding Movex in Edsbyn's Resource Network

Enrico Baraldi

Introduction: IT-related opportunities

Few technologies have been surrounded by so high expectations as Information Technology (IT). Visionaries, business consultants and academics alike regularly attributed to IT the power to open *opportunities* for firms to achieve efficiency and development. All this started 50 years ago, with the first applications of computers to Operations Research (Diebold, 1953; Herrman and Magee, 1953). Then, in the 1970s, IT-based 'integrated information systems' (Ramström, 1973: 15) offered the opportunity to monitor any contingency within a firm. However, these opportunities were not fully concretized because of social resistance to panoptical control (Zuboff, 1988: 320–4), irrelevant IT-borne information (Mintzberg, 1972) or excessive rigidity in computerized information systems (Hedberg and Jönsson, 1978).

Then, in the 1980s, the new potentials of making markets more efficient were attributed to IT. For instance, Malone *et al.* (1989) envisioned electronic markets whereby IT would allow 'frictionless transactions', offering the opportunity for large efficiency gains, mostly for buyers (Porter and Millar, 1985). But also the IT-related opportunities identified in the 1980s were not seized as expected: instead of using IT to open up business networks, firms took the opportunity of strengthening their existing *business relationships* with selected partners by means of, for instance, Electronic Data Interchange (EDI) systems (Gadde, 1997; Gadde and Håkansson, 2001: 74). The latest trend in attributing potentials to IT began in the late 1990s with the Internet and a new breed of IT systems called ERPs (Enterprise Resource Planning). Relying on greater computational power and the interlinking possibilities of the Internet, ERPs created the opportunity for seamless integration with suppliers and distribution partners (Kalakota and Robinson, 2000) and for knowledge management (Davenport *et al.*, 1998).

Against this historical background, the primary purpose of this chapter is to investigate the *opportunities* that IT opens for firms. This purpose corresponds with much of the IT literature's concern with the *possibilities* that IT offers to transform firms and make them more efficient, while re-engineering their processes (Davenport, 1992). This chapter opts however for a focussed notion of opportunities, seen here as chances to recombine resources to deliver improved value (see Ardichvili *et al.*, 2003: 108). Eckhardt and Shane (2003: 340) recognize the new working methods introduced together with IT systems as a specific type of opportunity. More precisely, the introduction of new IT tools entails new methods of production and of organizing, which are among the *five loci* of opportunities identified by Schumpeter (1934). But new IT tools open an even broader series of opportunities including improved service to customers (e.g., shorter lead-times or more customization) and improved routines for orders to suppliers. Thus, IT-related opportunities emerge whenever an IT tool allows a firm to recombine resources either *inside* or *outside* it, in relation to its customers and suppliers. The above historical overview shows however that it is difficult to exploit the IT-related opportunities. Therefore, the second purpose of this chapter is to discuss the *obstacles to seizing* these opportunities.

However, this chapter does not penetrate in the opportunity-development process, that is, the process whereby opportunities emerge and evolve, often unexpectedly. Instead of a process-like view on opportunities, for simplicity, a more *static* view is adopted: the opportunities envisaged at the time of making an IT investment are simply confronted with the obstacles that appear when a firm tries to seize them. Some of these obstacles have been singled out, although as very broad categories, within the management literature that identifies the factors affecting the exploitability of technology-related opportunities. For instance, Malerba and Orsenigo (1997) stress the following: (1) the relevance and availability of feasible (technical) solutions, (2) their appropriability against imitators, (3) the cumulative effects of previous investments and (4) the nature of the knowledge behind a certain technology. But such factors (and potential obstacles) are grounded in *industry-level* issues, such as appropriability regimes, sectoral knowledge codifiability and path-dependence. Are these types of *broad* explanations enough to understand what has happened with IT for the last 40 years? In fact, constantly renewed expectations made IT the most applied type of process innovation (Tidd *et al.*, 2001: 267), but the failure rate of IT projects is worryingly high (*ibid*: 47). To explain these failures, besides industry-level obstacles, the 'human factor' that resists change is another obstacle mentioned all too often (see Davenport, 1992; Tidd *et al.*, 2001: 57).

But the assumptions driving most IT investments already point at the difficulties to come when firms try to seize the IT-related opportunities: matching the potentials of technical solutions with models from microeconomics does not help firms really gain anything from IT. In particular, the assumption that more information and automation equals efficiency and development contrasts with a reality where IT and more information often do not drive efficiency or hinder innovation (Baraldi, 2003; Hedberg and Jönsson, 1978). These 'unexpected' outcomes and the implicit obstacles to exploiting IT can be easier understood by taking a *business network perspective* (Håkansson and Snehota, 1995), instead of focussing on firm-internal (e.g. employees' resistance) or industry-level (e.g., appropriability) issues. More precisely, this chapter uses the notion of *resource embeddedness* (Håkansson and Waluszewski, 2002) in business networks to frame IT-related opportunities and obstacles.

In summary, the *purpose of this chapter* is to apply a business network perspective to develop an analytical frame over (1) the opportunities offered by such IT tools as ERP-systems and (2) the obstacles to seizing these opportunities. Such a frame is developed inductively from a case study about Edsbyn, a firm that uses the ERP Movex. This chapter also contributes a deeper understanding of IT-related opportunities and obstacles, viewed in terms of resource re-combinations, starting from the IT tool but moving towards a whole resource network. This understanding rests on two questions: (1) which resource *combinations* and *commitments* let efficiency and development opportunities emerge inside the IT-using firm, across its dyadic relationships and in the whole business network, and (2) which obstacles to seizing these opportunities are created by the *embedding* resources inside the IT-using firm, across its dyadic relationships and in the whole business network?

But developing this understanding requires also two methodological and theoretical steps. The first step is to avoid considering IT as a black box in a model and to penetrate instead deeply into IT tools and how they actually function. The second step is to place IT systems within the *context* in which they are used, explicitly considering the resources embedding them. In fact, the IT-related opportunities and obstacles emerge from the interplay between the focal IT artefact and its context of installation and daily utilization. Therefore, the next section reviews theoretically the nature of IT and its installation and use context. Then, the section on Movex presents the empirical material about the furniture producer Edsbyn and its new ERP-system. From the case analysis and discussion, the next section builds a framework over the opportunities and obstacles related to this type of IT tools. Finally, the concluding section discusses the implications.

IT as facilities: the interplay with the embedding resources

IT-related opportunities and obstacles do not reside inside an IT artefact, but emerge in the contact points between IT tools and *other* resources. More precisely, a whole *network of resources* is the context that embeds IT tools and that includes four types of resources: *business units* and the *relationships* among them, the *products* exchanged between units and the *facilities* utilized to perform activities (Baraldi and Bocconcelli, 2001; Håkansson and Waluszewski, 2002). Resources are *heterogeneous*, that is, their values depend on which other resources they are combined with (Penrose, 1959: 25, 74–5) and they shape each other's features during long-term interaction processes (Håkansson and Waluszewski, 2002). Such processes shape the 'interfaces' between resources, that is, the contact surfaces along which resources interplay on technical, social and economical dimensions (*ibid*: 190–200). An example of a product-facility interface is the time required to perform certain operations on that product, and an example of a facility-relationship interface is the percentage of output dedicated to a specific customer. This 'resource interaction' perspective (Baraldi, 2003) digs deep into the resource layer of business networks (Håkansson and Snehota, 1995) and is helpful to discuss IT-related opportunities and obstacles in terms of (re-)combinations of resources.

IT systems are 'information processing facilities', that is, simply machines. Considering IT as facilities is a good starting point to bring IT down to earth and avoid attributing it supernatural powers and all-too deterministic effects. Placing a focal IT system at the centre of a context populated with other identified resources shows how opportunities and obstacles for the using firm emerge while the IT tool interplays with the other resources in business networks. This interplay concerns, for instance, the resource representations created by IT, the preconditions imposed by IT to performing certain activities, the monitoring and steering of resources made by IT, and the connections between units established via IT (Baraldi, 2003, and Baraldi and Waluszewski; 2005).

This chapter focusses on a special type of IT tools, ERP-systems, that is, *heavy* administrative systems that reunite, under a 'single roof', several linked databases and software applications that perform calculations (e.g., production scheduling) and emit transactions (e.g., orders). ERPs are 'mission critical' systems (Davenport, 2000) sustaining information-rich tasks and critical processes in a firm, such as purchasing, inventory management, production scheduling and logistics (Davenport, 1998). These IT tools are often profiled as 'navigational cockpits', able to supervise all the enterprise's resources and processes. In order to do this, resources are *modelled* according to the templates built inside ERPs. Such templates mimic 'best practices' prescribing how to perform activities and utilize resources (e.g., the MRPII method for production planning) or broader models, such as Value Chains and Balanced Scorecards.

Every company installing an ERP-system inherits therefore all these models and uses them to daily represent, monitor and steer its resources. But in order to produce such effects, ERPs, which are relatively standard application packages, require changes in the way a firm's resources are organized.

In some cases, installing an ERP-system requires a business unit to radically 're-design' its processes and resource combinations, if it wants to fully exploit the benefits of the above models. ERPs are, in fact, rather *rigid* and their models allow increasing efficiency only if the above 'best practices' are applied. This induces many firms who purchase ERPs to go through painful re-organizations, in so-called 'Business Process Re-engineering' projects (Davenport, 1992). All this, and the need to learn using the system, makes the very implementation of ERP-systems a crucial phase that can last over one year.

Opportunities and obstacles in the interplay 'IT-embedding resources'

Once in place, the ERP produces its effects on the resources *inside* and *outside* the unit where it is installed. These effects entail both opportunities and obstacles that emerge when the technical core of the IT system interplays with the embedding resources. Like all IT systems, ERPs manipulate a hierarchy of symbols to represent (i.e., produce information about) real objects, such as products, facilities or workers (Winograd and Flores, 1986: 86–90). Daily using the software and the models inside the ERP produces effects on the surrounding resources, including the using unit and the resources represented (or neglected) inside the ERP. These effects are both 'informative' and 'concrete' (Baraldi, 2003), as shown in Figure 14.1. The informative effects of IT (see the vertical solid arrows in Figure 14.1) derive from IT's capacity to create digital images of resources according to predefined models. IT tools also transfer this digital information inside and between business units. By providing information about resources, ERP-systems contribute to monitoring, controlling and supervising resources. Whereas these effects appear at a cognitive level, thanks to the *informative power* of IT (Zuboff, 1988: 9–11), the *concrete* effects of ERPs emerge at the level of resources. These latter effects (see the horizontal solid arrows in

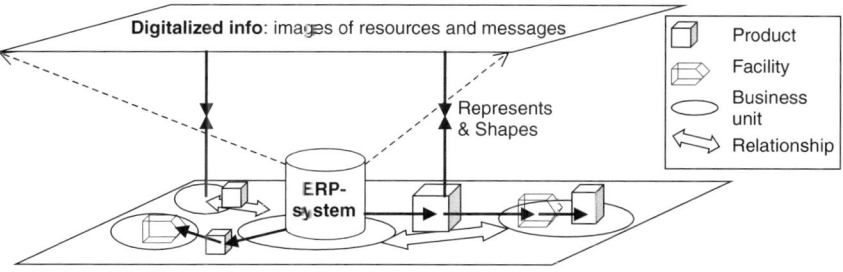

Figure 14.1 The effects of an IT system on resources
Source: Baraldi (2003: 36).

Figure 14.1) concern key dimensions of resources such as costs, quantities and times: for instance, the costs of running a production facility, the number of sold products, or the delivery lead-times. The concrete effects of IT are less straightforward than the informative ones, because they often spread across resource interfaces connecting several resource items. Transferred according to non-deterministic patterns, the concrete effects of IT are often *indirect* and *unexpected* (Baraldi, 2003).

This indirectness of IT effects can open unexpected opportunities – but also create obstacles – for firms using IT systems to handle resources. In fact, introducing an IT facility opens the possibilities to *re-combine* other resources (products, machines, units and relationships). This recombining entails (1) the creation of *wholly new* interfaces among resources, like in product development, or (2) the *refinement* (including the strengthening) of existing interfaces, like in improved production scheduling. When these new or refined interfaces generate value – inside the firm installing an IT tool, outside it (e.g., for a customer) or, both – the resource recombination opens business *opportunities* (Ardichvili *et al.*, 2003: 108). However, in order to move from simple, generic chances (*ibid*.) of recombining resource to actually seizing these opportunities, two further conditions must be met: (1) a concrete *resource commitment* is necessary and (2) the direct and indirect *obstacles* deriving from the resources network need to be first *identified* and then *overcome*. Committing resources implies making investments (time, financials and attention) to consolidate the wholly new resource interfaces or to refine the existing interfaces against potential obstacles. But certain obstacles emerging from the surrounding resource network may be so indirect to be virtually hidden, and even when these are identified, the commitment required to overcome them may be prohibitively costly.

In the case of a new ERP, resource commitment is evident firstly in the investment necessary to purchase and introduce the IT tool: beside the software licence (reaching sometimes Euro10 million) this costly deed requires time and concrete changes in routine, alongside the hurdles of learning to use a new complex IT system. Second, commitment is necessary also towards each of the single resources to which the IT tool is applied, which is also costly: some interfaces will need to be torn apart or opened up, others will need to be refined or strengthened and even others will need to be established from scratch. Committing resources to new resource combinations, in the pursuit of new business opportunities, can therefore easily clash with pre-existing investments and oriented interfaces. These inherited interfaces are likely to create a certain *resistance* because of the inertia that binds resource interfaces together socially (e.g., in business relationships) or technically (e.g., in established designs).

To summarize, resource heterogeneity (Penrose, 1959: 25, 74–5) and resource interfaces (Håkansson and Waluszewski, 2002: 190–200) imply business opportunities across the network, but also a resistance that can create obstacles to seizing them. More precisely, the obstacles and opportunities related to ERPs appear both in the *installation phase*, when their enticing potentials need to be confronted with the problems of any large investment, and in their *actual utilization* in several managerial tasks (from production scheduling to product development). ERPs have very pervasive effects, especially on how a firm utilizes and develops internal resources (e.g., own facilities) and external ones (e.g., suppliers' components). Thus, ERPs can open opportunities for *efficient resource utilization* (e.g., in production scheduling), and for *resource development* (e.g., in product development). But the opportunities for utilizing and developing resources created by a focal IT system need to be confronted with a series of obstacles and limits, which are explicitly presented in the empirical part of this chapter.

A note on methodology

The empirical material for the case study was collected through 60 interviews at Edsbyn, its key suppliers and customers and at the ERP provider Intentia. The case illustrates the opportunities and obstacles entailed by ERP-systems, but it is also the ground from which the analytical framework of the section on opportunities and obstacles in using ERP systems is inductively developed. Thus, the case sustains the theoretical discussion of the first two sections, to be continued in the section on opportunities and obstacles in using ERP systems. The focus on contextual factors impedes broad generalizations to other using contexts or to IT as a whole. However, the obstacles and opportunities identified for Edsbyn and Movex are common to many firms and cases of implementation of IT tools similar to those considered here: ERPs and the heavy administrative IT systems populating the back-office of many firms. In the case and in the discussion, opportunities and obstacles are viewed as deriving from the business network, but are seen from the perspective of Edsbyn, the focal firm in the analysed network.

Movex: a new IT tool for handling resources in Edsbyn's network

Edsbyn is a 250-employee Swedish office furniture producer that addresses organizational customers, to which it sold, in 2001, for Euro 30 million. Edsbyn's strength resides in its ability to adapt tabletops even for small orders. Since the mid-1990s, sales, customers and products have constantly increased, while product customization has become essential for securing new orders. Increased production volumes and customization made Edsbyn's outdated IT infrastructure unable to sustain ordering and production scheduling tasks that had grown too complex. Therefore, in 1999 Edsbyn decided to introduce a modern ERP-system.

Opportunities and obstacles in implementing Movex

Edsbyn chose the Swedish IT provider *Intentia* and its ERP-system *Movex*. Intentia, with annual sales of Euro400 million and 3000 employees, is an experienced IT developer, running about 200 implementations per year. However, a long vendor selection process and the complexity of Movex required postponing for the first time the expected introduction from the end of 2000 to early 2001. In order to reduce risks and expenditures, Edsbyn chose an almost standard system, with only 5 modules, all for internal use: order fulfilment, purchasing, accounting, personnel management and material and production planning. Thus, Edsbyn chose only what was essential to its current business activities, avoiding such features as e-business that would only complicate the installation of Movex.

Edsbyn focussed on modules that directly addressed its urgent problems. For instance, production planning, a fundamental task for Edsbyn that relies on production-to-order of customized furniture, had to be done almost manually and only once per week with the old system. This caused errors and delayed production, with negative effects towards customers and the impossibility to increase sales and capacity utilization. Also purchasing and semi-finished products control was done manually, with data made available with great delay. On the marketing side, product–cost calculations for adapted offering, so important for Edsbyn's customization strategy, required many hours. Movex was therefore the new tool to tackle these problems. Thus, Edsbyn envisaged a series of business opportunities enabled by Movex: (1) in relation to customers, Movex could help reduce lead-times, increase delivery precision and speed up customization calculations; (2) in relation to internal operations, Movex could help reduce inventories and better utilize production capacity. These opportunities derived from faster, updated and standardized information, and from avoided duplications.

A series of obstacles emerged already during the implementation project. Despite Intentia's experience and established project routines (the Implex method), Edsbyn met many unexpected problems that caused no less than 5 postponements of the official launch date. Apart from technical problems and difficulties in coordinating the schedules of Intentia's consultants and of Edsbyn's personnel, introducing Movex required extra time and efforts to adapt the whole organization, its processes and resources to the new IT system. Using the previous core IT system for over 30 years created a great resistance to the impressive learning and to the changes required by Movex in such tasks as production scheduling or order management. Moreover, the fear to abandon the known (the old system) for the unknown (Movex) were compounded by the 'critical mission' nature of this ERP-system: Movex handles so highly critical processes (e.g., order management or production scheduling) that if something went wrong on the launch day, production would be blocked and Edsbyn paralysed. Delays were therefore accepted, in order to have a fully usable system.

Opportunities and obstacles in using Movex

When Movex was finally installed, in 2002, it became essential for performing several tasks at Edsbyn with many effects on *internal* and *external* resources. To see these effects, we now delve into how resources are organized in Edsbyn's sales, production and purchasing, also in relation to external units. Edsbyn sells, via distributors, office tables to customers such as Ericsson, often within large furnishing projects. Edsbyn's most important distributor is SENAB, accounting for 30 per cent of Edsbyn's sales, while Edsbyn stands for 20 per cent of SENAB's turnover of Euro40 million. SENAB participates to project tenders and then assembles and maintains Edsbyn's furniture on customer locations. Another major customer group are public organizations (e.g., the Swedish Posten), reached via the central agreement stipulated by the state purchase agency FMV. This sales channel covers 20 per cent of Edsbyn's sales.

Edsbyn produces flat-line furniture, such as tabletops and shelves, with a production process that starts from applying veneers on MDF-boards and proceeds with milling and cutting tabletops. For this purpose, NC-millers are key production facilities, allowing precision and speed, but the sale increase of 2001 made them almost reach full capacity utilization. Thus, Edsbyn strongly depends on regular flows of inputs, such as the MDF-boards that the supplier Karlit must precisely deliver to avoid delays in an already constrained production flow. But delivery problems are occasioned when Karlit's other customers put pressure on its rigid MDF-line, causing either delayed MDF deliveries to Edsbyn or MDF delivered too hot for being processed. On the demand side, Edsbyn depends on regular customer orders, rapidly transformed into *production orders* that initiate production: because of production-to-order, most products become ready for delivery a few weeks after the order date (4 weeks for the standard range and 6 weeks for customized variants).

Movex is very useful to respect lead-times and balance capacity utilization. In particular, Edsbyn uses Movex for production scheduling, a task essential to keep delivery times by identifying for each customer order the right production slot. The result is a *production schedule* that steers the operations on the factory floor. To achieve this, all Edsbyn's internal manufacturing resources had been registered inside Movex's databases during its installation. Now Movex traces and monitors such resources as purchased *inputs* (MDF-boards and veneers), *WIPs* (e.g., veneered boards), *finished products* (e.g., tabletops), and *production facilities* (e.g., NC-machines). Then, Movex optimizes Edsbyn's production system, while respecting such constraints as the existing production capacity and the delivery times agreed with suppliers and customers. Movex's calculations utilize the *models* built into its databases and software. For instance, incoming customer orders are transformed into production orders (setting a start date and booking a particular machine) only after Movex has verified the availability of production capacity and of the inputs necessary to execute them. This model, known as 'MRPII', is repetitively applied by Movex.

A complete offering requires combining Edsbyn's flat-line products with complementary items, simultaneously delivered to customers. This holds especially for Edsbyn's major product, the 'El-Table', an electrically adjustable office desk. This table includes an adjustable *electrical stand*, developed and produced by the supplier Swedstyle. Producing, delivering and assembling into El-Tables this component (covering 2/3 of the product value) require high coordination between Swedstyle, Edsbyn, distributors and customers. Edsbyn and Swedstyle are located 700 km apart and most customers are located in between: transport costs can be therefore reduced by delivering tabletops separately from electric stands, from Edsbyn and Swedstyle factories, respectively. Distributors (e.g., SENAB) then assemble the two components at customers' locations. This requires high delivery precision and coordination from *both* Edsbyn and Swedstyle: delays in one component increase costs because assembly personnel must wait; while too early deliveries overload customers' offices with materials that hinder other furnishing tasks. Movex helps achieve this coordination by defining the exact dates when tabletops will be produced and deliveries can be made from Edsbyn. However, since Movex does not track Swedstyle's production, the detailed delivery coordination must be made manually between Swedstyle, Edsbyn and logistic partners.

Besides precise deliveries, respect of lead-times and efficient capacity utilization, Edsbyn strives to reduce inventories. Movex opens this opportunity: first, the MRPII method built into Movex purchases inputs *only* when they are about to run out of stock; second, such methods as the 'Wilson formula' minimize purchased lots in relation to the average needs to fulfil production orders. To summarize, while being constantly used, Movex became *embedded* into all resources intervening in Edsbyn's sales, production and distribution tasks. These resources are connected according to the network pattern presented in Figure 14.2. Placed within this networked context of use, Movex produces effects on the embedding resources (see the arrows originating from this focal IT system in Figure 14. 2). Let us now examine these effects and the obstacles and opportunities they imply.

The effects of Movex on resources: a source of opportunities and obstacles

Movex produces on the surrounding resources (see Figure 14.2) first 'informative' effects: it *models*, *monitors* and *calculates* inputs (MDF and veneer), WIPs (veneered boards), finished products (tabletops), production facilities, complementary products (stands) and supplier or customer agreements (lead-times and exchanged volumes). Movex measures these resources along quantitative dimensions (quantities, times, costs and article numbers),

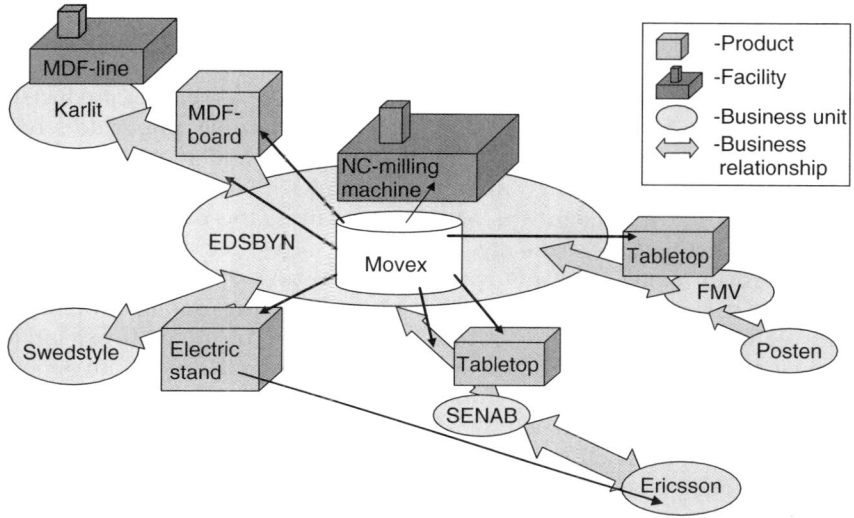

Figure 14.2 Movex and the surrounding network of resources

which are constantly monitored and calculated to create *information* that helps perform and improve central managerial task for Edsbyn, such as production scheduling or procurements.

Movex offers its greatest opportunities in those tasks that it fully *automates*, by performing all calculations about the involved resources and by providing all the information relevant for a task. The fully automated tasks are those where resources can be considered as *given*, with just a few quantitative dimensions as relevant. These automation opportunities are mostly evident in production scheduling, where Movex greatly reduced errors and accelerated information processing (to just a few seconds per scheduling run). Thus, Movex opens the opportunity to better meet customer needs, because Edsbyn can now schedule production daily and update its schedules continuously, as soon as new customer orders are received, instead of waiting for a whole week. This also contributed concretely to reducing Edsbyn's delivery times from 4 to 3 weeks. In parallel, Movex's ability to rapidly allocate production lots to the right machine gave the opportunity to utilize more efficiently Edsbyn's constrained production system, by making it easier to identify each single drop of free capacity.

Movex has many concrete effects on resources during production scheduling: it prescribes when tabletops lot can be produced and on which machine. Thus, Movex's internal models steer how resources can be combined. The more Movex is applied in scheduling and the more it becomes a precondition for performing the related activities, making Edsbyn dependent on Movex's schedules. The effects of Movex in other managerial tasks are instead more limited. For instance, in logistic management (essential to coordinate deliveries of Edsbyn's tabletops with complementary products), Movex offers no opportunity to improve coordination because it does not represent such external resources as transporters' routes and trucks, Swedstyle's production and distributors' assembly schedules. Since Movex does not cover the times and quantities of these resources, the detailed transport planning must be done manually.

But Movex alone does not either allow seizing opportunities (as its complete resource tracing does in production scheduling) or nullify them (as missing key resources does in logistics). Depending on how Movex interplays with the many resources involved in each managerial task, both opportunities and obstacles emerge. This happens, for instance, in the purchasing and inventory management task, concerned with ensuring timely input flows to launch production, while containing inventory costs. Movex's built-in models (MRPII and 'Wilson formula') allow containing costs by emitting purchase orders only when inputs are strictly necessary, but these models block the opportunity to exploit special deals (e.g., temporary discounts on veneers). In fact, Movex is not programmed to cover these external contingencies. But even the external resources that Movex actually covers do not always help procurements: Movex represents supply flows only as fixed lead-times, without tracing the current degree of utilization of suppliers' facilities (e.g., of Karlit's MDF-line). So, Movex does not react to a known overcapacity at Karlit with preventive orders (although manual overriding is possible). But the interplay of Movex with the surrounding resources produces unexpected 'concrete' effects in Edsbyn's inventory: Movex opened the opportunity to shorten Edsbyn's lead-times to produce tabletops; but Swedstyle's capacity limits impede to produce electric stands as quickly. This caused the disturbing indirect effect that Edsbyn, in order to quickly fulfil massive customer orders, needs to increase its stocks of expensive stands at its premises.

All the effects of Movex reviewed above concern tasks aiming at *efficient utilization* of existing resources. Which opportunities does Movex entail instead for *developing* resources, such as Edsbyn's products? Whereas Movex does not open major opportunities for *new* products, it contributes useful information for further developing *existing* products. For instance, competitive pressures and the search of new customers induced Edsbyn to improve the major product El-Table along two dimensions: (1) cost reduction and (2) range extension.

Whereas the largest cost reduction came from Swedstyle, which halved the number of components in electric stands and reorganized its subcontractor network, Movex was expected to reduce product-handling costs at customer locations: each table was burdened with assembly costs of Euro40 because tabletops needed to be drilled at customer locations, each stand model having different contact points with tabletops. Movex opened here an opportunity for reducing this cost, borne by distributors, by steering and scheduling the production of tabletops to have them predrilled in the exact positions required by the completing stand. The only information Movex would need is which stand each tabletop will be combined with. But while this Movex-enabled opportunity was being evaluated, Edsbyn launched so many new stand variants to make it too laborious to re-write all CAD/CAM instructions to steer NCs: this option was therefore abandoned. Moreover, this opportunity became less interesting because distributors had progressively learned to drill and assemble much quicker and did not need any longer predrilled tops so badly.

For range extensions, Movex provides much historical sales data, opening the opportunity to evaluate which standard items to include in the quick-delivery 5-day range. Finally Movex provides a marketing opportunity by calculating the price for customized versions within a few minutes (instead of hours, as it took before). But all in all Movex has limited effects for developing resources. Most opportunities to develop resources appear far away from Movex: most ideas and concrete recombinations are not represented inside Movex, either because they are too trivial (e.g., a roll-carriage to transport stands) or because they are outside Edsbyn (e.g., electric stand's construction and Swedstyle's subcontractor network).

Opportunities and obstacles in installing and using ERP-systems

Edsbyn's experience with Movex points at a series of opportunities and obstacles that ERP-systems create for the using organization. These opportunities are possibilities offered by the IT tool either to better *utilize given* resources or to *develop variable* resources. The empirical material also suggests that these opportunities are prepared well before starting using the IT system, that is, already during its installation, starting from the selection of IT tools. Afterwards, when the ERP is daily used, opportunities and problems concretely emerge while the IT system interplays with the embedding resources (see Figure 14.2). Let us now analyse the opportunities and hindrances related to Movex in its *installation* and in its *current use*.

Edsbyn's experience shows the difficulty to eliminate all problems in the installation of ERPs. Whereas it is relatively easy to identify a series of *abstract* opportunities and to select a matching technical solution, obstacles appear already in the implementation project. Despite the use of structured methods, such projects unfold in unexpected ways, mainly because they require IT provider and customer to closely interact around Movex. Moreover, the using firm needs to catalyse full support to the Movex project in order to overcome resistance (e.g., the high perceived risk and costly changes associated with a new critical system). The enticing, but abstract and future, opportunities that an ERP-system offers (e.g., fast and error-free calculations, improved processes, reduced lead-times) need to be weighed against the actual pains a firm needs to go through: organizational changes, need to unlearn and learn routines, and project delays. Thus, a heavy and critical system like an ERP needs to be treated both as a *strategic investment*, whose concrete benefits can lay much farther ahead of the pains it first causes, and as a *project* to be handled to keep its risks under control. Sadly, the opportunities that the IT tool will open are no guarantee, but they require sweat and pain to be first *planted*, during the installation, and then *concretized*, during the current use.

Among the opportunities opened by IT in Edsbyn's case one can distinguish those that lie *very close* to the IT artefact from those that appear in relation to resources *farther away* from Movex, in the network of Figure 14.2. In particular, the case points at these four types:

(a) *Information-handling* opportunities entail reduced costs or better quality in information handling (reduced errors, fast calculations, real-time data, etc.) and are closest to the IT core. These opportunities relate to the 'informative' effects of IT, that is, to how IT represents resources (Baraldi, 2003: 35–6). But such superficial opportunities do not justify the large investments in an ERP-system. And in fact the 'concrete' effects of IT on resources entail the following, more substantial, opportunities.
(b) *Internal efficiency-increase* opportunities appear a bit away from Movex, but still within Edsbyn's boundaries, and include reduction of internal lead-times and inventories or better capacity utilization.
(c) *Dyadic efficiency-increase* opportunities appear even farther from Movex, at the boundaries between Edsbyn and other business units, and concern improvements in the inter-organizational processes involving Edsbyn and its customers (e.g., faster customizations) or its suppliers/distributors (e.g., improved logistics or purchasing).
(d) *Network-level development* opportunities are farthest away from Movex and Edsbyn, in the network of Figure 14.2, and entail such resource developments as reducing El-Table's total cost.

The four types[1] of opportunities are presented in Figure 14.3.

The opportunities for improving information handling are very near the IT tool and cover only information. But moving from the centre of Figure 14.3 towards the external circle, we meet opportunities that can be seized through concrete effects on resources located increasingly far from Movex: suppliers' facilities, distributors or Swedstyle's subcontractors, in the case of the opportunities to develop El-Table at network level by reducing total costs. A key question is therefore: which types of IT-related opportunities are *easier* to seize for a firm using an ERP?

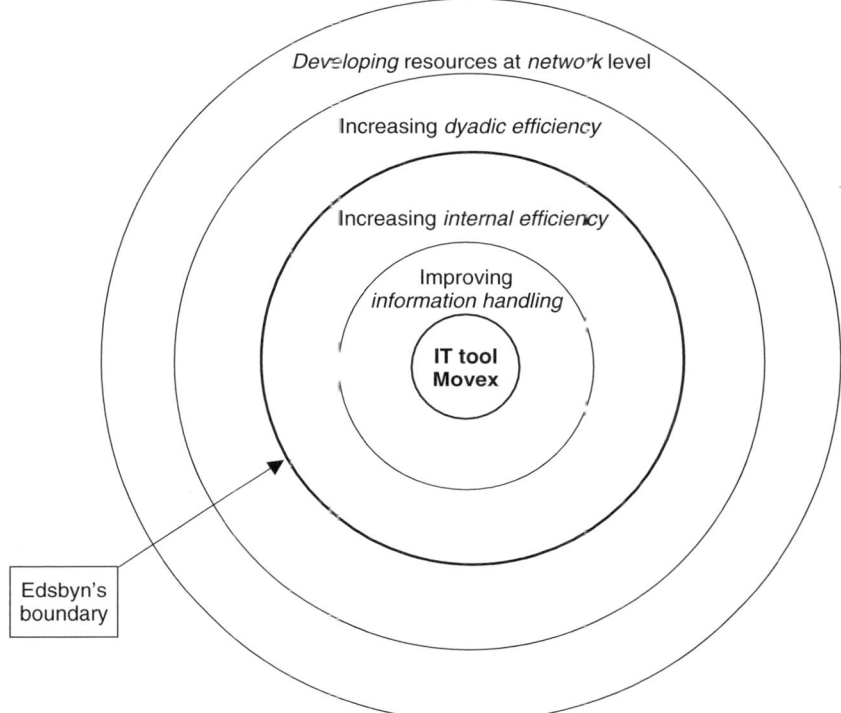

Figure 14.3 Four types of IT-related opportunities, closer to and farther from the IT core

Information-handling gains from IT are certainly easiest to seize, because these opportunities spring directly from using the IT system, unless the using unit does not apply it correctly. Things become instead complicated for the other three types of opportunities (*b*, *c* and *d*). In fact, when the ERP is constantly utilized, alongside expected opportunities emerge also obstacles to reaping the potential benefits from IT. These obstacles derive from how the IT system interplays with all the resources embedding it (see Figure 14.2), both inside and outside the using unit. However, some Movex-related opportunities appear easier to concretize. These are the opportunities to efficiently utilize resources, especially Edsbyn's internal resources, which Movex traces and monitors. Thus, Movex concretely increases efficiency in production scheduling and inventory management, thanks to such models as MRPII, capable to optimize given resources within closed systems (where resources are pre-defined and kept under control, like within Edsbyn's production system). These models nicely fit the needs of such efficiency-maintaining tasks as production scheduling, where Edsbyn allocates and locally optimizes resources (inputs, WIPs, facilities and finished products).

But things are more complex than what appears on the surface: seemingly easily-reaped internal-efficiency opportunities can become difficult to seize because of the obstacles created by indirect effects of IT that are spread across the network (the horizontal arrows in Figure 14.1). For instance, the opportunity to reduce Edsbyn's inventories is not seized because the Movex-enabled faster lead-times in producing tabletops require increasing stand inventories to guarantee quick and synchronized deliveries, since Swedstyle could not reduce its own lead-times. These indirect effects derive from the interaction among heterogeneous resources, causing the original IT effects to travel across their interfaces in the whole business network (Håkansson and Waluszewski, 2002). These effects deserve great caution because they are indeterminate and unexpected (Baraldi, 2003: 206), which implies that they may become obstacles to seizing the abstract opportunities of IT, even for internal efficiency.

Farther away from the focal IT tool lie opportunities that involve *external* resources, including those to *develop* resources: the empirical material points that Movex is of much less help in seizing opportunities involving external resources (e.g., logistics or purchasing), especially if these opportunities concern development (e.g., reducing product costs). What does this different contribution, compared to *efficiently utilizing internal* resources, depend on? Seizing resource-development opportunities requires treating resources as *variable*, within an *open* system enabling a *future-oriented* search for new features or combinations. Movex (like any IT system) treats instead resources as given, within a closed system, presenting only their historical features. However, this does not amount to claiming that IT tools are obstacles to seizing development opportunities: ERP-systems can help developing resources by measuring current resource combinations, by signalling problems and by comparing alternatives for decision makers. Besides providing information, ERP-systems can open development opportunities by reducing the information-processing costs of a new resource combination, as in the example of the pre-drilling option for El-Table tops. However, these opportunities are concretely pursued and exploited *only if* the embedding resources in the network (distributors' assembly competence or number of top-stand combinations) make these opportunities valuable to some actor: IT systems alone cannot 'oblige' all the nearer and farther resources to make place for the opportunities they allow to pursue.

The contribution of Movex for seizing development and efficiency opportunities diminishes the farther the involved resources are from the domain it is designed to supervise, that is, from the boundaries of Edsbyn. In fact, Movex has limits in tracing external resources in a system as open as El-Table's logistics. Moreover, the broader the domain to supervise, with growing

Type of opportunity (see figure 3)	Example of opportunity in Edsbyn's case	Obstacles to seizing (because of resource embeddedness)
Improve information handling	More rapid and error-free order handling or production schedule.	IT tool's capabilities, low IT competence, old internal routines, resource modellability.
Increase internal efficiency	Increase machines' utilization; reduce stocks; shorten lead-times.	Besides the above, MDF quality, Swedstyle's capacity and times.
Increase dyadic efficiency	More precise final deliveries; better purchasing.	Limits to model *external* resources; distributors' schedules; too varying supply conditions for MRPII.
Develop resources at network level	Reduce total cost of El-Table for the downstream network.	Limits to model *variable* resources; too many top-stand variants; distributors' assembly competence.

Figure 14.4 Classifying IT-related opportunities and obstacles for Edsbyn

numbers of resources, and the more blurred and complex their interfaces become (Baraldi, 2003: 21–2), with many more indirect effects and obstacles that Movex is not programmed to handle. But such problems emerge surprisingly near Edsbyn's boundaries: it is enough to have a few external resources involved in a task to see the rigidities created by Movex's mechanistic MRPII model, which blocks opportunities, for instance, in purchasing inputs. Using the categorization of opportunities on Figure 14.3, Figure 14.4 classifies some of the opportunities that Movex opens for Edsbyn, while pointing at the obstacles to seizing them created by resource embeddedness and by certain specific interfaces across Edsbyn's network.

Conclusions and implications

This chapter discussed the opportunities associated with complex IT systems, such as ERPs, while pointing that the embedding network of resources is a source of both opportunities and obstacles for the IT-using firm. Even if no general results are provided, areas of concern for all firms employing these heavy and critical tools were identified. IT-related opportunities are many but they do not automatically transform into real gains. Seizing these opportunities is not easy, because opportunities and obstacles emerge from the interplay between the IT tool and the other resources surrounding it, in the business network where this is systematically utilized. The seeds for opportunities are planted already in the installation of an ERP, with the *selection* of a specific IT tool and its *implementation*. Since ERPs are important investments that can sign the future of a using firm, the many abstract opportunities envisaged at this stage should be weighed against actual costs and required changes in the using firm and its network.

But the opportunities and limits of IT become even more evident when ERPs enter in use and constantly interplay with embedding resources. At this stage, the abstract opportunities can be seized only when ERPs 'meet' the other resources, such as products, facilities, business units and relationships. A laborious process of interplay with and between these resources is necessary for diffusing those effects that allow exploiting the technology-related opportunities of ERPs. However, resource interaction can also create and transmit obstacles because of the indeterminate nature of the effects that ERPs produce on the resources in which they are embedded, inside the using firm and in the whole business network. These obstacles and unexpected effects increase the more external and variable resources need to be involved for seizing an efficiency or development opportunity. Such obstacles are hardly avoidable, but being aware of where they more likely emerge (i.e., in externally oriented development tasks) can put firms in guard and induce them to better sense the limits of their IT tools. Further research is required to systematize the emergence of and the possibility to seize IT-related opportunities. This should be ideally conducted with a process-like view capable to catch also the *unexpected* emergence of opportunities, even *long after* the installation of an IT tool.

Note

1. The classification in Figure 14.3 does not aim to cover *all* possible types of opportunities, but simply points at those surfacing in the empirical material of the section on Movex and at how 'far' they lie from the focal IT tool. In fact, combining the development-efficiency idea with the distance from the unit where IT is installed generates other opportunities such as 'developing resources at *firm-internal* level' or 'increasing efficiency across the network'.

References

Ardichvili, A., Cardozo, R. and Ray, S. (2003). A Theory of Entrepreneurial Opportunity Identification and Development, *Journal of Business Venturing*, 18, 105–23.

Baraldi, E. (2003). *When Information Technology Faces Resource Interaction. Using IT Tools to Handle Products at IKEA and Edsbyn*. PhD. Thesis, Department of Business Studies, Uppsala University.

Baraldi, E. and Bocconcelli, R. (2001). The Quantitative Journey in a Qualitative Landscape. Developing a Data Collection Model and a Quantitative Methodology in Business Network Studies, *Management Decision*, 39(7), 564–77.

Baraldi, E. and Waluszewski, A. (2005). Information Technology at IKEA: An 'Open Sesame' Solution or Just Another Type of Facility? *Journal of Business Research*, 58(9), 1251–60.

Davenport, T.H. (1992). *Process Innovation. Re-engineering Work Through Information Technology*, Boston, MA: Harvard Business School Press.

Davenport, T.H. (1998). Putting the Enterprise into the Enterprise System, *Harvard Business Review*, July–August, 121–31.

Davenport, T.H. (2000). *Mission Critical: Realising the Promise of Enterprise Systems*, Boston, MA: Harvard Business School Press.

Davenport, T.H., De Long, D.W. and Beers, M.C. (1998). Successful Knowledge Management Projects, *Sloan Management Review*, Winter, 43–57.

Diebold, J. (1953). Automation – the New Technology, *Harvard Business Review*, November–December, 63–71.

Eckhardt, J.T. and Shane, S.A. (2003). Opportunities and Entrepreneurship, *Journal of Management*, 29(3), 333–49.

Gadde, L.-E. (1997). Information Technology and Business Transactions, in *Yearbook for the School of Technology and Management at Chalmers University*, Gothenburg, 25–51.

Gadde, L-E. and Håkansson, H. (2001). *Supply Network Strategies*, Chichester: Wiley.

Håkansson, H. and Waluszewski, A. (2002). *Managing Technological Development*, London: Routledge.

Håkansson, H. and Snehota, I. (Eds) (1995). *Developing Relationships in Business Networks*, London: Routledge.

Hedberg, B. and Jönsson, S. (1978). Designing Semi-confusing Information Systems for Organizations in Changing Environments, *Accounting, Organizations and Society*, 3(1), 47–64.

Herrman, C.C. and Magee, J.F. (1953). 'Operations Research' for Management. *Harvard Business Review*, July–August, 100–12.

Kalakota, R. and Robinson, M. (2000). *e-Business 2.0. Roadmap for Success*, Harlow: Addison-Wesley.

Malerba, F. and Orsenigo, L. (1997). Technological Regimes and Sectoral Patterns of Innovative Activities, *Industrial and Corporate Change*, 6(1), 83–117.

Malone, T.W., Yates, J. and Benjamin, R.I. (1989). The Logics of Electronic Markets, *Harvard Business Review*, May–June, 98–103.

Mintzberg, H. (1972). The Myths of MIS, *California Management Review*, XV(1), Fall, 92–7.

Penrose, E. (1959). *The Theory of the Growth of Firm*, Reprint 1995, New York: Oxford University Press.

Porter, M.E. and Millar, V. (1985). How Information Gives You Competitive Advantage, *Harvard Business Review*, January–February, 149–60.

Ramström, D. (1973). *The Efficiency of Control Strategies Revisited*, University of Umeå, Department of Business Administration.

Schumpeter, J.A. (1934). *The Theory of Economic Development: An Inquiry into Profits, Capital Credit, Interest and The Business Cycle*, Cambridge: Harvard University Press.

Tidd, J., Bessant, J. and Pavitt K. (2001). *Managing Innovation. Integrating Technological, Market and Organizational Change*, Chichester: Wiley.

Winograd, T. and Flores, F. (1986). *Understanding Computers and Cognition. A New Foundation for Design*, Reading, Menlo Park, New York: Addison-Wesley.

Zuboff, S. (1988). *In the Age of the Smart Machine*, New York: Basic Books.

15
Creating New Opportunities from Old Resources through Contextually Determined Information Asymmetries

Anna Bengtson and Susanne Åberg

Introduction

Last time you used a credit card, did you stop to think about all the necessary activities performed, resources used and actors involved in order for you to get your money? Probably not. There are many services that we use every day without giving them a moment's thought, and using our credit cards, either to withdraw money from an ATM-machine or to pay for our purchases in a shop, is one of them. Every time you use your card it triggers a process involving a number of activities, resources and actors. A technological change that makes your daily performance easier in small and almost unnoticeable ways – for example the fact that the electronic payments are nowadays mostly on-line, meaning that the line behind you at the register does not add up due to your choice of paying by card – can have a substantial effect on things we, as consumers, do not notice. Some of the changes that arise in a technological area, for instance electronic payments, are based on change processes started to exploit opportunities that are found because of the way the resources controlled by involved actors are combined. The necessary resources (and often even the industrial actors) behind a service of this type are normally black-boxed (Latour, 1987; Rosenberg, 1994). Thus, our first contribution will be to try to open this black box enough to peek in, and thereby reach a new understanding of how firms' opportunities are affected by resource connections and interaction between actors in an industrial network.

In the first chapter of this book, the development of an opportunity is defined as 'the process of knowledge and resource combinations to attain new markets or products'. It is further stated, that the insights from the study of opportunity development can increase when an industrial network approach is adopted. Most researchers who have dealt with the concept of opportunities, however, have focused on individuals acting as entrepreneurs

(Eckhardt and Shane, 2003; Shane, 2000), or the opportunities facing a single firm (Penrose, 1959). Eckhardt and Shane state, for example, that 'researchers have tended to take a person-centric perspective, in which entrepreneurship depends on stable, enduring differences among *people*' (2003: 334). Both neoclassical equilibrium theories (e.g. Kihlstrom and Laffont, 1979) and psychological theories (e.g. McClelland, 1961; Brockhaus and Horowitz, 1986) assume explicitly or implicitly that fundamental attributes of people (such as taste for uncertainty (Kihlstrom and Laffont, 1979), need for achievement (McClelland, 1961) and willingness to bear risk (Brockhaus and Horowitz, 1986)) determine who becomes an entrepreneur. The focus is thus put on individual human attributes in order to explain opportunity discovery and change (Shane, 2000: 449).

The opportunity facing a single *firm* at a certain moment comprises, according to Penrose, 'all of the productive possibilities that its "entrepreneurs" see and can take advantage of' (1959: 31). This opportunity is thus a sum of the entrepreneurial opportunities of the people in the firm. Penrose declares as well that 'it is clear that this opportunity/the productive opportunity of the firm/will be restricted to the extent to which a firm does not see opportunities for expansion, is unwilling to act upon them, or is unable to respond to them' (Penrose, 1959: 32). Penrose finds that opportunities for the firm depend on two things: they are connected to the firm's production, and they are dependent on the actors' perceptions.

This chapter neither focuses on people as entrepreneurs, nor on single firms, but rather on connections and dependencies between resources controlled by interacting industrial actors as a means to study and understand technological change. Our chapter aims to show how technological opportunities may arise and become exploited within an industrial network context. In doing so, we will focus especially on the notion of information asymmetry. Based on the findings of our study, we will argue for a somewhat different view on information asymmetry than has been used by other researchers discussing the phenomenon to explain opportunity identification and exploitation (see e.g. Shane, 2000). Thus, our second contribution will be to relate the concept of information asymmetry from entrepreneurial theory to the phenomenon and theory of industrial networks.

Snehota's view on opportunities comes quite close to ours in that he claims that opportunities are in fact 'heterogeneity in knowledge of resource utilization' (1990: 70) and therefore they 'do not exist per se; they result from interaction between the parties'. In Snehota's view, opportunities are not only dependent on perceptions, they are also dependent on interaction between firms. The author further states that 'exploiting market exchange opportunities implies linking market actors, resources and activities in a novel pattern that provides value to some of the market participants' (*ibid*: 180). Before we continue our theoretical discussion, however, we will begin to delineate the empirical material used.

The chapter is structured as follows. In the next section, we will introduce the readers to the technological area dealt with in the study, the ISDN-net and the D-channel. Thereafter we expand on the theoretical framework used, and describe the study design and methods. Next we present the empirical study 'development and exploitation of the D-channel'. Finally, we draw some theoretical implications and make some concluding remarks.

The ISDN-NET and the D-channel

During an interview at the Swedish telephone company Telia a few years ago, a somewhat disillusioned product manager on the ISDN-side portrayed broadband technology as God: 'everyone has heard of it, many believe in its revolutionary force, but few or no one knows for certain if it really exists'. Today broadband connections are becoming more and more common in Swedish homes and companies (among other things, several municipalities are presently negotiating municipal contracts on broadband extensions with Telia's network company Scanova), while the more than ten years older ISDN-net already has reached its total extension on the Swedish market. As they say at Telia: 'Today all the profitable ISDN customers already have it', which in national terms equals 85 per cent of all companies and 80 per cent of all private customers or households. Instead of focusing on the new hot broadband area, however, this chapter will illustrate how companies through interaction with others extend their knowledge of the ISDN-net's usage potentials and thereby also learn how to make more money on an old and already established resource.

ISDN is the acronym for Integrated Services Digital Network. It is not a complete network (in the sense that the Internet is), but rather a digital communication channel. ISDN is used as a digital transmission channel for communication instead of analogue transmission, used for example in ordinary, 'old', telephone lines. One of the advantages with ISDN is that one infrastructure (the ISDN) can be used for both telephone services and data communications. Other advantages include the fact that ISDN contains a separate channel for signalling, which has been shown to be useful also for supplementary services. It is the separate signal channel, the D-channel, and one supplementary service, electronic payments, which will be studied in this chapter.

There are two kinds of ISDN access, basic access and primary rate access. In the Swedish system, these are called *ISDN duo* and *ISDN multi*. The ISDN duo is a single access connection aimed at small companies and private customers, whereas the ISDN multi is connected through telephone switches and used by big companies. The ISDN duo connection, which is what we will be focusing on, consists of a single ISDN line. Each line is made of two bearer channels, B-channels, of 64 kbs each, and a D-channel providing 9.6 kbs, running on a data network called the X.25-net. The system adheres to international standards. The main purpose of the D-channel is to function as a signal channel, so that the considerably bigger B-channels can be kept off-line. When someone wants to send a message (a telephone call), the B-channels are opened up for the actual data traffic.

ISDN is accessed by the user through ISDN adapters, terminal adapters, located in the user's home or office. A terminal adapter can be said to be, for the digital system, what the modem is for the analogue telephone system. It works as a translator to translate asynchronous and synchronous data to protocols mainly used on the ISDN.

Focusing especially on the use of the ISDN D-channel for electronic payments, we find that most payments by bank- and credit cards in shops today are of the electronic kind. An electronic payment requires some sort of terminal, either a stand-alone terminal such as the ones in small shops, or integrated systems like those in big supermarkets. After the card has been used in the terminal, the information from the terminal is sent over the ISDN D-channel and through a terminal adapter. The terminal adapter translates the information so that it can be sent over the X.25 net to the transaction-handling firm. The transaction handler is in turn connected to the banks for information handling. The resource collection that has been described this far and which forms the basis for the D-channel based electronic payment system is illustrated graphically in Figure 15.1 below.

We have now introduced the technological area we will be dealing with. This introduction, however, does not give any clue as to the processes that were necessary in order to develop the solution as it is constructed today.

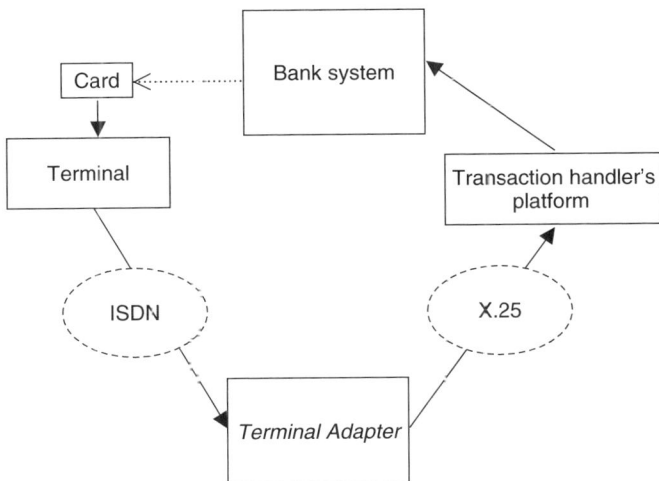

Figure 15.1 The electronic payment resource network

Later in this chapter, our material will illustrate that the development of the electronic payment system can be described and understood as a process through time. This process involved the interaction of several resources and the need for cooperation between several actors, based on different perceptions of opportunities by different actors, throughout the process that preceded the current solution. Before we move on to describing the six actors in the development of the electronic payment solution, however, we will first develop our theoretical tools a bit further. It is especially the opportunity concept, in connection to an industrial network view, which will be in focus.

Adopting an industrial network view on opportunities

The opportunity dealt with in this chapter, that is, the use of the already established D-channel of the ISDN-net for a new application in electronic payments, was created by already established industrial actors within an existing industrial structure. An important, if somewhat obvious, starting point for an analysis of the opportunity creating and exploiting behaviour of actors in technological change situations of this type is the fact that no change starts from zero.[1] There is always something there to build on, that is, a context of the change. According to, for example, Kirzner 'appropriate entrepreneurial incentives do, at any given moment, offer themselves in regard to the path relevant to the realities *of that moment*' (1992: 31). Pettigrew also emphasises the importance of temporal and spatial embeddedness of change in stating that 'actions are embedded in contexts and these contexts limit their information, insight and influence' (1997: 339).

Less agreed upon than the statement that context matters is, however, how this context should be dealt with in analysing opportunities. Based on thoughts from the Austrian economist theories in general and Kirzner (1973) in particular, Shane (2000) argues against both neoclassical equilibrium theories (e.g. Kihlstrom and Laffont, 1979) and psychological theories (e.g. Brockhaus and Horowitz, 1986; McClelland, 1961). These two theoretical fields claim that attributes of people are the fundamental contextual factors which determine entrepreneurial behaviour and therefore opportunity creation and exploitation. Instead it is, according to Shane, an uneven distribution of information, based on people's education and background that determine entrepreneurial behaviour and thus opportunities. 'Given that information asymmetry is necessary for entrepreneurial opportunities to exist, everyone in society must not be equally likely to recognize all opportunities. Rather, only a subset of the population is able to recognize any particular opportunity at any particular point in time' (Shane, 2000: p. 451).

Context is also at times discussed in terms of a structure (Barley, 1986; Giddens, 1979) or a network (Bengtson, 2003; Granovetter, 1985; Holmen, 2001; Snehota, 1990) involving both material and immaterial factors, which in different ways impact positively and negatively on change. This enlargement of the context to encompass also material items comes closer to our findings. The article will thus follow the IMP research tradition (Ford et al., 1998; Håkansson, 1987, 1989; Turnbull and Valla, 1986) in analysing context in terms of networks of relationships. We will analyse the opportunity seeking and exploiting behaviour of industrial actors in accordance with Granovetter's statement that 'economic action and outcomes are affected by actors' dyadic relationships and by the structure of the overall network of relations' (1992: 33).

Penrose alleges in her famous *The Theory of the Growth of the Firm* (1959) that 'opportunities to produce new products arise from changes in the productive services and knowledge available in the firm ... and from changes in external supply and market conditions as perceived by the firm' (p. 111). Adding the importance of interaction with other parties, e.g. suppliers and customers, to the thoughts of Penrose, it can be said that opportunities arise from the changes described by Penrose, which in their turn result from interaction between the focal company and other parties in its network context. Both the 'objective' productive opportunity, that is, what the firm is able to accomplish, and the 'subjective' productive opportunity, that is, what the firm thinks it can accomplish (*ibid*.: 41) are thus determined by the interaction that takes place in a focal firm's relationships to various counterparts, for instance its customers and suppliers. Hence, it is through these relationships that the firm develops resources such as information and knowledge and it is through these relationships that it is able to find and explore new opportunities, to test its capabilities and to create expectations of future performance.[2] A network view on opportunity creation and exploitation thus becomes a question of an interaction process through time between parties that have specific information about each other and certain resource connections to each other In this chapter, we will focus especially on the resource connections, where information is one important resource, and thus the resource dimension of the Industrial Network Model (Håkansson, 1987), thereby investigating the explanatory power that can be found in analysing the resource contexts of involved actors in this specific development (i.e. this opportunity). In the next section, we will talk about the design and methods of the study, after which we will come back to recapitulate the empirical story.

Study design and methods

Keeping the reasoning on opportunity creation and exploitation in mind, we will now return to the purchase of food at the register in the supermarket in order to describe what happened 'behind the scene' just a few years ago. We will take a fixed resource (resource constellation) as our point of departure and discuss the opportunity discoveries and exploitations that have taken place during the last years in this area.

The material for the D-channel study has mainly been collected through personal interviews with people responsible for the technical area in question, or in marketing areas in which the technology has an impact on the efforts made towards customers in one way or the other. The study has been conducted within a larger research project in which the uses of the D-channel for electronic payments in the Nordic countries of Denmark, Norway and Sweden, were investigated, plus an investigation of the situation in Finland on a smaller scale. In total 24 interviews have been made. This chapter focuses on the Swedish material and is based on eight interviews, combined with some additional secondary sources such as reports and technical product descriptions collected at the involved companies.

The study is outlined so that the role of each one out of six actors involved in, and central for, the development of the use of the D-channel for electronic payments in Sweden is described. The net of actors is graphically illustrated in Figure 15.2 below. After the empirical description of the actors involved in the development, we will analyse the findings based on the theoretical discussion made in the former section; some of the implications for management of technological opportunities in single firms will also be discussed.

Development and exploitation of the D-channel

As already mentioned, this chapter describes six actors involved in the development and exploitation of the D-channel for electronic payments in Sweden. We start by presenting the supplier of the ISDN infrastructure, Telia, and one of its main suppliers. Then we move on to one of the card suppliers and their subcontractor. Next we move closer to the shop by presenting one of the suppliers of card terminals, and, finally, we end up in one of the big supermarket chains where the transaction takes place – in this case ICA. In Figure 15.2 these actors and their technical connection to each other in the electronic payments network is illustrated.

The net-owner Telia

The development of payment solutions over the D-channel depended, from Telia's perspective, on the realisation in the late 1990s that the existing bandwidth was unused, that is, the 9.6 kbs D-channel was not fully used by the current signal traffic. To assemble all customers that needed to be on-line on the X.25-net in a common infrastructure, instead of spreading them on different small cables, was also a way to reduce costs. From the customers' perspective the development can be explained by an increasing need for information handling, and the need to send many small amounts of data often and at reasonable price. At the time of development, many retailers worked towards an increased use of plastic cards, and more and more shops had started using bonus systems to increase the rate of repurchase. In

Creating New Opportunities 295

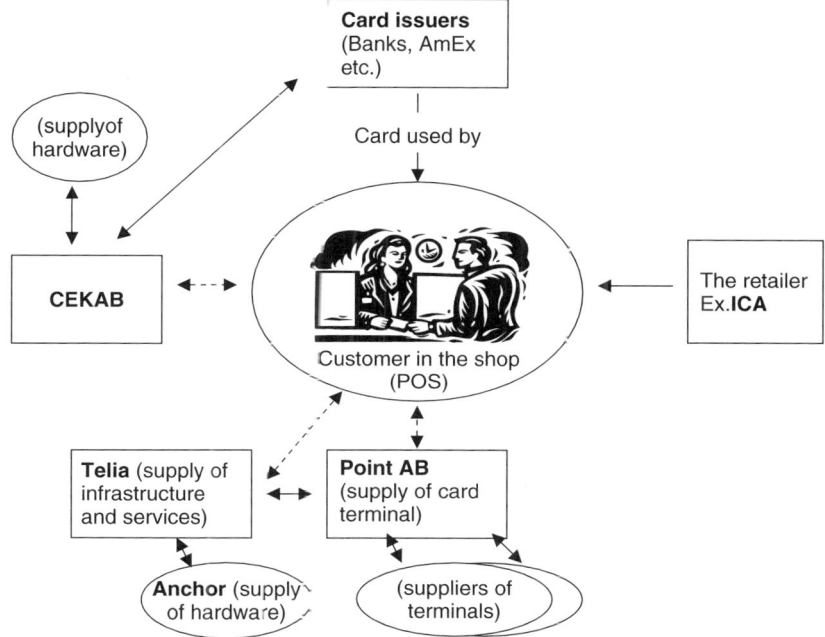

Figure 15.2 Some of the actors involved in the ISDN network

addition, other information flows, like games and volumes of consumption, had increased in scope. The low price demanded was difficult to achieve with the old solution since the customer was connected to the telephone network on a pre-rented line, at a fixed cost per minute.

It was fairly simple from Telia's point of view to see the opportunities related to an extended use of the D-channel. However, developing a well functioning use of the D-channel for electronic payments demanded several years of development work and continuous efforts performed by several parties who all had to see opportunities worthy of the efforts they put into their work. And all of these efforts were made in the shadow of the much trendier broadband development, which eventually may replace the ISDN-infrastructure that the D-channel is part of.

The data communication supplier Anchor Datacomm

An important counterpart for Telia during the development phase was Anchor Datacomm in the Netherlands. Anchor is one of Telia's most important suppliers when it comes to hardware, terminal adapters, for the ISDN solution over the X.25 net. When Telia started up the ISDN venture in

1998, they cooperated with both Anchor and Motorola, but Anchor was the one company willing, at this early development stage, to make changes and adaptations in its product to suit Telia's needs. Today Anchor is Telia's only supplier of terminal adapters, and the company is described by the people at Telia as a very flexible counterpart, prepared to make both customised products and quick changes, should this be demanded.

The Swedish efforts to extend the use of the D-channel to include payments services rhyme well with the product range and skills at Anchor at the time. Anchor develops and produces professional data communication products. The company started out by producing modems, but was at this time working more with X.25 related solutions, and its main product range is now within the field for digital infrastructures and X.25 leased lines. Telia has continued as one of its most important customers, together with other large telecommunication companies such as KPN Telecom and China Telecom. The main product range today is the X.Sagitta, and it includes many models and is based on modules. The product range includes ISDN terminal adapters, routers and gateways. Anchor has outsourced the production of hardware to suppliers and focuses on design and software in-house.

Hence, for Anchor the opportunities related to the Swedish development of electronic payments over the D-channel was extremely important for the development of the company. Telia, as a big and demanding customer, provided Anchor with knowledge about customer needs within the area, and also improved the knowledge about its own products (and how they could fit into a customer's resource base). Increased knowledge also meant more business with Telia, which in itself was important for expansion. A sign that Telia is still considered an important customer within the telecom segment is that Anchor uses it as a reference customer (e.g. on its home page on the Web).

The card issuer SEB Kort

In order to make electronic payments available to customers, another group of actors is of course necessary, that is, banks. Banks both issue cards and handle the transfer of money. An increase of electronic payments instead of cash payments has many benefits from a bank perspective. Besides the risk reduction on behalf of cardholders and shops, it is easier for a bank to handle 'electronic money' than 'physical money', and as a consequence, several routines can be simplified and the number of employees reduced. Despite the obvious opportunities in the development from a bank point of view, the banks do not seem to have taken a very active part in the development of the D-channel service.

SEB is one of the biggest commercial banks in Sweden, and SEB Kort AB is one of their daughter companies. SEB Kort is responsible for issuing cards, collecting and paying card transactions. The company handles SEB's bankcards, that is, Visa- and MasterCards, Diner's Club cards, Eurocards, and a number of 'loyalty cards' – bonus cards etc. Visa and MasterCard are so-called open networks, which means that there are an unlimited number of card issuers and payers in any given country, whereas Diner's Club only have one issuer/payer in every country. A Visa or a MasterCard issued in Sweden has to work in 29 million different places all over the world, a fact that gives some perspective on the level of standardisation needed for the system to work.

The collecting service provided by SEB card consists of three basic services. The first one is the control, the authorisation, of the card. This includes controlling that the card is valid, that it has not been freezed, that there is money in the account and so on. The second service is to collect all the transactions, and the third service to pay the selling company its money. In every transaction, there are four parties involved: a customer using the card, a seller accepting it, a collector performing the three services mentioned above, and a card issuer. The authorisation is always made in real time, and this is one of the reasons why SEB card uses a sub-contractor for this service, namely CEKAB. Being on-line for authorisations requires a great deal of resources, and it is better to use one company for this than having all banks on-line all the time.

The transaction handler CEKAB

Despite being a small company, CEKAB is one of Telia's biggest customers. In addition to being an important customer, they also had an interest in the development of the D-channel, since this facilitated their work. CEKAB was founded in 1989 by a number of banks to handle ATM machines. The reason why CEKAB exists is on the one hand to have a 'neutral' actor – any bank should be able to use CEKAB – and on the other hand to provide their services cheaper than it would be for any bank to perform the service in-house. CEKAB also has a very high level of availability, which means that their systems are available even if the banks have problems with their own systems. In 1994, the company started handling POS (point-of-sale) transactions as well, that is, card payments in shops, and today CEKAB handles all kinds of electronic payment solutions for most Swedish banks and for card issuers like American Express and Diner's Card. This involves, among other things, both ATM machines and card payments.

Although CEKAB is a rather small company, with about 45 employees, they are, due to all the transactions handled, one of Telia's 35 biggest customers. Most of the traffic into CEKAB's systems is handled by Telia and run over the ISDN network. If it concerns transactions outside Telia, it is collected by them and transferred over a B-channel, whereas the ATMs and the shop terminals use the D-channel. The main service CEKAB performs when it comes to electronic payments is to collect all the payments in their system. When a customer in a shop uses his or her credit card, the transaction is sent to CEKAB, who in turn sends it to the bank for confirmation. CEKAB then collects all transactions going to, for instance, SEB – both for ATMs and for shop purchases.

An important aspect when it comes to electronic payments is security. CEKAB is involved in setting the criteria for, among other things, the terminals. The terminal providers, like for example Point, have to follow these criteria, and CEKAB personnel then check the terminals to see that they are secure. The security controls deal with, for instance, what happens if the terminal is opened, if anything can be taken away, if anything can be added so that the PIN-code can be copied and so on. A terminal should be constructed so that if it is opened there is a power cut and no information can be retrieved.

The terminal producer, Point

The importance of terminal providers grew when electronic payments became more common, hence they are relatively new actors. When the first terminals for electronic payments were introduced in Sweden, the banks bought them and then gave them away, or leased them, to the shops. Point AB is, with about 80 per cent of the market, by far the biggest terminal provider in Sweden. Over 60,000 customers use Point terminals in Sweden today. Point was founded in 1989 in Norway, and the mother company is still there, although the Swedish market is now the dominating one. Whereas Point's expertise lies in the software, or the programming of the terminals, there are two different companies that produce the terminals sold by them today: CKD Moneyline in France and Banksys in Belgium. Both these companies are very big in their respective market, but since bank rules and regulations are different in all countries, it would be difficult for them to operate on the Swedish market.

Point AB originally had contacts with Telia through the Swedish banks, but early on the two parties saw a need for joint development on technological aspects. If a customer wants to start using a terminal, he or she has to contact both Telia and Point (or one of Point's competitors). Telia provides the telephone line, and the transmission capacity, while Point delivers the terminal. A few years back, the customer would have had packages delivered from both Telia and Point, and was then expected to connect the bits and pieces by himself. Today Point handles the order from Telia, and sends everything out in one single package. The customer still has to connect the terminal, but at least it is only one supplier involved. The contacts between Telia and Point are described, by both parties, as very good. Point tests its equipment in Telia's labs, and the companies work together to develop terminals that work satisfactorily. As an employee at Telia puts it, 'If they sell a terminal, we sell a D-channel. So we have worked a lot together with them.' This interaction has been going on since the electronic payment service was first provided by Telia in 1998.

The retailer ICA

Fast electronic payments are interesting for all shops, but perhaps especially for big retailers with hundreds of customers every day. By using the D-channel for these payments, the time every customer has to wait can be reduced considerably. This is one of the reasons why, in 1999, the big retail company ICA became the first application user, working as an active counterpart in cooperation and a potential customer for Telia in the development of payment solutions over the D-channel.

The importance of ICA's involvement in the development was expressed by Schultz, Telia's manager for the ISDN-net, in the following way: 'It was ICA that delivered the service. Without their cooperation, nothing would have happened. All development needs to be sustainable in business, and to get this project accepted internally we needed a customer to show the potential uses. Only a small number of development paths evolve into something viable, but if you have a big customer something happens'.

For ICA, the development also provided a possibility to reduce its information handling costs. They had started with the so-called ICA customer card (*ICA kundkort*) which has a bonus system attached based on the customers' volumes purchased. The bonus registrations induced a high cost of information handling, however, and the first version of the system was not profitable as a whole. Another problem, which they shared with many other chain stores, was the fact that cash handling required a lot of security routines. If the store could get the customers to use cards to pay for their purchases, this problem would be solved. The incentives for consumers to use plastic cards were small, however, and card users were often, as mentioned earlier, considered a nuisance at the cash-point. The average time for a card transaction used to be about 25–30 seconds, and this of course led to queues forming whenever someone chose to pay with a card. Through the use of the D-channel, this time has decreased considerably so that the printing of the receipt takes the most time now.

In the next part of the chapter, we will discuss the theoretical implication of the study that has just been presented. The chapter will then end with some concluding remarks.

Theoretical implications

The opportunity to use the already established D-channel for electronic payments that has been described shows a process in which several resources became connected to other resources in new or modified ways, and in which actors interacted more with other parties in order to start using the D-channel for electronic payments. The process has some theoretical implications that differ from, or that extend some implications from, earlier studies on (technological) opportunity-driven behaviour. These six implications will be discussed in this section.

Implication number one states that *other resources besides information are of vital importance for opportunity recognition*. The D-channel study describes several resources, besides information, which were absolutely vital for the opportunity recognition of the involved actors. Understanding why the development was started and why the creation process looked as it did therefore requires an understanding of a larger resource context of the involved actors (Bengtson, 2003). For Telia, it was the existence of a partly unused resource, the D-channel, and the cost of using other resources that sparked the opportunity recognition. In the case of all six actors we have illustrated that the development added more value to their already established resources, and that their established resources (such as relationships to certain suppliers or customers, a certain knowledge base and/or a specific product range or production equipment) were prerequisites for opportunity recognition. Thus, information is only one resource needed in order to recognise an opportunity.

We agree with Shane (2000: 451) that there is an uneven distribution (or asymmetry) of information, which determine the likeliness of entrepreneurial behaviour of different actors. In addition to Shane's discussion, however, the second implication argues that *the information asymmetry, which has been presented as one important determinant for opportunity recognition, is based on different resource contexts of the actors*. Our study shows that the various actors involved in the development control, directly or indirectly through relationships to others, various resources that form the very basis of the opportunity created and exploited, i.e. the new technological application. Shane's (2000: 452) statement that 'each person's idiosyncratic prior knowledge creates a "knowledge corridor" that allows him/her to recognize certain opportunities, but not others', could thus be extended by claiming that each firm's existing resource collection (which results from earlier interaction with customers and suppliers) creates a 'resource corridor' (cf. Håkansson and Lundgren, 1997). This 'resource corridor' makes certain actions – resource development efforts, recombination efforts, etc. – an opportunity to this specific actor if developed properly. Whether the information that the ISDN D-channel could be used for electronic payments was an opportunity or not for a certain actor was determined by its situation, that is its already established resource context at that time. Information asymmetries is therefore not a question of different amounts of general information available to different actors, but rather a question of whether or not a certain actor can use the information to create an opportunity due to its resource context.

This argument leads us to the third implication that *rather than opportunities available for any actor who may find and explore them, a situation that prevails may be an opportunity for a certain actor due to these information asymmetries*. Taking the reasoning on information asymmetry one step further, an important distinction, besides the claim that other resources apart from information are of vital importance for opportunity recognition, can be made. We claim that not only information but also opportunities are specific rather than general. The resources differed between the actors, and therefore the opportunities, as perceived by the various actors, were different. Thus, each actor had its own reasons for perceiving the use of the ISDN D-channel for electronic payments as an opportunity. In Telia's case it was the underused capacity of the ISDN D-channel, and their knowledge of it, that was the starting point, whereas ICA perceived the development as an opportunity due to their new customer card system and the problems of cash handling at the cashiers. For the card issuers electronic payments increase security, through on-line check-ups, and reduce handling costs. By taking a fixed resource (resource constellation) as our point of departure, the empirical material has illustrated that the use of this resource, by being perceived differently, could be extended. Thus new resources could be created in the form of new uses, more value and new products, which also made it possible for new actors (such as Point and Anchor) to emerge, or at least to grow. Hence, we argue against a view on general opportunities recognised by some market participants and ignored by others, and towards a more resource specific view on opportunities. In all situations, certain opportunities will be created and exploited by certain actors due to their resource possessions, while there will not be any opportunities, or other opportunities facing other actors at that moment.

One more characteristic of opportunities is presented in implication number four: *The discoveries of opportunities result from a constant orientation of and interaction between various resources within an industrial network structure*. Another theoretical implication of our network focus can be added to Shane's (2000: 451) proposition that entrepreneurial opportunities are discovered without actively searching for them. According to Shane (*ibid*.) 'people do not discover entrepreneurial opportunities through search, but through recognition of the value of new information that they happen to receive through other means'. In accordance with Shane, we argue that superiority in search and discovery of opportunities is situation-specific (2000: 457), but enlarge the concept of situation to encompass more than the knowledge and mind-set of the involved actors. In our view, a large number of opportunities, like the one examined in this paper, are embedded in (Granovetter, 1985) an already established resource structure. It is thus when these resources are constantly combined and recombined through interaction that opportunities can be found (cf. Snehota, 1990: 65).

Taking this reasoning one step further, our fifth implication states that *sometimes enough changes in resource use are made to, in retrospect, call it a discovery and exploitation of a certain opportunity*. The study illustrates that the results of the actors' aspirations in relation to the D-channel for electronic payments development were not known, at least not in detail, to any of the involved firms before or even during the development. New resource combinations among the established resources created new opportunities for further recombination opportunities and so forth. The ability to use and exploit the opportunities of electronic payments connected to the D-channel were created by several interacting actors rather than discovered by a single actor (cf. Snehota, 1990). Thus, it was not so much an opportunity that was found at one point in time, as it was a gradual development through interaction between industrial parties and their resources. Hence, this gradual development created the opportunity that can be viewed in retrospect. The discovery of an opportunity is thus, based on this view, a consequence of these interactions. That is, rather than a conscious search for specific opportunities, sometimes enough new resources or even new actors are created in interaction processes to, *in retrospect*, call it a discovery and an exploitation of a certain opportunity.

The emphasis on the words 'in retrospect' illustrates our last theoretical implication for the term opportunity, namely that *creation and exploitation of a new technology are parallel processes that cannot be isolated from each other*. Whereas some earlier studies on technological opportunities (Eckhardt and Shane, 2003; Shane, 2000) have focused on market exploitation of what is perceived as already existing technologies, our material emphasises that creation and exploitation of the technology are two simultaneous processes that, like two sides of a coin, cannot be isolated from each other. Although less discussed in articles that explicitly use the term opportunity, this view is firmly grounded in several studies of technological development (Lundgren, 1995; Rosenberg, 1982; Tyre and Orlikowski, 1994; von Hippel, 1988). Tyre and Orlikowski, for instance, point out that 'users' efforts to apply technologies reveal problems and contingencies that were not apparent before introduction' (1994: 98), whereas Lundgren finds that 'the essentials lie beyond particular technological innovations, in their relation to the context in which they occur and of which they become a part' (1995: 37). Lundgren continues by claiming that 'the focus on radical innovations and heroic inventors has furnished important insights into the process of technological change', but this focus 'deemphasizes the subsequent adjustments and improvements in technology and economic structure'. It is claimed by Lundgren, and illustrated empirically in this study, that the technological change process cannot be described as a linear process, starting in a discovery or invention, which develops into an innovation from which certain market opportunities can be exploited for economic gains. Rather the D-channel study shows a situation in which a technological opportunity and a market (or exchange) opportunity were created and exploited in parallel to each other. To quote Lundgren: 'development is not a cumulative sequence but a cumulative synthesis' (1995: 39).

Concluding remarks

Some theoretical implications of a network view have been discussed, but what are the implications of our results for management of technological change in single firms? Our material suggests that the key to opportunity recognition and creation is interaction with counterparts such as customers and suppliers and that it is through this type of every-day business exchange that opportunities are exploited. The study also shows a situation in which several firms found a mutual path to follow for different reasons – there was no need for common goals, a common definition of the opportunity faced and so on, but rather the dynamics created by the differences in the perceptions of the involved actors resulted in actions and changes that we as observers with hind sight can recognise as one opportunity.

A somewhat paradoxical note, finally, is the fact that the resource contexts of an individual actor, which has been claimed in this article to form the basis for information asymmetries and thus also for opportunity recognition, creation and exploitation, simultaneously form the basis for resistance to changes of this type. The resource contexts of the involved actors have been built up through long-term interaction in order to reach even higher levels of perfection in performance on behalf of the actors and their resources. Much of the invested time, knowledge and such others will loose some of its value when new opportunities are created and exploited in a never-ending construction/destruction process. As pointed out already by Penrose in 1959, any opportunity facing a firm (like the one described and analysed in this article) is, viewed from the perspective of anyone of the involved companies, 'merely one of the components of the whole productive opportunity of the firm' (p. 111). In other words, 'it is one of a number of possible uses of the resource of the firm, in each of which the firm believes it could make profit.' Any specific opportunity may or may not be considered by the firm to be the most profitable course of action: 'the firm may pass/ the opportunity/over, believing other things would be more profitable or considering that the action required is not worth the risk or does not justify the amount of resources that would have to be committed' (*Ibid.*, p. 112). Whether the considerations taken by the actors were 'correct' can only be judged in retrospect, when even we as observers can identify the opportunity, and from that perceive the courses of actions of the firms involved as successful or not.

Notes

1. We believe that this statement holds for opportunities discovered by non-established actors and individuals as well, but the issue is not investigated in the reported study.

2. Cf. Dubois's (1994) discussion about awareness boundaries, and Kirzner's (1992: 3) discussion of the market as a systematic process of mutual discovery (and elimination of ignorance) by market participants, concerning 'overlooked market gaps' and 'exploitable opportunities for pure profit' (*ibid.*, p. 49).

References

Barley, S. (1986). Technology as an Occasion for Structuring: Evidence from Observations of CT Scanners and the Social Order of Radiology Departments, *Administrative Science Quarterly*, 31, 78–108.

Bengtson, A. (2003). *Framing Technological Development in a Concrete Context – The Use of Wood in the Swedish Construction Industry*, Doctoral thesis, Uppsala University, Department of Business Studies.

Brockhaus, R. and Horowitz, P. (1986). The Psychology of the Entrepreneur, in D. Sexton and R. Smilor (Eds), *The Art and Science of Entrepreneurship*, Cambridge: Ballinger.

Dubois, A. (1994). *Organising Industrial Activities – An Analytical Framework*, Doctoral thesis, Chalmers University of Technology, Department of Industrial Marketing, Gothenburg.

Eckhardt, J. and Shane, S. (2003). Opportunities and Entrepreneurship, *Journal of Management*, 29(3), 333–49.

Ford, D., Gadde, L.-E., Håkansson, H., Lundgren, A., Snehota, I., Turnbull, P. and Wilson, D. (1998). *Managing Business Relationships*, Chichester: Wiley.

Giddens, A. (1979). *Central Problems in Social Theory*, London: MacMillan.

Granovetter, M. (1985). Economic Action and Social Structure; the Problem of Embeddedness, *American Journal of Sociology*, 91(3), 481–510.

Granovetter, M. (1992). Problems of Explanation in Economic Sociology, in N. Nohria and R. G. Eccles (Eds), *Networks and Organisations: Structure, Form and Action*, Boston, MA: Harvard Business School Press, 25–56.

Håkansson, H. (1989). *Corporate Technological Behaviour; Co-operation and Networks*, London: Routledge.

Håkansson, H. (Ed.) (1987). *Industrial Technological Development: A Network Approach*, London: Croom Helm.

Håkansson, H. and Lundgren, A. (1997). Paths in Time and Space – Path Dependence from a Network Perspective, in L. Magnusson and J. Ottosson (Eds), *Evolutionary Economics and Path Dependence*, Cheltenham: Edwar Elgar.

Holmen, E. (2001). *Notes on a Conceptualisation of Resource-Related Embeddedness of Interorganisational Product Development*, Doctoral thesis, University of Southern Denmark, Institution for Marketing.

Hippel, E. Von (1988). *The Sources of Innovation*, New York: Oxford University Press.

Kihlstrom, R. and Laffont, J. (1979). A General Equilibrium Entrepreneurial Theory of Firm Formation Based on Risk Aversion, *Journal of Political Economy*, 87(4), 719–48.

Kirzner, I. M. (1973). *Competition and Entrepreneurship*, Chicago: The University of Chicago Press.

Kirzner, I. M. (1992). *The Meaning of Market Process*, London: Routledge.

Latour, B. (1987). *Science in Action*, Cambridge, MA: Harvard University Press.

Lundgren, A. (1995). *Technological Innovation and Network Evolution*, London: Routledge.

McClelland, D. (1961). *The Achieving Society*, Princeton: D. Van Nostrand.

Penrose, E. (1959/1995). *The Theory of the Growth of the Firm*, Oxford: Oxford University Press.
Rosenberg, N. (1982). *Inside the Black Box: Technology and Economics*, Cambridge: Cambridge University Press.
Rosenberg, N. (1994). *Exploring the Black Box: Technology, Economics, and History*, Cambridge: Cambridge University Press.
Shane, S. (2000). Prior Knowledge and the Discovery of Entrepreneurial Opportunities, *Organizational Science*, 11(4), 448–69.
Snehota, I. (1990). *Notes on a Theory of Business Enterprise*, Doctoral thesis, Uppsala University, Department of Business Studies.
Turnbull P. and Valla, J-P. (Eds) (1986). *Strategies for International Industrial Marketing*, London: Croom Helm.
Tyre, M. and Orlikowski, W. (1994). Windows of Opportunities: Temporal Patterns of Technological Adaptation in Organizations, *Organizational Science*, 5(1), 98–118.

16
The Emergence and Exploitation of Opportunities in Business Networks
Benjamin Ståhl

Introduction

> A wise man will make more opportunities than he finds.
> Francis Bacon

Economic organization concerns the coordination and exchange of resources. An "opportunity" is commonly understood as a chance, often a product of luck, to actively coordinate so as to generate above-normal rents that would not be forthcoming without such coordination. But somewhat of a logical conundrum is inherent in the equilibrium market hypothesis, evident in the following joke: Two economists were walking down the street. One of them spotted a hundred dollar bill and told his friend, who promptly replied "Nonsense! If there were, it would already have been picked up!". In other words, since the equilibrium market hypothesis assumes that markets are complete – that is, that with perfect information and homogenous resources, the value and price of a resource will always be correctly determined by supply and demand. This means that opportunities do not exist. Acquiring resources in the present that generate an above-normal rent stream in the future can only be attributable to luck (cf. Barney, 1989). This chapter, like this book, challenges this assumption by looking at inter-organizational interaction, the "space" where opportunities are realized.

The interaction approach to industrial marketing (see Håkansson, 1982; Håkansson and Snehota, 1990) starts from the assumption that resources are heterogeneous and interdependent. The value of a resource depends on its combination with other resources and the activities surrounding it. Knowledge about resources is also heterogeneous and distributed. While prices constitute one kind of information concerning a resource or a product, more or less idiosyncratic knowledge about how to produce it and how to use it (Dahlqvist, 1998) usually interact for resource development to occur. Much of such interaction has been shown to take place in business relationships. Here, "opportunities" depend essentially on resource interdependencies existent in business relationships. Opportunities reflect possibilities to improve exchange effectiveness through adaptation between business actors (Hallén *et al*., 1991), investments in relationship-specific activities for higher efficiency (Dyer and Singh, 1997), establishment of cross-functional communication between business actors (Olson *et al*., 1995; Ragatz *et al*., 1997), and enhanced understanding of the production system in which exchanged products are to be used (Dahlqvist, 1998; Mattsson, 1978).

The interaction approach does not necessarily imply determinism. While stability in terms of business counterparts indicates a lack of dynamism, most business actors find themselves in a situation where continuous development occurs in terms of product development, innovation, changing customer requirements, changing supplier offering, new markets and so on. Thus, the content of business relationships is often very dynamic in terms of development of the resources and activities involved. Business relationships are vehicles for interaction, enabling actors to develop products and production processes (Lundvall, 1985; von Hippel, 1988) and exchange information about business opportunities (Ottum and Moore, 1997).

However, studies concerning what constitutes opportunities *outside* of existing business relationships are sparse. We know more about why relationships exist, and how they evolve, than we do about how they emerge initially (Ring and Van de Ven, 1994). The dominant line of research on relationships has focused on such motivational factors as trust and commitment (Anderson and Narus, 1994; Morgan and Hunt, 1994; Ring and Van de Ven, 1992, 1994), factors that are less amenable to discussions concerning situations where they do not yet exist. The purpose of this chapter is to investigate the link between the existing business network, opportunities and the creation of new business relationships. I argue that opportunities are essential for understanding network dynamics, but that they are simultaneously dependent on the existing network engagement and interactive efforts between counterparts.

The discussion starts with an in-depth study of an opportunity, which emerged and was subsequently exploited by a world-leading industrial tooling company (hereafter referred to as ITC). The investigation focuses on the development of a "preferred supplier" product and marketing concept, where the ITC is the supplier. The concept has been developed in the ITC UK subsidiary since the mid-1990s, in collaboration with customers and suppliers. The aim was to capture the business volume at customers through greatly increased embeddedness from a legal, technical and social point of view. In brief, the ITC offers greater productivity at the customer plant through productivity analysis of cutting, milling and drilling operation and of the tools involved. This has been codified in a software package that enables ITC application engineers to re-engineer customers' operations, and document the cost saving and productivity gains of such re-engineering. In this process, the customers accept conversion to ITC tools where it is cost-effective.

The ITC also offers automated, real-time stock control and consignment stocks, again as a method to increase the productivity of the customer and decrease their costs. In this capacity, the ITC takes on the distributor role of tooling requirements, also for competitors' products.

The next section outlines a conceptualization of opportunities in networks. After that, the case study is presented. The case study highlights some important implications of opportunities in business networks. The case is analyzed and conclusions regarding the emergence, capturing and exploitation of opportunities in business networks are drawn. Opportunities arise out of general developments in the network, ongoing business activities and existing resources, but also require belief, commitment and effort to be exploited. Moreover, opportunities, while subjective, are always to some degree mutual – that is, the viability of opportunities depends on the impact they have on all parties in a business relationship. The chapter concludes with implications for practice and theory.

Opportunities in business networks

The opening chapter of this book discusses the concept of opportunity at length. In this section, the concept is briefly discussed to lay the ground for the case study. Opportunity is a word difficult to define clearly, though often used. Some definitions from dictionaries include: "a favorable juncture of circumstances," "an occasion or situation which makes it possible to do something that you want to do or have to do," "suitable time combined with other favorable circumstances."[1] These definitions imply that opportunities are specific, subjective and uncertain. They are specific in terms of "a situation", "a juncture," and such specificity also implies novelty and a temporary nature – "suitable time." The dimensions of time and space are more clear in the etymology of the term: from the phrase *ob portum veniens*, coming toward a port, in reference to the wind, from ob, "to, toward" and portus, "harbor." Possibly this relates to the sudden appearance of wind that could be utilized for a ship to get safely to harbor.

An initial definition of opportunities in business networks thus relate to some change, or development, in the network, for example, the emergence of a new technology, such as the internet, or new institutions, such as a derivative market in a commodity, or new ideas and practices, such as just-in-time supplies. This development is the "juncture of circumstances" and therefore opportunities relate to *general developments* in the network. However, the specificity of opportunities furthermore begs the question of how they are discovered, and by whom (Kirzner, 1973, 1997).

Opportunities are subjective in that they do not apply to all equally – the discovery of an opportunity relates to something that is deemed desirable by the actor, and within the actor's ability to actually accomplish (Kirzner, 1973, 1997). The subjectivity indicates that opportunities appear to firms in the context of their existing resources, activities and capabilities – it concerns something that is at least deemed feasible to achieve with the resources at hand. Thus, since capabilities, knowledge and information are unequally distributed (Hayek, 1945; Kirzner, 1973) discoveries of opportunities is likewise subjective (Shane, 2000) and depend on related, prior knowledge (Cohen and Levinthal, 1990; Venkataraman, 1997). This defines for whom an opportunity is "favorable," and thus opportunities depend on *existing resources and capabilities* of actors.

Finally, opportunities entail a degree of uncertainty. This is also evident in the derivative "opportunism," a label for political behavior with a negative connotation, which means taking advantage of situations without regard for consequences or principles. The presence of uncertainty indicates that *belief, effort and commitment* are also part of the meaning of opportunity, that it is a decision problem and some action is required for an opportunity to be taken advantage of. In other words, the concept of opportunity is meaningless unless related to action (or inaction). The process of acting on opportunities is entrepreneurship.

Entrepreneurship takes place in interaction, it depends on differences in information and capabilities in business exchange activities (Casson, 1982). In industrial markets, products and services are bought primarily as a means to produce and/or exchange something else. Capturing an opportunity means convincing a counterpart that it constitutes an opportunity also for them, that it enhances their performance – opportunities in business network imply *mutuality*. Thus, an opportunity relates to the possibility of improving the situation of a counterpart.

The point of this brief exposé is to establish a definition of opportunities suitable for an interaction perspective. In conclusion, an opportunity is said to exist, in this discussion, when there is a juncture of circumstances, arising out of the current activities of a firm and emerging needs of its counterparts, which is discovered, judged to be favorable and capable of being achieved given a certain amount of effort, and being acted upon, in other words, on some general development in the network, existing resources and capabilities, and belief and commitment to change.

Case study

This section provides information concerning a particular opportunity that emerged and was seized by a tooling company in the UK. The study as presented here highlights the background, the development of new tools and concepts deemed necessary to exploit the opportunity, and how they are used and how they are experienced by customers. The study was carried out through in-depth interviews with employees from the ITC in five countries, in subsidiaries and at headquarters, as well as with ITC customers. In total, 18 interviews have been conducted with employees of the ITC, including the

CEO, managers, development engineers, application engineers and salespersons. Furthermore, three customers have been visited and representatives from them (construction engineers, purchasing managers and production managers) have been interviewed. During the case study, the ITC kindly let the author work at their premises and access archive material, meeting memos, presentations and agreement templates. Due to the novel and in some dimensions sensitive nature of the case, the ITC has requested to remain anonymous for the time being.

The international tooling company and the preferred supplier concept

The ITC is a leading, global supplier of carbide tools for the machining industry. It has a centuries-long history and has been producing cemented carbide tools since the 1930s. The current product range includes milling, turning, drilling and holding systems, with the bulk of sales coming from cemented carbide inserts. The applications are very broad, from fabrication of metal components, for example, shafts and engine blocks, to form casting, for example, for plastics. The company is present world-wide with more than 30 wholly-owned subsidiaries and more than 90 percent of the turnover is generated outside the home market.

The UK subsidiary is one of the biggest in the group, and has one of three "technical centers" outside the home market. The relative size is in terms of sales and customers, as the subsidiary does not carry out much production activity – production in the ITC is centralized to a few markets, with the bulk in the home market. Over the past six years the UK subsidiary has developed a "Preferred Supplier" (PS) marketing concept.

PS concept: the emergence of an opportunity

In the late 1990s, several concurrent developments occurred which prompted the development of the PS concept. The outlook was bleak as the UK market for tooling to the general engineering industry was, and had been, in decline. More importantly, there was an ongoing negative spiral of discounting among tooling suppliers due to the consumable and relatively standardized nature of the exchanged good, and the presence of several competitors with similar offerings, that is, the price of the exchanged products is relatively low (almost negligible), even in terms of total annual volume, compared to other manufacturing inputs. The wide range of specifications allowed suppliers to make frequent calls offering the latest versions and, more importantly, the latest discounts. Thus, business exchange was of an arm's-length character, with price as the major decision-making factor. Too much time was spent on customer calls, offering the latest product and competing by offering increasing discounts each year. The business was volatile as sales efforts led to piecemeal volumes that could be priced away by competitors or integrators.

At that time, the ITC UK subsidiary got a new manager, a Swede with long experience of the industry and the company who had built up the ITC subsidiaries in Japan and the US previously. Also, a couple of young engineers with computer programming skills had been recruited. All in all, there was a feeling "that change was possible," that there were people with "new visions" concerning how to do business (UK regional manager). Inside the UK subsidiary of the ITC, the rethinking had led to a decision that traditional marketing was not sustainable.

In 1997 a large customer (an automaker) announced that it would be moving all of its tooling supplies to an integrator. For the ITC and other suppliers, the alternatives were to either supply the integrator or lose the business. This move, which came without consultation, prompted an analysis within the ITC. They realized that they were not as strong in the marketplace as they had thought and that they could quickly lose significant volumes. They were also in danger of becoming distanced from their customers, as integrators and wholesalers stepped in as middle-men in the customer relationship. The motivation for customers to use integrators was mainly to regain control of their tooling supplies in terms of inventory, tool standardization and more efficient transaction handling (orders and invoicing). The ITC would have to offer similar services to stem the flow of business going through integrators.

As it happened, the new manager had made contacts with an American supplier of automatic dispensers for businesses. Their "supply bay" was used primarily in the dispensing pharmaceuticals and office stationary, but could easily be adapted to supply tools and inserts of a diminutive nature. The cost was high, but was expected to come down and moreover would constitute an offer for inventory control and stock reduction.

As such, the bleak outlook turned into an opportunity. The opportunity, as perceived by the ITC, was to offer more services to customers in return for a preferred supplier agreement. The basis of the service would be the ITC's superior competence of tooling and its impact on the production process, coupled with "integrator" offerings pertaining to inventory and transaction handling. A team was appointed, which developed a software package named PCA (productivity cost analysis, described in detail below). This software would enable application engineers to improve the productivity of the customers, thereby taking on a greater role in the customers' production process than merely supplying the tools. It took the UK subsidiary of the ITC two years to fully develop the PS concept, with much of the development and fine-tuning taking place at customers' sites, but without aid from other ITC units.

PS Elements: exploiting opportunities

The PS concept is a marketing concept and the ITC only receives revenue from their products, not their services. It is thus a vehicle for building volume and fixing prices, rather than a priced good in itself. The PS concept can be seen as having three main elements: a commercial element, a productivity analysis element and a stock element. The elements are in turn composed of a variety of tools and techniques. At the time of the study, the ITC had more than 70 PS agreements in place, approximately 40 percent of high-volume accounts. In PS accounts, volume increased by 83 percent in 2001, in a recessive market.

The commercial element

The ITC is primarily a product-driven company, and for any customer relationship, the product is the key to get the business. The commercial element relates to the product offering and discounts associated with the higher volumes that the PS concept entails. The ITC provides tools for milling, turning and drilling, as well as tool holding systems. The industrial machining applications these tools are used in are very demanding in terms of precision and quality. The tool often comprises several components, a tool holder and inserts. The tool holder is connected to a CNC machine and onto it an insert is fastened. Since the only limiting factor of CNC operations is material availability and cutter (inserts) wear, the tools are a small but critical input in the manufacturing process. Inserts are manufactured primarily in the ITC home market, while some tool holders are produced locally and to customer specifications.

For the PS concept to be viable, the product range needs to be extensive. Converting to the ITC range within the confines of the PS agreement requires that the ITC can offer similar or better products with minimal or no investment cost for the customer, at least in the first phase. The UK subsidiary is thus highly dependent on the home-market ITC units, with more than 90 percent of purchasing volume originating from there. It is also highly dependent on the home-market ITC for R&D and product development, although the subsidiary has a technical center and can carry out some application testing locally.

The actual PS agreement, a written contract, is not detailed but rather an indication of intent and allocation of responsibilities. The agreement stipulates that the ITC devices a methodology and initiates conversion to ITC tools, and that the customer undertakes to use ITC products where they can supply an equal or better cost effective product/machining solution. The decision parameter is thus holistic – it does not focus on the price of the individual tool, but rather on the cost effectiveness of the entire operation. Where the ITC can show higher or equal productivity using their product, the customer will switch to it. Moreover, success criteria are not piecemeal but evaluated in terms of annual tooling cost reduction and productivity gains.

The agreement's main purpose is to delegate responsibilities among the two counterparts, concerning how the actual work is carried out on site, with specific individuals identified and their responsibilities specified. An account manager and application engineers from the ITC work together with the customer's "tooling champion," their manufacturing process engineer, their purchasing and logistics manager as well as machine operators on-site. Initially, as the ITC team moves from cell to cell, the work load at the customer is heavy. The ITC team often has its own office in the plant in conjunction to the shop floor. The boundaries between the companies become blurred – ITC personnel are a common sight on the customer's shop floor, passing in and out of the building as any other employee.

The productivity analysis element

At the core of the PS is the productivity analysis element. This element is basically the PCA software and its application at the customers' plants. The software has been developed in-house at the UK subsidiary and is a simple program that incorporates a variety of factors influencing the productivity, tooling life and overall costs of a specific operation. The software does not constitute any new or complex knowledge, but can handle a large variety of parameters and greatly enhances the speed with which calculations are made. Engineers can and have done similar estimations with "pens and spreadsheets," but many time-consuming activities are automated with the software.

The PCA must be calibrated to specific operations. As such, PCA starts with benchmark measurements of a specific operation making a specific component. Taking into account materials, feed rates, tool changes etc. the PCA software indicates how a change in tooling affects the bottom-line productivity in terms of production speed and component costs. When it comes to speed and efficiency this is quite straightforward, but cost analysis rests on some assumptions that need to be agreed upon with the customer. While this is seldom a problematic area, ITC application engineers often find that their customers' knowledge about the real costs of an operation is low.

The productivity analysis establishes benchmarks for existing operations and then goes into "phase 2," where productivity is enhanced by altering operation parameters and substituting existing tools for the ITC product range. This is thus an essential part of the PS concept: by applying their knowledge and software, the ITC can enhance their customers' productivity and in the process build business volume, substituting competitors' tools for their own. There is also a "phase 3," which is a more comprehensive redesign of an operation to further productivity. This last step is dependent on the ability and willingness of the customer to invest in an operation, and is only suitable for high-volume long series production. The PCA also ensures that the whole process is documented, a key issue for both customers and the ITC. Since the PS concept entails an implicit understanding of cost-savings for the customers, it is crucial for the ITC to be able to show the bottom-line effects of their activities.

The stock element

Tools come in a large variety of dimensions and qualities, they wear quickly (tool life is measured in minutes) and must be replaced frequently. To control tooling in terms of logistics and inventory is a big challenge, especially if many suppliers are involved. The stock element of the PS concept entails the offer of consignment stock and/or automatic tool dispensers to the customer. For some customers, the stock element is the main reason for entering into the PS agreement.

Consignment stock means that ITC products are stored at the customer plant, but while the tools remain in stock the ITC retains title to it. Only when an operator takes a tool from the stock is the customer charged for it. Consignment stock has two main benefits for the customer: capital is not tied up in tools not in use and control of tool usage is enhanced. However, for the ITC this means more capital tied up in stock, which has prompted them to search for stock-control solutions. This is done by traditional instruments, but increasingly a new technology can meet this objective.

Automatic tool dispensers (ATDs), manufactured by a US company, have become very important to the ITC. ATDs look like vending machines, and their functionality is much the same. A machine operator has a smart card that he or she swipes in the machine and punches the code for a particular tool, which is then dispensed via coil-feed. This action is logged so that the inventory is always precise and the user/operation is identified. The ATDs come in two versions, an online model or one connected to a PC or local network. In the online case, the data is transmitted at regular intervals to servers in the US, belonging to the ATD manufacturer. This data is then processed in accordance with prearranged parameters and is forwarded to the ITC central warehouse in Belgium, which in turn ships the required products via DHL straight to the customer (or in some cases to a distributor who handles the restocking). The ATD manufacturer charges a subscription fee for this service, depending on the transaction volume. If the ATD is offline, it generates reports at regular intervals that are then manually transmitted to the Belgium warehouse (see Figure 16.1). For bulkier tools, a locker system with a barcode scanner can be integrated into the system and placed adjacent to the ATD.

ATDs thus have several advantages. The amount of stock is minimized and stops in the production process due to tooling shortages are eliminated. The ATDs are small and can be placed next to machining cells, reducing the time it takes for an operator to access the tools. They are accessible at all times. Furthermore, customers note a change in behavior of operators: "They realize that tools have a value. When they know that we know who is using a tool, suddenly they realize that it's not for free. There's no 'squirreling', we don't pay for the tools until we use them" (Customer purchasing manager). From the ITC point of view, stock control in general and ATDs in

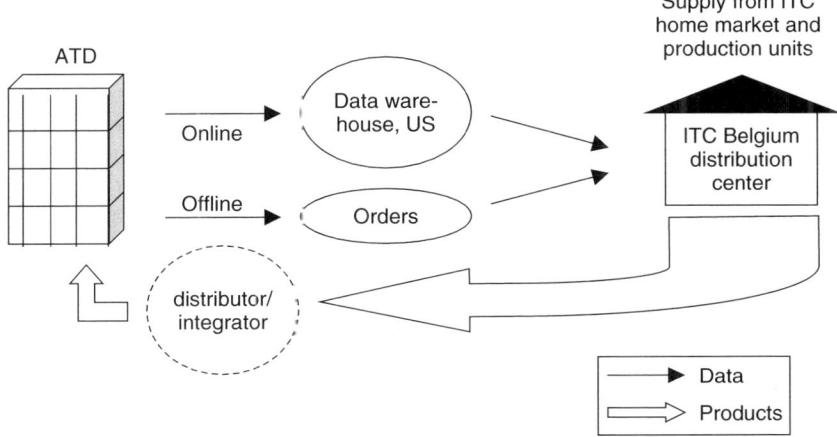

Figure 16.1 ATD stock, data/product flow

particular give them indications of high-volume tools that should be prioritized for conversion to their product range, thus quickly building up sales volume.

Summary

Each element on its own is a vehicle for building a business relationship, but their interactive nature means that the offering is significantly strengthened if combined. However, customer needs differ – an aerospace supplier making thousands of more or less customized components does not require PCA, since this builds around volume production, but may still be interested in standardization of tooling, consignment stock and ATDs. The current development of the PS concept focuses on catering for varying needs.

PS customers: building mutual opportunity

In this study, three customers with which the ITC had a PS agreement were visited and production and purchasing managers were interviewed. The objective was to get the counterpart view of the business relationship, and also to see how the PS works in practice. The three customers are in the engineering sector, but vary greatly in terms of size, products and customers. Alpha is a subsidiary of a US. first-tier supplier in the automotive industry. The plant in question (which has the PS agreement with the ITC) manufactures mainly rear axles and differentials. Beta is a British company with long traditions, producing telescopic cylinder tipping hoists. Delta is a multinational company that manufactures brake systems for trains.

Initialization

The ITC did not have a close business relationship with either of the customers prior to the PS agreement. In fact, they hardly sold anything to any of the customers. Common to all customers were that they were looking for a better solution regarding tooling supplies, which was most pronounced with Alpha. Their plant had just been acquired and new management put in place when a tooling standardization program was launched. At the time, the plant spent almost 1 million USD annually on tools. There was a great variety of even standard tools and many suppliers, with consequent high costs of ordering and large, uncontrolled inventories. All major tool suppliers were invited to investigate a part of the plant for a month, and come up with a specific and a general proposal that would increase the control of tooling. The ITC had virtually no business in the plant at the time, but were invited since Alpha had a good business relationship with them in the Benelux region. Coming up with the most holistic approach, the ITC won the contract by expressly avoiding a price focus.

In the case of Beta, severe cost pressure and downsizing, and a new, younger management made them open to a novel approach. The production manager at Beta had heard about the ITC's PS concept through mutual acquaintances, and asked their largest supplier at the time to provide a comprehensive tooling strategy. As they failed to do so, the ITC was invited to submit a proposal and show their abilities, which they did and got the business. In the last case, Delta's tooling wholesaler/distributor suggested to the new purchasing manager (appointed after a major restructuring and change of ownership) that the ITC was working with the PS concept. Delta then approached the ITC for more information, and also approached their biggest tooling suppliers at the time to come up with counter-offers. As in the other cases, the holistic focus won the business for the ITC.

Scope of the relationships

The scope of the relationships refers to what the customer representatives tended to stress as well as what the application engineers saw as prioritized in each case. These factors are related: for example, stock control results in cost savings, which results in increased productivity (if this is measured as output/cost). However, the different emphasis indicates the slightly differing rationales for each customer, with implications for relationship development and sustainability. Emphasis on productivity increase places more stress on time-consuming PCA to enhance output and freeing up machines. Cost savings stress conversion to standard tools. Emphasis on stock control entails conversion and setting up an efficient flow with the help of ATDs, with initially high but decreasing time-demands.

At Alpha, application engineers had prioritized projects but were on a daily basis interrupted by problem areas – due to the high costs associated with any stop in the production process, ITC employees were present or on call around the clock, and had their own office on the shop floor. The scope of the relationship in this case is a reflection of the customer's business – components to the automotive industry, high-volume series with continuous product development and cost reduction targets. Here, the PS concept is implemented to its fullest with all elements in place, and it is the ITC's biggest UK account. The high level of activity is evident in the following words, by the ITC account manager there: "They'd really like us to do everything, wouldn't they?" Essentially, the ITC had taken over responsibility for tooling in the customer's production process. This is sensitive, of course, despite the lack of resources on the customer side. At the start of the relationship, the ITC felt that there was some resistance from the tooling champion. However, as the PCA team solved an important problem for him, by increasing the output of an operation and thereby eliminating a bottleneck, "he's really come onboard after that" (ITC account manager).

At Beta, the pace is less hectic. ITC application engineers moved from one machine cell to the next, optimizing the operations using the PCA. Beta also has some consignment stock, but no ATDs. This was the most "cautious" of the customers visited, perhaps associated with their history of restructurings, outsourcing and redundancies. Of the three customers visited, this was the only one that had an explicit cost-reduction target in the PS agreement, of a 20 percent reduction on tooling costs the first year. Initially, operators had been skeptical to ITC's engineers, with redundancies and outsourcing fresh in mind, but this was overcome by the frequent presence of the engineers on the shop floor: "They're in the middle of things," "They've really got it across that they don't try to make [the operators] work harder – they try to get their machines to be more efficient" (Production Manager, Beta).

At Delta, stock control was the key to the business. At the first demonstration of the PS concept (at the customer's initiative), "his [the customer purchasing manager's] eyes lit up when he saw the ATDs" (ITC Regional Manager). The company had recently switched ownership, outsourced and divested some areas while merging with their biggest competitors. The tooling situation was a mess, and the new purchasing manager found that they were sitting on £100,000 worth of tooling in stock. Furthermore, each operator had his favorite tooling supplier, so practically each operation was using different tools. The outcome was that there was one employee dedicated full time to keep a warehouse of tools, which was on the far side of the floor and closed 16 hours a day. As such, inventory control through ATDs and conversion to standard tooling was prioritized, rather than PCA. The low-volume runs of course also contributed to this. Some initial resistance existed, which was largely overcome by a joint communication effort concerning the value of tools and the cost-savings provided by using the same tools. Again, the presence of ITC engineers on the shop floor contributed to the building of trust. The most emphasized "success factor" was, however, the documented costs savings in terms of standardized tooling, inventory control and transaction handling, shown on the basis of ATD-generated reports of tooling usage.

The different priorities in each customer relationship entail different demands in terms of application engineers' time – time that could be spent developing other customer relationships. One engineer was so occupied with Alfa – and had been for more than a year – that virtually no other contacts had been established. As the ITC does not charge for this time, it can be seen as a loss – at least, some engineers felt that ITC compensation schemes treated it as such. On the other hand, the close contact not only builds business, but increases the dependence of the customer on ITC competence. Although all customers visited were content with the relationship and did not consider abandoning the PS agreement, the less the involvement of ITC application engineers, the lower the feeling of commitment. It is conceivable that after systems are in place, optimization and conversion to standard tools has been made, a customer could switch back to a price focus.

Summary

The customers seemed content with the PS agreement and they all foresaw a continuation. A holistic approach, documented cost savings, tooling control and close interaction building trust appeared to be the main factors for quickly building strong business relationships. The following section analyses the case in more detail regarding the emergence and exploitation of the opportunity.

Analysis

Business relationships and networks emerge and evolve over time in a process whereby companies try to achieve their objectives. While much inter-organizational research has focused on incremental and rather slow processes of relationship development, this case study exposes a more conscious and rapid process. Since business volume was very low or non-existent in each of the emerging relationships, the study shows how a company can move purposefully, build relationships and change network structures. Figure 16.2 summarizes the general factors, responses and efforts contributed to the emergence and exploitation of the opportunity.

All these factors are interrelated, and together give rise to what may be conceptualized as an opportunity to develop exchange relationships and thereby the network. This move was dependent primarily on an extended scope of exchange and active relationship building, in effect a reconfiguration of existing competencies, resources and responsibilities. The ITC offers not only the product but also their knowledge of how to apply it. Business exchange moved from a "simple" product/price dimension to a more complex and multidimensional approach including tool handling and application knowledge.

	General developments Recessive market	Capabilities Application knowledge	Commitment New way of doing business
ITC	– Discounting spiral – Emergence of integrators – More remote from customer	– Development of PCA – Relationship with ATD supplier	– New manager – New engineers
Customers	– Focus on cost–cutting, productivity – Loss of competence	– Incapable of application optimization	– New management, ownership – Trust in ITC methods

Figure 16.2 Mutual opportunity in business networks

There were some *general developments* in the economy that influenced the emergence of the opportunity. The recessive climate in the general engineering sector in Britain had two important implications for the present discussion. First, customers were under pressure to reduce their costs and increase their productivity. This prompted many of them on the one hand to "buy the cheapest" at any moment, which led to a discounting spiral and price pressing on tooling. On the other hand, it prompted customers to seek total cost reductions in terms of industrial consumables (also cutting fluids, oils, handheld tools etc.) which opened up for integrators and distributors. Using integrators mainly reduced costs in terms of more efficient logistics and transaction handling. Second, the recessive climate had led to significant rationalizations at customers in terms of personnel. In particular, middle-management had been reduced so that there were less production engineers at customers, and those who remained had little time to proactively improve operational efficiency. In other words, customers had lost competence regarding how to best use the tools in their operations. These general developments impinged on both the ITC and their customer base – both parties to the exchange were pressured to look for alternatives. As such, the general developments became endogenous to the network as they affected the ITC's business. For example, the discounting spiral was eroding margins and increasing sales costs and the emergence of integrators were moving them further from their customers.

As such, these developments were particularly felt by the ITC through specific, existing relationships. A large customer that shifted their tooling sourcing to an integrator exposed the vulnerability of the ITC, as a supplier of low-value consumables. It was this event that prompted the analysis within the ITC to develop an alternative offering. It also provided a framework for what needed to be included in such an offering, especially regarding documentation – so that a position could be defended – and integrator-like services in terms of logistics and transaction handling. An ailing customer who in effect outsourced tooling to the ITC was also very important, even though it later went bankrupt. It provided a testing ground and valuable experiences for the development of the approach. In a sense, it showed the ITC that it was possible to take over the tooling of an entire plant, including competitors' products. Finally, the first PS account, that with Alfa, has also been very influential. Here, the ITC learned about how to convince the customer in the first place, by emphasizing productivity over price and a proactive stance, and that contacts should be made at a high managerial level (rather than sales to a production manager). Furthermore, this account has continued to be very important in terms of refining the PCA software and PS working practices.

If these general developments triggered change efforts, it was the current position that prompted the ITC to exploit the opportunity. In this sense, it was highly subjective, as it depended on *existing capabilities* as well as on some enhancements. As customers were losing the competence and ability to optimize machining in terms of tooling, and moreover handling the inventories and handling of tools, the ITC had – or could develop – the requisite application knowledge. Problem-solving was aided by the PCA and ATDs, but primarily dependent on the ability of ITC application engineers to mobilize their know-how of tooling in use. Knowledge about how products are applied is built up through experience of numerous applications across industries and markets. Application engineers witness a multitude of solutions at customers and in test centers, and their application knowledge commonly surpasses that of customer production managers and operators. The PCA software – based on known parameters and calculation methods – increased the efficiency and speed with which this knowledge could be applied. Moreover, enveloped by a PS commitment, they could spend more time on problems and follow them through, as efforts were seen in a bigger perspective than the specific tool and operation in question.

Another particularity of the UK market is the practice of offering consignment stock to customers. Since tools are critical to CNC operations, the supply must be uninterrupted and customers therefore usually have a significant buffer of tools. Coupled with the "squirreling" behavior of operators, this leads to significant capital that is tied up and unused. With the practice of consignment stocks, the cost of capital shifts to the supplier. This can be seen as an important reason why the ITC has been early in pushing and promoting the use of ATDs. The relationship with the ATD supplier is one of the specific business relationships that influenced the development of the PS approach. The machines are not particularly customized to ITC's business, other than carrying their logo. The configuration of the machine is done at the ITC and for each particular customer depending on the specific tools that go into the machine. Nevertheless, the internet version of the ATD depends on information transactions and database management that is provided by the ATD manufacturer and which integrates with the ITC's logistics and order-invoice system.

An important implication that emerges from this discussion is that the existing network is crucial for understanding the development of new relationships, that is, knowledge and resources that exist and are created in the ongoing relationships heavily impact the possibility of creating new relationships. In this case, this is especially evident in terms of the knowledge garnered by the ITC about customer applications, which can be leveraged to further relationship building. Thus, while each relationship is in some aspects unique, learning accruing from them can to a certain extent be systematized and applied in new ones.

The final factor influencing the opportunity can be traced to the *commitment* of specific individuals and groups of people to change the way of doing business. Opportunities are not automatically exploited but depend on the belief in their feasibility and active commitment to exploit them. In the case study, such commitment is evident from both sides. From the ITC's side, exploiting the opportunity was heavily influenced by the entrepreneurial action of a few individuals, particularly the new general manager, one regional director, and two new application engineers. They were new to the market or to the business. The general manager brought with him experiences from other markets and especially experiences of building a market from scratch. These experiences have instilled a heavy marketing focus, and a confidence that market shares can be built. The new application engineers brought with them new skills, particularly in programming, and were otherwise not hampered by existing practices but open for new ideas. From the customer side, they were proactive in their change efforts. At the three customers investigated, all had recently changed management and/or ownership, and had undergone considerable restructuring. Thus, what used to be considered a consumable that could be sourced at the lowest price was instead presented as a critical area with a large scope for improvement, with direct bottom-line effects. As such, this was an opportunity for the customer too.

The mutuality of commitment was particularly clear in terms of interaction in the relationship. The internal development of PCA was necessary for two reasons: to create a tool that greatly enhanced the speed and accuracy of application analysis, and to produce documentation that, in discussion with the customer, would be the basis for improvements and simultaneously a record of achievements. The explicit and easily understandable nature of information in the PCA established shared views on the cost savings that had come about with the PS agreement. The PCA helped operators to understand their machines better and to see the effects of changed behavior that would otherwise have been difficult to discover. At the managerial level, the documentation produced by the PCA was highly valued – bottom-line cost efficiency at the component level became explicit in an unprecedented way, in turn facilitating planning and budgeting. The reports generated by the

ATDs serve a similar purpose. The documentation and reporting also greatly enhanced the control over the tooling situation. Furthermore, stock control was a success factor in its own right. The effects in terms of reduced cost of capital, a more efficient transaction process and speedier logistics were critical for the relationships. The documentation of the working method was crucial for getting the business and for its continuation, as it articulates cost savings and productivity gains.

This methodology also depended on close contact and frequent interaction between application engineers and machine operators. The customers stressed that building high levels of trust early had been crucial to the development of the relationship. Resistance from the operators could be detrimental as benchmarks would be inaccurate and conversion slowed down. At the operator level, ITC application engineers were appreciated by all customers since they were out on the shop floor, rather than in offices. The engineers also emphasized continually that the measurements they were taking were not of the operators, but of their machines. They also encouraged input and suggestions from the operators. However, frequent interaction alone could not develop trust. Trust was predicated on ongoing, interactive problem-solving.

To summarize, the opportunity was specific as it arose out of the changes occurring in the business network on the one hand, and on the other, the existing competence accruing to the ITC through its extensive experience with tooling applications. It was mutual, since it reflected problems on the customer side for which the ITC thought they had a solution. Yet, it was uncertain and required commitment to create and work with new methods to be viable. As such, these three factors constitute the circumstances brought in conjuncture, forming an opportunity.

Conclusions

This chapter has discussed and investigated the emergence and exploitation of an opportunity in a business network. The objective was to enhance our understanding of opportunities using an interaction approach to industrial marketing. The case study and analysis indicate that the emergence and exploitation of opportunities depend on the interplay between internal resources, commitment and developments in the network. Specifically, a commitment to recombine existing resources, to develop new resources and a new supply relationship, coupled with network trends created the opportunity. The opportunity could be exploited by creating a holistic approach to tooling in the production process, common to both counterparts, and a methodology generating and documenting improved productivity. This suggests that opportunities are mutual – that is, that an opportunity for one party is an efficient solution for the other.

This study has some limitations. In particular, the investigation here concerns a special kind of product – a consumable, that is in some respects highly standardized, that nevertheless is traded in an industrial, business-to-business context. Moreover, the discussion concerns downstream opportunities – the applicability of mutuality may be different for upstream opportunities, such as shifting production to a lower-cost location through greenfield investment. Nevertheless, this chapter clearly shows the viability of utilizing an interactive approach for understanding how opportunities emerge and can be exploited.

References

Anderson, J. and Narus, J. (1994). A Model of Distributor Firm and Manufacturer Firm Working Partnerships, *Journal of Marketing*, 54, 42–58.

Casson, Mark C. (1982). *The Entrepreneur: An Economic Theory*, Oxford: Martin Robertson. 2nd edn, Edward Elgar, 1999.

Cohen, W. M. and Levinthal, D. A. (1990). Absorptive Capacity: A New Perspective on Learning and Innovations, *Administrative Science Quarterly*, 35, 128–52.

Dahlqvist, J. (1998). *Knowledge Use in Business Exchange*, Uppsala: Department of Business Studies, Uppsala University.

Dyer, J. and Singh, H. (1997). The Relational View: Cooperative Strategy and Sources of Interorganizational Competitive Advantage, *Academy of Management Review*, 23(4), 660–79.

Håkansson, H. (Ed.) (1982). *International Marketing and Purchasing of Industrial Goods: An Interaction Approach*, Chichester: John Wiley & Sons.

Håkansson, H. and Snehota, I. (1990). No Business is an Island, *Scandinavian Journal of Management*, 5, 187–200.

Hallén, L., Johanson, J. and Sayed-Mohamed, N. (1991). Interfirm Adaptations in Business Relationships, *Journal of Marketing*, 55, 29–37.

Hayek, F. (1945). The Use of Knowledge in Society, *American Economic Review*, 35(4), 519–30.

Kirzner, I. (1973). *Competition and Entrepreneurship*, Chicago: University of Chicago Press.

Kirzner, I. (1997). Entrepreneurial Discovery and the Competitve Market Process: An Austrian Approach, *Journal of Economic Literature*, 35, 60–80.

Lundvall, B-Å. (1985). *Product Innovation and User-Producer Interaction*, Aalborg: Aalborg University Press.

Mattson, L-G. (1978). Impact of Stability in Supplier-Buyer Relations on Innovative Behaviour on Industrial Markets, in G. Fisk, J. Arndt and K. Grönhaug (Eds), *Future Direction for Marketing*, Cambridge, MA: Marketing Science Institute.

Morgan, Robert M. and Hunt, Shelby D. (1994). The Commitment – Trust Theory of Relationship Marketing, *Journal of Marketing*, 58, 20–38.

Olson, E. M., Walker Jr., O. C. and Ruekert, R. W. (1995). Organizing for Effective New Product Development: The Moderating Role of Product Innovativeness, *Journal of Marketing* 59, 48–62.

Ottum, B. D. and Moore W. L. (1997). The Role of Market Information in New Product Success/Failure, *Journal of Product Innovation Management*, 14, 258–73.

Ragatz, G. L., Handfield, R. B. and Scannell T. V. (1997). Success Factors for Integrating Suppliers into New Product Development, *Journal of Product Innovation Management*, 14, 190–202.

Ring, P. S. and Van de Ven, A. (1992). Structuring Cooperative Relationships between Organizations, *Strategic Management Journal*, 13, 483–98.

Ring, P. S. and Van de Ven, A. (1994). Developmental Processes of Cooperative Interorganizational Relationships, *Academy of Management Review*, 19, 90–118.

Shane, S. (2000). Prior Knowledge and the Discovery of Entrepreneurial Opportunities, *Organization Science*, 11(4), 448–69.

Venkatamaran, S. (1997). The Distinctive Domain of Entrepreneurship Research: An Editors Perspective, in J. Katz, R. Brockhaus (Eds), *Advances in Entrepreneurship, Firm Emergence, and Growth*, Greenwich, CT: JAI Press.

von Hippel, E. (1988). *The Sources of Innovation*, New York: Oxford University Press.

Epilogue: Opportunity Development in Business Networks

Amjad Hadjikhani and Jan Johanson

This book project was initiated by thoughts on firms' growth and development on one hand and networks on the other. The connection is based on the belief for a need for deeper notion to understand network dynamic. Dividing the network relationship into the standardized/institutionalized which pertains to stability and the new uncertain interactions which relates to change and fluidity, the book relates entrepreneurship to the business network study. Entrepreneurship, creating new ventures, is generally assumed to be the central element in the dynamics of the market economy. The point of departure was, as Penrose (1959) states, that firms' business activities are of two kinds, standardized and entrepreneurial. The first is to administrate the prevailing business and generate stability and the second concerns the business dynamic and change in the firms' activities. The first one administrates market uncertainties and the next one creates new ones. Studying such behaviour is essential to understand how firms develop new markets or positions in the market. In line with these thoughts, the book focuses on business opportunity which the contributing authors have studied from different angles launching new notions. The initial idea was that the study of opportunity development should not only concern aspects like characteristics of sole individuals, as opportunity development is driven rather by interactions between individuals, groups and organizations. Actors – firms, organizations, organizational units or individuals – have previous knowledge and contribute different resources. This process contains the interrelated phases of opportunity development: recognition and exploitation.

While earlier studies have relied exclusively on economic and psychological theories, the contributions to this book are mainly based on network theory. With infusion of business network theory in particular, the authors have had the intention to generate new knowledge to the studies on entrepreneurship and business opportunity. The presumption was that the theoretical tools in the network theory would permit a different understanding of opportunity development. With their empirical studies the authors develop new notions and connect the network view to opportunity development.

The reason for selecting opportunity development in networks for studies was twofold. One was to introduce a concept packed with dynamism into the business network theory. The second was to study entrepreneurship in a network perspective. Several researchers have stressed the role of the entrepreneur's social network, but a network perspective means also that potential opportunities exist in a network context. While a market perspective implies that opportunities can be found in the market without reference to any specific actor the network perspective implies that opportunities are related to some specific actor or actors with potential wider relevance. The network perspective implies also that the potential opportunity will be protected by other committed actors which have an interest in the opportunity context. Another implication is that networks are cooperative structures as well as competitive. Information asymmetry is often stressed in discussions of entrepreneurship and opportunity seeking. In open networks we can always expect information asymmetries. In business networks, which is a typical case of open networks there is always asymmetry since relevant information on other firms' needs, capabilities, strategies and relationships is transferred mainly through business relationships. Nevertheless knowledge on other firms' and potential opportunities are almost always insufficient and have to be developed in various ways.

In this vein the development of business opportunity is viewed as interactions between individuals/units/organizations. In line with business network thoughts the book introduces a theoretical framework containing the three variables; specific knowledge, resource commitment and surpass value. The crucial assumption behind is that the extra value associated with the opportunity development is related to the experiential knowledge and resource contribution of actors. Shortcomings in knowledge or resource contributions affect the extra added value and economic failure. With these explanatory tools for analysis of real business it may become easier to understand why more than 80 per cent of all 'new entrepreneurial activities' go to economic failure. The epilogue elucidates some general aspects from the studies introduced in the earlier parts of this book. These concern the complexity, individual-organizational entrepreneurship, embeddedness and success–failure in opportunity development.

Complexity of the opportunity development

Articles in this volume expose a number of aspects of the complexity of opportunity development. One crucial aspect discussed concerns the temporal dimension in opportunity development. It views opportunity in a process in which different actors in interaction connect a variety of resources and knowledge in different phases. This view is different from the simple static view in which opportunity is given out in the market and is seen by some and not by others. The temporal dimension also reveals that opportunity can be initiated by one actor and be explored by someone else and exploited by still another one. A vision undergoes a change process in which the initiators do not need to be the same as those who explore and exploit it. In the process of resource combination some old faces disappear and some new faces appear. Further, the vision explored is not necessarily the same as the vision that initiates the process. A fundamental aspect in this temporal dimension lies in its incrementality. Idea generation and exploration involve actors having some experience and knowledge about the issue concerned. Their previous knowledge on where resources are available and how they are to be combined involves different actors in different phases. A low degree of experience will then increase the level of unrealized uncertainty threatening opportunity development. The more ambiguous the vision, the more likely that achievement is far from the plans. Shortcomings in knowledge or resource commitment in this process affect surpass value and produce fails in opportunity development.

Another dimension of complexity is related to the heterogeneity in the resource commitment. Opportunity development by nature relies on combination of new resources or new combination of the old heterogeneous resources. Both combination types are likely to lead to an incremental process of gaining surpass value development. The process of value generation may eventually lead to the fulfilment of a vision as the actors develop a new product or a new process affecting internal conditions of the firm and/or its relationship with others outside. When an opportunity is exploited managerial processes of standardization and routinization aiming at efficiency are introduced (Penrose, 1959).

The extent and depth of resource combination affect the degree of complexity in opportunity development. Simple visions demanding limited and simple resource combinations lead to simple processes. The higher the heterogeneity in the resource combination, the higher will be the complexity and degree of uncertainty involved in developing the vision.

Another dimension of the complexity reflects the place of initiation and exploring opportunity. In contrast to most entrepreneurial studies which only concern individuals and their external market, the view developed in this volume sees the opportunity development in a more complex setting. It sees the issue as a matter that concerns both internal and external affairs of business firms. New ideas can concern development of new technological means to increase the efficiency inside the firm and/or may concern relationship with old and new actors in the market.

Individual-organizational entrepreneurship

The role of the individuals in the world of entrepreneurship is well discussed. The idea in writing this book was not to go against it. Instead it aims at aiding studies in this line of thoughts. In this volume, individuals for their prior knowledge gained in interactions can push forward a vision which becomes developed by interaction with others. The earlier studies have a high emphasis on individuals' persistency, meaning that all initiation and exploration of new visions rely on the characteristics of these individuals. The business network perspective does not discard such a view. It is coupled with characteristics of the actors. No matter if the actors are individuals or organizations, the two notions of the knowledge and resource commitment are related to aspects like persistence and ability of the actors to combine these and develop a process leading to some goals. The whole idea of the book has been to provide a simple abstraction which can capture different aspects of the complex business world.

The emphasis of later studies on entrepreneurship has been to develop notions connected to social networks which can help understanding and explaining opportunity seeking of small business. This thinking is here expanded to incorporate other businesses and activities in the world of opportunity development. The business network perspective incorporates social, industrial and financial relationships affecting development process.

Embeddedness

Empirical findings in the papers of this volume reveal how the focal actors are embedded in a number of different relationships. For a deeper understanding, they have discussed the matter of interdependence between actors and their relationships. In this path the studies have demonstrated an important aspect related to the relationship strength and network structure. The interesting question raised has been how actors engaged in strong contra weak relationships can act for developing opportunities. Actors engaged in a strong interdependent relationship have the advantages of high knowledge and commitment, which facilitates and supports development of new opportunities. But, on the other hand, in a strongly coupled structure actors can lose their freedom to develop and explore new visions. A high interdependence can become a constraint for actors involved which blocks opportunity development. Some authors stress the weakness of relationship as a prerequisite for development and exploration of new visions. Jack and Anderson (2002) Hoang and Antoncic (2003) and Sarah and Anderson (2002) are among those few that discuss embeddedness in connection with social structure. They emphasize embeddedness with weak social structure as a prerequisite for development of entrepreneur. The dimension of weak relationship and its impact on opportunity development within the context of industrial markets is also discussed by some authors in this volume.

These contradictory findings have to be explained. One explanation can be related to the organizational bottleneck in the use of resources. Strong interdependence with highly embedded structure only can permit development of new opportunities if the actors have extra resources beside their ordinary relationship. Actors have to have risk taking resources for their future market activities. Devotion of resources for research and development in close cooperation with actors embedded in the relationship will produce opportunities which are more complex than those developed in simple exchange. This is because actors in such an embedded structure have high knowledge and resource commitment in their ordinary relationships. Devotion of extra resources can give more freedom to the actors to develop and explore their visions. Lack of input of extra resource will hinder development of new ideas. The important issue here is an efficient use of prior knowledge and resources in an atmosphere with more freedom in testing, checking and collecting resources and knowledge.

A network structure cannot necessarily be structured completely in weak or strong relationships. A network can contain different forms and structures. While one part contains strongly embedded actors, the other part may involve weakly embedded ones. This can affect the flow of new thoughts in between actors in different parts. In highly embedded business-network structures diffusion of new thoughts from parts having more freedom to parts strongly embedded in relationship can be associated with problems. Some parts of an organization may have enough market knowledge and realize a need for new products but may face problems when it has to gain internal resources. Integration of heterogeneous resources from parts highly interdependent to other activities can obstruct opportunity development.

Success and failure – some notes for future research

In this book, opportunity development process is presumed as added surpass value connected with combination of specific knowledge and heterogeneous resources. In this process, Figure 1.2 in the first chapter raises some crucial thoughts about the success and failure in the combination of knowledge and committed resources. While some articles in this volume have paid direct and indirect attention to the issue of failure of opportunity, others have considered the issue of opportunity success. Unfortunately, the aspect of failure is left untouched in the earlier studies on entrepreneurship. This trend may have had as the access to information its reason. Firms and organizations are unwilling to disclose their failure or obstacles in investment because of the market reaction. In fact studies of obstacles and fails can disclose facts interesting for both practitioners and researchers.

The aim of discussion on failure is also to recognize different obstacles in this development process. The nature of obstacles comes from the view that firms' activities in combination with new resources are based on past and present knowledge but opportunity development is based on future expectations. The crucial question is if the available knowledge is sufficient to explain the future behaviour of the actors. Though, opportunity development is connected with asymmetry in between now, what we have, and the future, what we will or expect to have. A high level of uncertainty in this asymmetry can explain why the majority of the opportunities fail.

Articles in this volume have discussed aspects like relationship strength, connections, competition and organization bottleneck which are interesting in understanding success or failure of opportunity development. In this research track, one interesting future research area, which really needs a deeper exploration, is the links that leads to the failure of opportunity development (See Chapter 1, Figure 1.2). In spite of the fact that the majority of the entrepreneurs in the real business world are witnessing the collapse or breakdown of new businesses, a large number of the earlier studies in entrepreneurship are trapped in the truck of success histories. Most of the research on entrepreneurship and opportunity development disregard such a fact. These researchers may have the hopes that the success histories can elevate knowledge necessary not to fall into negative development. Studying of obstacles or failure may open new doors for solving the problems before they hit the firms.

The notion of asymmetry in the business network and opportunity development can give some aids for development of new research ideas on opportunity development. The idea of asymmetry is constructed on two different but interrelated thoughts. One recognizes asymmetry as the driving force for opportunity development. It is relied on the asymmetry in the knowledge among actors in the market, for example, interrelated firms contra competitors. The driving force for the opportunity development lies in the notion that the extra knowledge of some interdependent actors is more than the competitors. If there was a balance and all different kinds of actors had access to all and the same knowledge, then there was no extra value in available knowledge and therefore the matter of opportunity development was not an issue.

The next thought is related to the question if the extra knowledge is sufficient and matches with the future needs of all actors, if for example, even those with weak ties or standing far away in the horizon of the business network context can derive the same value in future. But belonging to a specific business network necessarily means that one actor, because of its connections, has sufficient knowledge about all others in its network context, specifically, when it concerns knowledge about the actors' actions in the future. Each actor has its own business context and acts accordingly. Opportunity development is accommodated with change in the traditional behaviour, not only towards one, but also several others. Therefore, acting to change the behaviour of others is based on expectations that contain uncertainty. Uncertainty, for example, in the outcomes of resource input, can generate resistance which may lead to the failure of opportunity development. Actors in the end of the production channel with weak connections, for example, do not necessarily need to buy new developed products. This also elevates another fact on connections and impact on business development. It concerns the dilemma that a high interdependency in one hand increases the knowledge of the actors about the outcome of the resource combinations but on the other hand can block the opportunity development.

The view of opportunity development is constructed on the heterogeneous resource commitment for future expectations. An opportunity development can follow the expected process only when the new resources are combined 'rationally'. Since the idea of business network is built on the actors' incomplete knowledge on outcome of the resource combinations, the matter of failure of opportunity or obstacles becomes a serious issue. As mentioned earlier this may have been left untouched because the firms are reluctant to disclose information about their obstacles or failures and also researchers that choose the simplest means. But, despite the difficulties in studying these areas, there is a need to conduct deeper studies that elevate new facts and thoughts on opportunity development and obstacles. This becomes more urgent as the actors involved in different phases of the opportunity development are not the same. It is not unusual in real business life that those who develop an opportunity are not the same as those who exploit it.

References

Hoang, H. and Antoncic, B. (2003). Network-based Research in Entrepeneurship, A Critical View, *Journal of Business Venturing*, 18, 165–87.

Jack, S. L. and Anderson, A. R. (2002). The Effect of Embeddedness on the Entrepreneurial Process, *Journal of Business Venturing*, 17, 467–87.

Penrose, E. (1959). *The Productive Opportunity of the Firm and the 'Entrepreneur', The Theory of the Growth of the Firm*, 3rd edn, Oxford: Oxford University Press.

Sarah, L. J. and Anderson, A. R. (2002). The Effect of Embeddedness on the Entrepenuerial Process, *Journal of Business Venturing*, 17, 467–87.

Index

Åberg, S., 19, 288
absorptive capacity, 53
adaptive systems, 51
Adenfelt, M., 18, 164
Agarwal, S., 76
Ahuja, G., 102
Albert, S., 222
Alderson, W., 111
Aldrich, H., 7, 9, 72, 236–8
Allen, T. J., 141
Almeida, P., 91, 102, 105
Alvarez, S. A., 7–9, 51, 184
American bioscience firms and M&A, 205
Andersen, O., 82
Anderson, A. R., 4, 8–9, 27, 30, 36, 167, 328
Anderson, H., 202
Anderson, J. C., 111, 148, 202, 204–5, 307
Andersson, J., 254
Andersson, U., 13, 17, 27, 32–3, 79, 92, 93, 95, 98, 102–4, 127, 133–4, 141, 167
  subsidiaries, typology, 140
Angelmar, R., 132, 136
Antoncic, B., 9, 328
appropriability regimes, 270
Araujo, L., 92
Ardichvili, A., 9, 27, 30, 32, 165, 167, 236, 238, 270, 274
Areangeli, F., 95
Armbruster, T., 220–1
arms-length relationships, 134
Arrow, K. J., 146
Arthur Andersen, 219–20
Artisien, P. F. R., 81
Astley, G., 105
asymmetry
  in business network and opportunity development, 330
  information, 289, 300, 326
  in knowledge among actors in market, 330
ATM-machine, 288

Austrian economists, 3
Austrian School, 129, 292
automatic response to disequilibrium, 6
automatic tool dispensers (ATDs), 313
awareness boundaries, 304
Axelsson, B., 111
Axtell, C., 195

Baden-Fuller, C., 225
Bagby, D. R., 239
Balanced Scorecards, 272
balance/imbalance in opportunity elements, 14
Balmer, J. M. T., 221
Bandura, A., 151–2
bankruptcy, 16
Baraldi, E., 18–19, 202, 271–3, 284–5
Barkema, H. G., 147, 149, 150–2, 154, 158–9
Barley, S., 292
Barney, J. B., 79, 203–4, 223, 239, 306
Baron, J., 7
Baron, R. A., 235, 239
Barringer, B. B., 112
Bartlett, C. A., 92, 96, 127, 137–8, 225
Bauerschmidt, A., 149, 158–9
Baum, J. A. C., 14, 50
Beamish, P. W., 81, 147–8
  see also Lu and Beamish study
Beckermann, W., 148
Begley, T. M., 7
Belanger, J., 225
Bell, J. H. J., 150
Belussi, F., 95
Bengtson, A., 19, 288, 292, 300
Bengtsson, M., 17, 49–50, 53–5, 59
  classification of competitive relationships, 55
Benito, G. R. G., 149, 159
Bennett, J., 78
Berggren, E., 19, 235
Bergholz, H., 226
best practice sharing, 197
Bettis, R., 97
Beyers, W. B., 221

Index

Bild, M., 202
Bilkey, W. J., 80, 82
Birkinshaw, J., 77–8, 92, 96–8, 131–2, 136–7, 139, 182
Birley, S., 236, 238
Biscarri, J. G., 158
Blankenburg Holm, D., 13, 27, 77, 99, 112, 253–4
BMW, 120
Bocconcelli, R., 272
Boddewyn, J. J., 256
Boston Consulting Group, 223
Bouchikhi, H., 236–7
Bourgeois, III, L. J., 62
Bower, D., 197
Boyd, D. P., 7
Brahm, R., 63
Branson, R., 236
Bresman, H., 50
broadband technology, 290
Brock, D. M., 77–8
Brockhaus, R., 7, 289, 292
Brown, J. S., 52–3
Brown, T. E., 8, 73, 80
Bryman, A., 239, 248
Buckley, P. J., 81, 91, 95–6
Burns, T., 183
Burt, B. S., 62
Burton, F. N., 80
Burt, R. S., 29–30, 33–5, 37–8, 103, 114, 134–5
Busenitz, L. W., 4, 7–10, 51, 56, 73, 184, 239
business innovation, knowledge management, and corporate entrepreneurship in MNCs, 181
business networks
 adaptations, 99
 connections, 254–6
 characteristics of, 129–38
 dynamics, 4
 emergence and exploitation of opportunities in, 306
 genesis of, 239
 indicators of connections in the, 261
 studies of, 255
 for subsidiary, factors affecting 'productivity' of a, 96
 theory, 4, 325
business opportunity/ies, 1, 237–8
 characteristics of, 130
 and development process, 7–8
 in foreign markets, international experience and the recognition of, 146–7
 related to M&As, 215
 and subsidiaries entrepreneurship, 127
business opportunity mediator, 238–9
 concept of, 235
 in entrepreneurial process, role of, 235
 role and contribution in four case study, 246
 support from, 245
Business Process Re-engineering' projects, 273
business relationship
 and change, 252–4, 256
 indicators of areas of change in, 260

Campbell, K. E., 56
Cantwell, J., 91, 135, 141
Carlsson, S., 188
Casson, M. C., 29, 70, 91, 95–6, 236, 253
Castells, M., 181
Caves, R. E., 202, 204
Cavusgil, S. T., 82–3, 150
Centres of Excellence, 137, 182
chance, notion of, 236–7
Chang, S. J., 80, 152
Chatterjee, S., 204
Chen, C. P., 7
Chen, H., 81, 154
Chen, M-J., 63
Chen, T-J., 154
Child, J., 181
Chini, T. C., 127
Choi, Y. R., 29–30
Chrisman, J. J., 164–5
Chu, W., 27
Clark, T., 220
client/s
 and consultants, identity, image and reputation, 229
 creation of positive reputation of firm, 223, 229
closed network, 34–5
 with high degree of relational embeddedness, 42–3
 with low degree of relational embeddedness, 39–40
 and open networks, pros and cons of, 44

Coase, R., 95
codified knowledge, 29, 39–40
cognitive differences, 132, 136
Cohen, W. M., 37–9, 53, 58, 71, 184, 309
Cohendet, P., 167
Coleman, J., 28, 33–4, 38–9, 43, 152
Colombo, M., 181
commercialization or implementation, 50
commitment (or reciprocity), 56
communication
  capacity, 54
  fluidity, 181
competing, two ways of, 221
competitive relationships
  and cooperative relationships in networks, 49
  strong and weak, 55–6
  see also cooperative relationships
connected relationships, 255
connections and dependencies between resources, 289
consultancy firms
  knowledge management systems, 221
  top-ten in Sweden, 225
Continuous Improvement programme, 188
Cook, K. S., 34, 112
Cooke, F. L., 18, 180, 184, 195
Coombs, R., 181
cooperative relationships
  characteristics of, 54–7
  in networks, 61
  strong and weak, 56–7
  see also competitive relationships
corporate entrepreneurship, 164
  four different forms of, 165
  link between innovations and business opportunities, 185
  and opportunity development, 165–7
  organizational rejuvenation, research method, 167–8
Coviello, N. E., 15, 67–9, 76, 82–3
Covin, J., 164–6, 168
craftsman, 2
creation
  images and reputation, 224, 230
  knowledge through linkages with internal MNC network, 128
  of new products or services, 259
creation and realisation of value
  identifying, 110
  illustration of, 120
  model of, 118–19
credit card, 288
Crossan, M., 52
cross-border knowledge sharing, 198
cultural barriers, 150
cultural distance, 148–9, 154
cultural learning, notion of, 150
cultural similarities/dissimilarities, impact on firm behaviour, 159
culture as 'collective mental programming', 149
customer
  as innovator, 187
  relationships, established, 245
Cyert, R. M., 50, 62, 146

D'Aveni, R. A., 49, 59
Dahlqvist, J., 306–7
'damage-of-distance', view of intra-organisational social interactions, 105
Das, T. K., 221, 235, 237
Davenport, T. H., 269–70, 272–3
Davidson, W. H., 76, 150–1
decision-making rights, 132
Delios, A., 147
Denison, D. R., 153
Denmark, 153, 156
  study of firms, 147, 153–60
Denrell, J., 80, 130, 142, 203, 216
Dess, G. G., 4, 7, 13, 73, 148, 164–6, 168, 184
detection and exploitation of business opportunities, network view, 133–8
De Vries, M., 225
Dichtl, E., 80
Diebold, J., 269
Di Maggio, P. J., 27–8
Dimitratos, P., 17, 67, 69, 73, 83, 85
discovery process, 50, 259
domain redefinition, 165–6
Dosi, G., 140, 253
Dougherty, D., 132, 136
Dow, D., 150
Dowling, G. R., 221–3
Doz, Y., 135
Dubini, P., 9
Dubois, A., 304

Duguid, P., 52–3
Dunning, J. H., 72, 91, 103
Dutton, J. E., 228
dyadic efficiency-increase opportunities, 282
Dyer, J. H., 27, 307
dynamism in business network theory, 128

Easton, G., 55, 111
Eckert, C., 196
Eckhardt, J. T., 6–7, 27, 29, 51, 58, 70, 82–3, 165–6, 251, 253, 270, 289
economic organisation as network phenomenon, 112
Edsbyn, case study, 275
 classifying IT-related opportunities and obstacles for, 285
 internal resources, 283
 Resource Network, embedding Movex in, 269
 using ERP Movex, 271
Edwards, R., 77
efficiency-increase opportunities, internal, 282
Egidi, M., 13
Eis case, analysing, 213–15
Eisenhardt, K. M., 52
El-Ansary, A. E., 41
Electronic Data Interchange (EDI) systems, 269
electronic payment resource network, 291
Ellig, J., 63
Ellis, P., 27, 30
embeddedness, 9, 128–9, 328–9
 in business networks, 92
 concept of, 8
 and detection of opportunities, 134–5
 and exploitation of opportunities, 135–8
 four types, 28
 and network structure, impact on finding and exploiting opportunities by, 37
 of subsidiary, 78
 and success–failure in opportunity development, 326
Emerson, R. M., 34, 112
Engwall, L., 149, 225

Enron, 219
ENSR (European Network for SME Research), 80
entrepreneur/ial
 boldness and imagination, 184
 development, 236
 exploitation, 184
 mindset, 71
 opportunities, four case studies, 240–5
 profile of firms venturing abroad, six elements, 73
 recognition and exploitation, 51
 as small firms, 6
 two types of, 2, 237
entrepreneurial process, 70
 of opportunity perception and exploitation, 83
 conceptualization of, 68
entrepreneurship, 3
 as alertness to information gaps in the market, 238
 and development of entrepreneur, external factors, 247
 evolving, 236–7
 in network perspective, 326
 and strategic management, 69
 environmental context, 72–3, 84
 environmental determinism, 69, 72
Ericsson Information Systems
 merging into IT Industry, 207–8
 M&A, 205
Eriksson, C., 219, 224–5
Eriksson, J., 18, 49–50, 53–4
Eriksson, K., 127, 147, 150, 152
ERPs (Enterprise Resource Planning), 269
 obstacles and opportunities related to, 275
 opportunities associated with complex IT systems, 285
ERP-systems, 271–2
 opportunities and obstacles in installing and using, 281–5
Erramilli, K. M., 149–51, 154, 158
European pulp and paper industry, 110
evolutionary networks, 58
evolving entrepreneurship, aspects of, 239
exchange
 opportunities, 1
 of resources, 31
 value, 111

experiential knowledge, 13
exploitability of technology-related opportunities, factors affecting, 270
exploration of opportunities, 50–2
  flows of resources and information in, 52–4
externally embedded subsidiaries, 101
  adaptation to local environment, 136

Fagenson, R., 236
failure of opportunity development, 330
Faulkner, D., 181
Feinberg, R. M., 63
Financial Times/Price Waterhouse survey of top executives, 225
Finch, L. K., 73
Fincham, R., 222
finding and exploiting opportunities, 27, 30, 32–3, 36–8, 45
Finkelstein, S., 202–4
firm/s
  absorptive capacity, 184
  business activities, standardized and entrepreneurial, 325
  growth opportunity-seeking, 3
  international expansion, 151–3
  location choice, first step abroad, 150–1
  managerial experiential knowledge, 152
  and its network structure, characteristics of, 28
  'productive opportunity', 2
  related opportunities, 202–3, 215
Fischer, E., 150
Fleck, J., 184
Flores, F., 273
Florida, R., 4, 91
Floyd, S. W., 166
focal business relationship, evolution of, 255
Ford, D., 28, 112, 133, 147, 293
foreign market servicing mode, 75
foreign subsidiaries, 91
Forsgren, M., 13, 32–3, 79, 92, 94–5, 98, 103, 133–4, 137, 141, 167
  subsidiaries, typology, 140
Foss, N. J., 3, 6, 101, 131, 138, 204
Freeman, J. H., 72
Friesen, P. H., 74
Frost, T. S., 78, 101, 105, 137, 182

Gadde, L.-E., 269
Galaskiewicz, J., 63
Gardial, S. F., 7
Garrouste, P., 13
Gartner, W. B., 237
Garvis, D. M., 69, 73
Gaski, J. F., 41
Gassenheimer, J. B., 112
Gates, B., 236
Gemünden, H. G., 111
geographical markets, new, discovery of, 259
Geen, R., 74
George, G., 67
Geroski, P. A., 5
Ghauri, P. N., 1, 10, 15
Gherardi, S., 183
Ghoshal, S., 92, 94, 96, 105, 111–12, 127, 137–8, 152, 167, 225
Giddens, A., 292
Gilad, B., 13
Gioia, D. A., 221
Global Innovator, 139
global strategic mandate, 78–9
Gluckler, J., 220–1
Gnyawali, D. R., 57
Godfrey, P., 224
Goe, W. R., 27
Goldberg, W. H., 202
Gomes-Casseres, B., 255
Goodall, K., 100, 105
Govindarajan, V., 99–101, 127, 138–9, 167, 182, 194
Grabher, G., 27
Graham, E. M., 78
Granovetter, M. S., 27, 31, 33, 50, 56, 58, 74, 114, 134, 152, 254, 292–3, 301
Grant, R., 164
Graver, M. S., 6–7
Gripsrud, G., 149, 159
Grover, R., 197
Gulati, R., 27, 74, 131, 133
Gupta, A. K., 99–101, 127, 138–9, 167, 182, 194

Hadjikhani, A., 1, 15, 20, 60, 325
Hair, J. F., 156
Håkansson, H., 4, 9–10, 15, 27–8, 32–3, 56, 62, 110–12, 121, 133, 137, 140, 147–8, 204–5, 220, 251, 253–4, 269, 271–2, 274, 284, 293, 306

Halinen, A., 27
Hallén, L., 253, 307
Hamel, G., 49, 52, 181
Hannan, M. T., 72
Hansen, E. L., 236
Hansen, M. T., 32–3, 43, 102, 135, 141, 223
Harari, O., 49, 63
Harianto, F., 127, 131, 137
Harrison, J. S., 112
Hart, D. M., 4, 11
Havila, V., 202, 205
Hayek, F. A., 3, 5, 7, 10, 29, 51, 129, 309
Haynes, P. J., 237
headquarters (HQ)
  sources of power, 103
  and subsidiary communication, 78
  see also subsidiary
Hedberg, B., 269, 271
Hedlund, G., 77, 102, 132
Heitz Ltd,
  Information Systems Unit (IS-unit), 165
  organizational rejuvenation case study, 168–77
Hennart, J.-F., 76
Hernán Camps, 216
Herrman, C. C., 269
heterogeneity of information, 51
high risks and high returns, 239
Hislop, D., 183
Hisrich, R. D., 71
Hite, M. A., 57, 73
Hoang, H., 9, 328
Hofstede, G., 161
  four cultural dimensions, 149, 154
Hohenthal, J., 18, 127, 253
Holl, P., 204
Holm, U., 92, 95, 98, 104, 141
Holmen, E., 292
Holmen Paper (Holmen), and Springer, case study, 114–18
Hood, N., 77–8, 92, 137, 139
Hoopes, D., 194
Horan, C., 94
Hörnell, E., 148
Horowitz, P., 7, 289, 292
Howell, R. A., 203
Hu, M. Y., 81
Hunt, S. D., 41, 307
Hurmerinta-Peltomaki, L., 82

Hwang, P., 76
Hymer, S., 91, 152

Ibeh, K. I. N., 75
identity
  image and reputation built up through interaction, 229
  as organization's unique characteristics, 221
idiosyncrasy in information, 257
  for opportunity development, importance of, 256
IMP (Industrial Marketing and Purchasing Group), 111
Implementer, 139
incrementality, 13, 15
individual-organizational entrepreneurship, 326–8
industrial firms, study of, 251
Industrial Marketing and Purchasing Group, 28
Industrial Tooling Company (ITC), 20, 307
industry
  rationale in M&A, 204, 215
  related opportunities, 202–3
  see also firms
information asymmetries, 289, 300, 326
information-handling opportunities, 282
information technology, see IT
Ingram, P., 14, 50
Inkpen, A. C., 52, 198
innovation
  opportunities, importance of competition and cooperation for exploration of, 49
  in production technology, transfer of, 197
  propensity, 73
  and technological development, 253
innovative capacity, 181
institutional profile, 85
integrated information systems, 269
Integrated Player, 139
Integrated Services Digital Network, see ISDN
integrated subsidiary, 140
Intentia, 276
internally embedded subsidiaries, 100

Index

international business opportunities, 72
 and cultural differences, 148–50
 new, discovery of, 153
international entrepreneurship, 67
 culture, 67, 69, 73–4
 as field of study, 83
 process, 71
international exploitation, pattern of, 67
internationalization
 approaches, conventional, 68
 process view on, 158
international operations in firms, sample and tests, 153
international opportunity
 exploitation, pattern of, 8–3
 perception, 67, 69
 integration model, 69–72
international presence, 154
 importance for managerial experiential knowledge development, 158
 managerial experiential knowledge and choice of location, relationship between, 157
interpreneur, 128, 138
 activity, 138
 locus of, 139
intra-MNE business relationships, 104
Ireland, R. D., 166
ISDN-NET and D-channel study, 290–302
 access, basic access and primary rate access, 290
 adopting industrial network view on opportunities, 292–3
 Anchor Datacomm, data communication supplier, 295
 card issuer SEB Kort, 296–7
 D-channel, development and exploitation of, 294–9
 design and methods, 293
 network, 295
 retailer ICA, 299
 terminal producer, Point, 298
 theoretical implications, 299–302
 transaction handler CEKAB, 297
IT
 concrete effects of, 274
 as facilities, interplay with embedding resources, 271–3
 informative power of, 273
 opportunities and obstacles in using, 269
 related opportunities, 269, 285
 role of, 168
IT systems
 effects on resources, 273
 four types of related opportunities, 283
 indirect effects of, 274, 284
 as 'information processing facilities', 272
ITC in UK, case study, 309–18
 analysis, 318–22
 case study and analysis, 322
 commercial element, 312–13
 international tooling company and the preferred supplier concept, 310
 mutual opportunity in business networks, 319
 'Preferred Supplier' (PS) marketing concept, 310–18
 productivity analysis element, 313
 UK subsidiary, 307

Jack, S. L., 4, 9, 27, 30, 36, 167, 328
Jarillo, J. C., 8, 167, 184, 196
Johanson, J., 1, 10, 17, 20, 27, 72, 80, 94, 110–11, 133, 148, 150–2, 155, 159, 167, 325
 and Vahlne, internationalisation process model, 146
Johansson, J., 220
Jones, M. V., 17, 67–9, 82–3
Jönsson, S., 269, 271
Jöreskog, K-G., 156

Kahneman, 151
Kaish, S., 13
Kalakota, R., 269
Kale, P., 110
Kalling, T., 194
Kanter, R. M., 167, 184, 196
Keats, B. W., 72
Kelley, H. H., 112
Kenney, M., 27
Kets de Vries, M. F. R., 236
Khilstrom, L., 5
Kihlstrom, R., 289, 292

Index 339

Kim, W. C., 76
Kirzner, I., 2–4, 6–7, 10, 13, 16, 29–30, 52, 55, 71, 129–31, 152, 184, 202, 215, 236, 237–8, 251, 292, 304, 308–9
Kitching, J., 203
Klein, P. G., 3, 6
Klevorick, A., 251
Knight, G., 82–3
knowledge
  acquisition, 198
  and commitments of interrelated actors, 16
  and corporate entrepreneurship, 166
  creation and reputation building, 229
  dispersed, 30
  structure, 136
  transfer and intra/inter-organisational learning among MNCs, 180
knowledge sharing, 183
  communication links in MNCs, 190
  process at plant level, management of, 189
known ignorance, 29
Kock, S., 49, 55–6, 255
Kogut, B., 27, 32–4, 36, 38–9, 43, 95, 105, 149
Konsultguiden, 223
Kostova, T., 96
Kothandaraman, P., 112
Krackhardt, D., 167
Krugman, P. R., 78
Kulatilaka, N., 95
Kuratko, D. F., 164, 166

Laage-Hellman, J., 32
Laffont, J., 289, 292
Laffont, N., 5
Lafuente, A., 2
Lagerström, K., 18
Lam, A., 192
Lane, P. J., 37–9, 92, 101
Larimo, J., 76
Larsson, R., 53–4, 58–60, 63, 202–4
latent networks, 58
Latour, B., 288
Lawless, M. W., 73
Lawrence, P., 183
'leakiness' of flows in networks, 52, 54
  see also stickiness

learning
  across border, 180
  orientation, 74
  processes in interactions, 92, 252
Leonard-Barton, D., 181
Leonard, D., 222
Leonidou, L. C., 80
Leung, S., 92
Levinthal, D. A., 37–9, 53, 58, 71, 152, 184, 198, 309
Lim, J.-S., 80
Lindahl, D. P., 221
Lindbergh, J., 18, 146
Lindvall, J., 18, 219
Linneman, H., 148
Liouville, J., 75
Lipparini, A., 131
local environment of subsidiary, 137
local, external, business network, 128
Local Innovator, 139
location, SME choice of, 146, 150, 156, 158, 160
Longman Dictionary of Contemporary English, 2
Lorenzoni, G., 131, 225
Lorsch, J., 183
Lubatkin, M., 37–9, 92, 101
Lubatkin, P., 204
Lu and Beamish, study on prior experience of foreign direct investments, 152
Lu, J. W., 152
Lumpkin, G. T., 73, 148
Lundgren, A., 302
Lundun, S., 91
Lundvall, B.-Å., 92, 140, 253, 307
Lyle, S. W., 182

M&A (mergers and acquisitions)
  network opportunities and obstacles in, 202
  opportunities, realisation of, 202
  strategic path for firms, 202
  three types of opportunities in, 203–6
Madhavan, R., 57, 197
Madhok, A., 150, 152, 167
Madsen, T. K., 76
Magee, J. F., 269
Makadok, R., 49
Malerba, F., 270

Malmberg, A., 137
Malnight, T. W., 138
Malone, T. W., 269
management consultancy, 220
  firms, 222
  market, 221
  projects in public sector, 228
  work, 221
managerial experiential knowledge, 147, 151, 155–7
managerial process of standardization and routinization, 327
'Managerial Synergies', 204
Manimala, M. J., 2
Manwaring, T., 195
March, J. G., 30, 50–2, 59, 62, 101, 104, 146, 152
Mariotti, S., 149
market
  entry process, 253
  exchange opportunities, 289
  knowledge, 129–31, 253
  novelty and relevance, 130–1
  opportunities, 1, 29
  orientation, 74
  price and information, disequilibrium in, 5
  as systematic process of mutual discovery, 304
  uncertainties, 325
'markets-as-networks' (MAN), 94
Marsden, P. V., 56
Mattsson, L.-G., 10, 94, 111, 133, 220, 307
McClelland, D., 236, 289, 292
McDougall, P. P., 67, 69, 71, 73, 76, 82–3, 150, 155
McDowell, R., 112
McEvily, B., 27
McGrath, C., 167
McGrath, R. G., 236
McKendall, M. A., 4, 7
McKinsey & Co, 223
McLoughin, D., 94
means–ends relationships, 6
Medcof, J., 98
mergers and acquisitions, see M&As
Miles, M. P., 164–6, 168
Miles, S., 11
Millar, V., 269

Miller, D., 63, 74, 167
Minniti, M., 72
MIN-project, on international operations of large Swedish multinational corporations, 258
Mintzberg, H., 168, 269
Mises, L. V., 3, 6
  four factors, 6
Mitchell, R. K., 72
Mitchell, W., 49
MNC
  case study strategies for creating business opportunities and activities of knowledge management in, 187
  case study, innovations and knowledge sharing as process of developing business opportunities, 196
  dynamics of network relationships, case studies, 185–96
  evolution, 77
  innovations, knowledge sharing, and business opportunities in, 180
  learning and knowledge transfer in, 198
  as three-dimensional network, 182
MNE
  asset augmenting activities, 91
  comparison of influence of internal and external business networks, 91
  contingency theory perspective, 94
  features of internal and external business relationships, 96–100
  HQ, 98
  internal business relationships, 94–6
  involvement in different relationships, 164
  'markets-as-networks' (MAN) perspective, 94
  and 'opportunity development', 91–2, 164
  organizational rejuvenation, knowledge combinations, 177
  subsidiary business networks and opportunity development in, 91
Mokyr, J., 4
Möller, K. E. K., 111
monitoring, search, and creation, 51

Monti, J. A., 158
Moore, K., 182
Moore, W. L., 307
Moorman, C., 74
Morgan, R. M., 307
Morris, M. H., 8
Morrison, A. J., 78, 138
motivation, 74
Movex, 271
  effects on resources, 278–81
  new IT tool for handling resources in Edsbyn's network, 275–81
  opportunities and obstacles in implementing, 276–8
  related opportunities, 283
  and surrounding network of resources, 279
  see also Edsbyn
MRPII model, 283, 285
  method for production planning, 272
Mudambi, R., 98
Mueller, S. L., 67
multinational corporations, *see* MNCs
multinational enterprises, *see* MNEs
munificence, 72, 78, 83
  see also uncertainty
Munro, H. J., 76

Nagarajan, A., 49
Naidu, G. M., 75
Narduzzo, A., 13
Narus, J. A., 111, 148, 307
Narver, J. C., 74
Nelson, R. R., 152
network/s
  active, 59–60
  and alliances for knowledge sharing, 181
  analysis and inter-subunit business relationships in MNEs, 94
  approach on strategic initiatives, 167
  based modes, 69
  characteristics, 27, 57
  development opportunities, 282
  dynamics and opportunity discovery, 57–64
  focus and subsidiary organisational performance in MNE, 100–4
  function as a 'screening device', 134
  'hierarchical' structure, 34
  input from connections in, 257
  interplay between internal resources, commitment and developments, 322
  opportunities for technological development, 49
  related opportunities in M&As, 204–5
  of resources, 271
  slack, 59, 61
  structure as open and closed systems, 33–6
  structures, 28
  as unit of analysis, 113
  viable, 60–1
  view of detection and exploitation of business opportunities, 133–8
networking orientation, 74
Nevin, J. R., 41
new knowledge, 28
new methods of production and of organizing, 270
new ways of organizing business, 259
New Zealand, 153, 156, 158
  and Denmark and Sweden, study of firms, 147, 153–60
Newell, S., 194–5
Nohira, 94
Nohria, N., 127, 137, 167
Nonaka, I., 181, 196–8, 222
non-codified knowledge, 29, 38
Nordström, K. A., 147, 149, 158
Norrtälje maskiner, Rolf Fredrikkson case study, 240–1
'not-invented-here' syndromes, 141

O'Brien, M., 71
O'Donnell, S. W., 89, 94
Oakley, A., 59, 63
occurrence of opportunities, 251
Oliver, A. L., 49, 54, 56
Olsen, J. P., 52
Olson, E. M., 307
ongoing business relationships, 253
  exploring opportunity development for, 258–61
  five areas of change of, 262
  links between vertical and horizontal connections, 265
  two dimensions of connection in surrounding network, 262

open network
  with high degree of relational embeddedness, 40–2
  with low degree of relational embeddedness, 37
Operations Research, applications of computers to, 269
opportunism, 309
opportunities/y, 29–30
  aftermath of, 264
  basic considerations, 1–3
  in business networks, 9–11, 245–7, 308–9
  business theories, 6–7
  changes driven by, 265
  concept, 27, 127
  concept of key considerations, 28
  created by embedding resources inside IT-using firms, 271
  definition of, 263
  discovery or innovation processes, different descriptions of, 51
  economic theories, 5–6
  exploiting, 27, 38
  exploring, 50–2
  factors affecting exploitability of technology-related, 270
  finding and exploiting, 27, 30, 32–3, 36–7, 45
  international opportunity perception, 70–2
  by IT for firms, 270
  and IT, four types of, 282
  obstacles in interplay, 'IT-embedding resources', 273–5
  process, activities in, 27
  recognition, 300
  relational embeddedness and network structure, 27
  risks, 220–1
  value processes in networks, 113–18
opportunity development, 11, 250–2, 288
  areas of changes and connections as, 262
  in business networks, 325
  complexity of, 326–7
  failure of, 330
  for ongoing business relationships, 250, 265, 257–8
  in networks, 326
  process, 12
  process, obstacles in, 329–31
  relationships through horizontal connection, 256
  within multinational enterprise (MNEs), 91
organization/al
  content, subsidiary-based international operations, 77–9
  culture, 71
  as form of corporate entrepreneurship, 176
  global business experience, 153
  leveraging of technological knowledge, 128
  and management theories, traditional, 4
  rejuvenation, 164–6
  slack, 62
organizational context, 75–81
  international modus operandi, 75
  network-based international operations, 76–7
  resource-based strategy, 79–81
  trading-based international operations, 75
organizational rejuvenation case study, Heitz and IT, 168–9
  knowledge utilization at IS-unit, 172–4
  outcome of, 174–6
  rejuvenating enterprise IT-activities, 170–1
  seizing opportunities by, 169–70
· Orlikowsi, W., 302
Orsenigo, L., 270
Otto, J., 102, 105, 198
Ottum, B. D., 307
over-embeddedness, 43, 57, 135
Oviatt, B. M., 67, 69, 71, 73, 76, 82–3, 150, 155

Pahlberg, C., 17, 19, 92, 102–3, 127, 250
Paldich, L. E., 239
parent firm technology 'trajectory', 100
partner characteristics, discovery of, 99
Paterson, S. L., 77–8
path-dependence, 270
Paul, G. W., 8

PCA (productivity cost analysis), 310
  software, 313
Pearce, R., 91–2, 100
Pearce, W., 5
Pedersen, T., 92, 101, 138, 141
Pennings, J. M., 127, 131, 137, 150
Penrose, E. T., 2–3, 6, 10, 97, 112, 151–2, 167, 203–4, 250, 252, 264, 272, 274, 289, 293, 303, 325, 327
  distinction between routine and creative activities, 11
perception
  gaps in subsidiary-HQ relation, 136
  of international opportunities, 68
Persson, M., 17
Peteraf, M. A., 204
Pfeffer, J., 112
Phene, A., 102, 105, 167
physical distance/proximity factor in intra-organisational social interactions, 105
Pisano, G., 49, 52
Piscitello, L., 149
Plakoyiannaki, E., 69, 73, 83
planned search, 51
  for ideas, 52
population ecology perspective, 72
Porter, M. E., 41, 53, 63, 111, 181, 202–4, 269
Postrel, S., 194
potentially valuable opportunity, 131
Pouder, R., 53, 56
Powell, W. W., 49, 53, 56, 181
Prahalad, C. K., 49, 77, 97, 135, 151
Prandelli, E., 225
Prasad, S. B., 10
Prasad, V. K., 75
'Preferred Supplier' (PS) marketing concept, emergence of opportunity, 307, 310–11
processes
  of discovery, evaluation, and exploitation, 51
  of infusion and diffusion of information, 257
  of innovation, three different phases, 50
  production methods, new, development of, 259
productive opportunity, 264

psychic distance concept of, 148–9
Pucik, V., 181, 196

quality of the services, 221

Radner, R., 146
Ragan, S., 95
Ragatz, G. L., 307
Ramaswami, S. N., 76
Ramirez, R., 110–11
Ramström, D., 269
raw materials, new, discovery of, 259
Rayport, J. F., 222
Regnér, P., 92, 98
relational embeddedness, 30–3, 44
relationships
  between suppliers and customers, 255
  connection, 10
  development, 10
  embeddedness, 28
  knowledge and corporate entrepreneurship, 167
  specific dimensions of, 31
  strength (or bond strength), 56
rent accruing position in an open network, 35
reputation
  creating opportunities through, 221–3
  as opportunity and risk, 218
research
  on business network theory and knowledge-based view, 165
  on opportunity, previous studies, 5–9
  studies, later development, 8–9
resources
  based and head office assignment perspective, 69
  combinations and commitments, 271
  commitment in case of new ERP, 274
  dimension of Industrial Network Model, 293
  embeddedness, 202, 271
  heterogeneous commitment for future expectations, 331
Reuber, A. R., 150
Rice, M. P., 8, 49, 51
Richter, I., 183
Ricks, A. D., 67
Ridderstrale, J., 96–8, 102
Ring, P. S., 256, 307

risk attitude, 73
Ritter, T., 111
Roberts, E. B., 237
Roberts, J., 100, 105
Robinson, M., 269
Ronen, S., 149
Ronen and Shenkar, socio-cultural clustering of countries, 154
Rosenberg, N., 288, 302
Rosenzweig, P. M., 80
Roslagens kabel, Tommy Liljedahl case study, 241–2
Roth, K., 78, 96, 138
Rotschild, M., 146
Rowley, T., 27
Ruef, M., 102
Rugman, A. M., 78

Safab, Dan Larsson case study, 243–4
Salaman, G., 220
Salami, A., 204
Salancik, G. R., 112
Salas, V., 2
Salmi, A., 202, 205
Sarah, L. J., 9, 328
Sawhney, M., 225
scanning or monitoring, 50
Scapens, R., 239
Scherer, F. M., 204
Schlegelmilch, B. B., 80, 127, 147, 149, 158
Schmid, S., 93
Schneider, S. C., 132, 136
Schumpeter, J. A., 4, 30, 49, 70, 153, 165, 236–7
 discussion of innovation and creative destruction, 50
 entrepreneurship, 4, 82
 five 'loci of change' relating to entrepreneurship and innovation, 253, 259, 270
Schumpeterian models, intense competition, 63
Schuring, A., 93
Scott, J., 9
sectoral knowledge codifiability, 270
Servais, P., 76
Sevón, G., 62
Shaanan, J., 63
Shackle, N., 5

Shane, S. A., 6–7, 13, 27, 29–30, 51, 68, 70–1, 8–3, 129, 131, 134, 151, 153, 165–6, 184, 197, 220, 238, 251, 253, 270, 289, 292, 301–2, 309
Sharma, P., 164–5
Sharma, S., 156
Shea, J. D. C., 74
Shenkar, O., 148–9
 see also Ronen
Shephard, D. A., 29
Shepherd, D., 30, 129
Shoonhoven, C. B., 49, 52
Silicon Valley, USA, 11
Silver, L., 19
Simiar, F., 81
Simonin, B. L., 141
Simpson, P. M., 111
Simsek, Z., 27
Singh, H., 149, 307
slack in networks, utilization of, 61–4
Slater, S. F., 74
SMEs (small and medium enterprises), study of, 146
Smilor, R. W., 235, 238
Smith, A., 111
Smith, N. R., 2
Snehota, I., 10, 27, 56, 62, 110–11, 204–5, 220, 253–4, 271–2, 292, 301–2, 306
 view on opportunities, 289
'social capital' concept of intra-MNE relationships, application of, 96
social relations, 31
Sölvell, Ö., 50, 59, 95
Sörbom, D., 156
Sorvell, O., 198
specific market knowledge, 127
Spendrups, 213–15
Spendrups–Wårby merger, 208–11
Springer Verlag (Springer), 114
Springer, 120
St John, C., 53, 56
stability and long-term orientation, changes providing, 265
Ståhl, B., 20, 306
Stalker, G., 184
Steiner, P. O., 203
Stern, L. W., 41
Stevenson, H. H., 8, 80, 167, 184, 196
Stewart, W. H., 239

'stickiness' of flows in networks, 52–4, 60, 141
Stigler, G. J., 7
Storey, D. J., 238
Stöttinger, B., 147, 149, 158
strategic management knowledge-based view, 181
strategic renewal, 165–6
strategies for creating business opportunities at corporate level, 187
Strömsten, T. W., 17–18, 110, 202
structural holes, 33, 34
Sturdy, A., 221
Subramaniam, M., 102, 197
subsidiaries/y
  adaptation to local environment, 136
  autonomy, 78
  based modes, 69
  choice, 139
  contribution to MNE production and product development, 101–2
  credibility, 78
  embeddedness of, 78, 133
  as entrepreneurs, 138–42
  as exploiters, 127
  external, 140
  externally embedded, 101
  and HQ communication, 78
  influence of MNE strategy, 102–4
  integrated, 140
  intra-firm interactions, 95
  in knowledge transfer to other MNE units, 100–1
  local embeddedness and interpreneurial role, 140–1
  local environment of, 137
  mandate in MNC, 138
  market knowledge, 134
  in MNCs, 127–8, 142
  'negative' power of, 103
  'network focus', 100–5
  organisational performance, 100–4
  relationships with internal counterparts, 141
  semi-vertical, 140
  technological knowledge, 127
  typology developed by Andersson and Forsgren, 140
subsidiaries, business network for
  factors affecting 'productivity' of, 96
  internal versus external business networks, 97
  and opportunity development in multinational enterprises, 91–3
success and failure, 329–31
Sudarsanam, S., 202, 204
Sullivan, D., 149, 158–9
surpass value, 12, 15
surprise, element of, 52
sustained regeneration, 165–6
Sweden, 153, 158
  beer market, 205, 209
  and New Zealand, Denmark, firms study, 147, 153–60
  study top-ten management consultancy firms in, 223–9
  survey of small- and medium-sized firms, 239
Swetech, Jens Marklund case study, 242–3
Szulanki, G., 101
Szulanski, G., 52, 141

Takeuchi, H., 181, 222
Tan, C., 92
Tasoukas, H., 99
Tavares, A., 78
technology/ical
  development, 49
  innovations, 184
  knowledge, 130–3
  market linkage, 136
  opportunities, 30
Technology network (TechNEt), 11
Teece, D. J., 49, 52, 181, 204
Telia, 290, 294
Teng, B. S., 221, 235, 237
Tesar, G., 80, 82
Thakur, S. P., 8–9, 15
The Theory of the Growth of the Firm, 250, 293
Thibaut, J. W., 112
Thilenius, P., 19, 60, 250
Thomas, A. S., 67
Thomke, S., 187
Tidd, J., 270
Törnquist, G., 50–3
Törnroos, J-Å., 27
Toro Bioscience, 211–13, 215
Törrönen, P., 111

trading-based modes, 69
transaction cost/internalisation literature, 95
transference of information, 51
trust, 56
Tsai, W., 94, 96, 105, 111–12, 194
Tsang, E., 181
Turnbull, P. W., 147, 293
Tversky, 151
Tyre, M., 92, 99, 302

uncertainty, 72, 149, 309, 330
  see also munificence
UNCTAD, 95
unknown ignorance, 29
Uppsala University, 148
use value, 111
Utterback, J. M., 181
Uzzi, B., 27, 32–3, 35, 43, 57, 133, 135, 141

Vahlne, J.-E., 72, 80, 147–8, 150–2, 155, 158–9
  internationalisation process model, 146
Valla, J.-P., 147, 293
value
  concept, 111
  creation and realisation, 114–18, 120–2
  definition of, 111
  firms and industrial networks, 111–13
  Holmen and Springer case study, 114–18
  processes in industrial networks, 110, 122
Value Chains, 272
Van Den Bosch, F. A. J., 53
Van de Ven, A., 307
Vaughn, K., 6
Venkataraman, S., 6–7, 13, 70, 131, 165, 197, 251, 253, 309
Vermeulen, F., 147, 152
Vernon, R., 78

vertical integration, 255
Vihanto, M., 5, 7
von Hippel, E., 92, 99, 137, 140, 187, 222, 253, 302, 304, 307

Wagner, J. A., 4, 7
Walker, G., 152
Wallenstål, M., 149
Walsh, J. P., 136
Walter, A., 111
Walter, G. A., 203–4
Waluszewski, A., 15, 111–12, 121, 137, 205, 251, 253–4, 271–2, 274, 284
Webster, F. A., 2
Weick, K. E., 81
Whetten, D. A., 222, 224
Wiedersheim-Paul, F., 148, 150
Wiklund, J., 129, 239
Wilson, D. T., 112
Winborg, J., 239
Winograd, T., 273
Winter, S. G., 32, 152
Wood, S., 195
Woodruff, R. B., 7
Wooldridge, B., 166
Wright, R. W., 67, 77

Yamin, M., 17, 91–2, 95, 98, 102, 105, 198
Yang, Y. S., 80
Yaprak, A., 80
Yip, G. S., 150, 158
Young, S., 67, 73, 77–8, 146

Zac, J., 105
Zaheer, A., 27, 63
Zahra, S. A., 67, 69, 73, 75, 78, 80, 148, 165–6, 177
Zander, I., 95, 198
Zander, U., 32, 127, 138
Zawacki, R. A., 182
Zeithaml, V. A., 111
Zuboff, S., 269, 273
Zukin, S., 27–8